Cruel Habitations

Cruel Habitations

A History of Working-Class Housing
1780-1918

ENID GAULDIE

'All the earth is full of cruel habitations'   *Psalms* 74 v.20

London   George Allen & Unwin Ltd
Ruskin House   Museum Street

First published in 1974

© George Allen & Unwin Ltd 1974

ISBN 0 04 942120 4 hardback
ISBN 0 04 942121 2 paperback

Printed in Great Britain
in 10 point Times Roman type
by William Clowes and Sons Limited
London, Colchester and Beccles

Preface

I am grateful to my husband and to Dr Donald Southgate for their patient and careful help, to Professor J. N. Tarn for his early encouragement and to Professor H. J. Dyos for his generous offer to read my manuscript and for his constructive suggestions; to Mrs Lyn Leece and Mrs Barbara Gray who shared the typing; and to the staffs of Dundee University Library, Dundee Public Reference Library, Edinburgh Central Library and the Library of the Royal Institute of British Architects for their tolerance. I should also like to thank Mr Jeremy Lowe of the Welsh School of Architecture for his informative correspondence.

Contents

Illustrations

All the half-tones and line blocks in this book are reproduced by kind permission of *The Builder* with the exception of plates IV, V, VIII and IX which are reproduced by kind permission of the Dundee Public Libraries.

Table of Statutes on Housing

Towns Improvement Clauses Act, 1847	10 and 11 Vict. c. 34
Public Health Act, 1848	11 and 12 Vict. c. 63
Common Lodging Houses Act, 1851	14 and 15 Vict. c. 28
Lodging Houses Act, 1851	14 and 15 Vict. c. 34
Common Lodging Houses Act, 1853	16 and 17 Vict. c. 41
Dwelling Houses for the Working Classes (Scotland) Act, 1855	18 and 19 Vict. c. 88
Metropolis Local Management Act, 1855	18 and 19 Vict. c. 120
Nuisances Removal Act, 1855	18 and 19 Vict. c. 121
Metropolitan Building Act, 1855	18 and 19 Vict. c. 122
Labourers Dwellings Act, 1855	18 and 19 Vict. c. 132
Nuisances Removal (Scotland) Act, 1856	19 and 20 Vict. c. 103
Metropolis Management Amendment Act, 1857	19 and 20 Vict. c. 112
Common Lodging Houses (Ireland) Act, 1860	23 and 24 Vict. c. 26
Metropolitan Building Amendment Act, 1860	23 and 24 Vict. c. 52
Entail Cottages Act, 1860	23 and 24 Vict. c. 95
Burgh Police and Improvement (Scotland) Act, 1862	25 and 26 Vict. c. 101
Labouring Classes Dwelling Houses Act, 1866	29 and 30 Vict. c. 28
Labouring Classes Lodging Houses and Dwellings (Ireland) Act, 1866	29 and 30 Vict. c. 44
Sanitary Act, 1866	29 and 30 Vict. c. 90
Labouring Classes Dwellings Act, 1867	30 and 31 Vict. c. 28
Public Health (Scotland) Act, 1867	30 and 31 Vict. c. 101
Police and Improvement (Scotland) Act, 1868	31 and 32 Vict. c. 102
Artisans' and Labourers' Dwellings Act, 1868 (Torrens)	31 and 31 Vict. c. 130
Metropolitan Building Act, 1869	32 and 33 Vict. c. 82
Public Health Act, 1872	35 and 36 Vict. c. 79
Building Societies Act, 1874	37 and 38 Vict. c. 42
Working Men's Dwellings Act, 1874	37 and 38 Vict. c. 59

Artisans' and Labourers' Dwellings Improvement Act, 1875 (Cross)	38 and 39 Vict. c. 36
Artisans' and Labourers' Dwellings Improvement (Scotland) Act, 1875	38 and 39 Vict. c. 49
Public Health Act, 1875	38 and 39 Vict. c. 55
An Act to explain and amend the 22nd section of the Artisans' and Labourers' Dwellings Act (1866) Amendment Act, 1879	42 and 43 Vict. c. 8
Artisans' and Labourers' Dwellings Improvement Act (1875) Amendment Act, 1879	42 and 43 Vict. c. 63
Artisans' and Labourers' Dwellings Act (1868) Amendment Act, 1879	42 and 43 Vict. c. 64
Public Works Loans Act, 1879	42 and 43 Vict. c. 77
Artisans' and Labourers' Dwellings Improvement (Scotland) Act, 1880	43 and 44 Vict. c. 8
Public Health (Scotland) Act, 1882	45 and 46 Vict. c. 11
Metropolis Management and Building Acts (Amendment), 1882	45 and 46 Vict. c. 14
Artisans' Dwellings Act, 1882	45 and 46 Vict. c. 54
Housing of the Working Classes Act, 1885	48 and 49 Vict. c. 72
Local Government Act, 1888	51 and 52 Vict. c. 41
Local Government (Scotland) Act, 1889	52 and 53 Vict. c. 50
Working Classes Dwellings Act, 1890	53 and 54 Vict. c. 16
Public Health Amendment Act, 1890	53 and 54 Vict. c. 59
Metropolis Management Amendment Act, 1890	53 and 54 Vict. c. 66
Settled Land Act, 1890	53 and 54 Vict. c. 69
Housing of the Working Classes Act, 1890	53 and 54 Vict. c. 70
Public Health (London) Act, 1891	54 and 55 Vict. c. 76
London Government Act, 1899	62 and 63 Vict. c. 14
Small Dwellings Acquisition Act, 1899	62 and 63 Vict. c. 44
Housing of the Working Classes Act, 1900	63 and 64 Vict. c. 59
Housing of the Working Classes Act, 1903	3 Edw. 7 c. 39
Housing and Town Planning Act, 1909	9 Edw. 7 c. 44
Housing Act, 1914	4 and 5 Geo. 5. c. 31
Housing Act No. 2, 1914	4 and 5 Geo. 5. c. 52
Increase of Rent and Mortgage Interest (War Restrictions) Act, 1915	5 and 6 Geo. 5. c. 97
Housing and Town Planning Act, 1919	9 and 10 Geo. 5 c. 35

Introduction

There is still a great deal to be learnt about urban history and, in particular, about the history of housing. A few interesting and careful studies of local housing history have been made, but there are still large areas of the country and long periods of time about which very little is known. It is difficult to detect a pattern in a puzzle from which so many pieces are still missing. On the other hand, students of the subject, working perhaps on the housing of their own district, need a general framework of reference against which they can measure their own findings. While local variations in housing patterns must appear, caused by geographical and economic factors and by differing forms of local administration, it seems nevertheless possible to find more points of similarity than of difference between regions. This book has been written in an attempt to gather together in one place as much as possible of what is already known about the history of working-class housing. I hope that it will make it a little easier for those interested in housing to pursue their interest and that more detailed local studies will follow.

'Working class' is a term that has had so many different meanings for different people at different times that it seems sensible for me to try to define what I have meant by it while writing this book. I shall, for instance, always include people who were not strictly 'working' at all, those once described as 'lower than working class...they get their living as they can', the casuals, the unemployables, the aged and the sick. They are, in fact, the core of the problem.

In this book, then, I have meant by 'working class' all those for whom the provision of a decent house by their own efforts was impossible or so difficult as to be attained only by those with exceptional energy and initiative, as well as those working people whose skills ensured regular wages and whose wages made available to them, in some areas at least, houses designed especially for their needs.

The word 'decent' has also to be defined. While today the remotest agricultural cottage is not a 'decent' home without a bathroom, at the beginning of the nineteenth century a 'decent' house might very well be one that claimed no more than to be weatherproof, ceilinged and floored, and to have right of access to some outside source of water. By mid-century 'decent' would mean large enough for unmarried grown-up members of the family to have separate sleeping accommodation—the word has acquired an overtone of morality—as well as served by adequate drainage and with a regular water supply. An indoor lavatory did not become a necessary or even an expected part of a 'decent' house for working people until the twentieth century. Perhaps the nearest meaning that would serve for all periods is 'watertight and able to be cleaned'. The degree of effort necessary to keep it clean would vary very much with the period. How much the standard of cleanliness would vary we cannot know for certain. We know that at all times, even before sanitary reform, it has been considered desirable that a house should be clean. What we cannot know is what different periods meant by 'clean' or 'dirty'. Clean may sometimes have meant little more than 'not verminous'. But, whatever the period, a decent house was one which admitted the possibility of being cleaned by an industrious woman. To live in one was a privilege not open to so very large a proportion of the working class.

The Victorians believed that it was not necessary to worry about the housing of the very poorest because, by concentrating on improving standards for the better-off worker, the poorest must eventually benefit. The persistence to this day of a large class of slum dwellers living in disgusting sub-standard housing proves the failure of the notion that the lowest would inevitably be raised up the rungs of the housing ladder by the improvement of those already on the higher rungs. The presence of a slum quarter degrades not only those who live in it but those who tolerate it. It is necessary to try to understand the economic and social causes which taught society to tolerate slum-dwelling for a proportion of the population, a proportion which fluctuates but does not disappear.

I have concerned myself with the attitudes of those who worked to achieve legislation on housing because it seems to me that the failure of all such legislation to achieve real solutions was caused by inadequacies, limitations, in the aims and attitudes of those who designed it. However inclined to radical solutions governments may be they cannot lead a united public where it will not be led, and the sixty years in which Shaftesbury's Act lay a dead letter on the statute book illustrate the point.

The attitudes of the middle-class electorate which defied attempts at improving legislation are of even more importance than the attitudes of the legislators. It is not easy to accept how large a part fear played in determining middle-class attitudes to social reform. Fear that the deterioration of the living conditions of the poor might be producing a truly degraded race of sub-human beings, a kind to be recoiled from, a kind whose reactions might be animal, revengeful, unpredictable, played a part in demands for early social reforms. Fear of the mob demanded sops to the mob. It was fear which, lying quiescent for long periods, could be fanned into life again at a spark from the Continent, as in 1848, a breath of combined action from working people, as in 1867, by the advance of returning patriots in 1918. It was not, of course, the only, perhaps not even the dominating impulse affecting reform. The Victorian zeal for improving all around them was based on genuine Christian belief in man's power to do good, to change for the better, to fight the evil in man's soul and in his environment with the same energetic faith. Christian faith was complicated and limited by economic pressures, by a self-protective wish to preserve the balance of society, with its favourable tilt towards the established classes, as well as by fear of the consequences of change. But it ought not to be dismissed and disparaged because we can now see that faith to be less straightforwardly altruistic than its holders believed. Christian belief as taught in their churches, allied to what became almost unassailable economic superiority, gave the middle classes their certainty, the certainty that led Miss Hill's young ladies into the evil-smelling slums, the same certainty which lit the conscience of Lord Salisbury in his stumblings towards housing reform.

Within Parliament, work to achieve legislation on housing did arise from some real concern for the condition of the people. It is striking, however, that outside, among the mass of the population who were badly housed, there was at no time until the twentieth century any strong pressure for housing reform; no rioting with improved housing as its aim, no petitions, processions, secret associations or lobbying. Even the meetings held with trade union backing to discuss overcrowding were middle-class inspired. The attention of the working class was turned towards campaigns for the shortening of working hours, the right to vote, the right to combine in unions. The right to live in a decent house was not clamoured for and I think this was because the working class believed as sincerely as did the gentry that self-help was proper and that, given the other conditions—a say in the running of their country, a working day short enough to leave some leisure hours for self-improvement, and trade unions with power to press for better wages—they could indeed house themselves respectably. Government answered parliamentary anxiety about the condition of the people with legislation about their housing not because that was most pressed for, but as a sop to quieten agitation on other matters.

In spite of all the official surveys and reports which exposed the miseries of the poor, in spite of the social-problem novels which enlisted sympathy for the poor, it was a failure not of purpose but of imagination which delayed real housing reform. Victorian writing reported but did not convey experience. It was as if all the reporters drew back on the edge of real experience and used stock political attitudes to fill in the gap left empty by their imaginative failure. They could read what Carlyle called 'Dr Alison's Scotch facts', feel dismay about the sty-like conditions of their brother citizens, and then fall back to preaching about self-help and self-improvement for the poor. Charity became almost a dirty word to Victorians because it could appear to support without improving, to encourage shiftlessness rather than to remove distress. Even the most conscious-stricken of observers, even those who broke through the barrier of inertia and self-interest to work towards improved housing, found it necessary to protest against charges of philanthropy, to insist upon their business-like intentions.

While social theory was developing towards a new view of the role of the state, the attitudes not only of the electorate and the administration but of the social theorists themselves were limiting that role, setting boundaries of caution and self-interest to the regions in which it could act.

To discuss the attitudes of our predecessors with any usefulness we must admit to attitudes of our own. It is not possible to think and write about the problems of housing without acquiring a point of view, even if one had not come to the subject along a path which already determined one's view. My own attitude to the failures of the Victorians is limited by my awareness of the slums that still exist. It seems to me useful to try to understand the attitudes of the past in the hope that we may learn to understand the ways in which our own society is affected by built-in patterns of response to poverty and slum dwelling.

PART 1

Housing in Pre-Industrial and Rural Society

Chapter 1

A Bitter Cry from Rural Britain

'Worse housed than your hacks and your pointers'
CHARLES KINGSLEY

It is very easy to assume, because the decay of Britain's cities and the appalling living conditions of her working people became noticeable and impossible to ignore in the period following her rapid industrialisation, that industrialisation caused those conditions. But to understand that the roots of the Victorian housing problem lie deeper, in social and economic causes existing in a pre-industrial society, we have only to look at the housing enjoyed by working people in the period before industrialisation and in those parts of Britain which remained non-industrial throughout the Victorian era. There, untouched by the growth of cities, herded together by causes other than lack of land around them, were rural slums of a horror not surpassed by the rookeries of London. The touching picture of country people leaving neat and pretty thatched cottages for the sins and slums of the city is easily dispelled by a closer look at the pretty cottages. If in this chapter we seem to dwell upon horrors it can only be stressed that the evidence, from the accounts of parish ministers at the beginning of the century, from the reports of the Poor Law Commissioners, between the lines of Royal Commission reports like that on the hand-loom weavers and from the late-century reports on the dwellings of agricultural labourers, shows that the decent cottage was the exception, the hovel the rule. Even those agricultural surveys which find estates that can be praised for the provision of housing for their workers prove the point by the minimal conditions they choose for extravagant praise.

This is not to say that the countryside was untouched by the processes of industrialisation: the relative prosperity and comfort of farm workers in arable areas near the manufacturing towns could disprove that. It is only to say that those circumstances which make houses unfit for human habitation—overcrowding and lack of the means of keeping warm and clean—were present both in town and country. The decay of the towns caught the attention of the reformers if only because of the smell. In the country the homes of the poor mouldered slowly away with much less notice. If we pay any attention at all to the dearly-held Victorian belief that it was the dirty, shiftless habits of the poor that caused the misery of their surroundings, it should be remembered that those habits had been formed by generations of slum dwelling before country dwellers came to town. Cobden[1] spoke of villagers in Dorsetshire living 'in dwellings worse than the wigwams of American Indians'. Milton Abbas, built as a show village of pretty thatched cottages in 1786, had deteriorated by the 1840s into a slum of ruinous, overcrowded, filthy houses.[2] New, sound thatch makes fine protection from the weather. Decaying thatch is neither wind- nor rain-proof and makes, besides, a first-rate harbour for vermin. Because the cottages had neither ceiling nor flooring, the droppings from the roofs fell directly upon the inhabitants and their bits of furnishings and added to the muddy filth underfoot. Agricultural improvements had cleared people from the farmlands of Dorset into the villages, with the result that cottages built to house one family were, sixty years later, inhabited by up to thirty-six persons at a time.[3] The villagers arranged among themselves that one cottage should be used entirely by the women of these extended families, another by the men. One is continually struck, when reading nineteenth-century reports of housing conditions, by the extent to which the poor strove in the almost impossible circumstances of their lives, to conform to middle-class standards of morality. In this century we are less shocked by hints of moral deterioration, so very effectively used by all the Victorian reporters in their campaigns to shock the public into accepting reform, than by the revelations of just how bad conditions can become and still be accepted by the poor.

Dr Alison described, in 1840, the houses of day-labourers in Tranent and Haddingtonshire, where fowls roosted in the exposed rafters of the roof and the pigsties were just under the window; 'but these are scarcely nuisances, the odours being comparatively sweet and pleasant to those emanations from the heaps of manure and ashes...and even from the people and houses themselves.'[4] With unplastered stone walls and mud floors these houses offered little comfort and contained nothing in the way of furnishings to soften their bleakness. A pile of straw served as bedding and nails in the walls held what small possessions the household owned. One house visited by Dr Alison, and it was not unique, had another addition: 'the only furniture I observed was an old bedstead with some bedding. I think straw was spread in a corner for a bed, and on one side of the fireplace: on the other side of the fireplace there stood a large horse, sharing the apartment, with its back at no great distance from the roof.'[5]

And, lest it be thought that the Scots peasant lightly endured the proximity of livestock and conditions which would have caused rebellion south of the border, look at the village of Wark Castle, in

Northumberland, as described by James Caird, the *Times* Commissioner, in 1850:

'the very picture of slovenliness and neglect. Wretched houses piled here and there without order—filth of every kind scattered about or heaped up against the walls—horses, cows and pigs lodged under the same roof with their owners, and entering by the same door—in many cases a pigsty beneath the only window of the dwelling—300 people, 60 horses and 50 cows, besides hosts of pigs and poultry—such is the village of Wark.'[6]

In the Vale of Aylesbury in Buckinghamshire cottages of mud walls with earth floors and thatched roofs were criticised for their defective construction and its effects on the health of the inhabitants:

'The vegetable substances mixed with the mud to make it bind, rapidly decompose, leaving the walls porous. The earth of the floor is full of vegetable matter, and from there being nothing to cut off its contact with the surrounding mould, it is peculiarly liable to damp. The floor is frequently charged with animal matter thrown upon it by the inmates, and this rapidly decomposes by the alternate action of heat and moisture. Thatch placed in contact with such walls speedily decays, yielding a gas of the most deleterious quality.'[7]

If things could be worse they were worse in Wales: Richard Cobden described to the House of Commons in a speech on Free Trade on 12 March 1844 the deplorable condition of the half-starved Welsh farm-labourers:

'They live in mud huts, with only one room for sleeping, cooking and living—different ages and sexes herding together. Their cottages have no windows, but a hole through the mud wall to admit the air and light, into which a bundle of rags or turf is thrust at night to stop it up. The thinly thatched roofs are seldom drop-dry, and the mud floor becomes consequently damp and wet, and dirty almost as the road; and to complete the wretched picture, huddled in a corner are the rags and straw of which their beds are composed.'[8]

Of course it can be argued that Cobden, pleading the case against the Corn Laws, had, if not an axe to grind, then at least a point to prove. But he had no need to exaggerate or invent. While there did exist working people in the country who were decently housed— rural areas had a 'superior artisan' class as well as towns[9]—they were the exception and, for the most part, as we shall see later, they lived under patronage, either of great landowner or manufacturing employer, their continuing tenancy depending upon their good behaviour. It is quite clear that there is no part of the kingdom which could not show the majority of its rural inhabitants living in damp and squalor. Even more disturbing is the fact that there is no period of the nineteenth century in which the agricultural labourer was not miserably housed. The Royal Commission on the Housing of the Working Classes whose report was published in 1885, describes a state of affairs in the countryside not very different from that described in the Reports on the Sanitary Condition of the Labouring Population in the 1840s or the Agricultural Surveys at the beginning of the century.[10] Many good cottages were built during the century and a real improvement took place, just as it did in the towns, in the housing of the better-paid worker in the more prosperous parts of the country. But the condition of the poorest grew worse rather than better, again paralleling the situation developing in the towns, as the cottages, which were inadequate when built, perhaps sixty years earlier, grew steadily more dilapidated.

Considering only places already described, we find in 1884 that in Dorsetshire cottages were still 'generally in a bad condition' and very overcrowded;[11] that in Buckinghamshire the typical cottage was still built of mud with two rooms each 8 ft square, with no conveniences whatever.[12] On the estates of the great lords considerable improvements had been made, but outside their protection little or nothing had occurred to make the living conditions of the rural worker approximate to comfort.

In Scotland the clergymen who contributed to the *Old Statistical Account* in the last decade of the eighteenth century, took a close, if condescending, interest in the welfare and living conditions of their parishioners. They produced incidentally an account of the housing of the rural worker, whose detailed reporting and stressing of the need for change came before any other national survey of dwelling conditions. Scotland's housing was traditionally bad, so bad that work slowed down during the winter months while the people subsided into a state of near hibernation to endure the cold, damp and darkness of their homes. An even earlier report had shown the hand-loom weavers 'but ill-accommodated in houses' to such an extent that productivity was severely affected during the winter months.[13] Not only did the cold and damp and poor diet lower their energy but the houses provided no safe storage for the raw material of their trade, the flax-fibre which needed a dry atmosphere to prevent mildew, cleanliness, which was hardly possible, and protection from fire-risk. And the lack of glass or large window-space did not allow enough light to enter the house to make work at the loom possible. Most houses had 'little poor windows and doors that nobody can go in or out without breaking their head except they remember to duck like a goose'.[14]

The *Statistical Account* remarked everywhere the existence of 'small, dark, dirty hovels',[15] 'ill-secured from the effects of weather, and scantily provided with fuel',[16] 'generally low, and consequently very damp in the floors';[17] 'nor is there, for the most part, any access to the houses of the lower ranks, but over a dung-hill, which reaches to the very threshold.'[18]

And yet there is here a clear impression of improvement in the homes of the agricultural labourer. Little additions to the comfort of the household are often noted. Kettles and clocks begin to be fairly common, and properly-made furniture, sometimes of a good, solid quality, appears in the homes of the better set-up rural worker.[19] This increased comfort at the end of the eighteenth century was, however, heavily dependent upon the spectacular but short-lived prosperity of hand-loom linen weaving, for almost every country family in Scotland and the north of England wove in the time spared from the land. The coming of steam-powered weaving brought an end to what one writer called 'the daisy days' of the weavers. Their wages dwindled, the possessions which had made their stone cottages habitable were sold, the loom room was very often let to lodgers to pay the rent.[20] When the Commission to Inquire into the Condition of the Hand-Loom Weavers met in 1834 it heard evidence from all quarters of the miserable living standards to which they had fallen. The agricultural population, accustomed to supplement a meagre living by spinning or weaving, fell back even further into the miserable condition they had known before the brief spurt of prosperity. An unusually perceptive eighteenth-century writer described them like this: 'Our people proceed as if half-asleep, without any lively spirit in contriving and executing',[21] and another backed him up: 'I have often thought that those sorry cloaths, houses and meals to which our commonalty has been accustomed, instead of being assistants, as they may appear at first sight, were great enemies to our growing manufacture'[22]

That was published in 1761, but because it was written of the Scots and in another century it cannot be dismissed as bearing no relation to the truth about the condition of later agricultural workers. One must use the word 'shocking' sparingly when talking about housing because the occasions for feeling shock and horror come so frequently as to devalue the word and to dull the imagination; but if one may use it at all it is to describe the fact that, despite all the talk of housing reform, nothing whatever happened to improve the lot of the average farm worker in a hundred years. The reports collected by John Simon in the 1860s bear testimony on every page 'to the insufficient quality of the house-accommodation generally had by our agricultural labourers'.[23] And the Royal Commission of 1917 shows the persistence of miserably inadequate housing in the countryside.[24]

Low as was the condition of the worker on the land throughout most of the nineteenth century the lot of the industrial labourer in rural areas was often even worse and almost certainly worse than that of the manufacturing labourer in the towns. An extreme case was described in September 1864 in a letter from the Relieving Officer of the Chapel-en-le-Frith Union to the Registrar General:

'a number of small excavations have been made into a large hillock of lime ashes (the refuse of lime kilns) which are used as dwellings and occupied by labourers and others employed in the construction of a railway now in construction through that neighbourhood. The excavations are small, and damp, and have no drains or privies about them and not the slightest means of ventilation except up a hole pulled through the top, and used for a chimney. In consequence of this defect, smallpox has been raging for some time, and some deaths have been caused.'[25]

All the examples quoted have something in common besides the misery of their inhabitants. It is the intention behind their building. Houses without floors or ceilings, with unlined walls, unsound foundations and no drainage cannot help but become slums. They provide only the most basic shelter from the worst of the weather. They were intended for what their builders felt was an inferior class of human being, and so the provision of warmth and comfort was not necessary.

In this they were different from the dwellings of the workers in the towns. These, too, became insanitary hovels, 'unfit for human habitation', inhabited by a miserable population. But they were not, like the rural slums, designed to be so. Their eventual deterioration was not built into their original conception.[26] For the most part, the slums of the cities had been originally good, middle-class or tradesmen's housing, and had been brought into the state of decay in which the first public-health reformers found them, by multi-occupation and misuse. What is more, the overcrowding in the towns was a direct result of the miserable condition of the country dwellers. It was as much the lack of accomodation in the village as the attraction of the city that brought so many immigrants from rural Britain, and Ireland, into the overcrowded centres of the Metropolis, Liverpool and Glasgow and the other large towns.

One of the arguments much used by those who had an interest in delaying housing reform was 'the pigsty theory'. Give a pig a clean sty and he will soon turn it into a muddy, smelly den. There were a few who suggested that perhaps the sty made the pig, not the pig the sty. But it was a strong and perennial argument, and it turned up again as the 'coals in the bath' theory of the twentieth century. The great attraction of this kind of slogan thinking is that it does away with the need for action. Once it has been proved to the satisfaction of the majority of the public that 'it's no good giving decent homes to people like that—they'll only turn them into slums', then consciences are satisfied and pockets saved and nothing need be done.

Even those who advocated change found themselves unwarily providing backing for the pigsty theory, like Cobden when he warned of the deterioration in the habits of the country people which was inevitably following the deterioration in their housing accommodation:

'what a population they are thus sending to the manufacturing districts! And what are these villages but normal schools of prostitution and vice? Oh do not blame the manufacturers for the state of the population in their towns, while you rear such a people in the country, and drive them there for shelter, when the hovels in which they have dwelt fall down about them.'[27]

And Dr Alison, who used all the strength of argument his experience and his conviction could give him to counter those who believed that the poor could save themselves through self-help and who, therefore, could never side with those who would leave the pigs in their filthy sties, still sadly found ammunition for his opponents: 'whether the destitution without the filth or the filth without the destitution is more effectual in the production or extension of fever hardly admits of an answer, because...we have no destitution without filth; but we do have many examples of filth without destitution.'[28]

In the countryside of England, control over the appearance, management and convenience of villages and rural settlements lay in the hands of the great estate-owners. Their power was, in fact, absolute. They could choose to lay out convenient and pretty villages, carefully planned for drainage and water supply, or they could choose to demolish cottages to relieve the estate of the responsibility of caring for its poor. John Simon went so far as to suggest that it should be the duty in law of every large estate to provide house accommodation for its labourers and pointed out that it depended entirely on the whim of the landowner whether the house of the farm worker 'shall be human or swinish'. Whether or not the man who tilled the ground should have decent accommodation depends on the use which others may see fit to make of their 'right to do as they will with their own'.[29] While Simon questioned that right there is no doubt that the right existed in law. Large tracts of the best and most thickly-populated land of England lay in the hands of a few very rich men who had it in their power to see that no man was uncomfortably housed within their bounds. There are, of course, strong reasons why they did not do so and perhaps the strongest is the readiness with which it was universally acknowledged they they might do as they liked with their own property.

Chapter 2

'Pigs and Children': Economic Causes of the Housing Conditions of the Rural Poor

'Hands wanted'
ADVERTISEMENT

We have looked now at some of the worst conditions prevailing in rural areas before and coincidentally with the growth of towns. Now we must give some thought to the social and economic causes lying behind the deterioration of rural living standards which, by driving so large a part of the agricultural population into the towns, contributed to, if it did not cause, overcrowding and town decay. The housing conditions of the rural poor were of great importance both in increasing the overcrowding in slum areas and in conditioning the acceptance by the poor of the low standard of accommodation offered them. It was not, after all, the comfortably housed who left the country, but the already pauperised. The 'attraction to the towns' so often discussed was much more a repulsion from the countryside, not so much an incident of the Industrial Revolution as of continuing occurrence throughout the nineteenth century.

The factors most nearly affecting the condition of the agricultural worker were four: changes in population theories, land 'improvements', the effect of the Poor Laws on the thinking and practice of rural landlords, and the manipulation of the country-dwelling population to suit the needs of water-powered industry.

Population increase and housing shortage are obviously closely linked. It is almost certainly wrong to think, as some agricultural scientists did at the beginning of the nineteenth century, that 'the regularly acting check to population in this kingdom is not the price of corn—but the difficulty of finding habitation.'[1] Although shortage of accommodation acted locally to reduce the population in pockets of rural areas by sending the people elsewhere to find houses, we know that it had no national effect because the population as a whole continued to rise steadily. But there is no doubt that, even without the destruction of cottages practised by landlords throughout the century, the existing cottage accommodation could not fail to be insufficient for the increasing population. Very dramatic increases in town population have tended to mask the fact that in spite of enclosures and emigration, and in spite of statistics showing that a predominantly rural population changed to a predominantly urban one in the years between 1780 and 1840,[2] the rural population was also rising.

It was very obvious to middle-class observers, particularly their farmer employers, their doctors and their clergy, that by the beginning of the nineteenth century there were more of the rural poor than there had been. This was most often interpreted as meaning that country folk were producing more children which had important effects on middle-class attitudes to the rural working population.

Population studies are bedevilled by the paradox that the more work is done on the subject the less certain our knowledge seems to be. The long-accepted theory that advances in medicine were responsible for eighteenth-century population growth has been dispelled by a closer look at medical history.[3] With the important exception of smallpox vaccination, physicians had little advantage over their seventeenth-century forbears in either knowledge or technique. Methods of child-birth delivery had changed very little since medieval times, the only important introduction, the use of forceps, being offset by the increased risk of infection. Without reliable statistical evidence which was not available until after the Registration Act, 1837, in England and twenty years later in Scotland, it is difficult to be certain whether population growth was chiefly the result of longer life expectancy or an increasing birth rate. It would seem that both played a part in the increase and that the new economic activity, by stimulating a demand for labour, not only encouraged country labourers to marry earlier and so produce larger families but also enabled them to feed their children, giving them a greater chance of survival.

Country women were accustomed to conceiving and producing babies at intervals throughout their fertile lives. They were not accustomed to having many of those children survive their infancy. Cottages built to accommodate parents, countless short-lived infants and perhaps three or four surviving children now had to house large families of growing children and young adults. There is also some evidence that country families at the beginning of the nineteenth century were less willing than they had been to apprentice their children at a very early age to the poor-house. One landlord found that cottages with one bedroom which had been sufficient for his tenants were now overcrowded because growing children were being kept at home instead of leaving to serve as prentices.[4]

The eighteenth century saw attempts towards a scientific way of thinking about the relationship of economics and population. Traditional economic thought believed an increasing population to be essential to a thriving nation. In much the same way that modern economists talk about the need for 'growth' as paramount, traditional economists put forward the advantage of population growth. This theory was later rejected by the Malthusian view that a fast increasing population posed a dangerous threat to a growing economy. Malthus had great influence and his theories were the object of discussion among bodies like the newly-established Board of Agriculture and the Highland Society which sought to improve the condition of rural communities. But some economic historians have written as if the views of Malthus were known to every ploughman and his wife, who gave them due consideration before deciding whether or not to have a baby the following year. In a study of housing it is necessary not so much to understand the details of current population theories but to consider how those theories looked to the ordinary farming community and how the way in which they were interpreted affected agricultural policy.

The ordinary farming landlord had the increase in population brought to his attention in two ways: by the abundance of cheaply available labour and by the frequency of calls upon his purse for charitable purposes. His attitude to the first was entirely affected by how much labour he needed. So long as the French wars brought a continuing demand for corn at high prices he could use all the labour he could get. He was therefore not averse to the building of cottages on his land, or at least was prepared to ignore the intense overcrowding of existing cottages. After Waterloo, when prices fell, he found it impossible to absorb the increased population in productive labour. The extra hands upon his land therefore became something to resent. But even during the same period and among farmers affected by the same pressures there existed two distinct ways of thinking about the increasing agricultural population. They could be called the 'stock' theory, and the 'alien' theory. Those who thought of the people on their lands in much the same way as they thought about their stocks of cattle, of sheep, or of pigs, as a valuable asset to be comfortably housed and encouraged to be productive, found it difficult to reject that idea, although they were told by less 'old-fashioned' neighbours that it was out-moded and indeed dangerous. For them good land was land where 'population increases so that pigs and children fill every quarter.'[5]

Others, perhaps more 'progressive', perhaps simply conditioned by personal experience, thought of the surplus population as aliens, never to be encouraged to settle or establish rights upon the land, always to be moved on outside their territories. And here there crept in something new in relationships between country landlord and tenant. Because there was a surplus of labour and a shortage of house accommodation in the country from the last decades of the eighteenth and throughout the nineteenth centuries it became possible, even advisable, to choose which section of the population should be allowed to stay. It is not surprising that farming landlords chose, as even the model dwellings associations later chose, the least offensive members of the rural community. It became important to be 'respectable'. This was expressed quite clearly and without apology by those interested in the design of workmen's houses, for instance Colonel Dirom of Mount Annan who planned new cottages on his land in 1800: 'to render them comfortable habitations for industrious people and beyond the rent which can be afforded by vagabonds'.[6]

It is important not to think about one theory or attitude supplanting another, either suddenly or completely. Both, and a dozen minor variations of them, existed at the same time even within small communities. Both survived in some degree throughout the century. Even within the same national economic conditions local circumstances had their effect. Dairy land required more labour than upland sheep-runs and so cottagers found themselves more welcome there. It was not only the inhumanity of the Duchess of Sutherland and her factors, although in them we see the purest working of the alien theory, but the needs of her land that allowed the expulsion of between 5,000 and 10,000 people from the county of Sutherland between 1807 and 1821. Once the decision to turn cattle land into sheep grazing was taken, the crofters upon the land came to be an irritating surplus, inimical to the profitable use of the land.

Even in those Highland areas where a benevolent paternalism was substituted for the Duchess's cruelty the attitude towards emigration changed with the beginning of the nineteenth century. Opposed by most Hebridean proprietors up to 1800 even in the face of a very fast increasing population, emigration after 1820 came to be arranged and paid for by the island proprietors as a means of lessening overcrowding.[7]

The same thing happended at the other end of the country in the Vale of Avon, another sheep-rearing district where Cobbett called the Emigration Committee, whose job was to keep down the labouring population, 'the most cruel, the most unfeeling, the most brutally insolent...the *most base* of all the creatures that God ever suffered to disgrace the human shape'.[8] In the counties Cobbett knew best, Sussex, Suffolk and Surrey 'teeming with production',[9] the 'stock' theory was favoured and although he talked and wrote as a radical fierce in the cause of the labouring country man, he could not avoid some condescending paternalism in his attitude. When one compares, however, how the average Englishman feels about animals and how he feels about foreigners, there is little doubt that it was better for a labourer to live in those parts of the country where the stock, whether human or animal, was cherished into production. While attitudes were partly governed by disposition or by sensitivity to human needs there is, of course, no doubt that economic factors influenced the attitudes more.

Unimproved land, worked by heavy teams of oxen with old-fashioned unwieldy ploughs, required the presence of abundant labour, especially where fields were small and unenclosed. Enclosures were the first and most important step in reducing the population on the land. At one step an Enclosure Act deprived the labourer of his home and his job. Whereas owners of cottages might receive some compensation for their destruction, tenants never did. Not only could one large field be worked with the same labour as previously had been employed on three or four small plots, but the hedging in and ploughing of common land deprived the labourer of grazing for his own beasts and so of his means of livelihood in times of unemployment. What's more, under the old system of agriculture, there was work not only for the able-bodied men but for their dependants at the labour-consuming tasks of herding, gleaning and flailing. Light, well-drained soils ploughed by well-bred horse teams drawing new metal ploughs needed less labour all year round; and when steam threshing-machines were introduced, as they were early in the century, to Cobbett's disgust and horror, there was no work for the wives, the children and the old. Only young, single men were needed. So cottages were pulled down to discourage settling of cottar families. The few young women needed for dairying and domestic service were taken to live in the farmer's house and 'bothies' were built for the labouring men.[10]

Changes in land-use and agricultural improvements affected the demand for labour and affected attitudes to increased population and to the existence of cottages on the land. But we find in the *Old Statis-*

tical Account of Scotland in the 1790s, the Agricultural Surveys of the English Counties in the first two decades of the nineteenth century, and in the successive reports to Parliament on the condition of the agricultural poor up to and including the 1917 Report,[11] evidence of cottage destruction from all over Great Britain. There was, it is true, some cottage-building in its place, but this came seldom where it was needed by the agricultural population. Sometimes the building was due to the initiative of a landowner in bringing an industrial enterprise to his estate; not always, it should be said, in response to any favourable conditions for industry but more to the notions of possible fortune-making in his own head.[12] Sometimes building was carried on by landlords wishing to improve the appearance of their estates by erecting pretty cottages upon it, but only too often the romantic fancies of the proprietor and the Gothic taste of the architect combined to produce houses too expensive for the labourers who needed them.[13] Speculative cottage-building became increasingly common but as it was not, for the most part, permitted by the great landowners, it had to take place on tracts of land off the estates, away from the places of employment, forcing labourers to walk many miles at the beginning and end of their day's work. The fact that such inconveniently situated houses were taken up merely underlines the great need that existed. Cottage destruction began towards the end of the nineteenth century, rather earlier in Scotland, and continued throughout the century and was not confined to any one kind of agricultural land. Agricultural conditions, and particularly the adoption of labour-intensive farming methods, certainly increased the tendency, but are not enough, without the existence of some other factor, to explain the consistent expulsion of cottagers from the land. That other factor was the working of the Poor Law system.

The Poor Law of England, as traditionally administered, accepted that it was the duty of each parish to maintain its own aged and infirm and to provide the able-bodied with means of making a livelihood, if necessary maintaining him in the work-house. The means to assist the poor was acquired by assessing the proprietors of the parish at a rate varying with the current need. Increased poverty and a growing population, necessarily overloaded with the aged who were living longer and the infants who were increasingly surviving birth, made the system unworkable; or rather, made it so much resented by those on whom fell the burden of paying the poor-rates, that they were unwilling to maintain it efficiently or interpret it charitably. Parishes began to apply very strictly the 1662 Law of Settlement and Removal which allowed them to send out of their bounds people liable to become burdens upon the rates, and to accept as having rights to

2

parish relief only those who by birth or long residency had established rights of settlement.

In practice this could mean that all strangers entering a parish were met with hostility. Local variations in the need for labour and in the wealth of landowners produced great variety in the amounts charged as poor-rates, one parish perhaps being assessed four or five times as high as another. In parishes where the holdings of land were moderate the amount needed for the poor could be divided among a number of proprietors and might not be too harshly felt by any of them. But where the presence of great estates resulted in one man owning the whole of several parishes and being alone responsible for maintaining their poor that man necessarily was very aware of the burden of the rates. Even John Simon, who so deplored the complete and pathetic dependence of the country labourer upon his landlord, had to admit that it was inevitable that large proprietors 'feeling the burthen very definitely and considerably' should use their 'facilities, which are deemed not to be illegal, for shifting it away from themselves...any future can be foretold from the known interests of those who can control it; and it would be too much to expect that landowners as a class should be the voluntary bearers of a taxation, which the law leaves them option to escape.'[14] In other words the landowners could not be blamed for countenancing the constant 'moving-on' from one parish to another of unemployed people who wished to settle, or for pulling down cottages on their land which, by giving them house-room, might have encouraged the settlement of those who would become a charge upon the parish. There was a natural temptation to empty the land. Those who had once been happy to see themselves in the role of Christian dispensers of charitable relief, when the amount asked of them rose too high to be unthinkingly given, were reluctant to change their role to one of niggardly dispensation. They preferred to keep down the numbers on the land so that they might remain benevolent to a few rather than resentfully burdened with many.

Settlement rights were inconsistently and variously interpreted, but interpretation became harsher as the numbers of the poor increased. A legal finding of 1816 that keeping a cow established a right of settlement[15] resulted in fewer and fewer labourers being allowed land on which a cow could graze. This was a short-sighted policy, because their cows had often provided means of sustenance to the poor when wages fell. The removal of their right to keep cows only succeeded in putting more 'upon the parish'. This was eventually recognised and a campaign putting forward the benefits to all of 'cow-cottages' was mounted.

Nothing, however, could mask the fact that the amount required for poor-rates rose steadily. In the 1780s the amount was £2,000,000. By 1803 it had doubled.[16] In 1812 it had risen to over £6,000,000. There was nothing in the air after Waterloo to lead anyone to suppose a fall in the amount could come naturally. Corn prices fell and less labour was needed, just as returning soldiers swelled the country population in need of employment. The population continued to rise. Malthusian theories became even more attractive. A dangerous chop-logic which, having noted that population increase and increase in poor-rates came together, deduced not that the population rise caused the rate increases, which was at least partly true, but that the payment of poor-rates caused a rise in the birth rate. Payment of charitable relief to the poor encouraged them to breed. It was a very attractive proposition for those who were looking for good reasons for non-payment, and it had such respectable adherents, from Malthus, who called the poor-rate 'a bounty on population', to Dr Chalmers and his anxieties about 'luring more of the poor' into existence. Arthur Young denounced the 'new and fashionable objection' to charitable treatment of the poor 'that men and women thus placed in a state of ease and comfort will breed children most intolerably'.[17] Cobbett rode round Britain in a rage denouncing the parsimony of farmers and clerics who had taken from the English labourer his rights in the land of his fathers and who would take from him now his last inheritance, his right to relief in hardship. But neither the good sense of Young nor the eloquence of Cobbett influenced rate-payers as much as did the steady lightening of their pockets.

Pressure upon the government to do something about the Poor Law became very great, although, in fact, little pressure was needed to persuade a government largely composed of great landowners that the pressure of the poor-rate upon their own purses should be lessened. A Royal Commission on the Poor Law was set up in 1832 and its proposals embodied in the Poor Law Amendment Act, 1834, which was given an easy passage through Parliament because it was represented by its proposers as a concession to the landed interest. Its effects aroused less enthusiasm among country landowners than they had expected, partly because the new body of Poor Law Commissioners came to represent that centralisation of authority they so much detested, partly because of the very unpopular energy of the first secretary to the commission, Edwin Chadwick.

If the new Act became unpopular with the middle classes because it lessened their hold upon their own parishes it proved disastrous for the rural labourer, the last step in the steady eroding of his rights which had been operating for half a century, for many the last spur to his leaving the land for the towns. The Act aimed at abolishing, or at least drastically reducing, out-door relief, by allowing help only to those willing to enter the work-house.[18] With the same breath it was decided that the work-house must be made sufficiently unattractive not to harbour the indolent and vicious receivers of charity which it was then popular to fear hiding under every bed. The work-house inmate's lot was to be made 'less eligible' than the lot of the poorest in employment outside. This was quite difficult. The lot of the rural labourer had never been enviable. The failure of the domestic hand-loom weaving industry and the introduction of farm machinery had reduced it by the 1830s to a misery not easily surpassed. But Chadwick's certainty in the rightness of his own course and the energetic application of his new rules succeeded in making the new 'Bastilles' arising throughout the country places to which only those in the most abject need would turn, places where the poor must leave behind the last vestige of human rights. Yet even so, the population in the work-houses of England rose steadily up to 1843. As E. P. Thompson writes: 'The most eloquent testimony to the depths of poverty is in the fact that they were tenanted at all.'[19]

The Act, in spite, or perhaps because of attempts at very harsh application, proved at least to some extent unworkable. Simon's Public Health Reports of the 1860s show landowners still feeling themselves unfairly burdened by the poor-rates and working people still suffering from the policy which moved them from parish to parish in case they became 'chargeable'. For many landowners, even those who had pressed the need for reform, the new system was too harsh, caused too obvious hardship. Middle-class doubts about the rightness and about the workability of this Act, joined with the horror caused by the revelations about rural conditions made in the Poor Law Commissioners' reports to begin a campaign for change. Because Edwin Chadwick's ideas were formed at a time when most people, however anxious for some reform, were muddled and unsure of their own opinions, this campaign for change was channelled into the sanitary reform movement. However necessary sanitary reform may have been, enthusiasm for it absorbed energies which might more profitably have been used to examine the real causes of the condition in which the poor, both rural and urban, were shown to be living, and which might, perhaps, have produced remedies more radical than street-sweeping.

However, what the campaign for sanitary reform, motivated, at least to some extent by the results of the 1834 Poor Law Act,[20] did incidentally achieve, was much needed publicity for the plight of the rural poor. The *Report of the Royal Commission on the Condition of the Hand-Loom Weavers*, published in the same year, added dramatically to the picture. It showed that for many years agricultural districts had been cushioned from the worst effects of dearth or sporadic unemployment by the demand for the products of domestic industry. The withdrawal of this demand left families entirely dependent upon wages from agricultural labour at a time when that labour too was unwanted and ill-paid.

So, one of the factors affecting the distribution of rural population and the pressure on house accommodation was the manipulation of the country labour force for the advantage of the new industrial capitalists. 'Manipulation' is not too strong a word. Chadwick's belief that 'the labourer gains by his connexion with large capital'[21] was not borne out by the evidence. It might seem true until that capital was diverted by the needs or opportunities of the economy to other outlets. Then workmen, drawn from one place to another by transitory needs and then deserted by capital, can only be said to have been manipulated to their own disadvantage. Railway building, for instance, provided an incentive for many thousands of labourers to leave their homes. When the railway mania subsided they were left to find their own way back from the navvies' settlements. The poor were quite helpless to control their own destiny. They must go where wages and homes were provided.

The first effect of national economic growth during the Industrial Revolution had been to increase the rural population or at least, by providing the means of maintenance for a naturally increasing population, to encourage stability rather than immigration. Increasing demand for manufactured goods did not mean an immediate cessation of country industries. In fact it stimulated them. Mechanisation, even in the most advanced industries, never reached every process simultaneously. Many steps, particularly the preparatory and finishing processes, remained hand-operated until well into the nineteenth century, and, because wages were lower in the country, it still paid to have them conducted as domestic out-work. Especially in those rural areas within reach of the larger towns, and of the organising ability and free capital available there, there was plenty of work for country people with time to spare from the fields. Even in some very distant country districts entrepreneurs found it worth-while to arrange for the supply of raw materials and the collection of finished goods from out-workers. William Sandeman of Perth, for instance, employed spinners in Highland glens a hundred miles from his manufactories and found it paid to do so.[22] The textile trades, particularly, employed many thousands of cottagers. A highly organised system of administration had built up during the eighteenth century a commercial connection involving dozens of middle-men from hawker to exporter to collect and dispose of the products of cottage-based industry. Although it dwindled, this did not end with the coming of technological change. Cotton was soon mechanised and town-based, wool and flax very much later. Even after weaving became a factory operation, wool-combing, for instance, provided home occupation for workers in the Bradford district, lace-making in Nottinghamshire, sack-sewing in Angus. Not only textiles but the metal-based trades used domestic labour. In the Midlands nail-making remained a cottage trade until, by the 1830s, machine-made nails became cheaply available.[23] Near Sheffield, file-cutters and scythe- and sickle-makers worked outside the city in their own homes. Simon found overcrowding in rural areas 'aggravated by the influence of local industries—straw-plaiting, glove-making, braiding, shoe-making, etc.—which are followed as household occupations by young women who might otherwise be in service or married away from home'.[24] The most widespread of domestic occupations, however, was, of course, weaving, which in its palmy days, in the brief years after the invention of mill-spinning and before the power-loom, kept many thousands of families in comfort and independence.

Cottage homes were adapted for the pursuit of these trades and furnished by the proceeds from them. Children could be employed at minor occupations such as winding and reeling, young adults, who might otherwise have left their villages in search of work, stayed home to learn their fathers' trades. The effect on these domestic workers of, first, the mechanisation of their trades, and then a steady recession of demand was disastrous. It meant the selling of household furnishings, and, most bitterly felt, the giving up of independence. Men who had been little masters had to seek wage employment again, and at a time when agriculture had no need for more labour. The end of out-work meant the stranding in rural areas of a large population for whom there was neither work nor charity. It was the last step in the steady process of reducing the rural population and driving the people into the fast-growing towns. The degrading treatment of the agricultural labourer dependent on poor relief, and the very harsh putting down of any resistance in the form of riot or combination[25] succeeded in driving thousands either to emigration or to town employment.

Temporarily, however, some were attracted into different parts of the country by the needs of water-powered industry. The eighteenth century had seen a proliferation of small country mills, flour mills, fulling mills, lint mills, and so on. Arkwright's invention of water-frame spinning caused the injection of very large amounts of industrial capital into rural areas. Very few of the established commercial centres had water supplies sufficient for the demands of the new industry. Entrepreneurs were forced to go into the country to seek land with water rights on which they could build spinning mills. Within sixteen years of the publication of Arkwright's patent in 1769, more than £500,000 had been spent on the erection of mills using the water-frame.[26] Because the need for abundant water took precedence over everything else, these mills were not always, not indeed often, built in populated areas. It therefore became necessary to attract labour to them. A dislike of regular hours, of indoor labour, of mill-overseers, some well-based fear of fire-risk and a general suspicion of novelty meant that local people were often very unwilling to work in the new mills.[27] Employers were forced to seek out labour and to encourage the settling of large families to provide cheap hands, by providing house accommodation for them. Advertisements like these appeared in local papers:

'Families wanted, house and garden provided free, Seatonden mill.'
'A family that could furnish a few hands for the mill would be accommodated with house and yard, Douglastown mill.'
'Carding master wanted for Prinlaws mill. One with a family would be preferred.'[28]

Small industrial villages grew up around the water-powered spinning mills. Families settled there. Although it was reluctantly at first that men used to field work entered the mills, their children quickly adapted to regular employment and families became dependent upon mill wages; sadly dependent because in the cotton districts water-powered spinning lasted only one generation of workers, in flax districts perhaps two. Then steam power, more efficient, more subject to control, and, most important, able to be operated in the towns, supplanted the water-mills. The small industrial settlements in the country were left with full dams and silent wheels. Families who had come from other parts of the country, attracted by free houses and the hope of steady wages, were stranded and unemployed again. Sometimes whole villages were advertised for sale, but what happened to their inhabitants is not recorded. Discouraged in the parishes of their birth and unwelcome everywhere else, they had only the big towns left to turn to.

Economies in farm labour, the tighter application of the Poor Laws, the application of new mechanical methods to industries which had been handcrafts all reached a peak in the period between the end of the Napoleonic wars and about 1835, before the industrial depression which followed. The simmering revolt among agricultural labourers in some parts of the country, best known through the case of the Tolpuddle martyrs, whose impudence in attempting to form a union led to their transportation in 1833, only hardened opposition to attempts at alleviating their condition.

It has been suggested that this period saw the emigration from the country of all 'the ambitious, the sharp-witted, and the young',[29] leaving behind a slow, unprotesting rural population growing more sluggishly accustomed to slum conditions in their decaying cottages. In fact, it can be argued that something quite opposite was taking place. Time and again contemporary accounts report that it was the lack of somewhere to live that was the chief reason for people leaving the country. But it was the poorest, most degraded, least able class of farm labourers which was left homeless in the greatest numbers. The skilled artisans of the countryside, the shepherds, the game-keepers, the blacksmiths, the horse-men, the dairy-men, wheel-wrights and thatchers, for instance, were still valued in the rural community and there were still houses for them. It is sometimes forgotten that the country has its labour aristocrats too. These were not unintelligent people, nor were they unaccustomed to comfortable housing. It was in fact the least well-housed who reached the towns, the least able to improve their surroundings and the most likely to accept the deterioration of living standards, of health and comfort and privacy, in the decaying streets.

Chapter 3

Results in Housing: Design and Standard of the Homes of the Agricultural Workers

'Long, long in hut and hall,
May hearts of native proof be reared'
FELICIA HEMANS, *The Homes of England*

It is easy to fall into the trap of showing everything about this period in too sharp a light of contrast, as if there were only on the one hand rick-burning hordes of swinish oafs living in filthy hovels, on the other besmocked and docile, forelock-pulling yokels, living in pretty white cottages. So it is worth-while attempting to make a dispassionate study of the results of social and economic factors upon the design and standards of the homes of the agricultural poor. It is not easy to find uncoloured descriptions of working people's homes. Every man who visited and described them brought his own subjective ideas to their viewing. Some could see only the dirt. Some looked only for evidence of immorality. A few noticed the poverty and wondered about their diet. Not as many as one would wish took note of the size and number of rooms or the materials of construction. This was partly because cottage types, though varying from district to district, varied very little in construction (though not in state of repair) within one area, so that a local observer might see nothing worth his comment. Perhaps we can come nearest to an understanding of what houses were really like through descriptions and plans of suggested conditions which seemed ideal at the time. There were very many such plans especially in two phases, first at the turn of the eighteenth and nineteenth centuries when bodies like the then new Board of Agriculture were attempting to encourage cottage-building and then again after the middle of the nineteenth century when publicity about agricultural conditions had stimulated some interest in rural housing. It is fair to assume that actual conditions fell short of those which contemporaries thought Utopian, and from that we can arrive at an idea of the optimum standard of comfort available. There are only too many descriptions of the worst. The evidence points to the fact that bad conditions were more prevalent than good, but we must beware of words like 'bad' and 'good', as we must be careful not to deduce too much from descriptive terms like 'dark' or 'small'. How dark is dark? How small is small? How dirty is dirty?

So far, because we have been attempting to show the origins of the move away from the country which resulted in overcrowded towns, we have dealt mostly with the first decades of the nineteenth century. But the flow from rural areas into industrial cities was a continuing process throughout the century and now, because our purpose is to show that the extreme shortage of decent housing accommodation was one main cause forcing people away from the country, we deal with the whole of the nineteenth century in describing the kind of houses in which agricultural workers lived. It is clear that, while perhaps the very worst conditions were eliminated and the best slightly more common, the housing of country people changed only very little throughout the century. If one remembers that it was not until after the Second World War that improvement grants encouraged farmers to put running water into their workers' cottages it becomes less surprising that so little happened in the way of improvement in Victorian times.

Quite marked improvements in living conditions clearly had been taking place during the last quarter of the eighteenth century but this was set back by the end of a profitable war and the lack of demand for domestic industry. Similarly economic growth, combined with agitation for reform, produced a good deal of cottage-building and some raising of standards in the period between 1850 and 1880 after which the agricultural depression put a stop to farm improvement generally. There was considerable publicity in the 1880s for claims that the agricultural workers' lot had been improved by his beneficent landlords but the 1885 Commissioners' Report shows this to have been largely wishful thinking in response to pricked consciences. It would seem that while in times of economic depression house-building to satisfy market demand must cease, evangelical crusading for better housing becomes more vociferous, stimulated by the sheer increase in human need. To suppose that the periods in which housing was most talked about, when the shortage of housing was most clearly demonstrated, should inevitably be followed by periods of housing improvement, it to be misled. This is only a preliminary to saying that, when we come down to discussing the details of housing actually available to rural workers, what can be said about the beginning of the century can be said about the middle and the end as well. Standards of comfort and space changed very little. It seems certain that the Public Health Act, 1875, did begin to have a real effect upon sanitary conditions, in that new houses were seldom after that built with surface drains running into open ditches. But the evidence given to the Commission of 1885 shows that insanitary conditions were still most common. The failure of farming profits followed too hard upon the reforming legislation for its bite to take real effect.

It can be taken as axiomatic that standards of housing are affected by the intentions of the builder. To take an interesting example: in the parish of Flitwick, the wish to increase the number of dependable voters persuaded a builder, whose intention was to create new forty-shilling freeholds carrying a vote, to erect a number of cottages. Because the need for these cottages was temporary their construction was the cheapest possible—clay walls, turf roofs and not even a pretence of drains. They were erected for election purposes and when they had fulfilled the intention of their builder they were allowed to fall into decay.[1] Housing built in response to a temporary need, whether for speedy financial return, for shelter for casual labour or for election purposes is seldom of anything but the lowest standard. One eminently qualified observer seems mistaken when he claims that all rural housing after the end of the Napoleonic wars was built with charitable intentions.[2] This leaves out of account all building with temporary motivation and also oversimplifies the thinking of the wealthy landlords with whom he chiefly deals. Evangelical doctrine had certainly great influence among the wealthy and aristocratic gentlemen who controlled whether building should or should not take place over most of the populated parts of rural Britain, but there were many Utilitarians among them too. So while the intention of some was to fulfil God's purpose by building for the industrious poor on their estates (and one cannot doubt that houses so built were of the highest standard that then seemed possible), there were more whose understanding of the community good led them to wish chiefly the adornment of their own estates, and their building was affected more by romantic notions of the picturesque than by any real understanding of countrymen's needs.

One must beware of putting modern notions into nineteenth-century heads, of colouring our understanding of Victorian thinking with our knowledge of what has happened since. For instance, the idea that comfortably housed labour might be more productive and therefore conducive to national happiness is very much in accordance with Benthamite beliefs, but not even the most diligent Benthamite had reached so far. The converse, that dirt led to disease and so to loss of man-hours, was being tentatively put forward as a new and by no means generally acceptable idea in the evidence to the Health of Towns Committee, but the notion that comfort, as opposed to mere lack of disease, might be necessary was hardly yet given an airing. Similarly, Evangelicals were progressing towards the belief that workers, being human, should be housed not like animals, but in conditions befitting Christian souls, but this did not include any idea that the home should give pleasure. The intention of both Evangelicals and Utilitarians, then, was to provide basic shelter plus a clean well, no more. The extent to which their intentions were carried out was affected by their pockets, by their lack of understanding of the real needs of the people, and by their romantic notions. The one big change from tradition in rural housing in the nineteenth century was that it ceased to be provided for country workers by themselves and came to be provided for the poor man by his betters and designed by professionals with ideas about style. Thus the deliberately rather than accidentally 'picturesque' cottage appeared in the countryside, affected in style by a new interest in 'simple' country life, as described by romantics like Wordsworth and painted by Morland and Wilkie.

The motivation of those who built, then, was far from simple. That they were moved by charity must be admitted because we know that all the sums presented to them proved it impossible to build for agricultural labourers, and to let at an economic rent.[3] We need not decide, nor even discuss at this juncture, whether or not it was indeed impossible to build both cheaply and well; the important thing is that those concerned believed it to be impossible. But there were motives other than charity, among them a wish to have on their estates a docile, dependent people, a wish which became tangled up with the often expressed notion of the nobility of simple people. It was pleasanter to believe that the peasant was a splendidly noble, uncorrupted character who was nevertheless prepared to honour his betters than that he was a depraved, incestuous lout, only too ready to burn and destroy the envied property of his masters; and it was easier to believe if the visible peasants were housed in pretty cottages and the rick-burning rebels expelled from the estate.

So, because estate villages had great influence over the building practice of lesser men, because their estates were spread over so wide a part of the face of Britain, and because many of the same landowners who were building houses on their own estates had great political influence over the course of housing legislation, we must deal first with the 'closed' or estate villages.[4] These villages were closed in the sense that no man might build upon them without permission from the overall landowner. There could be no 'squatting' by labourers attempting to establish settlers' rights. There could be no competitive building by tradesmen for profit. And, perhaps most important, there could be no independent action by the villagers themselves, no do-it-yourself building or extending.

They were closed, too, in the sense that no worker not in the permanent employ of the estate could live there. The villages were for the essential estate workers. All the temporary and low-grade labour was evicted. Landowners did not cease to employ ordinary labourers, and they continued to need extra hands in seed-time and harvest, but they ceased to house them. It was the labourer who was most likely to become a charge upon the rates in his old age or in periods of unemployment and so labourers became unwelcome upon the estates. This meant that, on top of a long day's work in the fields, labourers were forced to walk five and six miles to the 'open' village away from the estate that employed but would not house them.

Within the closed villages lived the skilled and privileged country workers, housed as the fancy of the landlord led him. In the last decade of the eighteenth and the first of the nineteenth century, 'fancy' was the word. The Gothic revival led to some astonishing excesses in cottage-building, to the plastering on of elaborately 'rustic' detail, bearing no relation either to the interior of the cottage or to its scale. Professional architects and builders, now employed generally for the first time by landowners to build for their workers, had had little practice in cottage-building. The nineteenth century had to grope after a legitimate cottage style with some roots in tradition and some acknowledgement of new ideas about living standards, and its first gropings led in extraordinary directions. The 'cottage ornée' was taken up with enthusiasm by the rural landed gentry, seeming to add dignity, novelty and charm to the countryside and nodding towards the idea of quaint, fairytale peasantry. Deep eaves, which excluded almost all the light from the tiny, ornate windows, ornamental patterned slate roofs which could only be repaired at great cost, shakily fretted verandas, appeared among a profusion of other inventive but not very useful ideas. Unfortunately the cost of the cottage ornée was so high that it was seldom inhabited by those rural workers who, still in their mouldering ancient hovels, stood in need of new houses. It became the country home of the curate, the doctor or other reasonably well-to-do professional gentlemen with romantic tastes to suit their abodes and servants to clean the inconvenient rooms.[5] By 1860 cottages ornées were getting hard to let. One young Victorian in search of a home for his bride inspected several dark, damp and typhoid-ridden cottages at £45 per year, and was told: 'Large mansions might be hard to get but the "cottage orny" [as the house agent called it] was quite another thing. Here they were on the list by the dozens.'[6]

After the first flush of enthusiasm for the picturesque had died down, the work of various new bodies interested in cottage-building began to take some effect. The Board of Agriculture and the Highland Society, agricultural societies and farming clubs and a number of new organisations like the 'Cottage Improvement Society' concentrated the attention of the landowning public on the need for good, functional design in cottage-building, and, by offering prizes to architects and builders in competition, encouraged research into the basic principles of cottage design. From 1840 the new building journals published specimen plans and informative articles, and a wealth of new cottage pattern books appeared.

The result was that, by about the middle of the century, a compromise had been reached between the traditional tied cottage, which for all its faults had a natural affinity of appearance with its background, and the cottage ornée. It was a compromise which allowed at least minimum space requirements, while at the same time restricting cost. Something like a standard plan began to appear all over England with another more restricted form becoming common in the lowland areas of Scotland. Several causes tended to produce standardisation. The first was certainly cost. Although the cost of building materials varied throughout the country it was invariably dearer to build than in town, partly because of the cost of transporting materials, but equally because the demand was for small groups of houses rather than large and more economically built blocks. By the time the cottage plan had been pared down to its minimum it began to look much the same whichever hand drew the proportions. There was little in cottage design to attract the attentions of the most creatively original Victorian architects, although Butterfield and Street, for instance, were responsible for some good examples later in the century. This lack of interest, leaving the problem largely in the hands of the uninspired, tended to a certain mediocrity of style. Then, as mechanical production methods began to make bricks and slate of a standard type more cheaply available over a wider area, the use of similar materials brought about uniformity. Large landowners, the Duke of Bedford particularly, whose estates were widely dispersed from the Wash to Devon, set an example in cottage-building which inevitably influenced, through its publication in illustrated papers, the kind of cottage built by owners of smaller properties.

The most common plan was to build cottages in pairs, each having one main room of from 12 ft to 15 ft square, and two bedrooms upstairs. According to the generosity of the proprietor and to his view of what was important there might also be a cellar or pantry, a third bedroom upstairs, a pig-sty and 'necessary' in the yard and a lean-to wood store. Materials were, wherever possible, quarried on the estates until the use of machine-made bricks made brick construction more common and cheaper. In 1813, in Norfolk, Mr Robinson of Carbrook was constructing cottages of flint-work, with eighteen-inch-thick walls plastered on the inside with clay and pan-tile roofs.[7] These had one room up and one downstairs, each 15 ft by 11 ft, with two more tiny bedrooms and a wood-shed in a low lean-to. In Lincolnshire at the same time[8] cottages were regularly built of 'stud and mud'.[9] But in Lancashire the traditional rubble stone or 'post and plaister' construction had already given way to brick.[10] By 1851 Bedford was finding that the use of hollow bricks lowered his construction costs as well as making his cottages dryer and better ventilated.

Bedford's estates were so large and his interest in the need for good cottages so keen that he conducted his building 'with all the method of private speculation', using mass production techniques, giving scientific attention to costs, taking into account the future cost of repairs, and adopting new machinery with enthusiasm. He kept a hundred workmen in permanent employment in his own woodyard, foundry, smithy, carpenters', plumbers', glaziers' and painters' shops. Cottage plans were rationalised so that windows, doors and stairs were of uniform sizes and could be mass-produced indoors during the winter and put up during the summer, thus making economic use of labour as well as materials. A 25 h.p. steam engine powered planing machinery and lathes for the carpenters, blew the smithy fires, dried timber in the sawing shed and heated an oven for the workmen's dinners. The cottages were plainly constructed of nine-inch-thick brick walls, with the judicious addition of ornament in the form of concrete slabs bearing the ducal crest. Each had two ground floor rooms, one fitted with kitchen range, the other with a copper, two or three bedrooms upstairs, one of which had a fireplace, and out-buildings for wood and ashes. They were built in rows with a common oven for each row. Their cost was, in mid-century, from £90 to £100 and, letting at 1s to 1s 6d a week according to whether they had two or three bedrooms, it was reckoned that they gave a return of nearly 3 per cent on outlay.[11] As there was no site cost, and taking into account the economical scale of the Bedford enterprise, this would tend to support the claim of other landowners that the building of good cottages for labourers could not be indulged in without financial loss. The Duke, however, had a purpose other than financial gain in his cottage-building. By taking the letting away from the small farmers and into his own hands, and by letting only on weekly terms so that notice of eviction could immediately be given to undesirable tenants, he kept a very tight control over the residents on his land.[12] His claim was that: 'To improve the dwellings of the labouring class, and afford them the means of greater cleanliness, health and comfort in their own homes, to extend education, and thus raise the social and moral habits of those most valuable members of the community, are among the first duties, and ought to be among the truest pleasures, of every landlord.'[13]

Two important influences for change upon nineteenth-century land-owners were the implementing of the Public Health Act, 1875, and the work of the Enclosures Commissioners. The Public Health Act applied to rural districts in a way that previous legislation had not. Charles Dilke, chairman to the 1885 Commission, writing to the commission's secretary in September 1884 said: 'Enormous good seems to have been done by the working of the Public Health Act in these villages which were undoubtedly very bad indeed some years ago.'[14] He had just returned from the west of England where some of the most abject living conditions could be found.

The Enclosures Commissioners were appointed in 1845 to facilitate the loaning of public money for estate improvement without the need for expensive individual local Acts.[15] They appointed inspectors who, when a landowner applied for state help, reported whether the sug-gested improvements should or should not be approved. These inspectors interested themselves in cottage-building, encouraged it and laid down certain minimum standards. They refused to approve the use of poor bricks or unseasoned timber, insisted on the provision of adequate sanitary arrangements and sufficient sleeping space, and on occasion refused to condone unnecessary decoration. In the matter of style they were tolerant so that landowners could indulge their own taste in architecture within the limits of cost efficiency and reasonable living standards. They were 'willing to adopt any plan which affords a reasonable amount of accommodation and provides for the separation of the sexes, and for health, comfort and decency'. The need to win their approval put landowners in a mood conducive to being shown the most practical methods of cottage-building. Their influence was most felt in the North of England, the South being slower to apply for improvement loans,[16] perhaps because the larger landowners, like the Duke of Bedford, had capital of their own more easily available, and the smaller were in any case disinclined to improve. John Simon, who tried most conscientiously to be fair, found, however, that landed estates 'where at least no aggression has been made against the house accommodation of the poor...are...altogether exceptional and rare'.[17] He mentioned only the Dukes of Bedford, Rutland and Newcastle, and the Marquis of Exeter as being conspicuously different from the general run of neglectful landlords.

The extent of the Duke of Bedford's estates and, most important, the fact that he owned valuable land within the Metropolis as well as his country estates, meant that he was sheltered from the worst effects of agricultural depressions. He was more able than most landowners to provide for the poor man at his gate. It is the more pertinent to ask, then, what happened to those labourers he found unsuitable for residence on his estates, those who were too poor or improvident to pay their rents regularly, whose age or ill-health or large numbers of children might make them burdens on the rates, or whose spirit of independence made them bridle at the restrictions of estate life, so that they seemed rebellious and dangerous. Nineteenth-century landed proprietors could with an easy conscience feel that it was no part of their duty to provide homes for the immoral, the undeserving, the socially undesirable. Yet rural labourers could slide into one of these categories through sets of accidents quite beyond their control. And such people had to live somewhere.

One of the gaps left by the estate-owners was filled by the cottage speculator. Near to those prosperous estates where the demand for labour was not equalled by the supply of houses, builders extended the 'open' villages by the erection of rows of very cheaply constructed cottages. Making use of sites unsuitable for other purposes and there-fore usually marshy and unstable,[18] ignoring the need for land, street or house drainage and using shoddy materials, builders who were, for the most part, small-scale and under-capitalised, ran up cottage blocks which were designed to become rural slums. The most common plan was the row of two-roomed, two-storey cottages. It was common practice to build them with walls only half a brick thick, that is, 4½ in.[19] This meant not only that the walls were too thin for comfort, the cheapest bricks being often extremely porous and allowing the penetration of damp and draught,[20] but that they were unsafe, especially upon unstable foundations which produced settlement cracks. In nine-inch walls an occasional lengthways brick is bonded in to strengthen the structure. Half-brick walls could have no such safeguard. Wherever there was a possibility of a return these flimsy cottages were quickly run up, often financed by a huckster or shop-keeper in the existing village, who stood to gain by the increase in custom from the growing population.

Speculative cottage-building was common in Lancashire as early as 1795, when the cotton manufacturers' use of rural sites was attracting labour. Cheap brick houses, built in long rows, could then give a return of 10 to 20 per cent with rents at from £1 to £5 per year, 'if the rents are paid'.[21] It was a big 'if'. By the 1840s the natural objectives of speculative building in the country was to get a very quick return on a low outlay. No continuing profit could be counted on because of the unsteadiness of agricultural wages. This kept costs and quality abysmally low. By 1885 the commission found that building houses for agricultural labour to be let at an economic rent and yielding any financial return had been impossible for some years.[22] There had long since ceased to be any speculative cottage builders and so there was no longer a need to control their activities. The problem from then on was to encourage rather than limit cottage-building.

It is clear, then, that the greatest part of the rural population of Britain during most of the nineteenth century was living neither in improved estate cottages, of which there were necessarily few, nor in fact in new houses of any kind.[23] They remained in the traditional country workers' houses built by their ancestors and repaired and extended over generations by the workers themselves with or without the assistance of village tradesmen.

In Scotland the custom had always been, even for the most bene-ficent landowners, to 'feu' land to prospective tenants and to allow them to build their own houses upon it, sometimes providing timber and stone from the estate. It was not usual for the proprietor to commission the building himself although he sometimes had a feuing plan drawn up with some restrictions placed upon heights of houses built there.[24] As early as the 1730s John Cockburn of Ormiston insisted that only two-storey houses be built in his improved villages, saying 'good, handsome houses sets off the place, whereas ugly ones hurts the narrow thinking man that builds them.' When Claud Alexander of Ballochmyle feued land at Catrine to David Dale, Robert Owen's father-in-law, he, too, bound all those who built there to build their houses two storeys high, and to slate them.[25] Robert Rennie who, in 1803, drew up a model village plan, disliked two-storey houses without making it clear why, and would seem to suggest that earlier landlords' efforts to encourage two-storey building had been successful: 'Of all houses a high, narrow, thatched one is the least commodious...and unluckily in most villages such houses abound.'[26] He preferred a low, double cottage, not less than 22 ft wide inside and 10 ft high, with two large rooms on the ground floor, one used as a kitchen, 14 ft wide with an end cut off as a bed-chamber, the other 22 ft by 16 ft to be used as a loom shop; and with two garret-rooms 16 ft wide and 6 ft in the middle, lit by large skylights and used either as bedrooms or workshops. Too much weight should not be given to Rennie's suggestion that two-storey building was the most common form in Scotland at the turn of the century. In large villages and small market towns rows of two-storey cottages, with access to the top flat by an outside stone stairway, were common and can still be seen in places like Kirriemuir and Forfar. But in the predominantly agricultural areas the labourer's cottage was something like that described by Rennie, although less generous in size, and the many cottages built between about 1845 and 1860 to replace the meaner traditional houses were double, one-storey cottages, the better class of which had garret-rooms and dormer windows. These are the farm cottages still standing all over Scotland which have been improved in the last two decades by the addition of kitchens, bathrooms and front porches.

Scotland has few examples of what in England is thought of as an ordinary village and those few are artificially planted in their context by the fancy of a wealthy landlord. Two interesting examples are Fochabers in Morayshire and Gifford in Haddingtonshire, both of which were built in the eighteenth century, as was Milton Abbas in Dorset, to house tenants from 'untidy' settlements, which had been pulled down because they offended the proprietor's taste. The traditional Lowland Scots community was the 'fern toum', a huddling of workers' cottages around the 'mains' or principal farmer's house and steading.[27] This form did not attract settling by tradesmen other than those employed in strictly agricultural pursuits. The community was not large enough to support village carpenters or builders. People living there were necessarily self-sufficient and house-building was simply one of the necessary activities of life. By the last quarter of the eighteenth century it was becoming more common to employ stone masons,[28] partly because of the improving landlords' greater interest in the design of houses on their land, partly because more organised and regular field-work, or the extreme profitability of hand-loom weaving, was leaving less time for desultory spare-time activities such as wall-building, and partly because gradually introduced new building techniques, the use of dressed stone instead of rubble, of mortar instead of dry-stone, required more practised skills. But in less prosperous parts of Scotland than the arable farming Lowlands, old habits remained. In the southern counties, for instance, although walls and roof were provided for tenants, ceilings were an additional extra brought by the tenant and carried from job to job in the form of a bundle of boards and carefully hoarded nails along with other household goods.[29] Some carried and erected white-washed canvas instead. Their cottages were, in fact, built with the very minimum of joiner-work and interior woodwork had to be supplied by the occupant. In the Highlands of Scotland crofters even carried their own roof timbers with them, the house existing on the croft when they took up a new tenancy being literally no more than four low stone walls.[30] On these they rested their beams, which in a timberless country were of great value, and on which were then spread turves to keep out the weather. This casts a new light on those scattered and deserted crofts still to be seen in the north-west of Scotland and generally supposed to be 'ruined' dwellings. It may be that these are not houses fallen into ruin but, in fact, that they are still in the condition in which they were customarily left by removing tenants, stripped of turf-roof, rafters, doors and left to the elements as virtually indestructible stone walls, which being in any case only 6 ft high would crumble only slowly over a hundred years.

The traditional Highland 'black house' was beginning by 1884 gradually to give place to the slighly superior white house. The black house was built of stones gathered off the fields, and therefore rounded and unshapely, fitted roughly together. The walls were 5 ft wide and 6 ft high on all four sides, there being no gable wall. Roof timbers rested on these thick walls and were covered with turf thatching as much as 2 ft thick, slightly rounded 'like an elongated beehive',[31] but with no perceptible ridge. The house was fairly long, sometimes 30 ft, to allow accommodation for the cattle wintering at one end, and about 15 ft wide. The single window was about 1 ft square, admitting very little light through the thickness of the walls, but equally allowing little heat to escape from the peat fire burning in the middle of the floor. It was necessary to stoop on entering the only door through which both human occupants and cattle came and went. 'If your visit is in July, you make an unexpected descent of a foot down to the earthen floor. If your visit is in March, the inside level is higher than the surface of the ground, for you step upon a thick mass of wet cattle-bedding and dung, which has accumulated since the last summer.'

These were the miserable living conditions and certainly longer-enduring in the remote parts of the Highlands than elsewhere in Britain, but it would be wrong to imagine that only the savage crofter walked on floors spongy with decay. In the Home Counties of England too, thatch-roofed mud cottages had earth floors bound with vegetable matter, which decomposed and mixed with the 'animal matter' thrown upon it by the inmates to produce a damp and rotting mass.[32] At least in the Highlands use was made of the rotten flooring which every spring was cleared and laid on the fields as manure along with the well-rotted roof turves which were then replaced.

The last quarter of the century saw some improvement in crofter housing. A partial division between cattle and family became usual and fireplaces with proper chimneys built into gable walls began to appear. But reform was very much delayed by the, to say the least, insensitive way of Highland landlords in attempts to regulate building on their land. When they were hit by the idea of sanitary improvement, they attempted, through their factors, to enforce a code of estate regulations about the maintenance and erection of buildings on their land. Quite apart from the harassing effect of any new regulations upon a bewilderingly poor people, the new code contained in many cases a very real injustice: it compelled crofter-tenants to acknowledge the landlord as sole proprietor of houses which they themselves had built from materials on their crofts with their own labour. It laid upon them the obligation to keep houses already on the land in good repair, bound them not to destroy or take away any part of such buildings, yet rejected their claim to ownership of any additions or extensions or new buildings. At Easdale quarries a particularly resented case concerned 'white houses', each with a room and kitchen and closet built by the quarriers at a cost of about £50 each, the cost being high for the district because masons and joiners were employed. The stony ground on which they were built bore no earth and these tenants carried soil with which to make gardens. On the death of the old proprietor, with whom the tenants had only word-of-mouth contracts, a new factor began to extract rents of from £1 12s to £2 12s a year and to force the workers, who were of course dependent for their living on employment in the proprietor's quarries, to acknowledge that their houses belonged to Lord Breadalbane. By 1885 the proprietor was gaining a yearly income of between £400 and £500 a year from houses built by people who imagined themselves to be the owners.

There was in such treatment no incentive to improve land or houses or to conform to sanitary regulations. It was one more reason to add to the list of causes pushing Highland people away from their traditional lands and customs into the unfamiliar and unwelcoming cities. The large numbers of Highland people in the towns, their conspicuous non-conformity in dress, language and behaviour, the difficulty they experienced in settling to regular habits of industry and the depressed psychology which caused them to accept unprotestingly the most abject of living conditions, caused the Highlanders, even before the Irish, to be looked on by city dwellers with a measure of derision and distaste.

In England, as in Scotland, rural workers' cottages varied in standard and style from district to district. Whether the landlord was resident or absentee, prosperous or heavily mortgaged, interested in reform or reactionary, was important. The legal framework of house and land letting, whether copyhold, leasehold or freehold had its effect, conditioning whether or not a cottage dweller thought it worthwhile to attempt repairs and improvements on his own account. To reformers with the interests of the people at heart it seemed, for instance, that to encourage workers to become owners of small freehold properties was a desirable long-term project. But Poor Law administration which forbade out-relief to freehold cottagers discouraged labourers and even forced many to sell their freehold so that they might obtain charity in times of unemployment.[33]

The kind of farming prevalent in the district affected the kind of cottage; the type of soil on which they were built, the presence of local building materials, timber, reeds or straw for thatching, quarries for slate or stone, brickyards or tile works affected the style. What cannot be avoided is the general conclusion that the houses of most agricultural workers barely gave them shelter from the elements, and where they offered comfort it was the labour and ingenuity of the occupants that had achieved it. The very wide difference in terms of comfort between the best furnished and the most miserable cottage when both were basically the same was often used as an argument against the need for reform. If one woman could make a pleasant, neat and cheerful home out of four bare walls then only lack of diligence prevented others from doing so: that was the reasoning. But even the best of the old cottages seems primitive in the extreme by today's standards. On the Duke of Bedford's estates, regular inspection and estate maintenance, as well as careful selection of occupants, meant that the old cottages there were among the best in Britain. They were still one-roomed, thatched cottages with outside privies, with water supplied from rain barrels.[34]

From foundation to roof most cottages were unsound, largely because their construction was inadequate. It goes without saying that damp-proof courses were unheard of. Foundation making, as we have seen, was a science little understood. In any case the difficulty of finding land on which to build had become so acute that builders had little choice of site. Foundations were too often laid on roadside waste[35] or on marshy ground on sites generally unsuitable for other purposes and therefore, in fact, unsuitable for building without the expense of extensive draining and levelling operations which were not likely to be undertaken. Floors were most often of trodden mud or clay which, just passable when dry, became a morass in wet weather. In Ayrshire 'floors are frequently depressed a few inches below the street, and composed of clay full of inequalities so they are constantly dirty and generally wet; indeed, floors which neither admit of washing nor scrubbing cannot be otherwise.'[36]

This was the kind of thing generally forgotten when slum dwellers were criticised for failing to keep their homes clean. Too many of them had been reared in conditions where scrubbing was not a possibility. In Dorset a medical visitor reported: 'I have often seen the springs bursting through the *mud* floor of some of the cottages, and little channels cut from the centre under the doorways to carry off the water.'[37] In one house the door had been removed from its hinges so that the children, who were employed in making buttons, should have something dry to put their feet on. Where suitable stone could be quarried close at hand and carrying arranged, flagged floors were laid. In Halkirk, in Caithness, where the local stone occurred naturally in flat thin strata suitable for flags, stone floors were common as early as 1795.[38] But although Aberdeenshire at the end of the eighteenth century was exporting 12,000 tons of paving stone to London annually[39] this was for street laying, not for domestic floors, certainly not for floors for agricultural labourers. In the 1830s, Carnegie of Carmyllie in Angus invented stone-cutting machinery which facilitated and cheapened the laying of flags. Locally their use became common. It was claimed, for instance, that although the slums of Dundee were in every other way at least as horrific as those of London, they were in one respect much cleaner—their back courts were laid with even stone flags instead of being trodden earth, and so could be swept clean.[40] But transport costs ensured that stone floors could not become generally common in rural areas. Even where they were used they were far from ideal. Laid flat on the earth, they were liable to subsidence and soon became uneven and cracked. They were only a trifle less damp and cold than the earth itself. 'Another great deficiency is the bad floors. Even in the case of my parish, which is supposed to be a very superior parish, because I have a great number of gentry residing in it, the floors are often composed of little broken pieces of flag, with great holes, such as one could almost trip up in; it is impossible for any woman to keep such a floor as that tidy and clean.'[41]

It would, of course, be a ridiculous exaggeration to suggest that nowhere in Britain did country people walk upon dry and even flooring. Where timber existed locally and cheaply it was used for floors. By the 1880s imported boards were being laid as flooring in the better kind of cottage.[42] After the introduction of powered sawing and planing machinery in joiners' workshops in the 1830s prepared timber began to be more generally used. But for most country people board floors remained a luxury. Even in Sheffield city few houses had replaced flags with wooden floor-boards as late as 1893.[43] One witness, who persistently in his evidence to the 1885 Commission talked about 'good' and 'bad' cottages, was asked by Lord Salisbury to describe his idea of a 'good' cottage. He did not put his sights too high. A 'good' house, he said, should have walls, roof and windows that could keep out the weather, access to clean water, and a sound floor.[44] But he did not think it even remotely possible that such cottages were likely to be the lot of most agricultural workers, and, although there were plenty of individual examples of such cottages, he knew of no part of Britain where they could be said to be common. No one raised a voice to deny what he said.

Reformers generally were appalled at the existence of so many 'cob' cottages or mud cabins.[45] Arthur Young decried them at the beginning of the century. But in 1885 they were not only still very common but it was said that too vigorous an attempt to destroy them and replace them with 'better' homes would bring about a revolution.[46] These clay cottages had something to commend them apart from the extreme cheapness of their construction. Called *stud and mud* in the South, *wattle and daub* in the Home Counties, *post and plaister* in the North, they were all variations on the theme of a timber frame filled in with the local clay, with straw and branches for reinforcement. In Cornwall 'cob' cottages were constructed of rough stone and clay. Their great advantage was that merely to stay up the walls had to be very thick. This gave them efficient insulation against the weather, at least while they were new. If they absorbed and held the damp this made them perhaps not much inferior to the kind of brick most commonly used for labourers' cottages, which was often extremely porous as well as being liable to cracking. Lime-washed inside and out, these clay-walled cottages could be given a neat and clean appearance and it is not difficult to understand how they appealed to the romantic painters, their locally-found materials giving them a natural affinity with their environment. To the kind of mind which prefers a landscape to look as little man-made as possible, the cob cottage must have seemed to be as near to a natural habitat for the peasant as could be achieved. Their cost was certainly markedly lower than any other kind of construction. Mr Renton of Freiston in Lincolnshire was building stud and mud cottages with thatched roofs for £40 a pair, while brick and tile cottages of the same accommodation, one room up and one down, cost from £60 to £80 each.[47] This particular landlord was building, for letting to his tenants, cottages much the same as those they traditionally built for themselves, with the materials they were allowed to draw free from the estate.

Roofing again was of local materials, pan-tiles where the local clay was suitable for tile-making, but more often thatch. Slates were usual for workers' cottages in England only where they had easy access to a slate quarry, although 'estate' cottages were slated increasingly often throughout the century. In Scotland, partly because of the more frequent presence of stone, partly because long straw was not sufficiently abundant slate roofs for stone cottages were common. Thatch could be of good yellow wheat straw, of turf, as in the Highlands of Scotland, or even of flax straw.[48] Like clay walls, a thatch roof gave good insulation when new and sound. The trouble was that these cottages did not get the maintenance they needed. Even on good estates like the Duke of Bedford's, whose factor boasted to the 1885 Commission about his efficient organisation of cottage maintenance, white-washing of the old cottages took place only every six years and repairs had often to wait. Long hours of field-work left neither energy nor hours of daylight for the labourer himself to carry out repairs. Some of the worst-maintained cottages were those held on 'life-hold' terms. Roughly constructed in the first place, they were allowed to fall into disrepair towards the end of their term in the knowledge that the estate proprietor would certainly demolish them when their ownership reverted to him. Once thatch deteriorates it quickly becomes rotten and saturated with damp, letting through the rain and dropping particles of dirt and mud steadily on to the house beneath.

Joiner-work, being expensive, was kept to the minimum. Cottages seldom had more than one entrance. Window-frames, in particular, were beyond the skill of labourers and so windows were few and small. But the lack of ventilation, so loudly deplored by town slum visitors, was seldom complained of in the country. There were a hundred ways the wind could find its way into old cottages. Glass was not easily replaced, and the astonishing number of times one reads of windows being stuffed with old hats makes one stop to wonder where all the old hats came from. Even when one remembers how seldom nineteenth-century people ventured out with uncovered heads, one is hard put to it to understand why the turnover in hats should be rapid enough to stuff the windows of so many slum houses, even in remote country areas. It is tempting to associate this apparent surplus of hats with high mortality rates. Was it the headgear of the dead that so often stopped the draught? When the Highland Society began their campaign to improve labourers' cottages they first turned their attention to finding the best kind of window that could cheaply be fitted. They found many problems, not least the lack of standard sizing and the difficulty of keeping stocks of window glass available.[49]

Having described walls, roof, floor, windows and door, one has described the house. One cannot speak of average size. The 'average cottage' has no reality. But we know that rooms 8 ft square were everywhere considered mean and that rooms 16 ft by 12 ft were thought unnecessarily extravagant. It is reasonable, then, to suppose most cottage rooms to lie somewhere between the two in size. The fireplace served for cooking and heating water as well as for heat. On the large estates the best landlords installed ranges for cooking on, but the average country housewife made do with an open fire. The diet available to agricultural labourers gave them in any case, little need of an oven.

Sanitary arrangements consisted for the most part of a hole in the ground under a lean-to shed, emptied only when the garden plot needed manure. Underground drains were not approved of for cottages, even by fairly enlightened builders,[50] and where there was any waste removal at all it was conducted by surface drains, usually into the nearest ditch. 'Good' cottages had a well in the garden or at least one shared by a group of houses. Many others made do with rain barrels.

As in the homes of town workers, furniture was minimal, soft furnishings almost non-existent, but the degree of comfort achieved with so little varied very much. The 1840 Reports on the Sanitary Condition of the Labouring Population, for instance, contrasted the homes of the poorest workers, so primitive that the whole worldly possessions of the worst consisted of a pile of straw for bedding, large boulders for chairs, a jar for water and a piece of poker for breaking coal, with those of the best-provided, who had wooden furniture, beds, tables, chairs and chests which they cleaned with sand and water, and earthenware dishes, kept clean and used as ornaments. While reporters thought the contrast pointed to differences in moral character—the neat homes showing sterling worth, the hovels betraying dissolute ways—it is more likely that steadiness of employment made more difference than anything else. A small but regular wage could be husbanded to provide for cheap or home-made furnishings, while a wage not to be depended upon meant that furniture bought in good times had to be pawned in bad. Although, in the case of the worst conditions described, the cause was probably the harshness of the labour conditions. Where mother, father and children were employed long hours in hard labour, as in the colliery districts, there was neither time nor energy for making comfort at home nor much opportunity for enjoying it.

Chapter 4

Housing of the Industrial Poor in Rural Areas

'Are we eels or puddocks that we are sent to live in a loch?'
Royal Commission on Housing in Scotland, 1917, p. 187

However miserable the homes of the agricultural workers, the worst conditions were experienced in those pockets of rural areas where industry had been introduced. Where building labourers were employed in drain-, road-, canal- or railway-making, in rural collieries, brickyards and lime-works in what Simon called 'an adventitious throng of population . . . the accommodation will be of the vilest description'.[1] Against this it must be said that some of the best housing in the country could be found in rural industrial settlements, especially in the spinning villages.

The homes of the industrial poor in rural areas can be divided into two kinds, the paternally organised settlements and those of haphazard growth. Whether the accommodation was to be permanent or temporary affected its quality, although intended permanence could not be taken as a criterion of quality. The intention of the builder is not in this case sufficient guide to the kind of accommodation he offered, because in industrial settlement the intention was, of course, to make a profit; but in the case of men like Robert Owen, charity was much confused with profit-making and idealism with business sense. Perhaps the most reliable pointer to quality of living conditions is the availability or scarcity of labour. If the work offered comparatively high wages in a time of scarcity, as did most railway enterprises, for instance, then men flocked to the site without further inducement and could be housed as cheaply as the conscience of the instigator of the enterprise allowed. The extreme example of this is that already described, where labourers were left to provide shelter for themselves by hollowing caves out of piles of lime waste. If there was a need to attract labour, either because of rural suspicion of new methods or because of sites very distant from population centres, and especially where the labour of women and children was required, then housing accommodation had to be offered.

Owen was not the only entrepreneur to carry in his head a dream of a Utopian village inhabited by grateful workers. Something not unlike the Fabian dream of the garden village was very prevalent during the Industrial Revolution and in the years leading up to it. The need to entice country people to accept mill employment seems to have taught industrial builders to plan real communities, in the way that twentieth-century local authorities have only belatedly recognised as necessary. Shops, church and school were often included in the original conception, roads laid out at pleasant intervals and green space left for recreation. No doubt vanity played an important part in the psychology of industrial village builders, as the custom of naming the village after the manufacturer who built it would seem to show. Vanity which led to amenity could easily be tolerated by those employees who enjoyed the benefits of the planned community. If it was irksome for grown men to accept the restrictions of life in a paternally organised village—sobriety was almost always a condition of tenancy and public houses were not included among the amenities—their wives and children appreciated the wage packet not eroded by drink.

There were two main phases of village building by manufacturers, at the end of the eighteenth century and in the middle of the nineteenth, although the Health of Towns Committee found in 1840 that the building of cottages for workmen was very common then in the North, where the manufacturers' rows 'particularly eligible from every point of view, and very comfortable, of course' were contrasted very favourably with those built as an entirely commercial proposition.[2]

Of the first phase, perhaps New Lanark is the best known and the most interesting because of the future fame of its second owner, Robert Owen. In its original conception it was no different from many such villages built in the North of England and particularly in the middle belt of Scotland. The need to plan whole villages rather than add extra housing to existing villages was particularly strong in Scotland, partly because of the traditional lack of villages, partly because suitable sites for water power occurred most often away from towns. David Dale, Owen's father-in-law, planned his first settlement at New Lanark in partnership with Richard Arkwright, who was so delighted with the possibilities of the new site that he forecast the arising there of a new Manchester. While he was planning the mill village in 1792, Dale is said to have been very much affected by hearing of the plight of a large party of evicted Highlanders whose emigrant ship had been wrecked, leaving them stranded and without possessions. He saw the chance to solve his own labour problems while at the same time performing an obviously charitable action. Messages were sent to the Highland families, offering them employment in the new mills and homes in the new village. Dale promised, and kept his promise, to build 200 houses for them.[3] These slate-roofed stone houses, some of which are still standing, were built in long rows of two or three storeys, close to the mill. As a style of living, it must have been as strange to the people from the glens as high-rise flats seem to twentieth-century town dwellers. At any rate they did not settle down too well. Employers everywhere found difficulties in converting people accustomed to crofting to regular, indoor work patterns: 'As soon put a deer to the plough as a Highlander to the loom' said one witness to the Hand-Loom Weaving Commission. Dale was forced, until he could induce docile, Lowland labour to settle, to fall back upon the employment of pauper children, apprenticed at the age of 5 or 6, from Edinburgh poor-houses. What is interesting here is that we have some information about where the first inhabitants of the village came from. While census figures give the totals of people transferring from agricultural to industrial labour, we do not know too much about which kinds of rural workers first accepted employment and housing in the new villages.

When Robert Owen took over the management of New Lanark from his father-in-law in 1813, he ceased to employ pauper children. This is ascribed to his humanitarian, socialist principles, but of course it was an action made possible by the fact that adult labourers were beginning to accept the necessity of taking mill employment. By 1845 New Lanark was peopled by an industrious, respectable and respectful work force; 'compared with other establishments of the kind, remarkably decent in behaviour'; rather different from the situation described fifty years earlier when the village was infected by 'individuals who, either from ignorance or from violence and temper, will not listen to the cool voice of reason, who chime in with the ravings of the Friends of the People, as they call themselves'.[4]

Dale's earlier village, at Catrine in Ayrshire, had been built to a more rural scale, to which labourers must more easily have adjusted their own living patterns. A crescent of two-storey stone cottages was built along the river bank, leaving room for a village green. It accorded very well with the ideas of Robert Rennie, whose 'Plan of an Inland Village' had listed as requisites, a good, dry bleachfield for cotton work, 'which is of much consequence both to the feuar and to the landholder', and access to a main thoroughfare. 'Unless trade is in a flourishing state and some branch of a manufactory established,' Rennie wrote, 'it is in vain to think of erecting a village.' There were certainly many wishful attempts at village-building in late eighteenth-century Scotland which failed because they were based on what one writer called 'chimerical prospects' rather than the needs of industry.

That Dale changed his house plan from two-storey cottage to the stark tenement rows of New Lanark was due partly to the need to accommodate more labour, partly to economy. He was not the only manufacturer who found it necessary to adapt his original ideas. Many found that the kind of house they would like to have built for their workers could not produce an economic rent out of the wages paid. This was particularly so in the second, mid-century phase of village building, which was instigated not so much by an absolute shortage of labour as it had been at the end of the eighteenth century, as by a need for the right kind of labour. Experience had taught entrepreneurs the value of reliable, docile labour. Employers' logic now led them to believe that by building good houses for their workers they would raise the 'moral standard' of those they employed and so achieve a productive and docile work force.[5]

The fact that workers in tied houses become subdued by the fear of losing their homes was not lost sight of, but it would be wrong not to recognise the genuine altruism in some employers' motives. It led them at first to build houses so conscientiously designed to improve workers' living conditions that they were beyond their pockets: Edward Ackroyd planned at Copley, near Halifax, a village for his workers, 'with an eye to the improvement of their social condition'. The first houses, built in back-to-back rows, with eighteen houses to each front, had a living-room, 14 ft 6 in by 13 ft 6 in, and two bedrooms, one 14 ft 6 in by 10 ft with a fireplace, the other only 8 ft by 6 ft 6 in, without a fireplace. There was a stone sink supplied with piped water at the foot of the stairs. Each house had a cellar, a 'convenience' and an ash-pit, and drains emptied into the nearby river. The 'picturesque outline was adopted in a modified old English style', that is they had lattice windows and decorative arches over the doorways. These cottages proved too luxurious and later blocks were built 'more in the common style of the country', that is, with only one bedroom, parents using a box bed in the kitchen/living-room.[6]

Thomas Ashworth, who built cottages for his workmen in the country near Bolton, found, contrary to the experience of everyone else, that he was able to raise standards as he went along, but this may have been because his first houses were nearer the possible basic than others. He was building in the late 1830s. This was before the publication of the sensational reports on the living conditions of the poor had pushed employers towards the idea of improvement of moral tone through living standards. Ashworth found that his workers were willing at first to pay only for the very cheapest possible one-roomed house. After a few years' residence on his estate he found that they had raised their standards high enough to ask for more space and that, on moving into bigger houses, they began to show signs of growing self-respect and to aspire to comfort.

Another interesting and successful venture was the model village at Bromborough Pool on the Wirral peninsula, begun in 1854 by Price's Patent Candle Company, a London firm whose rapid growth and need for expansion had suggested the move to the North. Julian Hill, the company's London architect, designed a village laid out with gardens and open spaces, with two-storey brick houses built in terraces of four, with slate pitched roofs. Each had a living-room, kitchen and scullery on the ground floor, with two or three bedrooms upstairs. The living-room was 12 ft by 10 ft 8 in, kitchen 9 ft 5 in by 7 ft 1 in, scullery 8 ft by 7 ft 6 in. Although none of these rooms was large it will be remembered that most working people's houses of the time combined the functions of all three in one. There was no unnecessary ornament and the style was very much in the early nineteenth-century vernacular tradition, unaffected by the Victorian taste for decorative patterns in brick or the kind of 'Italianate' detail in which some took such pride. This has been called the 'first garden village',[7] a claim which can hardly be substantiated in view of the common occurrence of villages planned with gardens, yards and open spaces in the eighteenth century. It might, perhaps, be justly called the first employer-built garden village of the nineteenth century, and is, in any case, an interesting experiment.

Probably the most famous of all model industrial villages is Saltaire, built in 1854 by Titus Salt on an isolated moorland site to allow for the expansion of his Bradford works. His mills were built in the much admired 'Italian' style and the first 560 workers' houses designed to complement them with ornate chimneys and elaborate window and door detail. Salt planned for two types of housing from the start. The overlookers' cottages were built in blocks of ten with turrets at each end and contained, in the basement, wash-house, pantry and coal cellar; on the ground floor, parlour 16 ft 6 in by 15 ft, and kitchen 14 ft 6 in by 14 ft; and upstairs three to six bedrooms. Some had front gardens, all had back yards with conveniences. Cheaper houses were built fourteen to a row and had no wash-house in the basement, no parlour, slightly smaller rooms and no front gardens. Letting at rents of from 2s 4d to 7s 6d per week these houses, costing £120 for the cheaper, £200 for the larger, gave Salt a return of 4 per cent on his investment, but, it was said 'even in a pecuniary point of view, if all the saving effected by having steady, well-disposed, and well-behaved work people could be accurately measured, Mr Salt is a great gainer.'[8]

The 'well-disposed' is important. When it comes down to it there is not so much to choose between landed gentry and industrialist in their attitudes to workers' housing. There was in both of them a reasonable wish to have nothing on their land that they need be ashamed of, and increasingly as the century wore on, the Victorian middle classes did see need for shame in the misery of people dependent upon them . There was a genuine charitable intention to improve the lot of working people, and a real belief that this could only be carried out through a raising of their moral standards. Both shared the need to have docile people in their houses, people who would give no trouble, behave quietly and look respectable, and, preferably, show gratitude. Neither was prepared to house the unruly, the morally or physically crippled, the aged or the undependable. Farm workers were evicted for belonging to the Agricultural Labourers' Union.[9] Industrial strikes were easily broken by the threat of eviction. So the next question to be asked is: where did those considered unsuitable for living in the new villages go?

Among the clearly unsuitable were the Irish, upon whom were hurled all the abusive epithets of the middle classes and of those of the working classes who struggled to 'better themselves'. The Irish were shiftless, dirty, primitive, drunken, wild and generally to be deprecated. Certainly the social conditions they had left behind had taught them that steady industry and foresight would gain them nothing. They were prepared to work hard in short spurts and to spend their earnings in glorious outbursts of self-expression. They had not been affected by the teachings of Wesley as the English poor had been. They did not recognise sobriety, patience and forethought as virtues. Their independence has not been weakened by the paternal kindness of country estates. Unable to gain help from parish relief, they had not the same need to qualify, by making themselves acceptable to landlords, for settlement rights in villages. Because their strong backs made them physically suited to spade work and their psychological make-up made them find pleasure in the competitive expenditure of energy, they ended up in the navvy gangs. All over Britain in the first half of the nineteenth century, men were shifting earth by spadeful and barrowful, clearing the way for the constructions of the civil engineers. Lengths of road, rail or canal were let out to separate contractors, most of them in a fairly small way of business. To them flocked for employment not only the Irish but able-bodied single men from all over the country, particularly the rebels, those who, for one reason or another, did not fit into the gentle ways of village communities.[10] These contractors might, or might not, provide accommodation for their temporary hands. Very often the men were left to run up makeshift shelter for themselves. Where accommodation was provided it was of the cheapest and most quickly erected kind, usually wooden huts provided with neither water supply nor sanitary arrangements.[11] The settlements quickly became like the camps of barbarian hordes, their surroundings deep in mud and decaying remains of food and human filth. It was not surprising that, as Simon put it, it often happended that 'amid the adventitious throng of population, there is imported some contagious disease under circumstances which peculiarly favour its spread; and severe local epidemics of smallpox, diphtheria, typhoid fever, cholera, typhus, scarlatina have again and again owed their rise to such contagion from unclean industrial settlements.'[12]

Nor was it only, although it was chiefly, single men who were attracted to these settlements. Some of the men, for want of other homes, had their families with them. The hope of making quick profits by providing for the material wants of the navvies brought a trail of camp-following women and children. Where families were accommodated in huts they were obliged by the contractor to take in lodgers so that the 'houses' were necessarily overcrowded.[13]

But if navvies were miserably housed, and even if they knew that their next job was unlikely to bring improved conditions, they lived in hope because they knew the site was only temporarily occupied until the work was completed. Far more miserable were the occupants of those industrial settlements which, arising as a result of new exploitation of mineral resources, became permanent in their squalor. Mining settlements were, said Simon, 'foul, priviless, ill-watered, unscavenged, overcrowded lairs'.[14] The sanitary reports of the 1840s, too, had condemned the conditions in which miners were kept, the surroundings 'most intolerably filthy and unwholesome', the interiors of the houses unfurnished, filthy, and overcrowded.[15] By 1885 it was said of the pit villages near Newcastle that conditions were better than they had been: 'the coal owners have had to build better houses, there has been a great improvement, and the colliers expect to have better

1. 'Picturesque cottage' or 'rural slum'? *Above*: The home of twenty-six Christian souls. *Below*: A pretty prospect in Abergavenny

II. Traditional country workers' cottages near Carmarthen

houses than they used to have provided for them . . . There is an increased standard of comfort set up which induces the coal owners to compete with each other by building better houses for their workmen.'[16] In fact, the old story: only a shortage of labour would induce most employers to provide good housing for their work people. The same report showed that in less prosperous mining districts conditions had improved very little.[17]

There were certain special causes contributing to the evils of colliery housing. In English mining districts the most important was that mines were most usually worked on lease from the local landowner. The coal owner's interest, then, was in the underground workings only. He did not feel himself responsible for the land above, and, in fact, was discouraged from taking an interest in it by 'his landlord's tendency to fix on him, as ground rent, an exorbitant additional charge for the privilege of having on the surface of the ground the decent and comfortable village which the labourers of the subterranean property ought to inhabit'.[18] Speculators who might otherwise have run up cheap housing to meet the colliers' needs were equally discouraged by the exorbitant ground rents asked by landowners whose wish was as much to keep the unsavoury mining population off their land as to make high profits.[19] Short leases, usually only for twenty-one years, contributed to discourage house-building by coal owners to whom it did not seem worth-while to outlay capital on housing for leases which might only be temporary. The lack of security of tenure was certainly used by coal owners as an excuse for not providing housing. In other places, however, the length of lease caused bad conditions. Where long leases had been granted at the end of the eighteenth century for the working of mines then showing clear promise of long-term profit-making, cheap housing had been put up for workers. But towards the end of their ninety-nine-year leases, owners, noting the imminence of the time when the property would revert to the landowner, refused all repairs. In Wales, by 1885, cottages were in sad want of repair and many were tumbling down for lack of ordinary maintenance.[20]

The harshness of the labour, the long hours, the employment of women and children all tended to produce a dull-minded population unlikely to protest, however terrible their conditions. But the colliers' state of mind varied very much with the prosperity of the district. A depressed and degraded population in Scottish mining districts was said to take no interest in life outside the coal village, and to be remarkable for 'ignorance, prejudice and apathy in respect to almost everything except whisky, cock-fighting and the like . . . political, social, religious and all great and national questions are totally

3

uninteresting to the majority of these degraded men.'[21] The insides of their homes betrayed their apathy and brutishness. In the North of England and in Wales, a different and more independent spirit prevailed and Dr John Hunter commented on 'those signs of regard for order and cleanliness which, in the northern districts, are to be seen in the interior of a collier's dwelling',[22] in contrast with the poverty of the accommodation offered to him. But Scottish miners were, in the 1840s, at the most two generations removed from slavery. Until the very end of the eighteenth century miners in Scotland had been bondsmen, bound with their wives and children to work for their owner, who had power to bring back and imprison those who ran away and the right to sell his workers with his other property. Such an inheritance, and the utter isolation from contact with other working people, had left a brutish and degraded people, only too accustomed to misery, and a tradition among proprietors which did not spur them to improve the housing of their people. The Royal Commission of 1917 found that, even then, 'the shadows of the early bondage seem still to affect the miners of the present generation.' 120-year-old houses were still occupied and dampness and filth were the rule.[23]

Another kind of accommodation for working people which aroused great indignation among middle-class reporters was the 'bothy', a kind of communal dormitory building in which single men or women were boarded by their employer. Common in those parts of Scotland where labour economies were inducing farmers to evict cottage families and to employ only single labourers, they had always been frowned upon by clergymen who saw these all-male communities as fostering grounds for drink, gambling and immoral talk. When improving landlords introduced them into English farming they roused the explosive anger of Cobbett who saw in them only a degraded way of living far removed from his notion of comfortable and self-respecting cottage life:

> 'The treatment of labourers all over England [was fair] before the Scotch nobility urged the sharking landlords of England to throw farms together, and to bring up infernal Scotch *feelosofers* and scourging Scotch bailiffs to introduce the damnable "boothie" system into England. Ever since the system began; and stupid and greedy Coke of Norfolk was the beginning of it; ever since that system was begun, there has been war between the labourers of England and the owners and occupiers of the land.'[24]

Cobbett was laying a lot at the door of the bothy. He could not forgive the Scottish farm labourers he met because they seemed content with their way of living: 'What a Sussex chopstick would say if he were asked to live in one of these "Boothies" I do not exactly know; but this I know, that I should not like to be the man to make the proposition to him, especially if he had a bill-hook in his hand.'[25] At least one modern writer has agreed with him that in the bothies, the social degradation of the Scottish agricultural worker was complete.[26] This is to confuse motive with effect. The landowners' motives in depopulating the land were not admirable and their reduction of cottages did tend to produce a depressed, slum-dwelling agricultural population, but the effects of bothy-building were not all bad. However it may have looked to observers, working people were not discontented with the bothies. There are many country people alive today who remember their days of bothying with a pleasure that is not wholly brought about by the romanticism of age. A bothy was a large stone building with a stone flag floor and a big hearth at one end which was kept generously supplied with coals and on which the workers kept boiling pots of broth and porridge. Bunk beds were built-in round the room as in barracks, and there was little other furniture. But, however basic the accommodation, the community life of the farm-bothies produced a culture of its own, of which the 'bothy-ballads' are the flowering, which might be at least as worthy of interest as the over-publicised but very similar dormitory living of the nine-teenth-century cowhand in the American West. And if it seemed to Cobbett that the workers in bothies were housed only slightly better than the animals, that was in itself an improvement on the earlier situation in which many workers lived with the animals.

The bothy system could, however, be abused, and it was pushed to conditions of almost concentration-camp horror by some indus-trialists who adopted it as a cheap means of housing workers. It was particularly common in bleachfields, where the labour force was fluctuating, to provide bothy accommodation for the young women workers. In the country works, because the scale was small, the system worked well and the girls lived under the genuinely paternal care of their employer, locked in at night by the watchmen to safe-guard them from the attentions of the male workers. But as bleaching became an indoor process and the bleaching villages grew into towns, the numbers of workers grew and bothy conditions deteriorated. At the works of Messrs Cochran, Barrhead, 400 women were housed in one building in 1858, sleeping three to a bed, the sick with the healthy, and it was said that the close proximity produced a nervous state which resulted in violent outbreaks of quarrelling and that the health of young girls suffered to the extent that they might not be capable of normal child-bearing.[27]

Hugh Miller described some very rudimentary shelter offered to him in his days as an itinerant mason—earth floors, stone slab beds, leaking roofs and open gables. One laird who was criticised for leaving a crazy old building standing near his new farm steadings replied that it was not through lack of taste he spared the hovel! He found it of great convenience every time his speculations brought a drove of pigs or a squad of masons that way.[28]

In 1917 some migrant workers described a haybarn provided for their bothying as 'a roof-covered tank of green stagnant water three quarters of a foot deep . . . Are we eels or puddocks', they asked, 'that we are sent to live in a loch?'[29]

But whatever his home in his working days, the end for the country labourer was only too likely to be the work-house. Houses tied to employment implied eviction for those too old to work and agricultural wages were neither steady enough nor large enough to allow for saving. The poor-houses built in parishes all over England during the eighteenth century in response to the 1723 Act (which empowered authorities to provide accommodation for the poor) were small-scale, of local materials, not too different in appearance from other local buildings. Thus Crabbe, whose county was East Anglia, spoke of 'Yon house that holds the parish poor, whose walls of mud scarce bear the broken door.' In Dorest, too, walls were of clay, and floors of earth,[30] while in the North the work-house, like the local cottages, might be of brick or stone. The Poor Law Amendment Act envisaged buildings very different in character and in scale, designed and intended to be barrack-like and inhospitable in appearance, comfortless and repressive indoors. Building could not keep pace with the rise in pauperism and so the full effect of the Act was never achieved. The attempt to achieve it, however, and the fear of the work-house that it taught, was an important step in driving the country poor into the towns, there to increase the overcrowding, the unemployment and the disease of fast-growing town populations.

One of the first causes of town decay, then, was increasing poverty and homelessness in the countryside brought about by more labour—intensive farming, a decreasing need for domestic out-workers, and the destruction of cottages by landowners ridding themselves of an uncomfortable responsibility. Thousands left the rural areas and the town population shifted over and made room for them. The results are still with us.

When it at last began to be recognised that the depopulation of the countryside had gone too far, the scarcity of good cottages had become irreversible. So great was the need for new cottages in rural areas by the twentieth century that the government, still in principle convinced that private enterprise should be able to house the population, announced in 1913 plans for the building (by the state) of houses for agricultural workers. The Housing Act, 1890, gave rural district councils powers to build. The Housing and Town Planning Act, 1909, gave the Local Government Board authority to urge the councils to begin building houses. But so few districts responded to this encouragement, only 315 houses having been built in rural areas between 1909 and 1912, that Ministers felt prepared to take the step of direct interference by the state in local affairs.[31] The principle of public responsibility for housing was still far from being generally accepted and urban districts were not yet within reach of this kind of government action, but in rural districts the need for housing to arrest the drain of people from the countryside had become urgent even beyond the needs of the town slums.

Housing and Public Health

PART 2

Housing and Public Health

Chapter 5

Town Decay

'Putrid miasmata'
NINETEENTH-CENTURY MEDICAL TERM

Traditionally the rural labourer who wished to do so had been able to find land and materials to build his own house. The agricultural revolution, together with the replacement of instinctive habits of feudal care by theoretical concepts of country management, had made it increasingly hard for him to do so. While the idea was spreading that independence should be encouraged and self-help approved, it was being made more and more difficult for the working man to provide for himself. He was being pushed out of the country and into the towns by a deliberate policy which extolled the virtues of doing without charity while at the same time making independent action to house a family almost impossible. The towns filled up with country people searching for homes as much as for employment.

What they found in the town streets and alleys cannot have been encouraging. Even at the beginning of the century the pace of population growth was too fast for the builders and scores of families were crowding into houses built to accommodate one or two. The shortage of accommodation sent town rents for decent housing beyond the pocket of the labourer, and cellars, shacks and subdivided rooms were all that was left for him. Unpaved and undrained streets degenerated everywhere into quagmires. Refuse piled up. Water ran dry. Roofs leaked rain, floors rotted, walls bulged and the back-courts overflowed with sewage. While money was spent to improve town centres for the prestige of mayors and councillors, or to widen, drain and cleanse streets in the more prosperous parts of town, 'nothing whatever has been done to improve the condition of the districts inhabited by the poor...or the filthy, close and crowded state of their houses. No prudence or forethought can avoid the dreadful evils to which they are exposed.'[1]

The smell alone must have been nearly intolerable. To a generation which spends thousands of pounds on scents and deodorants to ensure that we are never aware of the odours of other bodies, it is astonishing that the smell of the 1830s could have been (even temporarily) endured. Yet thousands of families lived with years' old accumulations of filth permanently accosting their nostrils. It is at least arguable that if human excreta did not emit offensive odours the British public health movement might never have succeeded. To those middle-class officials who were driven by the execution of their duty into city slums the misery of the people was apparent, but it was the smell which was truly shocking. And when it is remembered that nineteenth-century people had an almost mystical fear of the powers of smell, believing that the source of infection and disease was actually created in the noxious gases emitted from decaying matter, it is easy to understand their horror. They believed that the 'putrid miasmata' lying over the filthy streets and closes could attack them through their noses. While there were eminent doctors who disagreed, the most influential body of medical opinion believed that 'the immediate or the exciting cause of fever is a poison formed by the corruption or the decomposition of organic matter.'[2]

One Irish tenant with a gift for words said that 'the smell was bad enough to raise the roof off his skull.'[3] The court where he lived in Leeds was 'inundated with filth, having a most intolerable stench... proceeding from two ash-pits in the adjoining courts having oozed through the wall, the liquid portion of it had oozed through in consequence of the imperfection of the wall...the landlord flagged the floor to prevent it oozing through but it still oozed through.'[4] There were cellar dwellings nearby where a hole was broken in the floor to allow the filth and water to flow there, and where the family bed was placed over the hole. In Liverpool one particularly noxious home was inhabited by a family 'who had collected about three cart-loads of manure out of the streets and courts and kept it in this cellar where they lived'.[5] In the old part of Hull, within the docks, where interconnecting courts in series had only one narrow-arched entrance to the road for eighty houses, 'six weeks' accumulation [of night-soil] had to be dragged through houses where people sat at breakfast.'[6]

All experienced visitors agreed that Glasgow was worst of all, where 'penury, dirt, misery, drunkenness and disease and crime culminate to a pitch unparalleled in Great Britain.'[7] Edwin Chadwick, along with the distinguished doctors Alison and Cowan, made a 'perambulation' there on the morning of 24 September 1840:

'We entered a dirty low passage like a house door, which led from the street through the first house to a square court immediately behind, which court, with the exception of a narrow path around it leading to another long passage through a second house, was occupied entirely as a dung receptacle of the most disgusting kind. Beyond this court the second passage led to a second square court, occupied in the same way by its dung hill; and from this court there was yet a third passage leading to a third court and third dungheap.

There were no privies or drains there, and the dungheaps received all filth which the swarm of wretched inhabitants could give; and we learnt that a considerable part of the rent of the houses was paid by the produce of the dungheaps.'[8]

In Dundee one poor woman taking occupation of a new flat in 1847 was shown a locked wall-cupboard and told by the house factor that she could have the use of it if she cared to clean it out. It turned out to be crammed full of 'about two cartloads of dung'. When the woman declined the task of clearing the cupboard the factor locked it up again. Apparently she continued to live within its aura.[9]

It was, of course, not only the poor who suffered from the presence of evil smells. Queen Victoria is said to have found her Palace of Holyrood uninhabitable because of the odours assailing her windows from Edinburgh's famous well-manured meadows, although it may have been indicative of growing sensitivity on the subject that the Earl of Haddington claimed 'when George IV was there no complaint whatever was made.'[10] But the poor had less opportunity to do anything about it. They could not choose their place of residence but must go where there was employment. The Select Committee on the Health of Towns found that 'the wealthy and educated gradually withdraw themselves from these close and crowded communities' leaving them to the poor.

It might be thought, and the point was raised often enough, that some of the filth and smell of their surroundings was due to the uncleanly habits of the poor themselves, that the application of water and elbow-grease and the opening of windows might have made all the difference. Water, unfortunately, was seldom available to the poor. The Commissioners on the State of Large Towns reported in 1844 that of the measures adopted for supplying water 'all stop short of... carrying supplies . . . into the habitations of the poorer consumers',[11] and forty years later the 1885 Commission on the Housing of the Working Classes showed the situation to have changed very little as far as the poor were concerned. Water was not a free commodity. Where it was supplied it was supplied by profit-making water companies who charged a yearly rate to individuals or communities. By the time that rate had passed through the pockets of numbers of middlemen to reach the poor it was charged at so much a jugful. The houses of the poor were supplied either from public wells which were only too often affected by seepage from the sewers, from stand-pipes which were turned on only for short intervals during the day, or from waterbutts in the back-courts. In some towns water had to be bought from passing water carts. Where to have water meant expense and the labour of fetching and carrying, it is not surprising that it was often dispensed with altogether. In the Boot and Shoe Yard, in Leeds, there lived 340 inhabitants who had no water within a quarter of a mile, and who may be guessed to have existed without it because 'very few of the inhabitants possess vessels in which to hold or attach water.'[12]

Henry Austin, the architect and builder who later became Secretary to the General Board of Health and who was Charles Dickens' brother-in-law, described the situation in the Blackwall district of London.

'On the principal cleaning day, Sunday, water is on for about five minutes and it is also on three days a week for half an hour, and so great is the rush to obtain a modicum before it is turned off that perpetual quarrelling and disturbance is the result and water-day is but another name for dissension.'[13]

Even in towns with an abundant natural supply of water the want of the means of conducting it left working people without. Middleton, a town near Manchester which grew very rapidly at the beginning of the century, had a number of good, clear wells on its outskirts but

'the water of the town wells is acknowledged to be very bad and it is generally avoided . . . It happens sometimes that persons are obliged to come out as early as one o'clock in a morning to secure a supply of water for washing day . . . the water must be taken as it issues or it is lost. A large proportion of the population is therefore employed catching water as it flows. There is no intermission, excepting that period when the population is asleep and even that time is occasionally broken into. The people, therefore, even where water is abundant, see it escaping whilst they can secure so very little . . . The great trouble in bringing water home causes it to be used again and again, until it becomes exceedingly filthy and in this state it is employed at last to wash the floors. The labour is sometimes put on special water carriers, whose charge, even for the smallest supply of a cottage, comes to 8d per week while washing-day demands 1s 3d . . . Middleton, with a considerable supply of water, is in actual want of water in every cottage; with a free supply it is actually paying largely for it, and, with a comparatively pure supply in a few of the more frequented wells, it is stinted to impure water.'[14]

In Manchester the water company, established in 1809, provided a plentiful supply of water to houses in the better districts at 6s a year but a very large part of the town was supplied from rain-water cisterns or shallow wells with pumps.

'In the better class of houses it is generally filtered, but the poorer classes use it without any preparation. The custom is for owners of small cottage property to erect a pump for the use of a given number of houses; this pump is frequently rented by one of the tenants, who keeps it locked, and each of the other tenants are taxed a certain sum per month for the use of it. One poor woman told me she paid 1s per month.'[15]

But perhaps none reached such straits as the townspeople of Tranent where, at one time, 'so great was the privation that . . . people went into the ploughed fields and gathered the rain water which collected in depressions in the ground, and actually in the prints made by the horses' feet.' Tranent was supplied from ten wells with a very irregular supply: 'great crowds of women and children assemble at these places, waiting their "turn", as it is termed. I have seen women fighting for water. The wells are sometimes frequented throughout the whole night.'[16]

Lord Shaftesbury described in 1884 a state of things in London which he believed to have changed:

'In the old times the water was supplied sometimes only once a week, and at other times twice a week. In particular courts there was a stand-pipe put up and the water came up at a certain time and lasted for twenty or twenty-five minutes. All the vessels were arranged in single file on either side to catch the water, and an old woman was placed at an upper window to shout and give notice when the water supply was coming on. The people rushed to get the water as they could before the supply ceased; and many of them had to take it home and put it under their beds, where it inhaled all the noxious atmosphere.'

We see here that his Lordship had still an almost alchemical awe for the power of smell—water could inhale!

This state of affairs, in which even prosperous houses could not depend on a clean water supply and the poor were almost wholly without water, was brought about by the treatment of water as a commodity to be bought and sold like any other. 'Water companies possessed a colossal power of life and death for which . . . there has been no precedent in the history of the world.'[17] The bitter squabbling for the right to provide water which inevitably preceded the granting of a monopoly to a private company by a town council produced political in-fighting of a squalid and expensive kind with disastrous results for the citizens. The East London Water Company was proved to have distributed 'a most improper water'[18] leading to many deaths during the 1866 cholera outbreak. In the 1830s, Dundee, where the supply was so inadequate that people had to use the filthy water from the mill-cooling ponds, the municipality wasted £30,000 on fighting a legal action over assessment for water-rate which went as far as the House of Lords and left the once strong radical movement in the town splintered and weakened.

The Metropolis Water Act, 1852, laid down rules for the provision of clean water in London, including the filtering of all supplies, but the £200 penalty for contravention was as Simon said 'utterly incommensurate with the magnitude of the problem'. The Sanitary Act, 1866, obliged local authorities to supply water to their townships and thus should have put an end to both shortage and impure supplies. Yet in 1884 Mr J. W. Tripe of Hackney told the Housing Commissioners: 'We have no power to compel the supply of water for domestic purposes under any circumstances whatever . . . the water companies will not lay on the water at the request of the local authority unless the local authority will guarantee the payment of 3d per week [per house]; and they will not do that.'[19] The Commissioners' Report showed that while there had been some improvement, more in the purity than in the abundance of the water supplied, there were still high tenements with only one tap shared between hundreds of people, and the supply was too often uncertain. Water companies cut off supplies if the landlord fell behind in paying his water-rates so that tenants suffered even when their own rent payments were up-to-date.

The well-intentioned Public Health Act, 1848, failed to improve water supplies because it was framed before the publication of a very important and relevant scientific discovery.

Until Snow's proof in 1849 that cholera infection was water-borne, the need for a pure water supply was not properly understood. Where water could be seen to be clouded with impurities or where its taste was unpleasant, people naturally shunned it. But as long as the best medical opinion believed that disease was air-borne and general opinion believed the idea of water carrying infection to be rather laughable, attempts to improve water supplies were necessarily half-hearted. Even Chadwick, whose belief that sewage ought to be disposed of in a state of suspension in water was very advanced for his time, fought proposals to empty that sewage into rivers only on the grounds that it was a waste of valuable manure. The fact that by entering the rivers it could pollute the water supply and thus bring disease and death, as indeed it might by being spread on the fields as he preferred, was a piece of scientific knowledge still outside his reach. Not even Bentham himself believed in the strict application of unadulterated utilitarian principles, but until the lack of abundant, pure water could be shown to be dangerous to the community as a whole the climate of thought fed on Benthamism was unlikely to institute reform. The discomfort of the poor was not in itself of national importance and could not command government interference. Those who opposed utilitarianism as foreign to Christian principles arrived at the same conclusion and the same state of inactivity by a different route. What one writer has called 'The puritanism of those who saw the world, not as a home to be civilised and comfortably furnished for man, but as a spiritual gymnasium for the improvement of his soul'[20] led its adherents to believe that people could be taught and encouraged to improve their surroundings without any concerted action by the state.

In spite of powers given to local authorities by the Sanitary Act, 1866, closet accommodation was still, in 1884, 'most defective'. Parts of Westminster had only one closet for whole streets in which thirty or forty people were crowded into each house. All over London such closets as there were were blocked and overflowing, often not provided with a supply of water, and used as sleeping places by the homeless. Bristol allowed privies in living-rooms and in most parts of the provinces there was no closet accommodation and no indoor water supply at all in the houses of the labouring classes.[21]

How did they manage? The middle classes were quick to suggest that the poor did not wash at all, but then spoilt the argument by complaining about whole streets made impassable to carriages by lines of wet washing hung from house to house across the street. And there are many pathetic descriptions of poor women exhausted with fever and lack of nourishment struggling to wash the children's clothes in water laboriously carried over courts and stairs. 'She was propped up in a chair, looking terribly ill, but in front of her, on another chair, was the wash-tub, and the poor woman was making a feeble effort to wash and wring out some of the children's things.'[22]

Water was perhaps seldom enough turned to the purpose of house-cleaning in the city slums. Shaftesbury estimated that there were some 60,000 or 70,000 people in London who never stayed more than three months in one place, who simply 'deposit their filth and go', but his statement was qualified by the report that: 'There are houses inhabited by the poor the floors of which a woman could not scrub because they are absolutely rotten and the more that is done to them the worse they become . . . the most cleanly woman could not be clean, even if the supply of water were at all times sufficient.'[23] The crumbling structure of their homes, the shortage of water, the lack of incentive and the poverty pushed many a woman over the edge into slovenliness when she had lived and bred her children in the slums; but a strong puritan tradition of cleanliness survived among the working classes ready to show itself when the merest chance of more comfortable living occurred.[24]

The Sanitary Act, 1866,[25] an amendment of previous Public Health Acts gave, in Section 10, 'power to the sewer authority to require owners to connect their houses by sufficient drains to sewers where they exist or into adequate covered cess-pools and where the owner does not comply to perform the work and recover expenses from him.' But in spite of the fact that this Act was prepared with adequate information about the scientific necessity for water to be pure and abundant, it provided only that 'the sewer authority may, *if it think it expedient to do so*, provide a supply of water for the use of the inhabitants.'[26] Section 35 gave the Secretary of State powers to put the Act in force authorising local authorities to make the necessary regulations. The Act was ineffective. It gave the possibility of power but did not enforce it. Few towns availed themselves of the opportunities the Act could give them. Most working-class areas in the cities remained without even an attempt at adequate provision of water.

In 1874 the powers of the Secretary of State, in so far as they applied to this Act, were transferred to the Local Government Board, but, the Report of the 1884 Commissioners found, 'the mere putting in force of the enactment would be of no avail unless the authority were both willing to make the regulations and when made to enforce them.'[27] In many cases it seemed 'that the authority had almost forgotten that they had the powers . . . even where the authorities have had their memories refreshed by energetic officers of health the result has often been the same.' Committee reports on the subject were indefinitely postponed and 'difficult' chairmen deposed. The Sanitary Act, 1866, was found to be a dead letter.

John Simon, who had been responsible for providing the scientific evidence and the moral persuasion which brought about the Act, believed that the failure of the Act to produce sanitary reform on a national scale was due to the inefficient working of local government,[28] but the new Local Government Board, when created, did little to change the situation. Nothing of importance, neither the supplying of water, the demolition of slums, nor the building of houses, could be done for the working classes until a new way of thinking about their needs could be taught to the people in power and to the voters who put them there.

The last quarter of the century saw an undoubted improvement. Flushing water-closets, introduced into a few wealthy houses at the end of the eighteenth century, were still not generally available for the poor a century later,[29] but a few of the more enlightened towns were beginning to see the advantage of the system by the 1880s, if only because of the saving it made in rates for sewage disposal. Croydon, Dover, Salisbury and Liverpool were said to be 'largely water-closeted' by 1884. Stricter application of the nuisance clauses of the Public Health Acts of 1848, 1867 and 1875 had resulted in the provision of a regular service of removal and, as Chadwick admitted, frequently-emptied privy pans were neither too objectionable in use nor too dangerous to health.[30] If working families had usually to 'go down the yard' at least they did not find there the disgusting mess usual in the 1840s, where a few planks on end might be all that served as a screen and the 'bog men' would break up seats and walls to make their task of emptying easier.[31]

Facilities for washing clothes began to be provided either as wash-houses with boilers in back-courts or as communal wash-houses provided at a small charge by the town council.

Drinking water had still, in most cases, to be carried at least from the head of the stairs, and most nineteenth-century reformers, like Octavia Hill, thought that the provision of one tap per floor was quite sufficient. Professor Pollard found that piped water was not common in the houses of the Sheffield working class much before 1914, and there is no evidence to prove Sheffield untypical.

The Housing Act, 1890, and the new Public Health Act of the same year[32] laid down rules for the provision and maintenance of new housing which might have changed the situation. Unfortunately the almost total stoppage of house-building for the lower income groups between 1890 and 1918[33] left most working people in old houses without water. It was still a struggle to be clean and a struggle beyond the energies of many working women.

The squabbling round the stand-pipes so often reported in the first half of the century became unnecessary with the provision of regular instead of intermittent supplies. There was still the labour of carrying water but no longer the fear of doing without. Those outbreaks of fighting over water were, of course, we now know from modern environmental studies, the kind of stress signs to be expected in human beings living in severely overcrowded conditions. British town dwellers of the first half of the nineteenth century were herded together in densities not previously experienced.

Chapter 6

Overcrowding

'Where houses thick and sewers annoy the air'

MILTON

The first census reports on urban housing densities seemed to belie the evidence of contemporary reporters of the situation, for they show an actual, though small, fall in the number of people per inhabited house between 1801 and 1841 at a time when the population rose steeply and eye-witness accounts of increased overcrowding are abundant.[1] London's population grew from 1,088,000 in 1801 to 2,073,000 in 1841, Liverpool's from 82,000 to 286,000, Glasgow's from 77,000 to 275,000, Birmingham's from 71,000 to 183,000, Manchester's from 75,000 to 235,000, Dundee's from 26,000 to 166,000, Leeds's from 53,000 to 152,000.[2] If the census figures are correct it would be necessary to believe that building kept pace with the increased demand for housing to hold the average number of persons per inhabited house steady at 5.6 from 1801 to 1831 with a drop to 5.4 in 1841.[3]

The want of statistics on house-building in the first half of the nineteenth century makes it impossible to check either the inhabited house figures in the census which proved that overcrowding should be declining or the impression of the slum visitors that overcrowding was certainly getting worse. Weber's index of residential construction shows a steep increase in house-building in Liverpool between 1838 and 1842, from 46.2 to 89.1, but this makes no distinction between villa building for the well-to-do and low-cost building for the poor nor does it tell us anything about the situation in the rest of the country.[4] Shannon's brick index[5] includes not only high-cost residential building but railway and factory building too, and so can have little usefulness for our purpose. We are thrown back, for this period, on impressions gathered by contemporaries.[6]

Chadwick's explanation was that a mistake had arisen from the lack of definition of the word 'house' in the census forms. Where large middle-class houses built for one family had been broken up into separate flats or single rooms for working tenants, as was the case in so many large towns, this fact was not revealed in the census, each room appearing as a 'house' if separately occupied. So the gross overcrowding resulting from the occupation of one six-roomed house by five or six separate extended families could be represented as an increase in house accommodation by the census, the same house which had appeared as a unit in 1801 appearing as six units in 1841.

Professor Flinn has also pointed out in his admirable introduction to Chadwick's Sanitary Reports that

'the increase in *per capita* income during the first four decades of the century must certainly have produced some improvements in housing densities which are most likely to have increased house space for those in the upper half of the income scale. Many of these would be upper working-class families who would use the rise in incomes to reduce the number of people per house . . . In this event, the constancy of the national density over the whole period must, as a result, have increased crowding of those in the lower income groups.'[7]

This, of course, is arguing with the advantage of knowledge not available to many people in the 1830s and 1840s. Taken as they stand, without any other evidence, the census figures for numbers of people per inhabited house could be taken to prove that there was no pressing need for further building. Other evidence, fortunately, was available, including the evidence of their own eyes, for those who penetrated the slum areas, and it was not lost on the speculative building firms who mushroomed to take advantage of the lucrative concentration of population in employment areas.

In Glasgow, for instance, the population of Blackfriars parish had increased by 40 per cent between 1831 and 1841 while the number of houses had remained the same.[8] Working people, in their effort to find somewhere to live in districts where they might also find somewhere to work crowded into decaying mansions abandoned by more fortunate families, using cellars and attics as separate homes, subdividing living-rooms and halls. And not only the number of people in each house but the number of houses per acre was important. Every mother knows that the presence of numbers of small children in one house is endurable if they have open space outside to run to, trying in the extreme if they have not. In the most crowded areas of the towns every scrap of land was built over in the rush to make money from house-letting. Corner sites and the open-ends of quadrangle courts were built in first. Then building took place within the courts themselves so that only pedestrian ways were left between warrens of houses crammed together, windows looking into high walls. Where the rich had once kept gardens, low-cost housing sprang up within the garden walls, sometimes with access to the road only through the existing house.

The towns most affected by overcrowding were those ancient ones which had originally been enclosed within walls, the City of London, the old town of Edinburgh, the dock area of Hull, where the difficulty of spreading outwards caused huddling on to narrow sites of houses without space, light or air. But even where town geography made urban spread possible the central areas, where there existed opportunities for casual labour, attracted crowds beyond their capacity to house. The poorest, those without regular employment, were those least able to move away from the commercial centres, forced by their need to be near the mere chance of a day's work, to live in the worst crowded areas. The first suburbs, spreading around the edges of London boroughs, of Liverpool, of textile towns experiencing urgent need for labour like Dundee and Leeds, were taken up by people in work with regular starting times. These first suburbs were, in any case, designed to be overcrowded, planned not only to save expenditure on land by covering sites as closely as possible, but also to avoid the expense of road-making as far as possible. Row upon row was built with only pedestrian access and in the shape of cul-de-sacs to take advantage of end-sites. 'A carpenter and builder unite', said Nassau Senior, 'to buy a series of building sites (that is, they lease them for a number of years) and cover them with houses. In one place we found a whole street following the course of a ditch because in this way deeper cellars could be secured without the cost of digging, cellars not for storing wares or rubbish, but for dwellings for human beings.[9] Overcrowding then, was of two kinds: accidental, caused by the attraction of population to built-up areas, and deliberate, caused by the speculative builders' need to put as many houses as possible on a site.

With hindsight it seems almost absurdly obvious to say that immigration from the countryside and from Ireland, plus the natural increase in town population, brought about overcrowding and that overcrowding brought about the breakdown of town administration, the decay of city centres, the demoralising of a dispirited population and the dangerous separation of urban working class from middle class. Towns whose wells had once supplied adequate, clear water, and whose scavenging contractors had provided a reasonably efficient service, found themselves helpless in the face of mountains of filth, with areas where once professional people and workers had lived together in neighbouring streets now never entered by any but the poor and desperate. Yet the effects of urban overcrowding on British society have been consistently under-rated. The nineteenth century admitted and deplored the fact of overcrowding, and attempted to treat some of the results of overcrowding, the epidemic diseases particularly—even, quite ineffectually, forbade overcrowding[10]—but never at any time did it consider treating the disease of overcrowding itself rather than its symptoms. Although the community had always accepted responsibility for the housing of paupers it did not even imagine the possibility of supplying for people above the level of pauper the only antidote to overcrowding, that is, the right kind of house in the right place. The connection between overcrowding and epidemic became increasingly obvious. Even while the precise cause of epidemic remained a mystery it was clear that fever flourished where human beings crowded. The need to curb epidemics became urgent and so the removal of the filth caused by overcrowding became the reformers' goal, leaving overcrowding itself not only untreated but increasing. Removal of piles of human dung from the streets and closes was undoubtedly a good thing, tending to make the occupation of slum houses more tolerable. It was irrelevant that the town reformers believed that the gases from the dung-hills had caused fever. Whatever the reason for the clean-up it was better that the towns should be clean. But in the pressure to provide sanitation the fact that the filth had been caused directly by the lack of houses and the subsequent overcrowding of people within houses was lost sight of. The provision of more houses was not pressed. Instead of being treated as a subject in its own right, housing became one part, and a neglected part, of the public health campaign. The paradox we have to deal with is that the public health movement is at the same time an important part of the history of housing and totally irrelevant to it. While it is true that attention to the subject of urban housing conditions was first drawn not by the philanthropists but by those interested in public health it is also true that the treatment of housing as part of the public health problem instead of as a subject for separate economic study and political action is a chief reason for failure to provide successful remedies.

The proof of this failure is clearly to be seen in the facts. By the end of the nineteenth century the killing epidemic scourges had been almost completely controlled. Successive waves of cholera had dramatically less drastic results and the epidemic of 1866–7 proved to be Britain's last.[11] Typhus appeared less often and less fatally. Yet the general physique of town populations steadily deteriorated in comparison with people in less crowded areas to the point where Boer War recruiting officers found as much as four inches average difference in stature between young men from the slums and from more favoured areas.[12] While epidemic disease was decreasing in its power to kill, overcrowding in some areas steadily increased. The efforts of the public health reformers to improve the towns actually increased the evils of overcrowding. Because nineteenth-century improvement schemes were chiefly demolition schemes they invariably increased overcrowding. Some writers on the history of housing have been surprisingly optimistic about the results of early town improvements. Charles Allan, for instance, in an otherwise excellent account of

Glasgow's pioneering work in the housing field, writes: 'There is little doubt that the sweeping away of the worst slums shoved people into better houses', although the City Improvement Trust had displaced some 25,375 people by 1876 and had built only 1,646 new houses by 1902.[13]

It is really necessary in circumstances like this to stop and consider the people involved as individuals rather than as units among thousands displaced. What happened to the people moved out of the worst slums? They moved into neighbouring areas, often to share houses with other members of their families. If, as Mr Allan suggests, this represents a move from a very bad area into a slightly better one, it also represents a step downhill for that neighbouring 'slightly better' area, which now becomes increasingly overcrowded.

Philanthropic attempts to improve housing conditions produced similar effects. Octavia Hill, for instance, bought up houses and courts in the worst areas she could find with the intention of showing what could be done to improve existing houses: 'As soon as I entered into possession, each family had an opportunity of doing better: those who would not pay, or who led clearly immoral lives, were ejected. The rooms they vacated were cleansed, the tenants who showed signs of improvement moved into them.'[14] She accepted for re-housing those who showed signs of wishing to improve their condition and took no further interest in those who did not. Where did they go once displaced from their former homes? They moved, inevitably, into other slum areas, increasing the overcrowding there, some of them joining the throng of ''appy dossers', as they were called, who slept on stairs and doorways and even in privies, wherever they could find, not a bed, but a space to huddle in. A London police magistrate wrote: 'I have often said that if empty casks were placed along the streets of Whitehall, in a few days each of them would have a tenant, and these tenants would keep up their kind.'[15] There were so many homeless people in London that any form of shelter must immediately find an occupant.

Miss Hill's evictions were small-scale, but the principle behind her action was accepted by all the larger model dwellings' associations who displaced slum dwellers when they acquired sites and accepted as tenants only the more respectable among the applicants for their houses. Even Lord Shaftesbury could not defend himself against the accusation that the most needy, those who, through poverty, might fail in regular rent payments, were not accepted as tenants by his association.[16] 'The poor', as James Hole wrote, 'are not always a *desirable* class of tenants, for they are troublesome, uncertain, and changeable.'[17]

Exactly the same thing happened in the towns as had been happening for decades in the rural areas. Housing was available for the respectable, the upper reaches of the working class, those who, in fact, had it within their own power to improve their situation. Those who through illness, age or economic circumstances found themselves homeless or in squalid conditions were most often not acceptable as tenants of better housing. Even now we find it difficult to accept that people must be housed whether they deserve it or not, that shelter must be provided for layabouts, drunkards, the rebelliously dirty, that the question of what they deserve is irrelevant. If we find this concept difficult the Victorians found it impossible. They could not accept that the undeserving and the deserving had identical needs. They saw, as inevitably they must in the light of their traditions and teaching, a large proportion of slum dwellers as undeserving. This left many thousands of people displaced and in need of housing who were forced to sift into the interstices of other crowded areas, to the financial advantage of landlords' middle-men and the detraction of the town's amenity.

The philanthropic housing associations showed at least some concern, if little practical help, for those made homeless. Railway companies, pushing their new lines through the most densely populated areas, demolished without compunction. Henry Austin was among the first to draw attention to the squalor in which people displaced by railway schemes were living when he was acting as surveyor to the Blackwall railway company.[18] Professor Dyos has estimated that 76,000 people must have been displaced by railway operations between 1853 and 1901. Pressure upon government to place limits upon railway companies' site clearance operations in towns resulted in the issue, in 1874, of new standing orders requiring railway companies to give eight weeks' notice before taking possession of working-class houses and to provide alternative accommodation. The regulations were easily evaded and even after 1885, when they were more strictly enforced, they did not succeed in re-housing the most needy of those displaced.[19] The extent of overcrowding in London has been most graphically described by A. S. Wohl in *The Housing of the Working Classes in London*[20] Medical officers who knew of extreme cases of overcrowding did not report them because they knew the families concerned had nowhere to go. Other towns shared the problem, people sleeping five or six to a bed, three beds to a room, two or three families to a stair, dozens of houses around one back green. It was a situation which grew only worse throughout the century, every move to improve working-class conditions seeming to increase the pressure on available housing.

Speculative builders were less likely than the model dwellings' associations or the railway companies to have engaged in large-scale demolition before their building started. Their habit was to make use of already available cheap land, sometimes odd corners left within the built-up areas, sometimes lots of land newly put on the market by

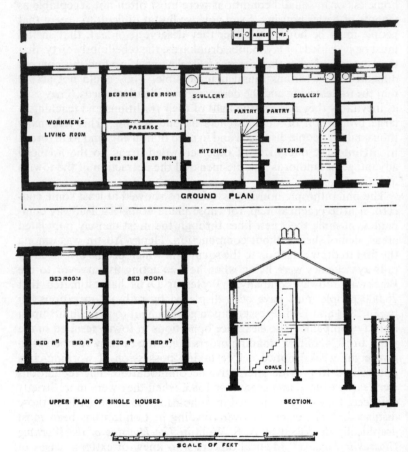

1. An ingenious plan combining accommodation for single male workers with separate family accommodation within one block

owners anxious to take advantage of rising values. But if they displaced fewer city dwellers by their building they were no more likely to re-house the poorest of those in need of homes. Because of their wish to get the greatest financial return on their first outlay and sometimes because the land itself carried restrictions on the building of houses below a certain ratable value, many speculative builders let only to the superior artisan class. George Smith, for instance, an architect in Old Jewry, claimed in 1840 to have built 2,000 houses for the working classes in the Commercial Road district, and to have covered sixty acres in fourteen or fifteen years. But further questioning showed his tenants to be 'seafaring men, mates of vessels, clerks in public offices paying £14, £16, £18 a year' and when asked if any of the houses were 'inhabited by common street labourers' he answered: 'Not of that class certainly.'[21]

In the North the situation was not markedly different in effect. Because there was not so large a market for middle-class housing the building of small, cheap cottages was found to be the most profitable to the builder. But it is clear that there was no real understanding of market requirements. Thomas Ashworth, for instance, a Bolton manufacturer, claimed in the same breath that one-roomed cottages gave the best financial return to the builder and that there was a real demand for better cottages by his workmen. When asked how he reconciled the two he said only: 'The ways of men are as various as the roads they take.'[22]

It would seem that builders provided the kind of housing for which there seemed the most urgent local demand but that new houses were seldom available for those who might prove irregular payers. Not unnaturally all landowners strove to keep up the respectability and therefore, of course, the value of their estates, by excluding unsatisfactory tenants.

This unwillingness, or inability, to provide housing for the poorest had repercussions not only upon the poor. Wherever there was a fluctuating or sporadic demand for labour there was bound to gather a population whose ability to pay rent was unreliable. In the dockyard areas of all ports, wherever there was navvying to do, and in manufacturing districts where employers would take on extra hands to meet a press of orders, people crowded together to be near their work. Because they must have homes, and because they were acceptable as tenants only to a class of landlord with no interest in the maintenance of his property but only in the extraction of as large a rental as possible, they were permitted to occupy houses in numbers far beyond their reasonable capacity. Where the district was crowded past its ability to absorb more bodies the people overflowed into neighbouring better-class districts, sleeping in holes and corners everywhere so that every district was affected by the existence of the homeless and overcrowded poor.

We know that, at least in some districts, a great deal of building was going on in the first half of the nineteenth century. Two hundred miles of new streets were constructed in London between 1839 and 1851 with more than 60,000 houses,[23] and Weber's index of building in Liverpool shows a rise from 46.2 in 1838 to 163.9 in 1845.[24] There is very little evidence of house-building in other towns until after 1856.

It might seem that even if these new houses were relatively seldom available to the poorest working people they must have eased the pressure on existing accommodation to a noticeable extent and, by emptying the slums of the better-off workers, made more room for those forced to stay there by the need to be near their work, the inability to pay higher rents, or the kind of apathy which makes major change too difficult to contemplate. Change was frequent enough. Indeed the poor of the slums were an almost nomadic tribe, changing homes at very frequent intervals, with their goods pushed on hand-barrows. But the removals were invariably within a district. They represented change without improvement. In fact, as many workers found mass production methods threatening their cost of living the change was most often downhill, from a cheap home to an even cheaper one. Whatever the, admittedly sparse, building statistics show, there is a wealth of reported evidence that overcrowding in the towns was affected by the amount of new house-building, chiefly for the worse.

Such information as we have about the extent of house construction during the nineteenth century is contained in the reports of the Inland Revenue Commissioners on Inhabited House Duty, in census returns for numbers of houses in the United Kingdom, and in some local studies of approved building plans. A. K. Cairncross's *Home and Foreign Investment, 1870–1913*, Habakkuk's *Fluctuations in House-Building*,[25] and B. Weber's *New Index of Residential Construction, 1838–1950* digest the available information and provide statistics of house-building which can be usefully measured against population tables. Professor Parry Lewis in *Building Cycles and Britain's Growth* adds to and discusses Weber's work. They would seem to show that house-building kept pace to a marked extent with population growth during the nineteenth century.[26] However these figures relate to house-building of all kinds, from the mansions of the northern textile barons to the cheapest labourers' cottages. Overcrowding was the result, not of an overall shortage of houses, as the large numbers of unoccupied houses in cities show, but of ill-distribution of housing from area to area and income group to income group. While the top section of the working class was being creamed off to join the lower middle classes in the rows of new houses in the suburbs, the heavy weight of the poorest continued to increase in density in town areas in which many of their former homes had been demolished. Their chances of earning a regular wage made it difficult to pay the kind of rents demanded for good house property. In fact, the frequency of their periods of unemployment made steady rent paying impossible and accounts for the habit of short-term occupancy and frequent removals, often executed at night to avoid the rent man.

The population of England and Wales doubled between 1801 and 1851. Scotland's took another decade to double. The period of swiftest population growth was also the period of uncontrolled building for profit. Before the towns began to be so filthy as to be actually lethal, when the average age of mortality was still rising, builders responded to the demand for housing without restriction.[27] As epidemics, malnutrition and poor living conditions began to lower the average age of death again so that population, while still growing, grew less dramatically, the campaign to improve the towns and regulate the builders' excesses began. But by then reformers were faced with the results of generations of building over open spaces and baffled by the problem of clearing almost impenetrable warrens of houses. Overcrowding, in any case, was not confined to the older houses. In the new working-class suburbs of London speculative builders planned houses specifically for the accommodation of lodgers. Very few were designed as one-family houses, because it was acknowledged that, without an extra income from lodgers, working families could not pay the kind of rent which would give a London builder a healthy return on his capital outlay. Houses which were an exception to this rule, like those in Bethnal Green 'which may be called more huts than houses, built in swamps, at a cheap rent, for the purpose of being let out to weekly tenants at as much money as they can get for them',[28] were so small, as to be overcrowded by the presence of one family. In the provinces, although more working-class houses were built for occupation by one family we know that, in textile towns particularly, the taking of lodgers to help with the rent was exceedingly common and remained so until the provision of council housing with its restrictions on subletting.

Custom and social usage, of course, affect tolerance to overcrowding. The sharing of beds with siblings, for instance, considered undesirable in the twentieth century, was acceptable to middle-class as well as poor Victorians. Until modern studies on family structure can produce more conclusive evidence, we cannot even know very much about the size and make-up of families. Some facts seem to emerge. Children of country families tended to leave home earlier than town children, finding work as farm or domestic servants, where they would also be given lodging from 12 or 13 years of age. Town children remained at home until, and sometimes after, marriage, sharing the family trade or scrounging casual work on the fringes of urban industry. Fertility seems to have been lower in towns, partly as the result of deliberate family limitation by town dwellers with access to information not available to rural workers.[29] Lowered fertility combined with high infant mortality in towns to keep family sizes down. In Nottingham, for instance, only 18.4 of working-class households in 1851 had four or more children.[30]

Much discussion went on about the minimum space required for healthy living. The Poor Law Board allowed paupers in health 300 cubic feet each, the sick 500, criminals in prison were supposed to have 1,000 cubic feet.[31] 'Expert' opinion seemed to agree that 300 was the minimum desirable.

But not only family size, the presence of lodgers, the space available within the house, and working-class custom affected acceptance of overcrowding. The decisive factor was the over-close proximity of other family units, and it is certain that nineteenth-century town overcrowding passed the limits of tolerance easily sustained without some form of breakdown of stability. Frequent drunkenness and the regular use of dangerous narcotics to quieten crying infants were natural and necessary responses, however undesirable, to the conditions of overproximity in which town dwellers lived.

Without a regular wage, a rare enough luxury in the nineteenth century, it was, then, seldom possible to provide comfortable accommodation for a family and often enough, especially within the Metropolis, even a regular wage could not command a home fit for human habitation by modern standards.

Chapter 7

Standards of Comfort

'Two old chairs, and half a candle
One old jug without a handle'
LEAR

The working man's family had most often not enough space, not enough warmth, not enough light, not enough furniture.

The builders of the 'back-to-backs' of England and the barrack-like stone tenements of Scotland have been condemned, and justly so, for the greed with which they covered land and their lack of concern for quality of materials or amenity of surroundings. Back-to-back speculative housing designed for the accommodation of low-income-group families was, especially in the first half of the century, shoddily built, on insecure foundations, of materials not even adequate for keeping out the rain. In some cases new estates were built on sites still heaving with refuse, lightly cemented over to provide a surface which, if temporarily flat and dry, soon split to produce settlement cracks, rising damp, and unpleasant smells.[1] Builders too often were men of little capital, sometimes groups of tradesmen combining together in a speculative enterprise involving none of them in too great an outlay. Such arrangements naturally resulted in skimped materials even to the extent that the collapse of new-built houses was not at all infrequent.[2] Scottish tenements were less often structurally unsound, the traditional use of stone requiring both greater outlay, which attracted sounder capitalists, and the employment of more skilled labour in the mason-work. The higher density of inhabitants made possible by high building, however, combined with the meanness of lavatory and tap provision to make tenement living less comfortable than it might have been. But whatever the evils of speculative building the new houses had some advantages over the ancient multi-occupation houses in the town centres. Original construction for single occupancy meant, for instance, that too few rooms were designed for living in or had means of heating and cooking. The reformers' obsession with ventilation, naturally in view of the medical profession's belief that most infectious disease was air-borne took little account of the poor family's great need for warmth. New houses had grates in at least one room, often in one of the bedrooms too, and proper kitchen ranges became more commonly introduced throughout the century. But the older slums seldom had the means of heating the individual rooms. Warm food had to be bought outside, hence the prevalence of street sellers with braziers, hawking hot potatoes, pies and chestnuts.

Room sizes varied very much but something like 8 feet by 10 feet seems to have been, if not average, at least very common. New houses had, most often smaller rooms than the older divided mansions. In Leeds the exterior size of the average working man's back-to-back cottage was 15 ft by 15 ft by 9 ft. Each contained a cellar, a kitchen, or *house* as the occupants called it, and an attic chamber.[3] Subtract from the overall 15-ft frontage the thickness of walls and space for even the narrowest of staircases and the largest room must have been about 10 ft square. In Liverpool the usual size of houses was from 10 to 12 ft square and contained a cellar, a ground-floor room and two chambers above. This typical speculative house type needed 28 square

2. Manchester cellar dwellings

a. Interior of a cellar shop: business and the family

b. Access to other cellar dwellings: death in the dirt

yards of land for each house, giving it a 12-ft frontage and a depth of
13½ ft.[4] Room sizes then were noticeably smaller in Liverpool than
was usual in Leeds, the two upstairs rooms being very small indeed,
with head-room only in the centre of the room. Birmingham back-to-
backs, catering for a superior artisan class in regular employment, contained an extra storey, a cellar, a ground-floor kitchen, a chamber floor
and an attic room above, but were not markedly bigger overall.[5]

Rooms with individual access were preferred to those entered from
a common stairway but many families suffered the inconvenience of
having access only through other people's homes in much subdivided
flats. Cellar dwelling was always condemned by public health campaigners and housing reformers, chiefly because rooms below street
level seemed inadequately ventilated at a time when ventilation was
thought all-important. But this is only one instance of the gap in understanding between those who wished to help the poor and the poor
themselves, for cellar dwellings were not disliked by their inhabitants
unless they were desperately in need of repair. Cellars had the great
advantage of having their own front door, giving their inhabitants, as
Richard Cobden pointed out to the Select Committee on the Health
of Towns, 'a complete domain of their own'.[6]

A degree of privacy was invaluable to a family attempting to preserve some self-respect or to prevent itself being dragged through the
worst dirt of the slums and the humiliations of the shared staircase.
The worst cellars were those originally intended only for the storage of
coals and having neither proper access, lighting nor air. The best had
been intended for the living quarters of servants of the original big
house upstairs or had been built, as was often the case in Scotland,
specifically for the purpose of separate letting. In Dundee, for instance,
the steeply rising nature of the ground resulted in the building of a
kind of cellar known locally as 'sunk flats'. 'They are very comfortable
houses, the back of the house being upon a level with the area or close
and the other, fronting the street, having sunk windows with excellent
areas around them, with the pavement covered with gratings which is
quite sufficient for ventilation.' Some of these cellar houses were lit
and aired by an ingenious piece of building construction. The shops on
the ground floor above them had boxed-out windows into which the
cellar window projected upwards about 2 ft, up to the sill of the shop
window. This opening was boxed in on either side within the shop area
but permitted the entrance of the air to the cellar at its lower level.[7]

The difficulty of knowing anything certain about the homes of nineteenth-century working people is made worse by two contradictory
facts. The first is that almost all those who were interested enough to
make reports on living conditions were led to describe the worst of

what they knew, either from a wish to shock the public into reform or from the journalist's wish to tell a dramatic story. The second is that what might seem the most concrete of all evidence, houses actually surviving from the period, is necessarily misleading, because what now exists is a sample selected by time, almost certainly better than the average for its period or it would not have survived.[8] We can only take the evidence of the reformers, balance it with judgement against what little we know of actual measurements and furnishings, and attempt to produce something like a true picture of working-class life.

We can note, for instance, the description by James Pennethorne, a surveyor, in 1840 of back-to-back rows built within the back courts of existing tenement houses. Each had two rooms, one up and one down, the upstairs one being reached by a ladder staircase. No privies, sinks or taps were provided.[9] We can compare the genuinely existing red-tiled alleys of Hull, 'where narrow archways like the entrance to a bee-hive lead to areas crowded with dwellings . . . no drainage of any kind, woodwork decayed, windows gone, rotten and filthy',[10] with Dickens's description of Bleeding Heart Yard in *Little Dorrit*.

'A place much changed in feature and fortune . . . walled and subdivided out of the recognition of their old proportions. It was inhabited by poor people who set up their rest among its jaded glories . . . As if the aspiring city had become puffed up in the very ground on which it stood, the ground had so risen about Bleeding Heart Yard that you got into it down a flight of steps which formed no part of the original approach, and got out of it by a low gateway into a maze of shabby streets, which went about and about, tortuously ascending to the level again.'

Interior furnishings varied not so much in their extent as in the ingenuity with which small hoards of collected objects could be cherished and arranged to provide comfort or neglected and scattered to produce misery. Whether the house was an old one subdivided or a new one shoddily built, working-class occupants had seldom the comfort of a home kept in decent repair. The overcrowded state of the cities made it possible for landlords to let rooms whatever their state, which left little incentive towards maintenance. Housekeeping, then, for people without the money to buy materials for repair themselves, was largely a matter of spreading what little was owned in the way of curtains or mattings to cover the holes in floor and walls.

Henry Mayhew was one of the best observers of interiors, bringing to the squalid slums of London the kind of eye for detail with which Vermeer painted the gleaming tiled rooms of Flemish merchants. A journalist and philanthropist and a pioneer of sociology, his *London*

III. Thatched cottage roofs in disrepair, Somersetshire

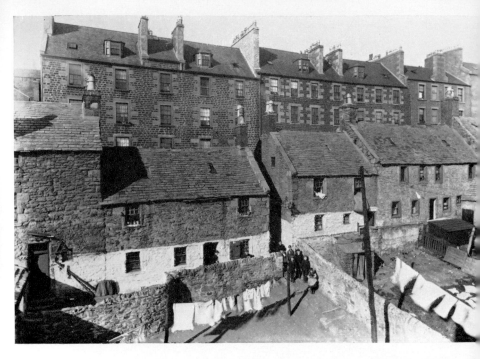

IV. Typical example of town infilling: early cottage-type housing over-looked by later tenement building, Dundee, *c*. 1890

V. The inhabitants of 'sunk-flats' taking an airing, Dundee, *c*. 1890

Labour and the London Poor is as complete a record as we are likely to find of the circumstances in which the poor lived and worked. He contrived to make dispassionate descriptions which, in fact, in every word condemned the system which allowed such hovels to exist. Take the Jew-boy's lodging in a back garret:

'The boy lived with his father (a street-seller of fruit) and the room was very bare. A few sacks were thrown over an old palliasse, a blanket seemed to be used for a quilt; there were no fire-irons or fender; no cooking utensils. Beside the bed was an old chest, serving for a chair, while a board resting on a trestle did duty for a table (this was once, I presume, a small street stall). The one not very large window was thick with dirt and patched all over.'[11]

Or the room of 9 ft square reached by climbing a flight of tottering and broken stairs:

'The ceiling slanted like that of a garret and was the colour of old leather, excepting a few rough white patches where the tenants had rudely mended it. The white light was easily seen through the laths, and in one corner a large patch of paper looped down from the wall ... They had made a carpet out of three or four old mats. They were "obligated to it for fear of dropping anything through the boards into the donkey stables in the parlour underneath".'[12]

Mayhew had a case to make and took care lest lack of restraint should spoil it. He contrasted at every turn the lot of the man with a regular wage and that of the man forced by lack of employment or the introduction of machinery to compete with his fellows for piece or *slop* work. The homes of the 'society' men showed in their comfort and little luxuries the benefit of sick insurance and savings. The competitive trades forced men to work all hours and still to live in bare rooms from which everything pawnable had gone.

Dickens was, in spite of attempts by such men as Edwin Chadwick to enlist him as an agitator on behalf of sanitary reform, always more concerned with the structure of his story than with any overt plea for social reform. But his descriptive powers reinforce the impression gained from parliamentary reports of the living conditions of the poor. His toy-maker in the *Cricket on the Hearth* lived in a house described a hundred times to the Health of Towns Committee and those other committees that followed it and might have been one of the doll-makers interviewed by Mayhew:

'Caleb Plummer and his blind daughter lived all alone by themselves, in a little cracked nut-shell of a wooden house, which was, in truth, no

4

better than a pimple on the prominent red-brick nose of Gruff and Tackleton. The premises of Gruff and Tackleton were the great feature of the street; but you might have knocked down Caleb Plummer's dwelling with a hammer or two, and carried off the pieces in a cart . . . The blind girl never knew that ceilings were discoloured, walls blotched and bare of plaster here and there, high crevices unstopped and widening every day, beams mouldering and tending downwards. The blind girl never knew that iron was rusting, wood rotting, paper peeling off; the size, and shape, and true proportion of the dwelling, withering away.'

Caleb's room was sparsely enough furnished, but it had table and chairs, delf and earthenware pots, a kettle and pillows on the beds, which was more than many houses in real life could boast.

Andrew Mearns's *Bitter Cry of Outcast London* may have felt the hand of a journalist with a knack for the spectacular,[13] but it was based on the collecting of honest evidence and independent witnesses back up its findings. The 'pestilential human rookeries' described there made Caleb's house and furnishings seem luxurious: 'As to furniture —you may perchance discover a broken chair, the tottering relics of an old bedstead, or the mere fragment of a table; but more commonly you will find rude substitutes for these things in the shape of rough boards resting upon bricks, an old hamper or box turned upside down, or more frequently still, nothing but rubbish and rags.'[14] Although this passage dates from 1883, a general lack of possessions by the working classes was true of the whole period up to the end of the nineteenth century.

On the one hand mass production was putting a greater and greater abundance of cheap factory-made furniture and imported gewgaws on the market which it might have been supposed even the insatiable appetite of the Victorian petit-bourgeoisie for stuffing its homes might not have exhausted. On the other hand eye-witness accounts throughout the century report the bareness and want of furnishings of the workman's home. Even those whose intention was certainly not to emphasise the prevailing poverty accidentally illustrate the paucity of material possessions, like the landlord of one of the better houses in the St Giles district of London in 1849 who 'pointed in triumph to a clock and some crockery in one of the rooms'.[15] They were clearly more than he expected to see in the houses of his tenants.

The contents of the pawn-brokers' shops, again described by Mayhew, provide a bitter comment of how little the poor possessed by showing how little they had to pawn even when in the most desperate straits of unemployment.[16] He reports how reluctantly they would part from the coloured prints with which they liked to cover the bad patches on their walls. The rag and bone man, repository of goods sold by the poor, said: 'For pictures I've given from 3d to 1s. I fancy they're among the last things some sorts of poor people parts with.'

Dr Cowan described the tenements of Glasgow in the 1840s as 'to an incredible extent destitute of furniture. In many there is not an article of bedding and the body clothes of the inhabitants are of the most revolting description. In fact, in Glasgow, there are hundreds who never enjoy the luxury of the meanest kind of bed.'[17] In Liverpool, piles of straw or timber shavings made frequent substitutes for beds.[18]

Thomas Ashworth told the Health of Towns Committee how workmen who had been in regular employment with him for some time and who had become tenants in his company housing would begin, after a year or two's tenancy, to think about furnishing their houses with something more than make-shifts. Up till then, 'They had not been accustomed to furnishing',[19] partly because they had never had enough space before.

This all seems less surprising if it is remembered how large a proportion of town dwellers were immigrants who had left their former homes because they possessed so little, who had walked into the cities carrying what little they owned on their backs, and who had found little opportunity to increase their stock since their arrival.

By the end of the century, while, again, the position of the poor had improved very little, those who had known a generation or two of something like regular wages had begun to accumulate household goods. A very interesting light on what working people owned is thrown by compensation claims of working-class victims of the 'Sheffield Flood' of 1864. Sheffield was an artisan town with a high proportion of skilled men in regular employment. The claims are unlikely to be under-played, so that it is reasonable to suppose that articles not claimed for were not usually found in ordinary Sheffield homes. Bedsteads, tables and chairs, as well as some form of storage, either cupboard or set of drawers, and the basic items of tableware were the usual household goods.[20] But the number of beds per family is very low by modern standards, children usually sharing a bed with three of four of their kin, and soft furnishings other than a few blankets and a few cheap floor mats were very rare. Goods bought on marriage were expected to last a lifetime because replacement out of wages was impossible so that most furniture was worn and perhaps broken. The introduction of cheap linoleum towards the end of the century brought floor-covering within reach of all but the poorest and factory-made carpet prices came down in competition. Flock mattresses instead of sacking palliasses filled with chaff or straw became common.[21] Curtain materials were within reach of the worker's purse where the housewife was handy with her needle, which was far from usual among girls who started work at an early age. By the first decade of the twentieth century, when Robert Tressall wrote *The Ragged Trousered Philanthropist*, this description of his best room was probably a fair picture of the living style of the respectable artisan:

'The mantelpiece was of wood painted black and ornamented with jagged streaks of red and yellow, which were supposed to give it the appearance of marble. On the walls was a paper with a pale terracotta ground and a pattern consisting of large white roses with chocolate coloured leaves and stalks. There was a small iron fender with fire-irons to match and on the mantelshelf stood a clock in a polished wood case, a pair of blue glass vases and some photographs in frames. The floor was covered with oil-cloth of a tile pattern in yellow and red. On the walls were two or three framed coloured prints such as are presented with Christmas numbers of illustrated papers. In the centre of the room was a round deal table about 3 ft 6 in across, with the legs stained red to look like mahogany. Against one wall was an old couch covered with faded cretonne, four chairs to match standing backs to wall in different parts of the room.'[22]

Because Tressall was a house-painter to trade he could make improvements beyond the skill of most householders, and all of his furniture and floor-covering was being paid for, with great difficulty, on the instalment system.

Fred Jowett, Bradford's labour councillor at the turn of this century, found people who moved into the city's first council houses after the demolition of their slum homes very worried about furniture. They had no practice in the purchase of furnishings and knew neither what was necessary nor what was good value. He arranged for them to be issued with a catalogue showing them how their new rooms could be laid out economically and well.[23]

Chapter 8

Publicity for Squalor

'A lousy set of devils'

O'CONNOR

For the greatest part of our period, then, and over most of the towns of Britain, working people lived in crowded squalor, in dilapidated or shoddily built houses without the relief of comfortable furniture. In the second half of the century there was a great deal of pious probing of the sore. Reformers of every persuasion talked about, wrote about, lectured about the conditions in which the poor were living, but in the period up to the late 1830s only a few middle-class people were fully aware of the massive scale of town deterioration in Britain. They knew that the commercial centres of their own cities in which their homes as merchants and professional men had been traditionally gathered had become quite uninhabitable by people with the means to leave; and they had left, to build substantial villas in more salubrious quarters and, eventually, to move into 'the county'. Afterwards their wives and daughters saw nothing of the town's poor and the masters as little as their trade or profession made necessary. There were whole areas, in the older cities particularly, never entered by anyone except their inhabitants who had, as in Hull's dockland, 'their own customs, their own shops, their own language even'.[1]

Six factors of importance worked together to confront the people of Britain with the appalling conditions existing in their towns; the publication of census figures and mortality rates in 1831, and the Registration Act, 1836, the reports of the Poor Law Commissioners following the Poor Law Amendment Act, 1834, the forming of a number of societies interested in statistics and social studies, the continuing and accelerating threat of riot and revolution, and the attack in 1833 and 1848 of King Cholera.

The establishment of the office of Registrar-General in 1837 and especially the appointment to it of Dr William Farr[2] as Compiler of Abstracts gave those interested in public health the first reliable statistics with which to fight for reform. The returns from the Registrar-General's office gave information on age distribution at death, and on local variations in the incidence of disease and in mortality rates. Farr took the important step of publishing in his reports comparisons between the life-spans of people in 'healthy' towns and those less fortunate. He compared a country death rate of 18.2 per thousand with a town-rate of 26.6 per thousand. Later work backed him up and showed even more shocking figures of the great variation between one part of a town and another. Edwin Chadwick warned, in his report on 'The Comparative Chances of Life in Different Classes of the Community', of the danger of making judgements from gross national returns. Examination of local registers showed that the death rate within one town could vary from district to district as much as from 1 in 57 to 1 in 28. In Liverpool in 1840 the average age at death of the gentry and professional persons was 35. The average labourer died at 15 years of age, this average being kept down by the enormous figure of 62 per cent of labourers' children dying under 5 years old. Infant mortality was high in all classes of the community, ignorance of the science of bacteriology, malnutrition through ignorance of dietary requirements, very little, if any, improvement in methods of delivery since medieval times and total absence of after-care caused high rates in death immediately after birth, whatever the income group, and infectious disease accounted for high rates in the under-fives who survived their first weeks of life. But even within the national figure the wide variation in infant mortality shocked.

People had to face the fact that conditions in their towns were bad enough to kill. Even while the national death rate was still falling steeply, that is before urbanisation had affected the major part of the population, the early census figures showed urban death rates to be very noticeably higher than rural rates. But, as the unfavourable environment of the towns began to affect a second generation of urban dwellers and to increase its lethal tendency, the rising urban death rate actually moved steeply enough to counteract the national decline in mortality. Farr's cool statistics betrayed more tellingly than emotional ranting the terrible fact that a child's chance of life was affected by his place of birth to such an extent that if he were born in a town he had only half as good a chance of living as a country child.

These figures were exactly what was needed to strengthen the case of those already perturbed by the condition of the poor. The Poor Law Amendment Act, 1834, had proved, as we have seen, unworkable partly because those who had framed it had seriously underestimated the existing need for relief. But the administrative framework set up by the Act had, for the first time, made possible the collection of evidence about the needs of the poor on a national scale. The first reports of the new Poor Law Commissioners revealed a state of shocking poverty and squalor which aroused in those who had to administer the law, in those who were affected by its results, and in those who were simply hearing about such conditions for the first time, an overwhelming sense of horror and dismay. Not least affected by what he learnt as he attempted to put the Act into operation was the man who had done so much to put the stiffening into it when it was framed. Edwin Chadwick moved from a stern belief in the efficacy of withholding relief from the able-bodied to as stern a certainty that prevention must henceforward be more important than cure. The conditions which had succeeded in reducing so large a part of the population to pauperisation must be treated. If epidemics caused widows and orphans to become a burden on the country and if, as his medical colleagues assured him, epidemics were caused by filth, then the filth was directly the cause of the rising taxation for poor relief and it must be swept away.

On 14 May 1838, the fourth report of the Poor Law Commissioners was sent to Lord John Russell, the Home Secretary, along with a letter asking that the Commissioners be given powers to indict for nuisance. This would have had the important effect of giving a body with national authority power to act where accumulations of refuse or pollution of the water supply was affecting the health of the community. There was no official response. It was too obvious that if the Commissioners were to have these new powers they would also have to have extra funds to meet the additional costs which could not fail to be incurred. While those who adminstered the Poor Law districts had come to believe that small sums spent on the removal of filth would prevent large sums having to be spent on the maintenance of paupers, it was not easy to convince Parliament that any extra expenditure, however long-sighted, was desirable. The House of Lords debated the first reports and their accompanying letter without arriving at any conclusion.

In the following year Dr Thomas Southwood Smith's 'Report on the Prevalence of Fever in Twenty Metropolitan Unions' was published as an appendix to the fifth Poor Law report. This was very widely read and had sufficient influence to cause the Bishop of London to rise in the Lords in August to move an inquiry into the condition of the labouring classes. Edwin Chadwick, as Secretary to the Poor Law Commissioners, was instructed to organise a sanitary inquiry which would give a true picture of the condition of the people of Britain and their needs. The thoroughness with which Chadwick worked, the vicissitudes of the Whig government during the next years, and the practical difficulty of finding men of both knowledge and conscience to produce the surveys over the whole country, delayed the production of Chadwick's report on the sanitary condition of the labouring population of England, Scotland and Wales until 1842. When it was eventually published it contained such a mass of evidence of the plight of the poor and of the need for effective administrative action that it needed a major psychological effort to assimilate its implications.

Meanwhile in June 1840, Richard Slaney had acted precipitately in the House of Commons to obtain a select committee on the Health of Towns. While Chadwick attacked this committee's report as containing 'off-hand and easy generalities', its evidence was effective enough to persuade Lord Normanby, who had succeeded Russell as Home Secretary, to bring in three new Bills with important bearing on the subject. They were the Bill for the improvement of certain burghs, the Bill for the better drainage of large towns and villages, and the Bill for regulating buildings in large towns. The House of Lords passed all three and sent them to the Commons on 6 May 1841.[3] There they had an interesting history, interrupted by the fall of the Whig Government in September 1841. Normanby had given Chadwick orders to halt his inquiry until the fate of these new Bills was known.[4] Lord Melbourne instructed him to continue it.

During May, June and August of 1841 the select committees set up to consider the three Bills were bombarded by petitions against them from towns and individual landowners[5] who considered them 'detrimental to their properties, rights and interests'. The opposition was partly the expected outcry of threatened property owners and officials afraid of diminished power, but partly the result of faulty preparation of the Bills. Not enough work had been done in discovering the state of professional opinion on the measures proposed. Building Regulations, in particular, needed, as the recent twentieth-century committee has discovered, long and detailed study before a satisfactory measure of agreement could be arrived at.

Sir James Graham, the Tory Home Secretary who inherited the three Bills, was not one to lead reform. He stopped them at their second reading. The Drainage Bill was lost altogether, but the Building Regulations and Burgh Improvements topics had select committees appointed in March 1842, which reported on 27 June. Their reports, although ineffective in producing legislation, added to the body of evidence mounting now about the disastrous state into which our towns had subsided.

Unpreparedness and lack of thoroughness was something of which Edwin Chadwick could never be accused. Scorning Slaney's report as 'concocted by Home Office lawyers and palace architects',[6] his own was a model of careful preparation. It used assistant Poor Law Commissioners, local doctors, ministers and clerks, knowledgeable individuals of all professions to make a survey of all types and sizes of towns and villages. It dealt with the physical geography of an area, its drainage and water supply, or the want of them, the cleansing of streets, the prevalence of fever, the general condition of the residences of labourers, their internal economy and domestic habits and the comparative chances of life in different classes. It discussed, more controversially, the existing principles of legislation, the present state of local executive authorities, condemned the inefficiency of both and suggested remedies.

It was far too forceful a collection of documents to be ignored even by a Home Secretary with as little liking for change as Sir James Graham and a Prime Minister whose over-riding faith was that things were best left to right themselves. A Royal Commission on the Health of Towns was appointed in 1843, its first report on the State of Large Towns and Populous Districts being published in July 1844, the second a year later. These reports showed, as all the foregoing evidence had done, the failure of all previous Acts, both local and general, to bring drainage and water supply to the poorer districts and emphasised the need for building regulations to prevent the waste and inefficiency prevalent in the building trade. But they also betrayed the terrible ignorance both of the true condition of the people and of the means of changing it which was then general. The inability of the commissioners to conceive of the idea of legislative interference in what seemed to them private matters gave little hope that their report would be effective.

Government committees were necessarily limited in their attitude to the evidence at their disposal by their knowledge of what Parliament would find tolerable. The new societies of individuals interested in the collection of statistics felt no such limitation. They had more scope both in their means of collecting evidence—they could conduct house-to-house surveys which would have been bitterly resented if instigated by a central authority—and in the presentation of their results.

It is not easy to be certain why the 1830s should have produced an interest in the study of statistics so urgent and widespread as to assume the status of a new intellectual movement. It has been suggested that the new actuarial methods of life assurance had aroused curiosity about estimates of the duration of human life. It may have been a reaction by men of scientific interests to the emotional basis of so much of the local campaigning for public health. It may have been a simple response by an intellectual section of the public to the shock they felt at the exposure of so much human misery. Whatever the origin of the new interest, it resulted in the formation of a number of lively and hard-working societies. The Statistical Society of London broke away from the parent British Association for the Advancement of Science in 1834 after a disagreement with the B.A. President who felt that statistical inquiries into social problems probed unjustifiably 'into regions where they would touch on the mainsprings of feeling and passion'.[7] Reconciliation must have quickly followed, however, for a paper prepared by members of the Statistical Society on the condition of the working class was read at the Liverpool meeting of the British Association in 1837. Liverpool men in the audience were shocked into disbelief by the statistics of their town given in this paper but it is to their credit that they went home to organise a survey of their own to check the results. Richard Cobden reported in 1840 that they had found the statistics, if anything, under-stated.[8]

The Manchester Statistical Society was formed in 1833, a little earlier than the London Society, its object 'the collection of facts illustrative of the condition of society'.[9] These two societies have survived until the present day, but the 1830s saw the birth of others with similar aims in Bristol, Leeds, Birmingham, Liverpool, Glasgow, Aberdeen and Belfast. Their painstaking efforts to collect hard facts and to present them by statistical method in a manner too irreproachable to be ignored had real impact both on the communities in which they worked and at national level. By the mid-1840s there was little possibility of any section of the middle classes remaining entirely ignorant of the problems which threatened their new industrial society.

The evidence and the facts were, however, backed most powerfully by fear that the cracks appearing in that society would open into chasms capable of swallowing the dominant classes and all their works. It would be much too simple to say that slum conditions produced political discontent in the working class. There were grievances other than the misery of their housing to account for the resentment of the people, especially the conditions of their labour and the fluctuating demand for it, and there is nothing like enough evidence for a historian to draw conclusions about how the people most affected felt about their circumstances. The worst affected were the poorest, the least educated and the most inarticulate. Echoes of what they felt reach us through those middle-class workers who visited them for philanthropic or administrative purposes but we have only responses to set questions and the questions were too often leading ones. Even for contemporaries it was difficult to make judgements about the extent to which living conditions contributed to political grievance. It was possible for sensitive and thoughtful men living in the same period and speaking of the same conditions to differ radically in their conclusions.

When Slaney first presented the motion which resulted in the Health of Towns Inquiry he asked the House 'to inquire into the causes of discontent among great bodies of the working classes in populous districts' and suggested that the most important ground for complaint was 'the want of legislative provision for the preservation of their health and the comfort of their houses'.[10] It is perhaps indicative of government fears that there might be an uncomfortable amount of truth in the suggestion that the then Home Secretary, Lord John Russell, was so quick to sweep the idea away, objecting to 'the political tendency of the motion . . . As to the civil condition of the working classes he had no objection to an inquiry, but he thought it not wise to institute inquiries into their political condition.' Thus an important opportunity was lost. If the problem of housing the people had been considered as a political problem, the point at which government responsibility for housing was accepted might perhaps have been reached sooner, although not in the circumstances of the 1840s. Instead, housing was pushed into the safer province of public health, there to be lost in the pressure for 'moral and sanitary reform'. The inquiry[11] which eventually resulted from this abortive attempt to treat the matter differently concentrated on sanitation.[12] The question whether the people were discontented in their slums was frequently asked of witnesses by the select committee, and by the other inquiries which followed it, and it was invariably answered that the people seemed apathetic and unprotesting, not, in fact, likely to cause political trouble. Lord John seemed to be proved right when, in the debate which followed the first proposal to discuss the subject, he said: 'the growth of a disposition to turbulence by no means kept pace with the growth of population.' London, he pointed out, had a bigger population than any other town, and, he might have added, slums of greater extent if not of worse degree than any other. Yet there we had 'an example of an orderly population conducting themselves as well if not better than any other population of the same extent'.[13]

While no major political upheaval can be directly attributed to discontent with living conditions there were many minor disturbances caused by, for instance, evictions for non-payment of rent, when whole slum streets would rise up in defence of the evicted family.[14] Disgust with the squalor of their surroundings played an important part in bringing about what Slaney described as the want of 'attachment of the people to the institutions of the country'.[15] Economic causes alone were not responsible for the ferment of revolt which simmered among working people in the first decades of the nineteenth century. Russell was right in 1840 when he pointed out that economic distress was worse in the agricultural districts, which were quiet, than in the large manufacturing villages which were notoriously 'disorderly'.[16] It was the combination of unsteady employment, low wages, miserable housing and the impossibility of doing anything about it because of their complete lack of representation which caused resentment. While the main stream of Chartists, for instance, shunned land and freehold schemes as diversions from their political aims, they knew that it was always easy to rouse their following by reminding them of their pitiful surroundings, by calling them 'a poor, beggarly, lousy set of devils . . . without house or home or bread or clothes or fuel'.[17]

If Russell were right in describing London as more orderly than other towns, and of course the amount of petty crime shows him to be wrong and proves the Metropolitan population to have been quite wonderfully detached from the institutions of the country; but even if he were right he in fact brings arguments against his cause. For if indeed most political movements were begun outside London, in Tyneside in 1815, Manchester 1819, Derbyshire 1820, Newport 1839, and the London population expressed its discontent chiefly in drunken brawling, thieving and the defence of whole areas too dangerous to be entered by the middle classes, this can best be explained by the fact that squalor and misery were longer established and deeper seated than elsewhere. The difficulty of finding a home was greater, the home worse and more costly when it was found. London slum dwellers were reduced to sullen acceptance of their surroundings when the more independent spirits were still kicking against them because they had not yet become accustomed to them.

Chadwick was cunning enough, or perhaps he was honestly convinced of the truth of his own argument—it is never easy to be certain with Chadwick—to use the prevailing fear of mob violence as an argument for doing something about the high mortality rates in cities. The more mature section of the working people presented no threat to society, he said, but were orderly, docile, even prepared to come to their masters' aid in case of riot. 'They were generally described as being above the influence of the anarchical fallacies which appeared to sway those wild and really dangerous assemblages.'[18] The tragedy was that too few in the labouring districts reached maturity. The mobs were largely composed of hooligan boys lacking the influence of their sober elders. If conditions in the towns were improved so that mortality rates fell, a greater proportion of the working population reaching middle age would automatically subdue the discontent.

This was one case where Chadwick allowed his great desire to convince his readers of the need for reform to affect his selection of evidence. Very real grievances existed which would find an outlet in mob risings as long as no other means of expression was allowed and they could not be swept away as mere youthful hooliganism. It was because the new reports forced the middle classes to become aware of those grievances, grievances which seemed to thoughtful people genuinely unbearable, that they began to fear that the time must come when the poor would bear them no longer, that they would rise in a rage to overturn the society which had allowed such things to happen. The rationalisation of their own disgust caused middle-class people to fear revolution. The simmering resentment which made some streets unsafe to walk in and some towns prone to outbreaks of violence gave just enough evidence of its existence to justify that fear even when all organised protest seemed successfully suppressed.

Nothing, however, not even the fear of revolution brought panic so close to the British people as the cholera epidemics of 1832 and 1849. The relentlessness of its watched approach across the world towards our shores, the mystery of its means of infection, its apparently haphazard way of striking one household and not another, the terrifying suddenness of its onset and the speed with which death followed made the cholera epidemic a quite new experience of horror. Britain in 1831–2 was well accustomed to epidemic disease and death. Typhus alone killed every year almost as many as cholera in its sporadic onslaughts. But typhus killed the sickly, the under-nourished, the poor for the most part. Because it was louse-carried, it attacked dirty people living in filthy conditions, which seemed to the nineteenth century only just. Cholera was no such respecter of income groups. It hit active, healthy men in the prime of life. It killed the well fed, the comfortably housed, the prosperous. It crossed class barriers to terrify the middle classes with the possibility that God's punishing hand might fall on them in their virtue as well as on the paupers in their sin. There seemed no defence against it, no hope after it hit, no means of escaping its attack.

On the surface, the terror was masked by an acceptance of the inevitable as God's will. 'What can't be cured must be endured' was the prevalent philosophy. The poor bowed lower under the new burdens created by so many deaths, the burial expenses, the loss of wage-earners, the multitude of orphans. Those in authority first blustered, refusing to admit the possibility of any real threat to them: 'This overwhelming malady has as yet been confined, almost without exception, to the lower classes of society, whose irregularities, intemperances and general neglect of cleanliness afford strong pre-disposing causes; while the higher classes in Dundee, or in any other well-regulated town, have nothing to fear.'[19] Then they attempted to forbid it. They placed quarantine embargoes on ships arriving from cholera ports, embargoes which proved ineffective partly because cholera was not carried in cargoes, partly because the traders whose pockets felt the loss summoned effective enough pressure to have them lifted. Boards of Health were set up and medical officers appointed. When no cheaper course of action seemed possible and the force of public opinion was sufficient to make avoidance difficult, some public money was spent on cleaning out the worst parts of the cities, at least those courts where the human dung lay thickest.

But cholera did not last long enough to create a consistent demand for new social policies. Two summers and autumns of death and terror and then it was gone, as little apparent reason for its withdrawal as for its first appearance. The Boards of Health were disbanded, the streets again accumulated refuse and night soil. In the Boot and Shoe Yard in Leeds, where 340 persons lived in 57 rooms, 75 cart-loads of soil were taken out of their three 'out-offices' during the cholera but in 1840 it was reported that it had not been cleaned again in the seven years since the cholera scare had passed.[20] Cholera seemed easily forgotten and its immediate effect astonishingly small. The sanitary inquiries did not follow until nine or ten years later and seemed, on the surface, not to have been instigated by its results.

Cholera had no effect of a lasting nature on the cleanliness of the streets, the comfort of houses or the mobilisation of central administration in the service of public health. It had, however, two important, durable and more subtle effects.

The panic response of the working class, particularly to the 1832 epidemic, showed itself in fear and suspicion of the middle and upper classes. Rumours arose that the poor were being deliberately poisoned by their betters in a calculated attempt to keep down the population. Street riots occurred when the sick were carried away to hospital on professional orders, because the hospitals were accused of doing away with poor patients. Cholera epidemics coincided remarkably with depressions in trade, visiting the nation with one more crisis at times when economic conditions had already produced social tension and outbursts of protest. What Professor Briggs has called 'the equation of dirt, disease, and political disturbance'[21] was not a simple one. The coincidence of cholera and vigorous radical movements needs to be critically considered, and the last word on the subject has not been said. But the cholera epidemics did serve to point the chasm of misunderstanding which had opened between lower and upper classes, and, particularly after 1848, by heightening middle-class awareness of this terrifying gap, increased fears of revolutionary protest.

The other important way in which cholera epidemics influenced social development was in their effect on the few medical men who were closely involved with the poor in their fruitless attempts to treat the disease. Young doctors, uncomfortably aware, in spite of the oracular announcements from recognised medical authorities, of their ignorance of the origin of the disease and of any means of curing it, were induced to enter deteriorating parts of the cities long unvisited by professional people. There they were faced with the appalling effects of decades of urban neglect and with the impossiblity of helping by medical means people living in such degraded conditions. Those doc-

3. Open drains alongside houses, Bermondsey, 1855

tors who had experience of cholera responded to the crisis in different ways, evolving individual theories about the nature of the disease which eventually produced important schisms within the medical profession. But *contagionists*, who believed that contact with infected persons must take place before the disease could spread, and *miasmatists*, who believed that the disease had spontaneous origin in the noxious gases emitted by accumulations of filth, both became convinced that prevention must be their future aim. One school believed that the poverty of the people must be treated so that their physique could be improved to the point of withstanding infection and their homes improved by their ability to pay higher rents. Another school concentrated on the need for cleanliness as the best means of prevention. Until Snow proved, in 1848, that cholera was spread by infection from mouth to intestine, usually through the water supply, they were working in the dark. But while those medical men who were convinced that poverty was their worst enemy could produce no ideas about how poverty could be removed, there was an obvious course of action open to those who believed in the generation of fever from filth. The filth must be removed. In the conviction of those medical men who visited cholera victims in their homes, the campaign for public health was born. In their writings they exposed the conditions in which the poor were living so graphically as to arouse a determination among social reformers that the towns must be cleansed. People began to ask, at last, why such things had been allowed to happen and whether anything could have been done to prevent them.

Chapter 9

A Sense of Property

> 'The poorest man may in his cottage bid defiance to all the forces of the crown'
>
> PITT

In the face of these reports of the abject living conditions of the poor we must ask, as did those who first received them, what could have been done to prevent the situation and what were the causes which brought it about?

Almost all the nineteenth-century inquirers were agreed that there were no powers in the hands of those who administered the country during the period of rapid growth, that is in the last decades of the eighteenth and the first decades of the nineteenth century, which could have prevented the terrible build-up of the housing shortage and the public health problem. Yet machinery did exist and the fact that it was not used, or that it was inefficiently or dishonestly or inadequately used, was brought about more by the attitude of the administrators than by the inadequacy of the law. It was an attitude of mind shared by the first reporters and reformers which explains why they could not detect the failure of a previous generation, like their own, to use what powers they had.

This is not to say that legislative reform was not necessary but that the really revolutionary change of heart by the lawmakers which was necessary to bring about effective reform was no more likely to happen during three-quarters of the nineteenth century than it had been in earlier centuries. Given the kind of thinking which did eventually bring about the effective housing of the poor (to the extent that we can claim such a thing has been effected even now) the legislative machinery available during the Industrial Revolution could have been used to prevent at least the worst excesses of the slum landlords.

Study of such powers is made very difficult, however, by the lack of any central administrative authority or even any pattern of regulations over the country as a whole. Without making too rapid a descent into the complexities of town and local government it is necessary to consider in whose hands such powers as existed lay. England was divided into towns and 'manors', each of which had its own leet jury. One of the difficulties was that the framework had been designed for a very different distribution of population, so that as late as the 1840s Manchester, for instance, had still a manorial constitution, as if it were nothing more than a market town and Bolton was still under a court leet. In Scotland a burgh had its own 'sett' which controlled by whom it should be run and in what way. Even London was run as the series of villages it had originally been, each administered by a vestry which was little different from a village council. Primitive as were these institutions they did have considerable control over their districts. They could, if they chose, make rules, for instance, about the cleaning and lighting of their streets. If that alone had been effectively and consistently done much of the trouble which came later could have been avoided. Yet when the select committee set up to consider an early, and abortive, Bill about town and housing improvement made an analysis of replies from fifty towns in England to questions about their town cleansing regulations they found only one which was making effective use of its powers.[1] Councils could also order that water-courses and ponds be kept clear and pure and had the power to enforce penalties. This was a provision existing from medieval times and of an obvious usefulness. But as manufacturing interests made increasing use of a town's water-courses both to provide power and to carry away effluent it became increasingly difficult, or impolitic, to press the interest of the community as a whole; and particularly its poorest members, against the powerful claims of industry.

In the Metropolis and in those large towns in which sewers were laid, there were powers to control the connecting of drainage systems to the main sewers. This control was, in London and in some other cities, in the hands of the Commissioners of Sewers, in other towns in the hands of the town council. Those powers were most often used not to insist upon the connection of privately-owned houses to the sewers, but to prevent it.[2] The task was chiefly seen as one of preservation, the maintenance and repair of ancient sewers and the prevention of any action which might lead to undue strain upon them.

Accumulations of refuse, household manure and such delights as the offal from slaughter-houses were also the business of town and village authorities. Unfortunately, far from hastening their disposal, the councillors, or the Commissioners of Police who held the same powers in some towns, looked upon town dung as an important source of revenue and prevented its removal until the piles had reached profitable proportions. The point here is not only the unwisdom of the town councils in allowing their towns to grow filthier and filthier but the interesting fact that the matter was within their control. They were not entirely helpless in face of the growing health risks in the streets. They *chose* to ignore them.

In England as a whole the common law was not entirely incompetent to deal with nuisances of every kind. Built upon a series of precedents from cases won in the courts it could prohibit and exact penalties for anything of an obnoxious kind which offended either individuals or the community as a whole. Complaint had only to be made and the local authority had power to order the removal of the 'nuisance'. The fact that a nuisance had been tolerated over a long period did not, in law, give its perpetrators the right to continue it once it had been complained of. Scots law was, in this respect, less effective,[3] having little interest in nuisance as suffered by the public as a whole but only in litigations between individuals where one had suffered from a nuisance created by the other.[4] This meant that where the public was affected by a nuisance one private individual had to be found to bear the cost and inconvenience of a law-suit, possible in law, of course, but not easily achieved. In Scotland, too, the existence of a nuisance over a long period of years was taken to give it the right to continue, as in the famous case of the Edinburgh water meadows.[5] There were, undoubtedly, great weaknesses and inconsistencies in the law as it stood. However there was a law and it was certainly not used with determination or imagination. A law built upon precedent, as England's is, will allow of imaginative interpretation, and does so where the climate of public opinion is favourable.[6] But in the first half of the nineteenth century, in so far as a majority public opinion took any interest at all in the question of public rather than private health, it operated, for a variety of reasons as we shall see, against any interference with the *status quo*.

Where a town felt the need for wider powers it could, as Liverpool, for instance, did in 1825 and again in 1842, apply for a local Act of Parliament to suit its own particular needs. Liverpool's Building Act laid down rules for the provision of space around new buildings, the construction of walls, and the height of rooms. Bristol's, of 1842, made regulations about building materials, Blackburn's about the design of flues. London's Building Act was in some ways inferior to those of other towns, which was one reason why the Building Regulations Bill, which took London's Act as a model, ran into difficulties.

Scotland was in this respect more precisely provided for by traditional machinery than the rest of the country. Her Dean of Guild courts had 'full authority in all matters of building'.[7] It was provided that application must be made to the Dean of Guild for a warrant for any new building. Notice was then served on the neighbouring proprietors who had the right to object to any encroachment upon their property or supposed diminishing of amenity. The clerk to the Dean of Guild's court, on payment of a fee from the builder, issued the warrant. Jurisdiction extended also to alterations of existing buildings which must not encroach upon the thoroughfare or in any way adversely affect adjoining buildings. The Dean had the right to order closure and demolition of derelict buildings.[8] He could not control width of streets or height of buildings, unless the height was complained of by neighbours, but he could regulate thickness of walls in relation to the height. He could order newly erected buildings which did not conform to the provisions of his court and which had evaded notice by his clerk to be pulled down again, and on occasion did so.[9] He had powers to prevent what could be defined as 'an architectural nuisance'.[10]

Complicated, imprecise and inconsistent as they were, rules did exist which could have done something, if used with determination and honesty and not allowed to fall into abeyance, to prevent the towns deteriorating to the extent they did. There was no provision suggested in the proposed Buildings Bill of 1841 (the first attempt to bring out a general Act with national powers) for which there was not already a precedent in some part of the kindom. The principle of the need for control had in fact always been accepted in British law. For instance, Burton quotes this doctrine; 'It hath been holden to be a common nuisance to divide a house in a town for poor people to inhabit in, by reason whereof it will be more dangerous in time of infection of the plague.'[11] Yet the most powerful opposition to the 1841 Bill and to succeeding attempts at reform was mustered on the grounds of principle, not practicality. Joseph Fletcher, who had sat as one of the commissioners to inquire into the condition of the hand-loom weavers in 1834, in giving evidence to the Select Committee on Building Regulations, tried, and, it seems to us, convincingly, to put forward the view that: 'It would be no violation of principle to interfere in regulating . . . In the local Acts which already exist in the irregular system I have described there will be found contained in one or other of them all and more than all the purposes contemplated.'[12] But he was borne down. Many of those giving evidence of their own experience of the living conditions of working people, and whose every word seemed to prove the need for legislative action, still were troubled by the principle of interference with individual liberty.

To understand why the earlier regulations we have been looking at proved ineffective and why the new laws were so strongly opposed, we must consider this principle which Victorians saw to be involved and why it was so strongly held. On one level the highest concepts of Christian doctrine and statesmanlike philosophy justified inaction, at another inefficiency, dishonesty and ignorance made any action ineffective. The British dislike of centralised authority, religious support for self-help, the political theory of *laissez-faire*, and the belief in the sanctity of private property, united to form a middle-class creed of almost inviolable strength and vitality; while, at the level where theory stops and practice should begin, muddled officials, swayed by self-interest and not guided by informed opinion, contrived to make a bad situation worse. Even among medical men and scientists there was no certainty about means of preventing epidemics. Although many saw a connection between dirt and disease it was by no means universally acknowledged. There were some far-seeing minds who suggested that a man who was housed in miserable conditions might work less hard in support of his master's interests, but most people hardly gave the idea consideration. In the first decades of the century there were no hard facts with which to counter strong opinions. Science was in a state of anxious uncertainty at a time when middle-class values had never been more firmly held. The forces which would erode that wall of middle-class certainty were at work, weakening its foundations, but they put it in little danger yet.

One must try to understand what the words 'private property' meant to the nineteenth-century man—something different from the same words used today. To condemn the property owner of the early nineteenth century for putting his own interests before the good of the whole community, as it is fashionable now to condemn developers, is to miss more than half the picture and completely to fail in understanding the tremendous force of the 'private property' argument. 'Argument' is, in fact, hardly the word. The slogan 'rights of private property' had hardly to be breathed to send the first housing reformers scuttling back behind their barricades.

It was as if by becoming a property owner a man received an accolade from society. The simple view was that God would not have allowed him to attain such a position if he had not been worthy of it. Divine justice raised him to his comfortable status just as divine justice ensured that the shiftless and undeserving should remain poor and without property. This view was supported quite as much by the artisan who had just attained the status of owning his own tools and workshop as it was by the owners of vast estates. So long as there existed a possibility of the poor man becoming a property owner in however small a way, he would support the rights of private property.

Private property provided a barrier against the millions without property, distinguishing its owner satisfactorily from the common herd, raising him above them, but also giving him something to fear from them. Property had to be protected against the threat of uprising and this could justify keeping the poor in misery or even increasing their discomfort. In 1840 the Bradford wool-combers, a very depressed trade living in shocking conditions, were deprived of the only piece of open ground available to them for recreation by an Enclosure Act on behalf of the local landowner, because: 'This ground has been latterly used by the Chartists, and it has got into bad odour.'[13]

It was not only the property owned by each individual Englishman which was important to him, but the *idea* of private property which had an importance, almost a sanctity, of its own. Not only must a man feel secure from invasion of any kind in his own home but he must feel that the noble concept of private property was unthreatened by political notions which might undermine it. Private property stood as a defence between the state and the individual, giving the English the kind of strength which had in the past defeated attempts at despotic monarchy and ambitious parliaments. Thus the very idea of the creation of the inspectorate which would have been necessary to enforce building standards was interpreted as an intolerable attack on private property. Proprietors were represented as virtuous by reason of their ownership of property and the obvious respectability that conveyed—they obviously should not be threatened by intruding watchdogs of the state. The inspectorate, however, was resented not because it meant intrusion into the private homes of the lower-class tenants (who did not own the rights and dignity of private property), but because it represented an inspection of the property of the landlord, a questioning of his right to keep his property in any state he chose, which was seen as quite intolerable. There had taken place some narrowing of the principle of non-violation of the home since William Pitt had declaimed in a speech in the House of Commons: 'The poorest man may in his cottage bid defiance to all the forces of the Crown. It may be frail—its roof may shake—the wind may blow through it—the storm may enter—the rain may enter—but the King of England cannot enter—all his force dares not cross the threshhold of the ruined tenement!' This kind of objection to inspection as a threat to private property was one of the most powerful galvanisers of opposition to the Buildings Regulations Bill in 1842 and it helped to make Lord Shaftesbury's 1851 Act inoperable. At every turn, the property argument was used to prevent or delay reform. The select committee appointed to consider the Buildings Regulations Bill was bombarded with petitions against it both from builders and owners of land and from local authorities and officials, and the most commonly used phrase in all the appeals was 'highly injurious to rights and property'.[14] The petitioners were successful in getting the Bill dismissed. Such a conclusion was quite inevitable in view of the caution with which the Bill had been promoted. The Health of Towns Committee, in suggesting the need for a General Building Act, had reported that 'regulations should be framed so as to interfere no further with everyone's right to manage his own property than necessary'.[15] A little later, in 1844, new commissioners were appointed to consider the 'state of large towns and populous districts'. In their first report they made certain that nothing would be done about the situation which the great body of evidence put before them revealed, because of their inability to conceive of the idea of legislative interference with what seemed to them private affairs. They pointed out the need for change and then made certain it would not come about by adding the words: 'The greatest caution is necessary lest, while seeking to afford a remedy, injustice might be done to the inhabitants or their owners.'[16]

Very closely allied to the sense of 'Property's' importance was the English dislike of anything resembling or seeming to resemble a continental European type of strong, authoritarian central government. With only a hazy knowledge of other countries' administrative systems, Englishmen believed that in fighting the French they had been fighting not only for the defence of their country but against a tyranny which would regulate the individual's private life in an intolerable way. The inefficiency of small-scale local government was preferred to a possibly more effective central government because it appeared to be less far removed from an individual's control.

There was a very real fear that the growth of democracy must mean the establishment of an un-English tyranny and that fear limited all attempts to lessen or divide the powers of local authorities. But while that fear had been stirred up and excited in the last quarter of the century both by events outside Britain and by changing conditions within and had therefore been expressed more often, more loudly and in a more extreme manner than in the 1840s, when the first attempt at a General Building Bill was made, it was nevertheless an even more effective deterrent to legislation in the 1840s, than it later became. The dislike of authoritarian government was so firmly entrenched as to be in little need of defence.

The steadily deteriorating economic condition of large sections of the working population had weakened both their will and their ability to produce political pressure in favour of an improvement in their condition or even to prevent further erosion of their crumbling place in society. By the time parliamentary reform and the first Factory Acts had been achieved, those in favour of change found themselves fragmented, some diverted into not less worthy causes, some merely discouraged and disillusioned to find how little had been achieved. For a while, perhaps, the old order had been shaken and different men sat in the places of power but it was not a different kind of man. The owners of house property were still in a position where they could decide whether their own actions should be controlled or not. If they chose to build houses of materials so shoddy that they sometimes fell down before they were inhabited,[17] or if they liked to build whole estates of houses on land lately infilled with nauseous rubbish and still heaving with the gases of its decomposition, only committees of their peers could say them nay. It would be naive to show surprise that they chose to evade control where it either threatened to diminish their own powers or to create new powers in the hands of a central government or even of new committees of gentlemen like themselves but with conflicting interests. An interesting instance is the Act of 1833[18] giving Scots local authorities power to appoint Police Commissioners who would be in charge of the lighting, cleansing and street lay-out of towns, a sort of primitive Town Planning Act. This would have delegated to a differently elected, separate body of men powers which town councils felt should be in their own hands. The Act made it optional for towns to adopt the whole or a portion of the Police Act. It was taken advantage of only in a few cases. Similarly, English town councils disliked the existence of the Commissioners of Sewers as a rival power within their own domain. Much of the opposition to the Building Regulations Bill took the form of petitions from local councils against any transference of power from them to the Commissioners. Manchester town council went so far as to petition that such an action would place Property 'under the control of irresponsible parties'.[19] So while local authorities, representing the property-owning middle classes, fought any encroachment on their powers as an attack on individual liberty and could call upon the full force of traditional political thought as well as patriotic sentiment to defend their own interests, it was unlikely that any action could be taken to improve the condition of working people. In particular, because the home and the family were seen as the very shrine in which all the strong values of an Englishman, his liberty and his Englishness were most safely guarded, it was political suicide to support any measure which would affect the sanctity of that home. The fact that, for a large part of the population, home spelt misery rather than sanctity was quite irrelevant where a principle of such importance was involved. So the 'right' to look after one's own was easily confused with a 'duty' to do so, however impossible a burden that duty might be, and was firmly built into the traditional use of such controlling powers as existed.

From the churches, where some interpretations of Christianity might lead one to expect more understanding of the needs of the poor and ill-housed, there came only strong support for middle-class values. The doctrine of self-help had great attraction for the rising class of entrepreneurs fast becoming a more and more influential section of nineteenth-century society, who saw their own success as achieved by hard work and initiative without any help from outside agencies. To hear 'self-help' preached from the pulpit as a tenet of the churchman's faith gave great satisfaction. It was essential to middle class confidence to believe that material prosperity in this world was the reward of virtue. Those who felt some duty towards the unfortunates of society became increasingly aware that the problem of the slums and the housing accommodation of the poor was not an easy one. How pleasant, then, to be told that to do nothing, to leave the problem to self-help and a spirit of independence among the slum dwellers themselves, was not only the most expedient course, but the right one, backed by the doctrine of the Church.

Middle-class values, and particularly the doctrines of self-help, pride in property, social and moral respectability, were fed into the poor at their every turn, from employers, preachers, teachers and charitable workers. But there was no return, no way of putting the point of view of the hungry and homeless so that their plight could genuinely be experienced by those who could have helped. The hopelessness of communicating on any real level with the good men and women who came among them made the poor seem apathetic. Time and again it was reported that they seemed quite contented with the squalor in which they lived: Lord James Stuart asked a witness giving evidence to the Health of Towns Committee: 'Do you observe a great deal of discontent among the poor people?' He was answered: 'No, the great proportion of those people I should say are of the lowest class of Irish and I hardly ever see a discontented Irishman; he seems quite contented in whatever condition he may be.'[20] A builder was asked if the poor felt the evils of their living condition. He said: 'I am not quite sure whether they feel them so as to be fully aware of them.'[21] A doctor said: 'Amidst the greatest destitution and want of domestic comfort I have never heard during the course of twelve years' practice, a complaint of inconvenient accommodation.'[22] So while the revelations of the misery and decay of the towns were steadily penetrating into middle-class consciousness and cracks were beginning to appear in the solid front of confidence in their own system of values, the foundation of principles remained unshaken. These were the principles which motivated the petitioners against such attempts at legislation on housing as Parliament attempted and the same principles prevented the putting into action of such powers as already existed. Government officials, aldermen, professional men and committee men, builders and financial speculators, and all the minor officers of local administration believed themselves to be doing right when they resisted any encroachment of the state into the rights of private property, the activities of enterprising business men, or the independence of individuals. These were the principles of the bourgeoisie whose interests were very much involved. It was not perhaps surprising that it was from the aristocracy, who were not unaffected by the same considerations and had, of course, their own limitations, but who did not feel themselves so threatened by the contemplated reforms that the first parliamentary measures were introduced. The Drainage of Buildings Bill and the Buildings Regulations Bill were introduced to the House of Lords by the Marquis of Normanby, and rejected by the Commons.[23] Shaftesbury's long campaigning produced the Lodging Houses Acts of 1851 and 1853 and it was Salisbury's conversion to the principle of state intervention in certain circumstances which produced the Housing Acts of 1885 and 1890. They were measures which produced bitterly expressed opposition in the country as a whole and which were made quite ineffective by the failure of professional people and official bodies to adopt them with any show of enthusiasm.

The political principle of *laissez-faire*, then, was not countered by any volume of public opinion which would have persuaded Parliament to adapt it. Quite patently the natural law of supply and demand was not enough to control the market in housing and yet the belief in the effective working of unfettered economic forces and the dislike of arbitrary intervention remained unchanged. The extent of overcrowding showed that there was a demand for houses which was not being met, but those few who felt any need to defend *laissez-faire* principles pointed to empty houses in the suburbs as evidence that supply was there. The mistake, of course, was to confuse 'demand' with 'need'. People who had the most basic need for shelter were not in a position to create an economic demand for more housing. It would be a long time before this paradox could be admitted and a solution sought. The doctrine of *laissez-faire* had a very great natural attraction. It must always be easier to do nothing than to choose which way to act and so it is always satisfactory to have theoretical backing for inaction. Even after events had forced the abandonment of *laissez-faire* as any political party's philosophy it continued to have great force and to affect the judgement of those who sat on committees of all kinds. As late as 1880, the Duke of Somerset could say: 'continued interference by the state undermines and destroys the habit of self-reliance, which is essential to the independence and mental energy of man.'[24]

So, the chief reason for the failure to use effectively existing powers to control housing was that the old rules were framed to protect property, not to ensure health and comfort for the community. There was nothing written into the rules which need have prevented their adaptation to the problems of growing towns. Simon wrote: 'our present law is insufficient *for its understood purpose*.'[25] Lack of understanding of the new purposes for which existing laws needed to be used caused the delay. They could have been differently used. But it was the new theory, not the new practice, which was hard to accept.

Chapter 10

Reasons for the Non-Use of Existing Powers

'Petty and sinister interests'
EDWIN CHADWICK

However, even if the principles could more readily have been adapted there would have remained difficulties. In most cases action could only be taken by local authorities after their attention had been drawn to a cause for complaint. There was a built-in necessity to report a 'nuisance'. The 'nuisance' might be the fouling of a water supply by an industrial concern so that the drinking water of neighbouring houses was contaminated. It might be an accumulation of night-soil on the pavements and rising above the window-sills of houses fronting the street. It might be severe overcrowding or danger from a decrepit gable wall on the point of falling. It was necessary for those affected by the nuisance to make a complaint to the appropriate authorities. But those most likely to be affected by the most common and the most noxious nuisances in towns were those least likely to complain, the very poor, people having 'no standing in the community', the uneducated, lacking in social confidence. It was more than unlikely that such people could push themselves to the point of entering town offices and complaining about the condition of their streets and houses to the arch respectable council officers.

While towns had contained relatively mixed communities of people, the professional people, the reasonably well-to-do, living among or close to the poor, those who suffered had had a voice. But the withdrawal of the educated from the worst areas affected the situation in two ways. The kind of person who was likely to complain had left, which meant that nuisances multiplied, the area became more and more unsavoury and any chance of the respectable ever living there again became slight. And the evacuation of people with a reasonable standard of living left the next generation of the poor with no model to aspire to. Octavia Hill reminded her readers in 1875 how difficult it had become to find servants with any knowledge of good housekeeping and cleanly habits, and drove home the fact that girls brought up in homes where there was no possibility of cleanliness could never make good servants for middle-class families.[1]

The need for education grew. Without it the poor could have little knowledge of the ways in which their living standards could be improved, nor could they gain the kind of confidence which would spur them to complain about their conditions. As generation followed generation in the slums the pattern of a different way of life disappeared. There was neither knowledge of, nor hope for the kind of dwelling which meant home to the middle classes. The Report of the Select Committee on the Health of Towns published in June 1840 found it evident that 'the wealthy and educated gradually withdraw themselves from these close and crowded communities; which thus stand more and more in need of some superintending paternal care.'[2] It went on, after some description of the conditions prevailing in the larger cities, to suggest that 'to require them to be clean, sober, cheerful, contented under such circumstances would be a vain and unreasonable expectation.'[3] It was even more vain to expect them to protect themselves. They were 'exposed to the cupidity and defective arrangements of their landlords'.[4] So that while there remained the necessity of complaint before remedy could be found and while there was no one to complain except the poor themselves there was little likelihood of improvement in the condition of our towns. This was especially so because the slum dwellers knew that the very people to whom they were expected to complain, those who supposedly should have safeguarded their interests, were those on whom they were already too dependent—their employers and their landlords, who were only too often the perpetrators of the nuisances.

The inefficiency of local administration ensured that however suitably framed the law might be it could never be put into practice. There were a number of causes contributing to this inefficiency. Perhaps the first should be the self-interest and blatant corruption of the councillors, but almost as important was the bewildering complexity of the system of administration, the overlapping of functions and the rivalry consequent upon it; and a third cause was certainly ignorance, ignorance of the prevailing conditions, of the causes which lay behind them, and of the means of effecting a remedy.

The idea of serving on town councils held little attraction for the important merchant, the successful manufacturer or the professional man who might withstand the temptation to misuse the minor advantages given by this kind of petty authority. Working men were excluded from serving both by the franchise and by the hours of committee meetings, even if their lack of social respectability had not debarred them. It was the small tradesman or shopkeeper who was most often attracted to town council service, men of the class most open to temptation, for whom there was the greatest advantage in wielding influence over, for instance, the granting of contracts or the appointing of officials. It was not coincidence that they came from the same class to which the majority of investors in cheap housing also belonged, described by Thomas Cubitt, founder of the important building firm, as 'a little shopkeeper class of persons who have saved a little money in business'.[5] The building trade has always been most open to minor corruption. Even before the twentieth-century extension of bureaucratic government there existed a plethora of minor irritations which could be placed in the way of an uncooperative builder or swept away for one willing to make acknowledgement of help given by friends on the council. So the wishes of town councillors, builders and owners of house property were often seen to have remarkable agreement.

There is some evidence that in that minority of towns in which the working class had either a measure of electoral representation or were in a position to exert political pressure on the town council the condition of working-class areas was appreciably better. In Sheffield an economically strong class of skilled artisan cutlers forced the council to appoint an efficient, trained and uncorrupt surveyor at a much earlier period than was usual and later succeeded in pushing the establishment of a Health Committee against the wishes of the council.[6] In Dundee, although the majority of the working population was depressed and economically weak, it was led for a time by a strongly motivated heckling trade. Hecklers until after the breaking of a major strike by the introduction of machinery, were in the position to create a serious bottleneck in the production of coarse linens, on which the town depended, and so could exert some pressure on authority. Noisy, well-attended meetings forced Dundee to adopt the Burgh Police Act, 1833,[7] and to accept a much lower franchise than other towns, and forced the submission to Parliament of a local Bill instead of the General Act when it was revised in 1851. The local Bill retained the low franchise giving at least some working men a vote in local affairs, the General Act specifically excluded them by raising the qualification to £10 freehold. It was not surprising then that the General Act was bitterly opposed at public meetings by the working classes and supported by the wealthy manufacturers. 'It was monstrously unjust', reported the Guildry Incorporation, 'that an operative weaver's vote should go as far as the greatest manufacturer's in the town'.[8] But some remembered an earlier time, when workers had had no say in local administration as a time of 'alarming riots of frequent occurrence',[9] and one speaker threatened quietly that 'were he to be disenfranchised he would not take so much interest in the preservation of the order of the town as he did at present.'[10] The appalling state of Dundee's streets and closes between 1833 and 1851, the period when artisan representation on the body controlling street cleanings was strongest, might cause some doubt about its effectiveness; but, in face of praise of Dundee's Police Commission as a model for others by neighbouring towns and even by its usually critical rival, Perth, one must assume that without working-class influence things would have been worse.

For the most part, however, town government was in the hands of the petty bourgeoisie, the very weakness of whose position in society left them open to the suspicion that their motives were not wholly altruistic. If they were corrupt it was not always on their own behalf but on behalf of the rate-payers they represented. They were subject not so much to the temptation of bribery, although, certainly, money often changed hands to the advantage of both councillor and, say, building contractor, as to social, economic and political pressures even harder to withstand. Large rate-payers, on whom councillors might be dependent for patronage, for employment, for trade or for acceptance in town society, objected, not unnaturally in the climate of the time, to paying for town improvements which would benefit only the working classes. They could see the point of building magnificent council offices or of laying out the principal streets in a manner to excite the admiration of rival towns, but they begrudged extra rates for cleansing the slum areas, bringing water into streets occupied only by the poor, or demolishing dangerous buildings in districts never entered by the well-to-do. It was felt, for instance, that narrow streets were quite sufficient for the poor because they had no need of room for carriages.[11]

The need always to keep down the rates to please the voters left councillors prey to every kind of political pressure and seldom able to move towards any town reform which did not please the wealthiest and most influential townsmen who also paid the largest sums in rates. Political squabbles continually splintered councils, weakened their authority and deflected their interest and attention from matters which were properly their concern, such as the maintenance of all districts of their town in a state of decent order, health and cleanliness. Edwin Chadwick, in his Reports on the Sanitary Condition of the Labouring Population and in his evidence to the Select Committee on the Health of Towns, declaimed with so much passion against 'the petty and sinister interests'[12] dominating town councils that it is far from surprising that he met bitter hostility throughout the country and that too few of his recommendations were put into practice. But John Simon, who succeeded him and learnt from Chadwick's mistakes to express himself with great caution, could only confirm that all he said was still true twenty years later, and less involved observers spoke if anything more plainly:

'As a means of improving the condition of our towns, it would be very desirable to improve the character of the local bodies who conduct its affairs . . . in many places the most active political partisanship is rampant . . . Demoralising and expensive struggles take place between "blues" and "reds", and success often waits not upon the man most able to serve his fellow-citizens, but upon the most unscrupulous—upon him who will spend the largest sum on bribery, treating, and cab-fares. An improvement will be voted against, that the rival factions may show which has the greatest zeal for "economy". If a nuisance or an abuse has to be defended, it will not want defenders.'[13]

It was not only that the character of councillors was at fault but that the opportunity for bending or ignoring the law so often came their way. In many towns, for instance, rival water companies competed fiercely for custom, a competition which, as Simon pointed out, brought little benefit to would-be customers.[14] It was hard for councillors not to favour companies who favoured them. Again, in those towns where local Building Acts applied, there were rules about the laying out of streets to conform to regulations. But builders found it profitable to hasten the putting up of rows of houses before it was known where municipal drains were to run, to save the expense of connecting the houses to the drains. And they liked to lay out terraces in cul-de-dacs so that the next man to build on adjoining sites would have to pay to use the roads.[15] Both practices were frowned upon, but winked at. Thomas Cubitt suggested that his fellow builders were so unscrupulous and ingenious at devising ways round regulations that if the rules about widths of streets in relation to heights of houses were enforced 'I am afraid a house would become like a slave-ship, with the decks too close for the people to stand upright—they would put the floor and ceiling too near.'[16]

Many officials, building surveyors for instance, were appointed on a yearly basis. This made them, of course, extra dependent upon the pleasure of councillors for the security of their jobs and very unlikely to condemn the building practices of councillors or their business associates. The constant need to levy the largest possible amount of revenue from rates with least possible offence to the electorate had some interesting effects. 'Arrangements' were made with builders to collect and be responsible for the rates on slum properties, the builders theoretically obliged to keep the houses in good repair. Naturally the builder was inclined to stuff the houses as full of tenants as possible so that the rents he gathered compensated him for the rates he was bound to pay to the council, and naturally councillors paid no close attention to the overcrowding when so simple a means of rates collection was assured them.[17] Demolition orders too were easily misused, and one of the greatest causes of nuisance was also one of the greatest sources of revenue: the mountains of human dung which befouled the streets and blocked the courts and seeped through the foundations of every town in England were sold at intervals for profit to farmers to manure their fields. It therefore paid to allow it to accumulate. In some towns it was the right of landlords to make the sale, in which case they did not look kindly upon councillors who made accusations of nuisance and ordered disposal and cleansing. In other places the local authority itself had the right of disposal and drew revenue from the town's manure or 'night-soil' as it was euphemistically called.

In fact everything tended to support the councillors in their neglect of towns. Even after the Health of Towns Associations became active and fashionable in some parts of the country there was little public pressure for improvement and nothing like enough to counter the important influences working against change. As Chadwick put it: 'The public are passive and the adverse interests are active.'

The way was easy then for men like the surveyor appointed by Sheffield's town council who could neither read nor write and who devoted most of his little ability to his personal supervision of the sewage carts and most of the funds at his disposal to paving streets in the vicinity of his own dwelling.[18] The suprise was, as A. S. Wohl has pointed out, that any honest officials should have survived 'in face of great hostility from all sides (landlords, tenants, slum-owning vestrymen and rate-payers)'.[19] Great profits could be made by those who were not so much dishonest as willing to take opportunities that came their way, like the clerk of the courts in Dundee to whom builders wanting warrants to build must pay fees. During a period of building boom, as 1840 was in Dundee, his takings in fees were enormous.[20] Sanitary inspectors, and later medical officers of health, were often appointed with tacit instructions not to interfere too much. Wohl tells of one vestry chairman who greeted a newly appointed medical officer with the words: 'Now, Doctor, I wish you to understand that the less you do the better we shall like you.'[21] Simon spoke of Nuisances Removal Committees which remained in office 'in order to prevent nuisances from being removed' and of 'inspectors of nuisances . . . appointed on terms that implied a minimum of inspection to be required of them.'[22] And the *Pall Mall Gazette* suggested that to ask London vestries to enforce sanitary regulations was akin to asking poachers to enforce the game laws.[23]

Corruption, however, played no greater part than ignorance in the steps towards town decay. Even those councillors most willing to preserve the decent order of their towns could not look for a consensus of advice on how best to do so. Henry Austin, architect, described in his evidence to the Select Committee on the State of Large Towns the state of ignorance which existed about the drainage, about the strengths of building materials, about the laying out of foundations, the effects of street levels, the construction of chimneys, the optimum thickness of walls.[24] He, in fact, put this forward as a reason for not passing a general Building Act which he felt would be premature in the then existing state of knowledge about building methods. Different towns had different and conflicting regulations in their local Building Acts yet all had been advised by supposedly experienced men. London, for instance, laid down that timber supporting beams must project through and be exposed in outside walls, a practice thought exceedingly dangerous elsewhere. The Royal Institute of British Architects, which might perhaps have been thought of as a repository of information, concerned itself in its *Transactions* throughout the nineteenth century with such esoteric interests as the measurement of medieval buildings.[25] *The Builder*, which did play a leading part in gathering and transmitting information on the problems of low-cost housing construction, did not begin publication until 1840. If they could not hope for consistent advice about what was and was not acceptable, how could local councillors and their officials hope to distinguish between one set of plans submitted to them and another, except on the grounds of expediency and advantage to themselves?

Medical men were no more certain about the causes of disease and the connection between filth and epidemic than were architects about problems of construction. Or rather those who supported one cause were very certain of it but were countered at every turn by a body of opinion within their own profession which supported an entirely opposite cause with as much conviction.

However the delays to town improvement occasioned by the self-interest and ignorance of local administrators were as nothing compared to the delays inevitable because of the extreme complexity of the administrative system. A number of differently constituted bodies, some elective and some non-elective, moved in overlapping circles, often with conflicting interests, each with jurisdiction over one or more aspects of town government. The householder who today grumbles at 'the burden of the rates' will appreciate how much more irritating that burden was (even if it consumed a relatively smaller proportion of his income) when the rates for each separate function, water, light, sewage, town's-rates, poor-rates, police-rates, were separately demanded and separately collected at different times of the year and at irregular intervals. There existed, as well as the town council which was elected from the higher rate-payers, the Commissioners of Sewers, who were appointed and not elected. This might have been complicated enough but the Commissioners of Sewers

5

functioned only in the larger towns. In other places their function either did not exist or belonged to the town council itself, to the Board of Guardians for the administration of poor relief, or, in those towns which had adopted the Police Acts, to the Police Commissioners, who were elected on a different franchise from the town council. Similarly, the authority for the administration of the Nuisances Removal Acts when they came into being might be any one of the above bodies or a variety of others.[26] Some towns had anciently established town trustees with similar or overlapping powers. Highway boards and turnpike trustees had responsibility for the laying out of new streets and the maintenance of old ones. In some places the old courts leet still functioned. These juries were appointed from among citizens to walk their districts in a body, keeping an eye open for overcrowding, dangerous buildings or anything which might be complained of as 'nuisance'. When the towns had reached the dangerous condition of the nineteenth century the powers given to these courts leet had fallen into abeyance through disuse, although the courts were still appointed. Chadwick reported that it was because these juries had failed in their duties that the creation of Boards of Health became necessary.[27]

In Scotland there were different bodies again. The Board of Supervision for the Relief of the Poor in Scotland had powers similar to those given to the Local Government Board in England in 1871 and became, for instance, the authority to whom application had to be made for the adoption, in rural areas, of the Labouring Classes Lodging Houses Acts.[28] In the large towns as well as local councils and Police Commissioners, important powers attached to the Guildry, that is merchants' as opposed to crafts' guilds, whose Dean held complete jurisdiction over all building work within the town and whose clerk issued warrants to build and drew fees for them. But the magistrates' courts also appointed a clerk of works with power to issue warrants and draw fees, who also fell to be paid by intending builders.[29]

The appalling state of affairs in the towns can not then be attributed to a lack of officials but perhaps to a superabundance of them.

'In the same petty districts we have surveyors of sewers appointed by the commissioners of sewers, surveyors of turnpike roads appointed by the trustees of the turnpike trusts, surveyors of highways appointed by the inhabitants in vestry, or by district boards under the Highway Act; paid district surveyors appointed by the justices, surveyors of paving under local Acts, surveyors of building under the Building Act, etc. etc.'[30]

The surveyors were only too often men in the same trade as those requiring their approval and their business rivals 'whose dissatisfaction with work really fair and good may be governed by sinister considerations against which a fair builder will feel he has no defence; but the greater danger is to the public, that no dissatisfaction may be expressed with work that is cheap but unsound.'[31]

All this would have produced difficulties enough if the powers of the separate bodies were applied to the same districts. But the areas over which they held jurisdiction were seldom co-extensive, adding to the confusion and delay and to the resentment felt by householders against officialdom. The confusion was well recognised and the need for comprehensive legislation even used as an excuse for non-compliance with the law by bodies who at another time would do all in their power to delay comprehensive legislation.

What emerges clearly from the most perfunctory study of town administration throughout most of the nineteenth century is that the idea that local authorities would one day play the leading role in building and letting housing for the lower income groups was a very long way from realisation.

Chapter 11

The Public Health Campaign

'Washing and splashing, and twirling and rinsing, and spongeing and sopping, and soaping and mopping'
The Times, August 1854

We have seen the effect of rapid population growth and uncontrolled building on the towns and have considered the powers dormant in existing legislation and the factors which had prevented those powers being used. A series of government inquiries allied to the work of the statistical societies had made known to Parliament and to middle-class electors the conditions in which the poor were living, the lack of water and drainage, the crumbling, over-divided old houses, decayed to the point of danger, the shoddy new houses built in the back-courts or the new suburbs, the hopelessly filthy and airless streets.

After the publication in 1842 of the Sanitary Report on the Labouring Population, a new society, the Health of Towns Association, was formed with the purpose of considering what might be done to effect useful changes. Its aim, unlike that of the earlier statistical societies, was not so much the collection of evidence, of which there was by now a bewildering abundance, as the consideration of the means of improvement. Like the Epidemiological Society, established 1850, and the National Association for the Advancement of Social Sciences established in 1857, it acted as both pressure group and study group. How much these associations of conscientious, sincere, and sometimes clever men would have achieved on their own is not easily assessed. They might have made out a case pressing enough to be acceptable to governments for the need for legislation to improve working-class living conditions. They might, on the other hand, have degenerated into aimless talking shops. The point is an academic one because the situation and the need produced the man with the character, the knowledge and the drive to meet them. The public health campaign up till 1854 was Chadwick's campaign. His ability marshalled and ordered the facts, his beliefs governed the way in which they were presented and the way in which the needs of the people were interpreted to Parliament, his personality affected the extent to which they were made acceptable.

It was Chadwick, and of course those friends whose work he hurried to conclusion, who directed the turn the campaign for town reform was to take, his value judgements which determined which of the many evils thus exposed should first be dealt with, his interpretation of the scientific facts which controlled the weapons used to fight the war on disease. There was within the reports gathered by Chadwick as much evidence of the effects of economic depression and its fluctuating need for labour as of the effects of disease. There was as much indication of the need for control of building profiteers as of the need for control of water supply and drainage. But Chadwick threw his weight behind the reformers who put cleanliness before everything else, devoted his mind to studying sewage systems and the question of whether private or public water companies were most efficient. It was, if not his influence, which because of his intolerant manner was not great, but his efficiency which caused the campaign for social reform to be dominated by an obsession with sanitation. An interesting recent article on the 'imagery of anality'[1] in the works of Charles Dickens suggests that some Victorians had a view of the poor as excrement, their enthusiasm for draining and cleaning the towns being merely a rationalisation of their wish to be rid of the poor. It is perhaps not too fanciful to suppose that Chadwick's absorption with flushing and draining was not unconnected with his earlier and perhaps more straightforward expression of his wish to rid the country of pauperism. Clear away the filth, clear away disease, clear away the paupers. It was a simple and attractive logical progression.

The public's sympathy and indignation had been aroused by the publication of the sanitary report. It quickly became bored with the subsequent talk of 'washing and splashing, and twirling and rinsing, and spongeing and sopping, and soaping and mopping', the words with which the leader writer of *The Times* in August 1854 attempted to destroy Chadwick's policies. Small-bore sewers and soap and water make tedious conversation. The extension of the idea into reality must attack so many interests vested in the maintenance of the uncleanly *status quo* that Chadwick's campaign became unpopular almost everywhere.

Without the support even of the commission for which he worked there was little chance of Chadwick achieving what he wanted, a central administrative system controlling everything which affected the health of the community. Yet he did achieve an astonishing measure of success. He saw within his term of office the amendment of the old laws of nuisance, the interesting Towns Improvement Clauses Acts,[2] and the first general Public Health Act, 1848, which was based very largely on his unsolicited recommendation, to Parliament in 1844, of the lines which future legislation ought to follow.[3] It was in itself a great achievement to have *public* health as a concept recognised on the statute books. Individualism was the dominant philosophy. To have the welfare of the community considered as the responsibility of government was a not inconsiderable step. Perhaps the most important effect of Chadwick's Act was to have the idea accepted as something about which discussion was possible. Later legislation could start from the point where the best means of achieving a healthy society could be debated, because Chadwick's work already had forced acceptance of the notion.

Concrete achievement was not impressive. The machinery of public health control was set shakily in motion, but Chadwick failed to convince the government that an element of compulsion must be introduced. So local authorities were given power to appoint medical officers but were not compelled to do so. This was hardly a new step because it was already possible to appoint local medical officers under Town Improvement Acts as Liverpool had done in 1847 and the City of London in 1848. Inspectors of nuisances had to be appointed by towns adopting the Act but no qualifications for the office were prescribed[4] so that the job was given most often to ex-servicemen quite without the knowledge to fulfil their function as Chadwick had envisaged it. Local Boards of Health could be set up *if* the local authority requested it, *if* 10 per cent of the rate-payers requested it, or *if* the average death rate over seven years was more than 23 per thousand. If they chose, the Local Board could then be given the power to provide a continuous, pure water supply. The Act had no real effect on the condition of the towns partly because the machinery of petition, inspection and local inquiry was too unwieldy and slow to move, partly because local authorities were not ready to accept without compulsion the threat to their own interests implied by its provisions.[5]

On the subject of housing, the Act was even less effective. It did lay down that no new house might be built without adequate drains or without either a 'sufficient' water-closet, privy or ash-pit, but these requirements were too imprecise to be enforceable and the means of enforcing them was not built into the Act. The complete failure of this new legislation to improve the housing conditions of the poor was due partly to the granting of mandatory rather than compulsory powers to local authorities, more perhaps to a failure of imagination on Chadwick's part due to his obsession with the prevention of epidemic.

The 1842 Sanitary Reports had shown quite clearly that there was no town or region in the British Isles in which small pockets of shockingly bad housing did not exist. But the Act provided only for the extension of powers to those towns in which mortality exceeded 23 per thousand.[6] This left the bad areas of otherwise healthy towns quite unprotected. It built into the statute books the very wrong idea that housing must be bad enough to kill, and kill on a large scale, before anything should be done to improve it. It is perhaps not entirely fair to blame Chadwick for his lack of interest in housing as such unless it could be seen to play a part in the spread of disease. Where so much waited to be done anyone with his sense of administrative possibility was forced to select what seemed of most immediate importance. Now that we are free of cholera, typhus and typhoid we are not in the position to say he chose wrongly, although it is still necessary to point out that his choice did affect the thinking of reformers and the course of legislation throughout the century. The linking of housing and disease allowed housing conditions which did not kill but were otherwise intolerable to go unregulated. It has to be allowed that the coming into existence in the few years immediately preceding the Act of a number of model dwellings' associations may have made government action on housing seem less pressing. The very limited usefulness of those admirably conceived private societies could not then have been predicted.[7]

Chadwick did, in fact, turn his attention to the subject of housing more closely after he had completed his draft Bill of public health in 1844. His dominant interest in hygiene had led him to take an early interest in the possibility of using glazed bricks in housing construction to provide walls impervious to damp and capable of being washed.

In 1847 he had persuaded his friend Lord Fortescue to attempt the making of a machine-made, glazed surface brick with his tile machinery.[8] Lord Fortescue used the bricks in building new cottages on his estate. Lord Shaftesbury and Prince Albert in turn showed interest in the idea and the model cottages built at Albert's instance for the Crystal Palace Exhibition used these impermeable, washable bricks for the interior walls. Chadwick continued throughout his life to push the merits of glazed brick with his usual determination, brushing aside all arguments against them on grounds of cost as the expected obstructiveness of reactionary builders and proprietors. Up to a point, of course, he could only be as knowledgeable about building construction as the experts to whom he chose to listen. He was a little inclined to be taken by the novelty of whatever was the latest invention, becoming one year enthusiastic about huge hollow bricks, twelve times the size of ordinary bricks, which he believed could lower building costs by 25 per cent, another year converted to the use of prefabricated panels on the Nicoll plan.[9] His plan for the use of the extra size bricks was dismissed by Thomas Cubitt, the building contractor, because of the labour problems it would create: 'If I adopt that new and large form of brick, which requires the use of both hands to set it, my men will strike and I shall have the labour of overcoming resistance.'[10]

Early in 1866 the Department of Economy and Trade of the National Association for the Promotion of Social Science set up a committee of Members of Parliament and other interested people to consider how to improve working-class housing conditions. It was stimulated by the extensive demolitions of housing for railway construction in the preceding years. Chadwick was appointed chairman. The work of this committee resulted in the presentation to Parliament of McCullagh Torrens's original Bill on housing.[11]

Chadwick continued to find it difficult to hide his impatience with the slowness of government steps towards reform, the conservatism and self-interest of the public, the short-sightedness and ignorance of the working classes. He is still, thirteen years after his dismissal, angry at the 'utterly incommensurate amount of attention to the great subject'[12] of sanitation. Nor have advances in the science of medicine changed his attitude to the cause of disease. He still supports glazed brick because it keeps out 'the first class of evils of insanitary condition, those of damp and miasma'.[13] The opening sentence of a paper he wrote in 1867—'Dwellings for the poor characterised by cheapness combined with the conditions necessary for health'—shows that his approach to housing has not changed, it is still as a factor in the prevention or production of disease that housing has importance. Half the diseases of the wage classes, he says, are caused by 'local causes in or about their dwellings, together with the misuse of their dwellings by overcrowding'.

There had been, within the Sanitary Reports of 1842, tantalising hints of another point of view. At least one paper, W. P. Alison's, showed recognition that poverty was the chief barrier to improved housing conditions.[14] And Neil Arnott, who refuted Alison with another paper published at the same time,[15] and who was very much a believer in the need for ventilating houses to clear miasma, still showed in his evidence to the Health of Towns Committee,[16] his awareness that poverty was the root of the housing problem. He reported that their lack of fuel and insufficient diet made the poor feel the cold so much that they disliked open windows.

But Chadwick chose, when he drew the local papers together to make his report, to lay emphasis on the 'public arrangements external to the residences' rather than on the ill construction of the houses, the shortage of houses, or the difficulty in paying for better houses.

Whether Parliament would have been ready to accept any precise legislation on housing is another question. Lord Shaftesbury felt that a large section of the public was looking to the Lords [17] for a lead on the subject of how to prevent overcrowding and the troubles arising from it. But, while he and his advisers were convinced of the need for action on housing, they were not yet prepared to accept the implication of government interference in private contracts between seller and purchaser of land, builder and buyer of houses, landlord and tenant. If there was vacillation at the top, how much less clear was the opinion of the silent majority. It is almost impossible to disentangle the public wish for hygiene from the public wish for humane dealings with the poor. Both strands of thought inevitably existed within individual consciences. The extraordinary coincidence of outbursts of rebellion in Europe with outbreaks of cholera made the public fear the germ of sedition as much as the germ of disease, and confused the two in the public mind, especially after 1848. The same kind of panic was repeated during the economic depression after 1918 in the wake of the Spanish flu epidemic when the once hated Poor Law Board, now on the verge of dissolution, was portrayed as the bastion between the nation and revolution.

The campaign, which under Chadwick had been the campaign for sanitary reform, evolved in the second half of the century into the campaign for moral and sanitary reform. While, of course, there were plenty of voices crying out for a transformation of working-class morals in the first half of the century, the increased use of the phrase 'moral and sanitary reform' in the second half does seem to indicate a linking of causes in the fight against the threats presented by a growing working-class population in towns. The least useful, but unfortunately very common, response by middle-class people to the threat of disease and mob violence, was a turning away from what they described as the degenerate masses. People who live in squalid conditions do become unpleasant. Much the easiest thing to do is to keep away from them and to justify this philistinism as the only way of treating people so devoid of decency. Another approach, indulged in by those with a taste for the sensational, was to cry the need to remove overcrowding because it encouraged promiscuity. Illegitimacy and premarital sex were noticed as if they had not always been common. Hands were held up in horror as report after report pointed the wide difference that lay between working-class customs and values and those which the middle classes unquestioningly accepted as right. The word 'incest' began to be hissed or hinted at.

Under this rather salacious interest in working-class living conditions, however, it is possible to detect an increasingly sincere wish for change. The moral campaigners' central belief was that only through education could the poor be led to a better standard of life. The exposure by the 1851 census report of how small a proportion of the urban working class ever attended church shocked and alarmed the middle classes. On one hand it emphasised the gap that lay between them and the poor, on the other hand it showed one clear way in which improvement could be begun. The army of lady slum visitors grew throughout the 1850s and 1860s. At another level of usefulness, men like Lord Shaftesbury and the Bishop of London became more convinced that there was cause for shame in what had been allowed to happen and a need for atonement by working for housing reform.

The chief virtue of John Simon's scientific approach to public health was that it helped to defuse the emotional charge whose intensity Chadwick had only increased. Simon, of course, had one great advantage over his predecessor in that his qualifications for the job rested on more than his own conviction of the rightness of the cause. After his useful experience as Medical Officer to the City of London he was appointed M.O. to the General Board of Health in 1855. It was his steadiness which prevented the complete dissolution of the central health organisation and gained its transference to the care of the Privy Council where its work could go on scientifically and with less public attention. But apart from his professional qualifications, which were impeccable, he had the merit of producing good team work. He could work with people in a way Chadwick always found difficult, and his remarkable ability to spot excellence in young men not yet proved in their profession helped him to gather a team of disciplined workers whose researches and reports wielded great influence on the thinking of the next twenty years. While his chief interest had to lie in medicine and the prevention of disease because that was his experience and his training, Simon gave the subject of housing very close attention. His assistant, Dr Julian Hunter, conducted two careful, if restricted, surveys of the housing of the poor, the first, in 1864, concerned with rural housing, the second, in 1865, with towns. Simon extracted their results and presented them in his seventh and eighth reports to the Privy Council. These reports contained so complete a summing-up of the evils of the existing situation and of the steps necessary for their remedy that they formed the basis of the legislation specifically concerned with housing which was to concern Parliament for the rest of the century. If he had done nothing else he would have given reformers a useful tool in his careful definitions of the two most often used terms of criticism, 'unfit for human habitation' and 'overcrowded'. Places unfit for human habitation were 'places in which by common consent even moderately healthy life is impossible to human dwellers', places unhealthy because they were underground, dark and impossible to ventilate, or places 'in constructional partnership with privies', dwellings so placed that 'drain-water and sewage seep into their floors'.[18] Although he used the words 'by common consent' he was aware that consent to the idea that such houses were unhealthy was by no means common. One of the most common low-cost housing plans arranged back-to-back rows so that the central building of each block contained a common privy on the ground floor with a bedroom over it. Simon went on to condemn as unfit houses built too close together to allow light, air or outlook, and this was very advanced thinking for his time.

Overcrowding he defined as existing where people and space were 'in such proportion that no obtainable quantity of ventilation will keep the air free from hurtfully large accumulations of animal effluvium—cases where the dwelling space at its best stinks more or less with decomposing human excretions, and where, at its worst, this filthy atmosphere may (and very often does) have, working and spreading within it, the taint of some contagious fever.'[19] This, of course, is not scientific writing by modern standards. What, for instance, makes a smell 'hurtfully large'? And the profession's state of ignorance about the means of spreading infection is betrayed by the reference to the 'filthy atmosphere', that mystic miasma so feared by the nineteenth century. But the approach is cool and dispassionate and the descriptions more carefully scientific than anything else presented to Parliament on the subject.

From our present point of view even more importance attaches to

Simon's stressing that the health aspect of housing was not the only one which ought to concern Parliament. People living in the kind of houses exposed by Hunter's reports, he said, could never 'aspire to that atmosphere of civilisation which has its essence in physical and moral cleanliness and enhances the self-respect which it betokens'. This official suggestion by a medical man of position and influence helped to ensure that the Sanitary Act, 1866, the new public health legislation for which he had been working, should be accompanied in the same year by the first separate Act to deal with housing.[20] That neither proved effective was due not to faults in Simon's diagnosis of the health and housing problems but to inadequacies in the administrative system which became increasingly obvious after 1866. The Sanitary Act should have brought pure water to every town dweller, eliminated epidemics as far as medical knowledge allowed, and abolished overcrowding, which now became technically a nuisance and therefore a matter for prosecution. Simon's career after this was devoted to a study of its failure and to working for the reform of local governments.[21] In 1871 his office was transferred to the new Local Government Board which was now given jurisdiction over the Poor Law organisation and the central health department. Here while he continued to do useful work he ceased to have influence.

The course of social reform in the last quarter of the century was diffuse and unorganised, veering in one direction and another, lacking the clear direction it had been given, first by Edwin Chadwick, then by John Simon. The medical profession, the new town planners, the Fabians, the reformers within Parliament, all believed in the need for a central health agency but there was much academic dissension about the functions it should be given. Should moral reform necessarily precede the administering of relief? While the academics argued, public opinion grew steadily less and less interested. Professor Bentley B. Gilbert makes a useful point in his recent study of social policy after 1914 when he discusses the power of office-holders to resist social change: 'if he is comfortable, if he is unimaginative and his knowledge of social problems is slight . . . he may delay, he may dissemble; finally, when time is short, he may resist.' Too many of the men in whose hands lay control of health and housing in the decades after 1871 were of this kind. But Chadwick and Simon were not comfortable men. They achieved as much as was possible in the circumstances of their time because their social conscience and their respect for science would not allow them the comfort of inaction. The philosophy of public health dominated all nineteenth-century thinking about social reform, partly because of the effectiveness of these two men, so different in their ways but alike in their faith, partly because the idea of public health was acceptable where interference in housing was not. People had been led by the reports and surveys initiated by these men to feel threatened by the lack of public health organisation, so steps towards its creation were steps accepted as necessary by majority opinion.

So it was that almost all legislation on housing up to 1875 fell within the health laws. In the first period the 'Nuisances Removal Acts' gave power to councils 'to compel the erection of proper conveniences to every house already erected, or to be erected, to the satisfaction of the council'.[22] The trouble there was that councils were too easily satisfied. Speculators knew that they could disregard the regulations with impunity. In 1855 another Nuisances Removal Act defined overcrowding as a nuisance and gave medical officers with an order from a Justice of the Peace powers to enter premises to inspect for overcrowding. The Sanitary Act, 1866, which we have already considered, gave wide powers to councils willing to improve housing, and provided that central government might force reluctant local authorities to act.[23] But the 1885 Commission reported that 'it seemed that in some cases the authority had almost forgotten that they had the powers.'

In other respects legislative action to improve housing was to a degree dependent on the public health provisions already made. For instance, when Parliament passed, in 1866, 'An Act to enable the Public Works Loan Commissioners to make advances towards the erection of dwellings for the labouring classes'[24] known as the 'Labouring Classes Dwelling Houses Act', it provided that suitable authorities to receive loans were those already acting under the Nuisances Removal Act, 1855. Similarly, the Public Health Act, 1875[25] was very important for housing reformers because it laid down the principles for the purchase of land by local authorities. Both the 1875 and 1890 Housing Acts when making arrangements for the financing of local authority building use the phrase 'in like manner as if those purposes were the purposes of the Public Health Act of 1875'. In the very sensitive area of finance, housing had to tread ground already broken by sanitation. Because the importance of health had been accepted money was found for it, because money was found for sanitation it was possible to ask it for housing. The first steps had to be taken where the battle had already been won, and the battle to wrest public money for social reform was first won because the public feared for its health.

It is interesting, too, that the first rules governing the interior arrangements of houses were passed not under building legislation—we have seen how abortive was the early attempt to pass a general Building

Regulations Bill—but under Public Health Acts. The Sanitary Law Amendment Act, 1874, authorised local authorities to make regulations about the ventilation of rooms, the paving and drainage of premises and the segregation of sexes. The Public Health Act, 1890,[26] extended this to allow authorities to control the keeping of w.c.s supplied with sufficient water for flushing, the structure of floors, hearths and staircases and the height of rooms intended to be used for human habitation; to forbid the use as dwelling places of rooms built over privies and cess-pools, and the building of houses erected on ground filled up with offensive matter. This was the first general Act controlling the actual construction of houses, and it was slipped into the statute book under the heading of public health, because it was less likely there to attract too much critical attention.

Because the philosophy of public health was centred upon prevention, all these regulations were restrictive, destructive. They forbade, they demolished. They did not construct or create, and it was creative activity which was needed in the housing field. Demolition only increased overcrowding. Restrictive regulations only discouraged builders. A new kind of thinking about housing was needed and it could not come until the obsession with sanitation had waned, and the subject of housing could be considered as a quite separate issue, its problems arising from different causes, its solutions lying in a new philosophy.

When, in the last quarter of the century, it could be seen that the campaign for sanitary reform had been successful, although there were still a good many stubborn pockets of resistance, it became apparent that the housing problem remained. It had not been swept away with the refuse and the sewage and the germs. It had in fact grown larger and more acute. Only the most tentative steps towards a housing policy were taken before 1917 but at least after 1885 the existence of the problem was admitted. Reformers could no longer shelter behind the belief that the removal of filth, by reducing disease and the pauperism consequent upon it, would automatically produce a working population energetic enough, self-respecting enough, prosperous enough to house itself efficiently. The opposite was only too glaringly apparent in the slum centres of all the major towns of Britain from whence now not only the gentry, and the professional and middle classes but the tradesman and artisan class too had fled. Only the poor were left.

PART 3

Housing and Poverty

Chapter 12

The Recognition of Poverty

'Oh, I hate the poor. At least I hate those dirty, drunken, disreputable people who live like pigs. If they must be provided for, let other people look after them'
Blanche in G. B. SHAW's *Widowers' Houses*, 1892

The central belief of the sanitary reformers was that they could improve the living conditions of the poor by reducing epidemic disease and that by restoring health they could raise earning power sufficiently to allow the renting of decent houses. But when cholera and typhus had been quelled and a measure of sanitation been brought to all our cities, the housing situation was seen to have grown, if anything, worse. The number of persons to each inhabited house had increased throughout the century instead of being reduced by the efforts of the reformers.

The number of houses in England and Wales had grown from 1,575,923 in 1801 to 4,259,117 in 1871,[1] but in the same period the number of surplus families, that is the number of families over and above the number of houses available, had grown from 320,800 in 1801 to 789,999 in 1871.[2] In Scotland, the number of persons in each house had increased from 5.46 in 1801 to 8.15 in 1871.[3] It is interesting that the average number of persons in each Scottish family in 1871 was 4.52 so that the statistics suggest that most Scottish dwellings then housed two families. The difference between the number in each family, 4.41, and the number of persons in each house, 5.46, in 1801 is not nearly so marked as in 1871.[4]

These figures betray the fact that housing, sanitation and health are not as closely linked as the public health campaigners would have wished. Inability to pay economic rent may be increased by the prevalence of epidemic disease, but the same steps which will remove disease will not remove that inability.

While some people even before 1850 were aware of the connection between the poverty of the people and the low standard of their housing, it was in the second half of the century that public attention was brought to the problem. In the early 1860s, government inquiries into distress among operatives had shown how ineffective Poor Law administration was to reach those in most need. The publication, in 1863, of Dr Edward Smith's findings on the diet of the poor betrayed how impossible it was to exact a higher proportion of income for rent. John Simon underlined Smith's findings in his sixth report to the Privy Council:

> 'It must be remembered that privation of food is very reluctantly borne ... Long before insufficiency of diet is a matter of hygienic concern ... dwelling space will have been stinted to the degree in which overcrowding produces or increases disease—of household utensils and furniture there will have been scarcely any ... The home will be where shelter can be cheapest bought—in quarters where commonly there is least fruit of sanitary supervision—least drainage—least scavenging—least suppression of public nuisances—least, or worst, water supply—and, if in town, least light and air.'[5]

In other words, a man will not starve his family to pay the rent but he will pawn all his belongings and take them to live in a hovel in the attempt to fill their stomachs.

If the 1860s had found extreme poverty in some sections of the community, the trade recession and general unemployment which followed in the 1870s carried the threat of starvation into homes all over the country which had been accustomed to regular employment. The presence of poverty in Britain became very hard to ignore, as the difference between the great gains experienced by some sections of the community and the unchanged misery of the poorest became better known. And, while that section of the population not benefiting from the greater national prosperity diminished relatively, it increased in absolute numbers. Because the housing problem does not and cannot yield to *average* improvement, but only to absolute increases in numbers of adequate houses the overall improvement in living standards over the last quarter of the century did nothing to diminish it as a problem.

Professor Checkland quotes figures in 1867 of 1.3 million 'higher-skilled' workers, and 4.5 million unskilled and agricultural workers.[6] As both Booth and Rowntree, while defining their classes slightly differently, agree that workers below the higher-skilled level were unable to feed or house their families properly, this gives some indication of the size of the problem.

In contrast with the sobriety of the government publications on the condition of the people there grew up a literature of housing which laid emphasis on the degradation of the poor. *The Bitter Cry of Outcast London* by Andrew Mearns, recently reprinted and perhaps the best known, was very far from being first in the line. If it had, as is claimed for it,[7] more influence than many of the other, earlier, books and pamphlets, that was because its publication coincided with the culmination of a campaign for further government action. Before it had come a long succession of works whose literary merit and statistical accuracy may have varied, but whose cumulative influence was considerable. Among the earliest was the Reverend C. Girdlestone's *Letters on the Unhealthy Condition of the Lower Class of Dwellings*, 1845, which had a direct influence on the formation of the Hastings Cottage Improvement Society. Henry Roberts, the honorary architect to the Society for the Improvement of Dwellings of the Labouring Classes, published his *Dwellings of the Labouring Classes* in 1850, caught the attention of the Prince Consort and was commissioned to design model dwellings for display at the Great Exhibition of 1851. His own earlier experiment in working-class housing, in Lower Road, Pentonville, in 1844–5, had taught him that the problems were not only those of design.[8] Gore's *On the Dwellings of the Poor* followed in 1851, G. B. Tremenheere's *Dwellings of the Labouring Classes in the Metropolis* in 1856. By the 1860s the complexity of the problem was beginning to be better understood. Thomas Hare published his *Thoughts on the Dwellings of the People* in 1862 and wrote a series of letters to *The Times* on the need for better local government in London, followed by a pamphlet *Usque ad Coelum*, a paper to the Social Science Association in 1864 on the construction of dwellings for the working classes, and two articles in the *Fortnightly Review* in 1869 on public and private property. People with chastening experience of the difficulties involved in housing the poor poured their thoughts on to paper to an echo of disturbed applause from the newspapers and literary journals. Ebenezer Clarke, who was a member of the Central Cottage Improvement Society, wrote *The Hovel and the Home* in 1863. In 1864 the Society of Arts held a conference on the Dwellings of the Working Classes at which the Mayor of Leeds offered a prize for an essay on the subject with special reference to his own city. The winner was James Hole, a director of a large building society and member of Leeds Model Cottage Association. His *Homes of the Working Classes with Suggestions for their Improvement* was extended, for its publication in 1866, to include consideration of towns other than Leeds. It includes a great deal more factual information than most of the literature on the subject and it is not typical of its time in that it offers very radical solutions to some of the problems of poverty, even the provision of subsidies to 'provide by exceptional legislation and special arrangements for that small minority who cannot afford proper dwellings'.[9] Like most of his fellow authors, he was both optimistic in imagining that it was only a 'small minority' of the population who could not pay the rent necessary for good housing, and very quick to suggest that drink, gambling and thriftlessness were the chief causes of poverty. At the same time, however, he condemned those of the employer class who deplored the existence of slums while paying only subsistence wages, and suggested that in low-wage areas the keeping down of rents was not the way to improve housing. 'Low rents *make* low wages', he wrote, 'by lowering the *necessity* for a certain sum.' Employers would not pay one penny more than they were forced to do, workers would accept employment at any rate which would allow them to persist in life, however uncomfortable a life it might be. The only way to improve the situation was to build decent accommodation which would demand higher rents and encourage employers to give and workers to press for wages to meet the new rent levels.

It was, of course, an argument with no application to areas or periods in which a dozen men waited to step into any job, whatever its wage. Octavia Hill, whose *Homes of the London Poor* was published in 1875, was convinced of the need for a quite different course of action, tailoring the accommodation offered to the minimum standard required for healthy living and the small rents which were within reach of the very poor. She suggested that no attempt should be made to lay on water, for instance, or to do more than clean and repair existing slum property until the tenants had been educated by example to the benefit of spending as much as they could, or more than they once had, on rent. She had fewer illusions, either about the ability of the poor, especially one-parent families, to demand higher rates of pay, or of their willingness to change overnight from vandals inured to slum filth into respectable tenants.

Some of the millions of words written on housing had application to a particular town. Lord Kinnaird's *Working Men's Houses* published in 1874, was intended to stimulate action in Dundee, where, he claimed, 'a heavy responsibility rests on the owners of property and employers of labour . . . to see that those by whom their wealth is created have the means of providing themselves with dwellings where health and decency can be maintained.' *Squalid Hull* produced results in a conference held in the Town Hall, Hull, organised by the Charity Organisation Society to discuss 'Homes of the People' on 1 February 1884. George R. Sims wrote *How the Poor Live* and *Horrible London* after studying Southwark and the Mint, and, like Mearns, used the shock effect of descriptions of prostitution and vice to bring home to the middle classes the degrading effect of slum living on the poor. John Honeyman's *Dwellings of the Poor* was largely an attack on Glasgow's incipient 'municipal socialism', showing horror that housing might be used as 'a legitimate channel for that eleemosynary aid which the most advanced socialist would still hesitate to offer in the more direct though only equally objectionable form of food and clothing.'[10] Honeyman, an architect whose quite unashamed fear was that local-authority action and the effect of Building Regulations would make private enterprise house-building unprofitable, dreaded 'the absolute supremacy of the lower grades of society' and strongly objected to the idea that we should 'compel the steady and sober to pay more than the unprincipled and dissipated and to contribute to their support'.[11]

The direction of Honeyman's attack shows the very long way in which thinking about poverty had progressed in forty years. If socialism was rather further from threatening the established order than he thought, the idea that the poor should be helped to house themselves from government funds was at least one well-aired and therefore worth attacking. Shaftesbury had included clauses allowing government loans for the building of dwellings for the labouring classes in his Housing Acts of the early 1850s. It had not been necessary then to attack the notion because it remained unnoticed on the statute books, not only without the power to enforce its adoption but without even the force to attract attention. Early Victorians had feared the mob, anticipating riot and violence. They shunned unnecessary contact with the wretches in the slums, at the same time remaining ignorant of the gap widening between the sections of society. By the 1850s ignorance was not possible but the fear of uprising remained, expressed very clearly in the anxiety about the results of allowing excursions of working men from the provinces to attend the Great Exhibition.[12] Would the presence of so many thousands of workers in the Metropolis at one time cause trouble?

The last cholera outbreak in Britain in 1866 coincided again with European social unrest and produced the last flutterings of middle-class fear of revolution. But by then the masses were, on the whole, disciplined and not to be feared, safely to be allowed some outlet in organised trade unions, a modicum of education of a suitable kind and even the prospect of a say in the government of their country. It was not revolution and violence that the 1870s and 1880s dreaded but democracy, democracy which would swamp the educated middle classes in the baser tastes of the poor.

So the removal of poverty, with its appalling effect on moral character, came now to seem as important as the removal of disease. But if it had seemed to infringe on private and personal rights to legislate for sanitation it seemed unholier still to attempt the attack on poverty. To interfere in contracts between man and master, as would have been necessary to raise wage levels, or between landlord and tenant, as would have been necessary to prevent unfair rents, was almost unthinkable. Increasing social consciousness in a climate of steadily worsening economic crisis made it necessary at length to consider even propositions like these. While public opinion remained, on the whole, convinced of the virtues of self-help as a policy, intellectuals began to abandon traditional positions of economic science, to digest the statistical analyses of poverty produced in turn by Booth, Hyndman and Rowntree, and to arrive eventually at a new kind of thinking about the persistence of a class of very poor people within the established industrial society.

The beginnings of a public demand for state intervention in society were attributed by Beatrice Webb, who lived in the atmosphere of intellectual torment which the new social theories generated, to 'a new consciousness of sin among men of intellect and men of property'.[13] The literary propaganda on behalf of the poor by Dickens, Ruskin and William Morris, the analytical discussion of poverty by John Stuart Mill, Karl Marx, Henry George, Arnold Toynbee, the religious questioning of Kingsley, Booth, Samuel Barnett, Cardinal Manning, produced in middle-class homes a growing uneasiness that statesmanship, philanthropy and education had all failed to re-organise society.

It is in this light that we must consider that most important late entrant to the literature of housing, the article contributed by the Marquis of Salisbury to the *National Review* in November 1883 on 'Labourers' and Artisans' Dwellings'. As Joseph Chamberlain wrote in an answering article in the *Fortnightly Review* in December of the same year: 'the spectacle of Lord Salisbury demolishing the economists and entering into conflict with the Liberty and Property Defence League is not without a touch of humour.'[14] The opposition, of course, saw Salisbury's conversion to the housing reform movement as a Tory attempt to 'dish the Liberals' by robbing them of one of their claims to be the party of social reform. It was, in fact, not a conversion but a natural development of his own evangelical belief when his attention was drawn, by the findings of the Select Committee on Housing of 1882 and by the *Bitter Cry of Outcast London* to the true situation of the poor. A man of his Christian persuasion might succeed for part of his lifetime in ignoring social conditions but when circumstances had focused his attention upon them he was bound to act. His conclusion was that 'the difficulty in the case of the poorest class of town-workmen, as in that of the agricultural labourer, is their poverty. Until their wages rise they cannot pay for the bare cost of decent lodging.' His further suggestion, that the state should accept responsibility for the housing of the poor and should arrange low-cost loans for the purpose, met more opposition. But the acknowledgement by a man of such authority that it was poverty, rather than the mere lack of enforced sanitation, which was at the root of the slum problem gave a new direction to the work of the housing reformers after 1883. There had been, in fact, for some years little dissension within Parliament about the need for housing reform (as opposed to the form it should take) either between parties or between factions within parties, as Disraeli had found when the Cabinet discussed Richard Cross's Bill in 1874: 'These meetings have been eminently satisfactory: unanimous and very friendly, and never the slightest indication of there being two parties in the Cabinet.'[15]

It was, in this context, unfortunate that each successive step taken by Parliament towards the improvement of the environment had shifted the responsibility away from central government and on to the shoulders of the local authorities. The creation of Local Boards of Health, the power to appoint sanitary inspectors, to order demolition for slum clearance, to make building regulations and to borrow money for the purposes of housing and town improvement were all planted within the sphere of local government. This made it possible for the leaders of the country in Westminster, who were in touch with the developing line of thought of economic theorists and social philosophers, to voice their sympathy for the poor and homeless and their hopes that action would soon be taken to relieve them. But it was in the provincial council chambers that action had to be taken and local councillors were not among those most influenced by progressive social theories. John Honeyman's attitude to the poor was not untypical of rate-payers in those few cities like Glasgow where genuine attempts to tackle the housing problem were made. In Birmingham, where the council forced the removal of certain factories away from the crowded areas in the hope that the workers would follow them, the improvement scheme was almost crippled by the large amounts of compensation demanded by factory-owners for the move.[15] In Hull the manipulation required to push through a controversial Extension of the Boundaries Act left councillors in too weak a position to enforce their regulations against back-to-back building or to make use of the money and land already in their hands for the purpose of building working-class houses. They were 'not successful in creating the interest and securing the co-operation hoped for',[16] and spoke worriedly about the 'social propaganda which was forward again [which would make] every difficulty and complication ten times more difficult to deal with if these doctrines took hold within their own town'.[17]

In the provinces, as in the minds of most of Britain's citizens, poverty was still a sin. If the economic depression was making it increasingly obvious that the power to avoid poverty was out of the reach of most working people it was still generally thought foolish to reward the attainment of poverty with too much help. And, as Chamberlain declared, when speaking in Birmingham in 1894: 'local bodies cannot be much wiser than the constituencies which they represent . . . all legislation which is in advance of the sentiments of the people is nearly always a failure.'[18]

The sentiments of the people were eventually led, not so much by the expressed opinions of their leaders as by their disillusionment with alternative solutions, to recognise poverty as the chief cause of the housing problem. It had to be faced that the model dwellings associations had had more difficulty in attracting investors and less success in reaching the very poor than had been hoped; and that, in any case, the possible scale of their activities could not be commensurate with the scale of the problem. Shaftesbury's Housing Acts of the early 1850s, far-seeing as in many ways they were, proved absolutely ineffective in practice. Building societies generally failed to attract working-class members, the failure showing that not only present poverty but the fear of future poverty limited workers' ability to expend their income on housing. Improvement and slum clearance schemes served only to increase town-centre overcrowding and to raise the rents which could be extracted from bad property. Suburban estates seemed often to deteriorate as fast as they were built and, in any case, were not readily accessible to the poor until the late century cheap rail concessions. Cheap, clean lodging houses improved the lot of the transient worker and the single man but did nothing to help the families on whom the housing problem centred. All the schemes optimistically begun were seen to have failed. All hope that action based on sanitation and piecemeal charity could meet the situation faded away. But when the lack of drains and pure water had seemed the chief cause of slum conditions the course of action for reformers had been obvious, if still beset with opposition from the *laissez-faire* reactionaries. When poverty became the enemy the way to attack was much less clear.

Although the nineteenth century, then, became aware that a relationship existed between housing and poverty it had little understanding of the nature of that relationship. It was at once less simple and less difficult than Victorians thought; less difficult than it need have been because they put the notion of state subsidies towards the rent of the poor out of court and so badly handicapped their progress, less simple because the connection between wage and ability to pay the rent was not a straightforward one. Poverty affected housing in more subtle ways. Not only were there people too poor to pay the rent which would produce a comfortable house, there were people too poor to pay any rent at all, and there were people too poor *not* to pay exorbitant rents, people who were forced, by their need to be near the sources of casual employment and of credit at local shops, to remain in high-rent areas. 'By a strange perversion, as rents rise in the more central districts, the better off are more likely to be driven away, while the poor remain', wrote Charles Booth in 1889.[19]

It was the presence in towns of a large body of people living without any wages at all which caused the housing problem in the first place and allowed it to grow to unmanageable proportions. If it had been necessary only to house the *working* classes the problem might, indeed, never have arisen, for even a small wage, regularly paid, allowed the setting aside of a portion for rent. But, as James Pennethorne, surveyor, said in 1840, the worst slums were not inhabited by workers: 'But I should think they get their living as they can; they must be of the very poorest classes; they appeared to be worse than the working classes.'[20]

Mayhew has described the ingenious ways in which Londoners scraped a living from the streets, the ceaseless turning over of rubbish to extract half-pennies for food. Because so many towns-people, in the big cities at least, were forced to scrounge for a living rather than work for it, or were, at best, only casually employed, there were always takers for the most abject living conditions offered. No form of shelter was too dark, dirty and cramped for people whose days were spent, for instance, walking the sewer pipes in search of saleable objects lost down the drains. Cheapness, and even more important, time to pay, were the criteria which made a house desirable for too large a proportion of town-dwellers.

Because it was possible to let the foulest of accommodation, to stuff a crumbling house full of tenants 'in maggot numbers' there was little incentive to landlords to do better. Poverty caused the occupancy of rack-rented tenements, the building of badly constructed spec-housing, the overcrowding of central areas, and the illegal occupancy of condemned buildings. Poverty caused the destruction of house-interiors, by people who sold door-knobs and fittings to raise pennies for food, poverty caused the opposition of the poor to attempts at sanitary improvement. Poverty itself was caused not only by fluctuations of trade but by demographic changes which by increasing population in fixed areas increased the demand for housing and the rents which landlords could charge, so that, even during the general fall in prices in the last decades of the century, house rents continued to increase.

The biggest problem of all was what can only be called pre-existing poverty, brought about not by nineteenth-century economic causes at all, but inherited from the eighteenth century. The nucleus of very poor people accustomed to a low standard of living, existing on the pickings of urban society, composed of what would now be called 'unemployables', having, as one observer said, 'no notion of paying anything at all for rent'[21]—this was the core of the housing problem. And this did not change. This mass of people, abandoned by the Poor Laws, added to by each new step in technology and by waves of immigrants from rural areas, existed at the beginning of the century and had grown rather than diminished by the end of it. Octavia Hill and the model dwellings associations rejected them and they were still proving unsuitable for housing at the end of the century.

Housing reformers of all periods have indulged in the optimistic belief that catering for the needs of the average family, providing houses that can be paid for out of the average worker's wages, will, by a process of seepage, eventually better the condition of the poorest. The houses vacated by the newly-housed average man will, they think, become the homes of the poorer and the slums vacated by the poorest will be destroyed. It has never worked because the pace of town deterioration has always increased to match any housing programme and because the real needs of the very poorest have always been ignored. The unhouseable poor which inhabit the slums found few places in Peabody's schemes, could not (and cannot today) afford new council house rents. Their existence creates the slums, creates the housing problem, does not yield to the reformer's zeal, needs and has not yet had, special treatment.

Even when they have been very much diminished, the persistence of slum areas within otherwise beautiful cities is a source of shame which is in itself crippling. The shame encourages those in authority who have not found a way of removing the slum to grow a film over the mind so that they can justify lack of action. They learn to blame the character of the slum dwellers, or alternatively the limitations imposed by building regulations, both views as fashionable now as in the mid-nineteenth century, and, both, unfortunately, based on a version of the truth. Slum dwelling does produce apathy and lack of regard for other people's material possessions. Building regulations do often cause delay and raise costs.

The other inevitable effect of the resistance of poverty-stricken slum areas to reform is that the existence of even a small proportion of a city's population willing to accept such conditions removes the incentive to improve property, allows easy money-making by a Rachmanite kind of landlord. The availability of some property, however bad, to be let at very low rentals, keeps down the level of rent working people are willing to pay and makes the owning of house property by more scrupulous landlords less worth-while. The fact that the proportion of a town's acreage covered by slums has diminished hardly lessens the influence of the remaining slum property on the psychology of the middle classes or on the level of rent likely to be paid. The problem was aggravated by the lack of uniformity in the distribution of poverty. Some towns got off to a good start. Endowed by nature with easy drainage and plentiful water, by trade success with a population of skilled artisans, Sheffield and Birmingham, for instance, found builders who could make reasonable profits out of speculative building, and were able to make a success of building societies for working people at least until the 1870s.[22] In the company towns of the North and in other towns where textiles dominated the scene the general low wages of whole towns produced a general solution, if an unattractive one, in acres of low-cost housing specifically designed to be paid for out of the local wages. But in the larger cities like Liverpool, London and Glasgow the existence of abject poverty and marked prosperity within the same town made any solution difficult.[23]

Different forms of ownership of property again made general legislation difficult and produced different responses to the needs of the poor. Leasehold land was generally in the hands of large owners who in theory had control over the layout, standard of building and level of rents extracted over large areas, especially in London. But, although in the first period of rapid expansion when town estates were being quickly built over to meet population needs, metropolitan proprietors interested themselves in the manner in which their property was developed, they soon lost interest and handed over the management of the houses to factors. In those hands the property deteriorated steadily, repairs were not carried out, sub-letting and overcrowding were allowed and exorbitant rents collected, only a portion of which reached the proprietors.[24]

Freehold land was most often held by smaller owners and its piecemeal distribution resulted in unregulated layout of land, overcrowding not only of people within houses but of houses on land and, again, the extraction of maximum rents to produce large returns on small capital outlay. Both forms resulted in pressure on the poor but their different legal basis made relief difficult.

Even in those towns which had been relatively prosperous during three-quarters of the century, the problems of poverty began to affect the provision of housing adversely after the 1870s. The effect of more strictly enforced building regulations, increasing scarcity of land, and rising labour costs pushed up the cost of building. The effect of the trade recession discouraged investment and inhibited lending policies.

At the same time opportunities for investment overseas were drawing away capital which might have been attracted to the building industry. Unemployment caused inability to pay rents and made investment in working-class housing unattractive and at the same time drained strength away from the labour movement which had been beginning, tentatively, to exert pressure for housing reform.

In spite of the general fall in prices in the last quarter of the century, rents did not fall. It was this uncomfortable and perhaps hardly to be expected fact which finally overthrew the new theorists on housing, as completely as the public health men had been discountenanced by the failure of housing to respond to sanitary reform. The extreme difficulty of knowing what to do about the interaction of poverty and housing finally led late-century social reformers to a conclusion that would not have seemed too foreign to the adherents of *laissez-faire*. Just as the public health reformers imagined that the removal of epidemic would in itself improve housing, so now the belief took over that the growth of individual incomes in relation to the cost of living would gradually, and automatically, bring about a general improvement in housing conditions.

The idea of *unemployment* as an unavoidable state, not one deliberately chosen by an idle disposition, was not considered until the last fifteen years of the century,[25] the modern use of the word being until then quite unknown; but the eventual recognition of unemployment as a public responsibility produced first the attempt to provide employment through public works, then the campaigning by reformers for the labour exchange system which would distribute available work more effectively, then the various forms of unemployment insurance. But the determination of social theorists like Beatrice and Sidney Webb that the provision of insurance should be dependent on evidence of moral character showed that the real nature of the problem of poverty still had not been grasped when the new century arrived.

Chapter 13

Rents

'The dirtier a place the more rent you get; and the decenter it is, the more compensation you get. So we're to give up dirt and go in for decency'

Trench in G. B. SHAW, *Widowers' Houses*, 1892

Late-century studies of the housing problem were, of course, much hampered by the lack of statistical data on housing needs. Since 1917 quantitative material of every kind has been collected, but its usefulness is still limited. In the first place almost all figures relate to houses built, without distinction between mansion and two-roomed cottage. The provision of villas in the suburbs for the middle classes, for instance, could swell the tables without affecting the numbers of homeless in the slums. The existence of houses to rent in one area at rentals over £1 a week had little interest to prospective tenants of another area whose total wages when in employment amounted to less than that. Even when careful studies have been commissioned requiring detailed answers about housing needs from each local authority their results have been affected by local variations in the definition of such loaded words as 'unfit', 'homeless', 'need'.

But from the material available a few certain facts seem to emerge even if they must be qualified at every turn. The first is that house rents for working people showed an almost undisturbed upward trend throughout our period. An average annual increase of 11 per thousand took place according to H. W. Singer during the years 1845–1910.[1] This table is, however, affected not only by the inclusion of all housing but of commercial buildings as well. The tremendous variation that can be concealed in figures like these is shown in the Board of Trade figures for 1880–1900[2] which record an increase in all London house rents of 8.2 per cent while the increase in rents of houses under £20 annual value for the whole country during the same period was 17.9 per cent. Shadwell's index gives an increase in 'working-class' rents for the same period of 15.5 per cent,[3] and Singer's later index of house rents concluded that there had been a rise of 13.1 per cent.[4] Much greater increases of course took place in some areas in shorter periods, as much as 33 per cent in Hackney in 1894–1901,[5] and 50 per cent in Sheffield in the early 1870s.[6] However great the variation in annual increase the trend is steadily upwards, very steep rises in rents during boom conditions with only very slight, if any, falls during depressions. Rents simply did not fall into line with the general fall in prices during the last quarter of the century. Nothing perhaps illustrates the rise more clearly than the difference between the rentals fixed as defining working-class occupancy by the statutes of 1890 and 1909. In 1890 the sum for London was £20, in 1909, £40. In other large towns it was £13 or £10 in 1890, £26 in 1909. Elsewhere £8 in 1890, £16 in 1909.[7]

More interesting for our present purpose than the actual figures involved are the causes of the sustained rent increases and the effects upon society of these increases. The causes, the rising costs of labour and materials, the difficulties of obtaining credit, the consistent policy of destruction, the temptation of alternative investments, we will deal with later. The effects can best be measured against the pattern of the changing standard of living of late Victorians, a field in which recent years have seen very eminent economic and social historians unable to reach agreement.[8] Whether the price of the basic necessities of life fell far enough to compensate for the failure of unskilled labourers to obtain significant wage increases, or whether the increase in the number of expenses which had become necessities since the beginning of the century swallowed up an important part of the increased incomes of artisans will continue to be discussed.

It is reasonable to note that a contemporary student of the question considered that three-fifths of the wage increases experienced by working people in the preceding half century had been swallowed by increasing rents. Edith Simcox reported in these terms to the Industrial Remuneration Conference in 1885 in a paper on 'Loss or Gain of the Working Class during the Nineteenth Century'.[9] Certainly shelter is one of the necessities of life and if rents increased one of the major drains on income became more sorely felt. Equally certainly for many people, the difficulty of finding homes near their work drove them to live at a distance from it and made train or tram fares a new necessity. The fact that fares were adjusted to workmen's pockets in an attempt to attract travellers does not alter the fact that money had now to be found for a purpose which did not exist before.

In fact the figures for rent increases are much less relevant than at first appears either to the increasing severity of the housing problem or to the cost of living argument, for two reasons. The first is that, quite lost sight of in the tables which show average rent increases, is the fact that the amount of rent which could be extracted from the very poorest of tenants did not rise at all in almost a hundred years. It remained not only relatively but absolutely the same in the 1920s as it was shown to be in the 1830s. The second is that the amount people are prepared to pay for rent is affected much less by what they can in fact afford and much more by what they think they can afford.

Houses occupied by Irish families in Holborn in 1840 were let at
1s or 1s 6d a week.[10] This was then thought to be very little. Yet in
1885 houses were still available at 1s or 1s 6d a week[11] in Saffron Hill,
St Giles, St Luke and Clerkenwell in London, in Wiltshire, in Cam-
borne, Bristol and Exeter, as well as parts of Scotland.

Rooms at 1s a week could still be found as late as 1924, in Dundee,
for instance, where a rag-picker in a tenement known locally as the
'Blue Mountains' paid that sum for an attic room. This was a rent
lower even than the price of common lodging house accommodation
and represented rock-bottom. Rooms at this very low rent were,
however, available all over the country, if hard to find in the Metropolis and not common anywhere. Such cheap housing was not sufficiently common to affect statistical tables, but it did have an important
influence on society. Its existence resolves the paradox of how people
whose wages were not rising in a world where house rents did
rise contrived to house themselves at all. There was a small but significant housing sector which remained outside the trend of rising
rents, available to those unable or unwilling to stretch their inadequate
or irregular incomes towards a higher expenditure on rent. Landlords
letting houses at such rents did not, however, fail to achieve a high
level of profit. It was possible to house up to sixty people in houses
let originally at £35 per year and producing an income of £70, each
flat being sub-let, the individual rooms sub-let again, and beds
within the rooms relet again at 3d a night. Houses like this had no
water supply, no amenity of any kind, but it was possible to let them,
not only, it is important to add, because of the cheapness of their rents
but because they were available to people lacking the respectability to
be accepted as tenants in better property.

By the end of the century the asking for 'key money' and for a
character reference from a previous landlord[12] was becoming very
common in areas where houses were hard to find. This left for those
who had no hope of achieving either an accumulation of savings or a
'character' only the slums where the poverty of the accommodation
matched the condition of their lives. It was this class of tenant which
would not yield to any of the reforms attempted. As long as landlords
could make profits out of shilling-a-week sub-lets it would remain
impossible for a greater proportion of income to be extracted for
rents. Existing side by side with this class were the actually homeless,
the "'appy dossers', that surplus of families over inhabited houses
which persisted in the census returns, who contrived to live without
paying rent at all, moving about throughout the night and sleeping in
parks and public buildings in the daytime. In Glasgow, for instance,
where the Dean of Guild had powers to close unfit property but was

not always moved to demolish it, the boarding-up of doors and the banning of rent collecting was welcomed by the homeless who found their way into such buildings and lived rent-free as the walls crumbled away.

The persistence of a class of people living either rent-free or at levels like 1s or 1s 6d a week affected tenants' judgement of what was a fair rent. What people had been accustomed to paying affected their willingness to pay more. It must be remembered, too, that not only were town slum dwellers accustomed to low rents of this kind but that the towns also housed large numbers of rural immigrants many of whom had paid even lower rents, varying from 30s to 3 guineas a year, or had inhabited rent-free 'tied cottages'. Not only that, but many more rural workers had been used to depending on a source of extra income above their wages which they could set aside for rent-paying, from extra harvest work for women and children, from the produce of garden plot or cow, or, lingering on in some parts of the country till late in the century, from domestic handcrafts. Arrival into the towns meant the stopping of extra income as well as the need to find a larger proportion of wages for rent.

Wives had insufficient practice in budgeting, a deficiency which showed up more, not less, when wage rises gave them more money to manipulate and shops displayed a more tempting range of consumer goods. Husbands were affected by neighbourhood customs too, and the temptation to drink and gamble became something like a need in the face of slum conventions. Villages had provided a rigid social framework to which their inhabitants could only with great boldness fail to conform. Towns, and especially their poorer, most decaying sectors, had their own frame of convention which was in many ways hostile to improvement. Willingness to pay a greater proportion of income for rent was affected partly by what people had been used to paying in an earlier, probably rural, environment, partly by the style of living found admirable in the new environment, which sometimes set more store by a weekly debauch and a grand funeral than a comfortable home. One convention reinforced the other.

There are apparent contradictions in the argument so far which it is important to resolve. First, rents in general increased while wages remained on the whole static, making it difficult for the average labourer to pay for a decent home. But at the same time the very lowest level of rents remained static with two important effects. First, owners of very bad slum property opposed its destruction because they could still make high profits from it by cramming it full of tenants. But, secondly, it was not possible, because of the rise in the cost of building, to build new houses for letting at the very low rentals to which these tenants were accustomed. The people most in need of help, those who were poor enough, ill enough, apathetic enough, to accept the worst slum conditions were those most difficult to re-house. So, at the same time, two apparently conflicting facts—that rents were rising, and that some rents were not rising—led to the same conclusion, an increased difficulty, at all levels below that of the skilled labourer with uninterrupted employment, in paying rents adequate for good housing.

The great difficulty lay in the discrepancy between the very low sum of 1s to 1s 6d a week, at which level there was clearly a demand for rooms for families, and the lowest sum at which builders of new houses could afford to let them. One was in fact at least double the other. *The Builder* reported in 1884 that the poor 'cannot afford to pay more than a rental of from 1s to 2s per week, for their dwellings, of whatever size and construction, and wheresoever situate . . . but no practical plan has yet been devised by which dwellings can be built . . . which can be let at these low rentals and prove remunerative to builders'.[13] Builders of large numbers of new houses intended for the working classes told the 1885 Commissioners that they could not profit by letting at less than 2s–3s weekly. Sutton and Dudley, for instance, a large firm of London contractors, built something like a 100 working-class houses each year of brick and concrete construction, the smaller houses letting at 2s or 2s 6d weekly.[14] The Peabody Trust claimed that the *average* rental of their rooms was 1s 11½d,[15] but the lowest rent at which a single room was let was 2s 1¼d,[16] and large families were not allowed to take tenancy of single rooms. Peabody could not provide *homes* for less than 2s. London rents were reputed to be higher than those of provincial towns, but it is possible that the greater scale of building operations there, and sometimes the ready availability of cheaper building materials compensated for the higher land costs and allowed the letting of new houses at rents not noticeably higher than in the provinces. In Leeds, for instance, in 1865, 'one up one down' houses were let at 2s–3s a week but new back-to-backs could not be let under 3s 9d.[17] These rates had hardly changed, incidentally, in 1908 when a two-roomed back-to-back cost from 3s to rent and a three-roomed house from 3s 6d.[18] Leeds was among the lowest rented of towns surveyed by the Board of Trade in 1908. In Glasgow average one-roomed house rents in the northern district moved from 1s 6d in 1866 to 1s 9d in 1876, to 2s in 1891 and to 2s 5d in 1901.[19] In 1902 it was estimated that new single-roomed houses could not profitably be let for under 2s 6d. It seems to be less than certain that provincial builders could build for letting at rents markedly lower than London builders for the very cheapest property.

6

The greatest variation in weekly rents, in fact, lay neither between town and town nor between period and period, nor between charitable trust schemes and speculative estates; and even more surprisingly it was less affected than would have seemed likely by the presence or absence of sanitary arrangements.[20] The real variation lay in the number of rooms rented. The price per week per room actually varied very little, the poorest, if anything, paying slightly more rather than less than the prosperous on this reckoning.

For the working man the step from one room to two was a major one, involving at least double his usual outlay on rent. In boom conditions when wages rose fastest the move might be considered. But, because, as we shall see later, the supply of houses invariably lags behind in an improving economic situation, rents rose to meet the demand for larger houses. Of those who did successfully make the step towards improved living conditions many were forced by the succeeding slump and unemployment to return to living again in one room.[21] Trades which enjoyed the greatest wage increases in booms often suffered the greatest vacillation in wages in bad times. It is this kind of experience which makes house-ownership, so much advocated by the middle class as a solution for the artisans, impossible and even regular rent-paying difficult.

There was, in fact, a genuine demand for one-roomed houses from those who could not, in the long term, afford any other, and it was this which made the attempts to abolish cellar dwelling so difficult. Liverpool found, after its Act of 1846 had banned inhabited cellars, that they could not close too many in a year without intolerably increasing the overcrowding in other substandard housing; and was not successful in maintaining closure orders on cellars which, after a period of disuse, generally became tenanted again.[22]

In towns where enterprising builders had a real understanding of the needs of the population or of the possible profits to be made from those needs, one-roomed-apartments continued to be built long after successive commissions had deplored their existence. Just as Leeds smugly defied criticism and continued to build back-to-backs when their creation had been successfully discouraged elsewhere, Dundee and Glasgow built tenement blocks containing a proportion of 'single-ends'. There was, of course, a justifiable market for one-roomed flats for single men, widows and, especially in textile towns like Dundee, for spinster mill girls. But there was equally no way of preventing occupancy of single rooms by families. All the nineteenth-century regulations against overcrowding proved unworkable. 'Ticketing' and inspection, as attempted in Glasgow, never covered the whole area of slums and were not too difficult to evade. Medical officers hesitated to recommend, as they were empowered to do, the eviction of over-crowded families because they knew that a move would be unlikely to lead to improved conditions.

While poverty remained an intractable problem, continually with a large part of the working population and at least a dreaded occasional visitor in many more prosperous artisan homes, the need for very small houses predominated. While there had been no regulations about sanitary provisions the building of such accommodation had been very profitable. But under the new regulations the provision of water and drainage adequate for the supply of multi-tenanted blocks became expensive and less likely to yield high returns on the greater capital outlay involved. The building of very low-cost housing fell off at the same time as the improving of cities by slum clearance created a new need for homes.

Contemporaries often commented that no houses could be found in late nineteenth-century cities at weekly rents of less than 5s.[23] We have seen this to be less than true, for many working people paid rents of between 1s 6d and 4s 6d all over the country. It was certainly true that cheaper accommodation which was also large enough for a family, in reasonably good repair and able to be kept clean, was very hard to find. The very lowest rents bought only one room, probably without sink or grate. The range from 2s 6d to 4s 6d might buy one or two rooms with an attic, access to shared water-tap and privy, convenience depending very much on the age of the property and the district. Five shillings could buy tenancy of two rooms in a 'model dwelling' with all the comfort and conferred respectability that implied, or one of the larger back-to-back houses in provincial towns[24] or something approaching middle-class luxury in a town like Dundee where £7 a year was more or less the maximum working-class rent.[25] Model dwelling rents, 5s 6d a week for two rooms in Peabody Buildings, a little more in Waterlow Buildings and a little less in the Improved Industrial Dwellings Companies Buildings,[26] were said to be cheaper than private company houses, and in St Giles, St Luke and Clerkenwell the average rent of two rooms was 6s a week, although there a two-roomed house of sorts could be got for 1s 9d. In the suburbs of Newcastle 4s 6d was enough for two rooms,[27] in Bristol anything between 3s and 6s might be necessary.[28] Mr Shipton of the London Trades Council said in 1885 that the average rent paid by the artisan class was from 5s 6d to 9s a week;[29] in Sheffield in 1890 a four-roomed back-to-back could be got for between 3s and 4s,[30] although after 1900 there were said to be none available at less than 5s or 6s a week and the majority cost more than 7s. London suburban rents were said to be half the price of those in central London, and in 1890, a five-roomed suburban cottage could be rented for 6s 6d,[31] not so different a price per room from Sheffield, or indeed from central rents per single room. Five-roomed houses at prices within working-class capacity were, however, not likely to be found in central areas.

There are two main difficulties in discussing rents. One is that we have no infallible way of knowing how far houses of similar sizes and similar rents but in different districts were in fact comparable. Even if both were equal in terms of water supply and lavatory provision, were there considerations such as the space around them, the presence of shops and transport and especially the respectability of the neighbourhood which made one superior to the other? This is the kind of question which only detailed local study by qualified historians who also have real long-term local knowledge of their district can answer.

The other difficulty lies in the definition of working-class occupancy. Shipton's artisan who could pay 9s for a house and the Dundee ragpicker who paid 1s 6d were both working men but their lives were so widely different as to make them hardly members of one class of citizens. In the sphere of housing, as indeed of diet, the skilled worker must be considered as being of a different class and needing separate treatment. His housing problem would eventually have yielded to the initiative of private enterprise. But of Rowntree's four working-class groups, A with under 18s a week, B with 18s–21s, C with 21s–30s, and D with 30s or more, only the last could afford to pay rent adequate for the housing of a family of four to six persons.[32] It has been found that not until a family man's income passed a steady 32s a week was there any marked improvement in his dietary standards.[33] To improve his housing standard required a greater outlay, more forethought, saving and long-term planning. Improvement in housing was not likely, as Simon pointed out more than a 100 years ago, to precede improvement in diet.

The average British working-class expenditure on rent in the nineteenth century was 16 per cent of income, or slightly less than one-fifth. A. S. Wohl, quoting the 1885 Commission, gives the figure of 85 per cent of London working class paying one-fifth of their income and almost 50 per cent paying between one-quarter and one-half. D. J. Oddy has shown that an expenditure of 58 per cent of income on food left working-class families still undernourished. There is, then, little elasticity in budgeting to these figures. In Sheffield rent and rates took 13 per cent of a working man's income.[34] In Dundee, where the average late century wage was 16s and the average rent 3s, 18 per cent of income went on rent.[35] The working-class family spent a percentage of income inversely proportional to the size of its income, middle-class families spending an average of only 8 or 9 per cent of their income on rent. Workers in Germany, Poland and Hungary spent 18 per cent of income, in France 12 per cent, and in Scandinavia 12 per cent–15 per cent compared with Britain's average 16 per cent.[36]

The lowest paid workers, those who were necessarily already undernourished and therefore unable to stretch their expenditure on rent by spending less on food, were those forced by the circumstances of their employment to spend the highest proportion of their income on rent. If, in fact, landlords had not allowed great elasticity in the collection of rents, no week's budget would have met the needs of families in intermittent employment. Booth found evidence that landlords charged very high rents to cover themselves against the likelihood of non-payment of arrears.[37] Octavia Hill was sure that working-class property could be profitably let at low rents only if regular payment was inflexibly insisted upon, and she put her belief into practice.[38] The model dwellings associations, however, found it necessary to allow three or four weeks' arrears without eviction and they were seldom catering for the very poorest. Where possible, tenants in the same block of buildings would club together to pay the rent of families threatened with eviction during temporary financial difficulties.[39] The fact that there was no way even the most respectable of workers could prevent arrears of rent piling up during periods of unemployment is well illustrated in the Ragged Trousered Philanthropist's conversation with his wife over their difficulties:

'How much rent do we owe now?' asked Easton.

'Four weeks, and I promised the collector the last time he called that we'd pay two weeks next Monday. He was quite nasty about it.'

He began to reckon up his time: he started on Monday and today was Friday; five days, from seven to five. At sevenpence an hour that came to one pound four and ninepence halfpenny.

'You know I only started on Monday,' he said, 'so there's no back day to come . . . . If we pay the two weeks' rent that'll leave us twelve shillings to live on.'

'But we won't be able to keep all that', said Ruth, 'because there's other things to pay . . . We owe the baker eight shillings for the bread he let us have while you were not working, and there's about twelve shillings owing for groceries. We'll have to pay them something on account . . . . Then there's the instalments for the furniture and oil cloth . . . I've been paying that bit by bit all summer. I paid the last of it the week you finished your last job. Then you were out three weeks and as we had nothing in hand I had to get what we wanted without paying for it.'[40]

It was an inescapable situation. If even the skilled tradesmen at more than £1 a week fell into arrears during periods of unemployment, the casual labourer and his landlord accepted arrears as one of the facts of life. The labourer saw it as an inevitable block to better living conditions, the landlord as a reason for collecting as much for his property as he could, the rent-collector used it as a reason for threatening eviction without much intention of enforcing his threat.

Because, particularly in London, very large areas of urban property had been let on very long leases of eighty or ninety years at the turn of the century, by the 1890s a great many houses were approaching the end of their leases. This meant that repairs were not financially worthwhile during at least the last decade of the building's life and the structure was allowed to crumble to the point where demolition would not represent too much loss. The aristocratic proprietors and the Ecclesiastical Commissioners to whom the leases would eventually again fall due had long since lost sight of the uses to which their property was put, nor were they, for the most part, aware that the sum paid to them as overall landlords represented only a fraction of the profits made out of the tenants upon their land. Middle-men and factors profited from the system whereby rent-collecting was farmed out to those who would collect rents from whole slum areas for a percentage of the takings. Tenants could only lose from a system which put them at such a distance from the owner of their houses at the same time as it ensured that the profits from their modest rents should go not to the maintenance of their houses but to the pockets of the go-betweens.

The tendency noticed by Booth for the poorest to be forced into paying more for their housing then the better off caused the degradation of whole districts without the lowering of rents: 'Peckham is becoming poorer owing to increased rents driving better-class workers away. . . . Those who can afford it move out and those who cannot escape crowd in. Property becomes more profitable in a working-class district than in a middle-class district and even more profitable still when none but the poor are left as residents.'[41] The fact that the poor experienced a real need to remain near their traditional sources of labour and credit made them entirely dependent on landlords who could then profit from subdivision of property. And that dependence made it unnecessary for improvements or even repairs to be carried out to this much-divided property. The profits were not diminished, as they would have been in better-class districts, by expenditure on maintenance.

But the possibility of high-profit making from poor tenants existed only for owners of old, centrally placed property. To make profits from property properly constructed and maintained was certainly not so easy and whether it was in fact possible was much debated.

When councils eventually faced the task of providing municipal housing for those citizens of demolished slums who could not re-house themselves they had to consider two important questions: first, whether it was possible to let the houses at economic rents, and the evidence on this score was very conflicting, then, if that proved impossible, whether letting at uneconomic rents was either ethical or politically expedient.

The argument about whether council-house dwellers are able to or ought to pay economic rents is still not a dead one in 1973 and was very keen at the beginning of this century. But at whatever philosophy of housing the debate might finally arrive, the fact remained that private enterprise had not supplied the need for homes which the poor could afford. The number of houses being built in a year in England and Wales fell from 61,909 in 1901 to 38,178 in 1911, more significantly it rose from 37,803 in 1871 to the 1901 figure and then fell in 1911 back to something like the 1871 total.[42] The percentage of increase in the number of houses under construction rose from 13.5 in 1811 to 19.8 in 1841 and fell from then until 1911 when it was 12.5, less than the 1811 figure in spite of the vastly increased need brought about by increased population, steady demolition and improving sanitary standards.[43]

Weber's index of residential construction shows a fairly steady net increase in housing stock up to 1876, a fairly steep drop thereafter until 1898, a sharp rise until 1900 and a steady decline from then until the war. The drop after 1876 illustrates the effect of the Public Health and the Housing Acts of that decade, the demolition of slums and the disincentive Building Regulations, as well as decline in purchasing power of the often unemployed working class. The index includes all residential construction and the rise in the last years of the century is swelled by the vast acres of suburban villa-building of the middle classes. In Glasgow numbers of houses authorised to be built by the Dean of Guild Court grew from 2,880 for the four-year period 1862–6 to 21,052 for the four-year period 1872–6, fell steeply to 5,758 for 1877–81,[44] and had risen slowly to 17,068 in 1897–1901. In Dundee, where local knowledge made it possible to count working-class houses separately, a total of 20,567 was built between 1867 and 1914, the highest figure, 9,303 in the decade 1871–80. This fell to 1,783 in 1881–90, rose to 5,520 in 1891–1900,[45] and fell again to 2,236 in the period 1900–14. In Sheffield the number of working-class houses built was 1,648 in 1893–7, 4,670 in 1898–1902, 3,875 in 1903–7 and 2,493 in 1908–14.[46] In Oldham, Burnley and Preston, the cotton-mill towns, building figures were higher in the mid- and late-1880s than in the first half of the next decade or indeed ever again; and Birmingham, Bradford and Hull saw a recovery in house-building before the end of the 1880s.[47] So while the national peak of 1876 and the subsequent fall was reflected in all regions, the rate of recovery and the following fluctuations showed considerable regional variation due to local conditions.[48]

While the last spurt of building in the nineteenth century did make some reduction in overcrowding there were still 405,010 overcrowded tenements in England and Wales in 1911 and this was reckoned to represent only 7.8 per cent of the total overcrowded population. 3,140,000 persons were reported to be living in a state of overcrowding in England and Wales at the 1911 census.[49] By 1921 there was an actual deficit of 805,000 houses.[50] While cheap living space, however unpleasant, was available, the market for more expensive houses in better condition could not expand enough to keep down the rents of decent accommodation. This is the paradoxical situation which persuaded investors to put their money anywhere but in low-cost housing in the first decades of the twentieth century.

Among the first to consider municipal endeavour to house working-class tenants was Liverpool town council's Health Committee which in 1866 suggested the building of four-storey blocks of three-roomed houses to be let at 3s 6d a week. This hung fire until 1868 when the Corporation agreed to finance the St Martin's Cottage Scheme.[51] In Glasgow another very early municipal venture, the City Improvement Trust, charged its tenants £5 a year for one room and £8 for two.[52] In Sheffield the first council houses were let at 5s–7s 6d. The first council rents fit the observation that, in spite of steady average increases in house rents, the weekly rent which poor people could afford to pay did not vary very much at any period from the figure of about 1s 6d per room per week. Councils could, however, as the model dwellings associations had done, enforce rules against over-crowding and refuse to allow large families to take tenancy of the smallest houses. This meant that, however excellent the sample of the early venture in municipal housing, they could make little enough impact on those thousands of the still growing town populations who would pay only the lowest rents and whom private-enterprise builders naturally neglected.

Chapter 14

Building Costs

'It pays when you know how to work it, sir. Nothing like it.
It's been calculated on the cubic foot of space, sir'
Lickcheese in G. B. SHAW, *Widowers' Houses*, 1892

It might seem that, in spite of the increasingly well-proven fact that the rents which could be extracted from the poorest families moved only fractionally, the steep and steady increase in average rents would have tempted builders to speculate in housing for the next income groups. If those earning less than 18s a week provided no market for speculators, those over 18s would seem to have offered an outlet. Sixteen per cent of income, that is the average British nineteenth-century expenditure on rent, at 18s a week, is 2s 9½d a week. Those builders who did provide new houses in the 2s 6d–3s bracket admitted to making satisfactory profits from it. Indeed in some towns, in some periods, where there was still land available within the boundaries at reasonable prices there was large-scale building of low-cost houses,[1] even in the two decades after 1876 when the average rate of building had slowed to a near standstill.

There is a logic which ought to dictate the activity of the building industry. House-building depends on both the builder's estimate of how rent levels will affect the selling price of houses and on the investor's estimate of how profits from rents will move in relation to other investments. But the industry is notoriously one of the least logical and its numbers have always been swelled by small, under-capitalised contractors who have been easily tempted, especially during boom conditions, to begin speculative building enterprises on very loosely calculated risks. An apparent local shortage of houses did not, as we have seen, always indicate a real demand for houses by people able to pay for them. Between the builder and the tenant there had normally to be found a buyer of the houses who would then become landlord, investing his money in low-cost housing in expectation of a good return from rents.

Builders did not usually set about building houses with the intention of letting them but of getting them off their hands as quickly as possible.[2] This was especially so of small firms who were very often in the position of needing to sell the houses to pay for the materials, obtained on credit, with which they had been built. The activities of speculative builders entering on housing schemes without either safe financial backing or a wise estimate of the needs and possibilities of the market affected the housing shortage adversely in two ways. First the creation of temporary, local gluts of housing discouraged further building, sometimes for too long a period. The unfavourable effects of one disappointing experience in building could still be felt at the beginning of what should have been the next revival so that building activity did not catch up with the next shortage. Secondly, financially shaky or over-optimistic building firms gave the industry a bad name with the suppliers of credit on whom they were entirely dependent for the purchase of sites and materials. There has been some interesting discussion on the relative influence of small- and large-scale building contractors on the development of Victorian cities.[3] In this respect, that they made those with available capital wary about lending it, the small men had, in fact, too much influence. Financial institutions were, even without the example of too many bankruptcies before them, not enthusiastic about providing credit for building enterprises. Too often their own assets were in old housing properties whose rents might expect to be affected by the removal of a housing shortage. It was in their interests that the shortage should remain, the rents of old property stay high, and the value of mortgage securities remain unthreatened. In periods when house-building looked especially profitable, private finance might be made available but rates of interest were then often too high for small building firms.

Periods of intense building activity, such as that preceding the early 1840s, have been taken as guides to periods of profitability in building, but in fact the building trade is notoriously a poor forecaster of profitability. Small-scale contractors have always been peculiarly prone to financial failure because their over-optimism leads them to begin schemes with insufficient capital in the hope of quick profits, without accurate prediction either of the costs involved or of the demand for their products, which may or may not exist at the time of the scheme's completion. The fact that a great many houses were built in Liverpool in the years 1837–42[4] or in Dundee around 1840 does not necessarily mean that the then existing relationship between costs and returns was a favourable one. One does not know how many of the small-time operators went bankrupt in the attempt.

Indeed, while it is obvious that steadily rising rents did influence investment in the building industry, rent increase was not a reliable guide to profitability. The biggest annual increase in house rents, which took place in the years 1865–7, was in a period of rising building costs, and the rate of increase in rents throughout the century was only just enough to raise the value of houses in proportion to rising costs of replacement. Site rents in towns increased most at times when returns from rents were increasing only slowly. The increase in house rents was, in fact, only just enough to prevent site rents actually falling. It was not so much that house rents rose when building costs were rising, which is hardly surprising, as that they failed to fall enough when building costs were falling.[5] Some very valuable statistical material on rents and costs can be found in Professor John Parry Lewis's book *Building Cycles and Britain's Growth*. He quotes Weber's summary of the evidence for the influence of rents and costs on numbers of houses built: 'Variations in rents and house prices need not, and indeed are unlikely to, set off corresponding fluctuations in house-building if they are the consequence of changes in cost.'[6] The fact is that there are considerations other than rent increases which must influence intention to build. Builders themselves are influenced by apparent demand but also by availability of land, price of materials and opportunities for obtaining credit. Clearly land in towns which continued to increase their population became steadily less easy to find and more expensive. Demolition cleared central sites but did not necessarily make them available for speculative low-cost housing. In cases where the council cleared the land it held it for a period of years during which the decision whether to build or sell was delayed. In other cases increasingly profitable commercial purposes dictated the use of the land. In many cases the land was prohibited to working-class housing by a restriction on the annual value of property built upon it, a measure to maintain the value of the site.

One factor tending to encourage the purchase of land rather than the building of houses was the taxation system which, in mid-century, taxed house property at 10.5 per cent as opposed to 3 per cent on land.[7] The value of urban land is determined not so much by its actual use as by its most profitable prospective use. Because in London the great landowners held a monopoly of land the possibility of speculation in land was almost eliminated, London became what Steen Eiler Rasmussen has called a 'building speculation town',[8] characterised by the speed with which land was built over as it became available, the high value of the houses built upon the land, and the tendency for land values to fall very sharply towards the outskirts of the city.

In a 'land speculation town', on the other hand, there was a natural tendency to leave ground vacant, holding it until it seemed most profitable to sell, and to build very densely on land as it became available for building. The land speculation town then does not show the same steep drop in land prices from the central sites outwards but maintains the value of land out to the limits of building.

Rasmussen's two categories simplify the situation too much. There are, of course, reasons other than the monopoly of the dukes for the limitation of land-use within cities, for the tendency to build high and densely in some areas or to show very steep differences between central and suburban values of land. Rasmussen is, of course, right when he says that the varying kinds of ownership of land have affected the characteristic appearance of cities, but their geographical circumstances and industrial needs have affected their shape and their types of buildings as much. Property values in dock towns like Liverpool and Hull, for instance, have been affected more by their distance from the docks than anything else. Rasmussen's point is that property values affect the density of building, and that where it is possible to speculate in land the building will be either high or densely crowded.

The cheapest land in Liverpool in the 1860s was 1s per yard yearly ground rent or 16s per yard freehold. In Leeds at the same time freehold land could be obtained for 2s 6d–5s per yard.[9] Liverpool built tenement blocks by custom, Leeds built back-to-backs. Mill towns, like Dundee, Paisley, Oldham, were shaped by their need to be near the streams which were at first their source of water power. As the ground owned by the petty lairds of the Dundee district, for instance, gradually became available from the late eighteenth century onwards, it was snapped up by the linen manufacturers, then the only holders of reliable capital.[10] Dundee's land had been traditionally laid out, and continued during the nineteenth century to be *feued* or let, in very narrow strips of land, twenty-five to thirty feet wide. A typical ground rent for the kind of house built on this lot was £11 per year. The house was of four storeys and attics, accommodating fifteen or sixteen families in one- or two-roomed houses, at rents of £2, £3 or £4 a year.[11] In Liverpool, at the same time, cottages with 12-ft frontage, 13½-ft depth, containing a cellar, a ground-floor room and two above, rented at from £8 to £9 a year, cost £80 to £110 to build, with the cost of land running from £28 to £56. The cheapest land was £1 per square yard.

It was complained by builders objecting to the proposals for general Building Regulations in 1840 that to increase the size of the house in accordance with the new rules would increase the price by £9 10s for the cottage type, £34 10s for the court type tenement.[12] Land values increased throughout the century, tending to rise most during periods of depression, the rise being caused by what Professor Pribram has called the 'downward stickiness' of house rents.[13] Because lower building costs in times of depression did not bring about a proportionate fall in house rents, profit could be made from the owning of house property and land values accordingly increased. Although speculators in land could not deliberately bring about the rise in house rents they could time their sales and purchases of land to benefit most from the temporary difference between rents and building costs.

So, while both rents and the price of land rose in growing nineteenth-century cities, house rents rose most during periods of prosperity, because people flowed into the city for work, and because regular employment made the renting of better accommodation possible; land values on the contrary, very often controlled by speculators, rose in periods of depression.

For builders and investors this situation made the choosing of the right moment to build very difficult. For while costs for both labour and materials were lowest during depression, land costs were then highest. Building activity then is affected by the condition of the capital market. Temporary variations in the building industry show a correspondence with the movement of the general business cycle, but the actual phases of the two variations do not coincide. Builders seem most often to have chosen to build in the earliest phase of recovery from the low point of the business cycle, when interest rates were low and prices had barely begun to rise, which would suggest that land costs had less effect than might have been supposed on the decision to build. The price of land has affected the kind of building through the need for economy in land-use more than it has affected the time at which building commenced. It has been observed that the pace of house-building often slackens at the highest peak of the cycle, presumably affected by the cost of credit, materials and wages, yet it is in this phase of greatest prosperity that the demand for houses is most pressing and the rise in rents necessarily greatest. Unless builders have been building ahead of demand and producing a supply of empty houses, the shortage, at the peak of the cycle, during the downward turn and until the renewed activity of the first upswing, will be severe.

This was the situation which produced the serious housing problem described in the 1885 Report and all those reports which followed. The peak of building activity was reached in 1876 but the number of houses built during the preceding years was not enough to tide over the succeeding years when little house-building was taking place. Inevitably before the next period of activity, much delayed by the conditions of depression, a severe housing shortage was felt, resulting in high rents at a time when working people could least afford them.

This, of course, first affected the cheapest kind of housing. Residential building of all kinds is particularly sensitive to economic swings and slumps, often anticipating, as we have seen, a downswing before the peak has yet been reached. The first kind of building to be given up is working-class housing where profits are least certain and the first steps towards the paying off of employees in nearby works is immediately felt in failure to pay rents. In the few towns in which working-class housing has been counted separately from residential building in general it will be seen that while the trends of up and down are the same they do not start or finish at exactly the same points; and while house-building in general, that is including middle-class houses, continues to rise towards another peak in the first decade of the twentieth century private enterprise house-building for the working classes was decreasing steadily from 1902 onwards.

Building costs remained remarkably steady throughout the century, showing neither great reductions nor very steep rises until the First World War from which point costs rose very markedly up to 1920 and fell steadily, but not steeply, after the first fall in 1920-2, until 1936. Costs of materials took a very high jump in 1852-3, reflected in a very significantly much slighter rise in total costs, but even that steep jump did not bring materials back to their 1846 level. The fall after 1853 was steady but in fact very slight until 1872 when prices rose from 80.9 (index: 1930 = 100) to 90.4 in the following year. There was again a steady but not dramatic fall until 1889, a slight rise in 1889-90. Slight fluctuations followed during the next decade with a fairly steep increase in 1900, a fall thereafter until 1910, a steep rise up to 1920 and a steady fall until 1936. The price level of 1846 was passed only in 1873-4 and after 1915.[14]

Dramatic drops in prices or even a reasonable expectation of a steady fall in prices might have been expected to tempt investment. The opportunity of undertaking a building enterprise with low capital outlay might perhaps have encouraged a flow of investment into the industry. In fact the peak of building activity was reached in 1876, prices having only begun to take their downward turn in 1874. Those houses put on the market in 1876 were being sold at a time when the cost of building was lower than when their construction had been begun. It is the necessary time-lag in building which makes profitability so unpredictable. The importer of oranges seeing an increased demand allied to a supply of cheap fruit can have his oranges on the market in a very short space of time. The manufacturer of sacking can, and did, buy raw materials when they were cheap, store them against a future demand, go quickly into production and put his sacks on the market at the most profitable moment. But between the conception of a building and its construction and sale so many steps and so much time ensue that market requirements may be entirely changed in the interim. Although the Victorian era saw the emergence of the

4. Woodworking machinery, *c.* 1870

large-scale contractor, most builders were still small men operating from small yards or restricted premises. Even the largest contractor could not afford, either from considerations of space or finance, to keep on hand very large supplies of the bulky materials used in building. The ensuring of a steady flow of bricks, window-frames, roof-tiles, floor-boards, is still one of the major problems in the construction of any building under pressure of time. The supply of building materials depends more on the availability of credit than the actual price of the material in question.

Costs were not greatly affected by changes in manufacturing methods. Only two main technological changes affected the building industry, the introduction of powered machinery to the preparation of timber and the production of cheap machine-made hollow faced bricks. Both of these occurred in the first half of the century, a machine for mass production of floor-boards introduced in 1827 and improved in 1836 and brick-making machinery in 1856.[15] There were, of course, regional differences, hand-made bricks continuing in use until late in the century where under-capitalised brickworks and cheap labour persisted. Only the obtaining of a large contract for the building of the first, doomed Tay Bridge in 1871 spurred the installation of machinery to the brickworks in Pitfour in Perthshire, for instance;[16] but that was in an area where hand-dressed stone from local quarries continued to compete successfully with bricks. Joiners quickly adopted machinery for the production of long lengths of timber planking and the mass-production of standard size of window- and door-frames, floor-boards, and roof-timbers and stair-treads followed.

James Hole, writing in the 1860s, deplored the lack of advance in methods of building compared to the rate of introduction of methods of mass production in other industries. What the building industry needed, he said, was an Arkwright. But no single flash of inspiration brightened the industry. No one improvement of a particular technique could possibly have made for building the dramatic changes seen in the manufacturing industries. So much of the work of building involves the handling of heavy, bulky materials that it remained an industry dependent upon a supply of cheap, unskilled labour, having, in fact, the largest single group of workers outside agriculture in the British Isles throughout the century. The small-scale organisation of most of the employers and, at least in some periods, the organised militancy of the workers, combined to produce a reactionary tendency to cling to traditional methods. There was, perhaps, little scope for technological advance. There was certainly little search for it. Even where great changes in organisation occurred, as in the emergence of firms like McAlpine and the increasing dominance of older firms like Cubitt, the changes were in scale, not in method. The hundreds employed by McAlpine used for the most part the same tools and the same methods and worked at the same pace as the handful employed by the proverbial little man round the corner.[17]

Cubitt, indeed, had powered machines in its workshops in the 1840s but little enough is known about the general extent of mechanisation.[18] Nor were great economies achieved by advances in the scale of enterprises undertaken. Large-scale building was no new thing in the glorious free-for-all existing before the first Public Health Act in 1848, the uninhibited energies of builders had succeeded in erecting hundreds of houses at a time and covering acres of London and the large provincial towns with only the organising power latent in the small consortiums of artisan bricklayers and joiners then commonly in practice.

The introduction of restrictive building regulations was frequently blamed by builders themselves for keeping costs up, reducing profits and acting as a disincentive to investment. In Liverpool, for instance, the mere discussion of new regulations resulted in a rash of building speculation, attempting to make high profits from inferior building before the regulations could come into force.[19] Certainly the rate of building activity in Liverpool after the 1846 Act slowed, but whether this was because the regulations had limited profitability or because the market had been flooded is less certain. In the first regulations the extra outlay was forced by extra expenditure on land to meet the new requirements of space around buildings and to compensate for the room lost when cellar occupation was banned. Later regulations, by insisting on sink and lavatory provision, raised costs by introducing items which had not been provided in earlier low-cost housing. This represented not a rise in cost of materials but the introduction of new materials. Similarly, increased expectation on the part of tenants forced the inclusion of good grates, kitchen ranges and ovens where earlier houses had often had only open fires for cooking and heating.[20]

But the total cost of building was, in fact, dependent more upon labour costs than on prices of materials. Falling prices in some periods were compensated for by the fact that building operatives managed steadily to improve their position throughout the century. Building wages show no fall until 1883 and then only a very slight one which was reversed by a rise in 1889 and a steady rise from then until 1921. The rise in wages was not only absolute but relative to other trades so that the builders' position in society was improved. In 1859 the builder was inferior in wages to workers in agriculture in England and Wales (though on a par with farm-workers in Scotland) and to workers in ship-building and engineering. By 1883 he had gained a higher wage than the engineers, by 1884 he had passed the farm-workers and his wage never fell to the level of either of these groups again.

The vast amount of building of all kinds in Victorian England and the fact that in the building trade a man's labour did not have to compete with mass-production methods put the builder in a much stronger position than, say, the skilled cabinet-maker, whose wages were kept down by competitive factory-made furniture. Carpenters, masons, bricklayers, plumbers and plasterers all advanced their wage rates steadily and in step, from 1826–47, when all earned 5s per ten-hour day, until 1878 when all earned 7s 6d. By 1914 the plumbers had pulled slightly ahead, earning 9s per day to the 8s 7½d of the other trades. By 1920 plumbers had 19s to the others' 18s 8d. For labourers the rise was steeper, from 3s in the 1826–47 period to 4s 9½d in 1878, 6s in 1914 and 16s 8d in 1920. The labourers, therefore, had made greater strides than the others, doubling their rate for a ten-hour day between 1847 and 1914, while the other trades succeeded in doubling only after the war and just before the slump in wages and prices: between 1834 and 1861 operative builders' average number of hours worked was reduced from 60 per week to 56½ giving a short Saturday at the same time as the rate per hour was raised from 5½d to 8d.[21]

The Operative Stone Masons increased their membership from 1,078 in 1835 to 9,628 in 1862.[22] Until 1860 all the building trades except the stone masons had been without effective organisation. But the great lock-out of 1859–60, the employers' response to the unions' claim for a nine-hour day, taught the men the need for central organisation and effective administration. The result of the lock-out and of the employers' attempt to wean workers away from unionism by offering jobs in return for the signing of the infamous 'Document'[23] was to bring members flocking into the existing unions and to encourage the reconstruction of societies which had hitherto been half-hearted.

From 1860 employers were faced with a real power in the building unions. The stone masons, who had reached just over 9,000 in 1860, had doubled that by 1868 and had reached 26,330 by 1876. The Amalgamated Society of Carpenters and Joiners, with only 618 in 1860 had 8,736 in 1868 and 16,038 in 1876. The stone masons were adversely affected by the Great Depression, their numbers falling drastically after 1876 (as we saw, the volume of house-building decreased very much after that year), declining until 1890 but falling again after that without reaching the 1876 figure again at any time until after the First World War.

The Carpenters and Joiners were apparently unaffected in the numbers of their membership by fluctuations in house-building, showing perhaps a slightly slower rate of growth between 1876 and 1888 but no setbacks until 1908 and then only a short one followed immediately by a steep rise in members in the next years. The Carpenters were, however, not typical of the building unions, being, in fact, the only one not to lose members after 1876 and doing so only by methods to say the least unbrotherly.

Wages, which had risen steadily until 1876, remained at their 1876 level until 1880, and although a considerable rise was experienced then it was only shakily held until 1890. But while costs of materials fell almost eighteen points in Maiwald's index between 1876 and 1888, the ability of wages to avoid a decrease even in the worst years and to turn upwards when building increased meant that total costs fell by only eight points. Restrictive practices, rigid conservatism and inter-union rivalry made building operatives less able to present a united front to employers than might otherwise have been the case; but the sheer volume of building work undertaken in Victorian Britain, and the fact that industrial and commercial building continued at the peak of boom periods after house-building had fallen off, meant that the need for builders kept up wages. Wages tended to rise most in the closing stages of a boom. In 1876 and in 1899 there were large wage increases which raised total building costs to the point where further house-building was discouraged. It would seem that wage increases tended to put a check on building. On the other hand temporary reductions or standstills in wages and costs seem not to have provided enough incentive markedly to increase the output of houses.

Studies of average total costs are, in any case, only of limited usefulness. Very great regional differences and entirely local fluctuations in costs were not necessarily reflected in a marked divergence in the fluctuations of building activity in various parts of the country. The average cost of building one room was £37 in Liverpool in 1884, £62 in Newcastle suburbs,[24] £72 in Glasgow.[25] Yet, as far as we can tell from available information, house-building rose and fell with much the same rhythms in these three towns. In Hackney, building costs rose very much between 1880 and 1890,[26] a time when national average costs fell, and here again we come against the fact that the kind of house-building for which there was demand in these overcrowded poor districts of London was the kind first hit by rises in costs, the cheapest.

In England, as compared with both the Continent and with Scotland, the prevalence of the small-house system tended to keep up costs. The long-term leasehold system, as opposed to Scotland's system of 'feuing' land, favoured the building of small houses and affected the urban housing problem in two ways. It determined that there would never be enough houses for the poor. The covering of many acres of land with small houses could only be economically sound using the back-to-back system which was universally deplored by housing reformers. In Leeds, which held out stubbornly against this aspect of reform, back-to-backs were still being built in the twentieth century,[27] and made a contribution to the sheltering of the poor at low cost which encouraged the city to defend the system. But, where the need for houses was very great, as in London, the small-house system used up too much land, continually eating into the surrounding countryside at a cost in traffic problems and shrinking amenity that is still being paid.

The preference for small houses in England was not one based entirely on logical economic grounds, being mixed up with an emotional need to be king of one's own castle, however small, and confused by a leftover hankering for a rural, cottage life which seems to linger in the most urban Englishman. When the first council estates were being planned, the romantic notion of the superior status of the small individual house befogged the planners. Councillors whose drive might have gone to getting the houses built were diverted and drained by arguments about tenements versus cottage-type estates.[28] Fifty years earlier the charitable housing trusts had found that the only way to build cheaply enough for the poor was to build in high density blocks and even then they had found resistance to the idea of living in such barrack-like buildings. The speculative builders of the later century had to build what seemed to be demanded, which committed them to the small-house system with its higher costs.

But if the building of small houses was less economical than the building of larger blocks it could nevertheless be more easily undertaken by the small contractor. And, although the Victorian era saw the emergence of the large-scale contractor, the small men still predominated. It was not unnatural that the small contractor, not soundly financed but depending very largely on credit from his suppliers of materials should draw in his horns at the first hint of rising costs.

Chapter 15

Investment in House-Building

'He has em in St Gile's; he has em in Marylebone: he has em in
Bethnal Green. Just look how he lives himself and you'll see the
good of it to him'

G. B. SHAW, *Widowers' Houses*, 1892

It is the fact that there are two kinds of investor whose interests are
affecting house-building activity which explains housing's divergence
from the ordinary business cycle. The speculative builder is affected
by wages and costs and by interest rates on loans. Short cycles in
building activity are determined by his reaction to rises and falls in
these quarters. Long cycles are determined by the reaction of the
second type of investor in housing, the investor/house owner, who is
affected by the comparison between returns from housing and from
other sources of income.

If the thought processes leading to investment were in fact entirely
logical they would be based on the estimate of returns from rents and
the opportunities for other investment. Whether fortunately or not,
the whole philosophy of housing, not excluding investment in housing,
is clouded by ideas more emotive than logical. *Home* is an emotive
word, *security* another. 'Put your money in stone and lime' is a slogan
to match them and one which outlasted the periods of real profitability in property investments. If it had emotional overtones, however, the advice to put money in housing was based fairly soundly on
the knowledge that property survives periods of non-profitability.
For one content to wait till things were looking up again, one not
expecting enormous returns on investment, there was a comfortable
sense of security in seeing a row of houses still there in spite of
depression. In this respect, for the small investor, it compared very
favourably with other destinations for his money which could seem
like so many pieces of paper. Homes for the people remained necessary,
some portion at least of the rents continued to be paid when railway
manias and mining rushes had come and gone. Added to these
reasonable, if hardly enterprising considerations were the myths of
very large profits from housing which lingered on and had influence
into less profitable periods.

To understand the strength of these influences it is worth looking at
the kind of person who put his money into housing, buying a row of
houses from a speculative builder or commissioning another to build
to his requirements. Not nearly enough is known about these people,

but it is clear, from such studies as have been done,[1] that they were seldom big-time financiers. Widows, spinsters and orphans, for instance, seem frequently to have been provided for by the purchase out of family funds of a row of houses which was then expected to provide a small, steady income and sometimes a home within the property. It was through this kind of investor that lawyers exerted their very considerable influence on the housing market, advising investment in housing as a source of a small, steady income in preference to greater, but riskier opportunities elsewhere. Tradesmen and shopkeepers purchased rows of houses, living in one, sometimes a slightly superior corner house, and collecting rents from the others. In Scotland the owner of a corner-shop was sometimes owner of the whole block of housing, at other times the larger rent extracted from ground-floor shops increased the profitability of blocks of housing. For the most part, investors in housing were the very kind of people to have low expectations of returns from their investment, to choose safety in the form of a small yearly income rather than greater possible profits over a longer period of time. The kind of person who might have put in enough money, the very large sum which would have been necessary to exert a real influence on the development of housing, to ensure its efficiency or change its character, put his money elsewhere.

The average return to be expected on housing was something like 5 per cent. In the next chapter,[2] we shall see that the model dwellings associations did not find it easy to maintain even this rate of interest. Where the aim was to house the lowest income groups a rate of 3.5 per cent was more realistic. Those who hoped for more were inevitably disappointed. Henry, 9th Lord Kinnaird, had promised 6 or 7 per cent return on working-class house-building.[3] Those who believed him found him wrong. Henry Roberts became so disillusioned that he gave up all hope of housing the poor profitably, although he had once been among the most optimistic of campaigners.[4] Only in periods when depression, following over-investment abroad, diminished the attraction of overseas investments was money available for home investment. But even then housing had to compete for finance with other forms of investment. In phases of rapid growth at home, when the influx of migrants from country areas and the rise of industrial incomes increased the demand for houses, industrialists were liable to draw in their own funds to finance industrial expansion or to borrow from the kind of source which might otherwise have financed house-building. In phases of depression at home, emigration, especially to the United States, to some extent eased the demand for housing, and development abroad encouraged British investors to put their money in American concerns. Professor Phelps Brown[5] has simplified this theory with the sentence: 'Whether a house is built in Oldham depends on and is decided by whether a house goes up in Oklahoma.' Professor Habakkuk, however, investigating the theory that rapid growth and intensive use of resources in the two countries are inversely related to each other, has pointed out that it must be applied to housing only with caution[6] and Professor Saul found that 'the evidence for a complex interaction of the British and American economies, at least as far as investment in housing is concerned, is slender.'[7] In Britain, the need for housing was in long-settled urban areas where in America the need was for the creation of whole new towns, which meant that different kinds of financing were required. Not enough is known about regional differences in house-building activity to make hard statements about the effect of American investment possible. Professor A. K. Cairncross found a clear relation between foreign investment and house-building in nineteenth-century Glasgow,[8] whereas in Dundee it has been thought that house-building had been much more affected by factors of purely regional significance.[9] How widely different the effect of the same American economic situation can be on different regions can be shown by the impact of the Civil War. In Lancashire, the war produced the cotton famine which left thousands unemployed and unable to pay rent.[10] In Angus, the war and the lack of cotton stimulated the jute industry and made Dundonians and the many new immigrants to the city better able to rent good houses than ever before.

Until the 1870s house-building in Britain and America in fact moved closely in phase. From 1869 to 1872 activity was high in both countries. In America house-building declined abruptly after 1872 while Britain did not reach its peak until 1876. Here a building boom in Britain coincides with a trough in America. Thereafter, until 1914, during the forty years in which building fluctuation in Britain ceased to follow the trade cycle, activity in the two countries alternated.[11]

For our purposes it is only necessary to note that there were many counter-attractions to investment in housing. The fact that over-crowding in our cities was creating a need for low-cost housing had not enough weight to counteract the enormous potential for profitable investment in India, America and the Argentine. When such overseas investments became less profitable because of economic conditions in the countries concerned there were still a number of obstacles standing in the way of investment in low-cost housing. Even for those investors of low expectation with small amounts to invest the ownership of old, house-property was often more attractive than the building of new, because the old property was in the central urban areas where high rents could be extracted even when repairs were neglected. Lawyers and financial advisers who had, as we have seen, great influence on the kind of investments made by small owners of capital tended to prefer old property. While rents were free to move upwards with costs and demand there would remain some incentive to speculative house-building. Under this system those unable or unwilling to expend an increasing proportion of their income on rent were simply left out. The final blow to any hope of profit from the speculative building of working-class houses came with the Rent and Mortgage Restriction Act, 1915, which froze rents at their pre-war level. If low-cost house-building had been an unattractive prospect for investors in most of the years leading up to the war when rents were still rising steadily, it became now one not worth consideration. It has been usual for historians to say that private enterprise 'failed' to provide adequate housing for the poor. This assumes that builders and investors saw the housing of the poor as their aim, which is to misunderstand the Victorian attitude to poverty. There had been, indeed, some new thinking about the effects of rampant capitalism upon the labouring classes. The works of Henry George, and particularly his *Progress and Poverty*, were very generally read. Intellectual social reformers had reached a position which assumed some limited state responsibility for the care and accommodation of the poor. Leaders of the Labour movement had begun to teach the working man's right to have, as his share of the expanding wealth, at least a decent home and an adequate diet. But speculative builders and the investing public as a whole fell into neither of these categories. If they considerd the new social theories at all it was either to reject them or to consider the improvement of the poor to be desirable enough but certainly the responsibility of others than themselves. Their not unreasonable aim was to make a profit. To allot blame for not fulfilling an aim they did not hold is quite irrelevant. When housing ceased to give an expectation of profit they ceased to invest in it. The housing of the poor had to become the responsibility of those with aims other than profit-making. Eventually the development of social consciousness, a new awareness of human rights awakened by a sense of duty towards soldiers returning from the trenches to the slums, and the need to consider the demands and needs of a proletarian electorate would force the assumption of state responsibility for housing. Until then those who felt some individual responsibility for the condition of the poor worked for their better-ment through the philanthropic societies, or, as industrialists, built model estates for their own workers. Those who felt no such responsi-bility made a profit when they could. It was the fact that it became harder and harder to make a profit from the housing of the poor that reduced investment in house-property to a trickle.

PART 4

Private Enterprise Housing: Whose Responsibility?

Chapter 16

Employer Housing and Company Towns

'A bogus medievalism . . . symbolic of the reactionary trend,
away from dynamic urbanism'

MOHOLY NAGY

The fact that profits large enough to stimulate private investment
could not be made from building labourers' houses came to be recognised before the country was ready to accept the principle of state
responsibility for housing. There was a fairly general feeling that something should be done, a slightly less general recognition of the fact
that not much was going to be done by private enterprise, and only a
very rare acceptance of the logical conclusion that the responsibility
for housing those who could not house themselves should be borne
by the state. In this situation those individuals who felt bound by
conscience to shoulder some part of the responsibility for providing
shelter for the poor formed themselves into a number of different
agencies. These can roughly be divided into the employers, who built
houses for their own workers, the freehold land and building societies
who aimed to help the workers to help themselves, and the philanthropic societies who built for the poor as a charitable enterprise.

We have already seen how employers found it worth-while to provide housing at the end of the eighteenth century, and during the rapid
expansion of trade, because of their need to attract labour to the new
industrial sites; and how, at a later period, after the scarcity of labour
had lessened, the new need to improve the quality of labour had induced employers to build company towns for their employees. The
sanitary campaigns of the 1840s played a part in inducing manufacturers to provide a better standard of housing and hygiene for their
workers. Both the assault on their consciences of the increasingly common revelations of workers' living conditions and a self-protective fear
of the spread of disease persuaded some, at least, of the larger industrialists to plan the provision of company housing. To some extent
employers were feeling, indirectly, the effect of the workers' deteriorating living standards. The nagging ill health, the frequent absences, the
apathy induced by poor diet and sleeplessness, the despair brought by
constant infant deaths, the panic caused by rumours of fatal epidemics, the shiftlessness resulting from the impossibility of keeping clean
or looking respectable, all these added up to make a poor, unrespon-
sive labour force. The frequent early deaths of skilled and trained men
meant the wastage of time spent in training and the need to teach pro-

cesses and skills to a constantly replaced team of workers. The absence of the steadying effect of older men, when the average death of workers in towns was hardly into middle-age, left an unstable work force, easily roused to trouble-making, and, although fearful of openly expressed rebellion, often sullen with resentment.

The steadily rising standards of middle-class homes contrasted increasingly uncomfortably with the workers' situation as the century progressed. Yet the habit of building houses for workers, at least on any large scale, became increasingly uncommon after the 1850s.

The altruism of the Edward Ackroyds and Titus Salts ought not to be discounted. Their wish to improve the lot of their work-people was quite genuine. The unpleasantness of city streets produced a reaction in dreams of idealised medieval communities of contented workers dependent upon their beneficent employers. This dream fitted in with employer approval of the virtues of self-help for the labouring classes and a more realistic recognition that workers must first be given some shred of opportunity to begin to help themselves. In providing decent housing, employers were giving that opportunity, they were making self-help possible, and probably they were aware of it. There was also, in the creating of these ideal communities, some realisation, perhaps some dread, of the inevitable approach of the much feared 'democracy' and a kind of hopeless wish to postpone its consequences.

However mixed the motives of the company-town-builders it would be foolish to attempt to separate them from the profit motive. For the fact remains that in the second half of the century many of the factors which had induced building for workers were still there. Overcrowding in industrial areas had increased, not declined, and, although sanitary regulations had been introduced, they had made little enough impact on the poorer areas. But any wish to introduce hygienic living conditions was self-defeating. In the first half of the century an employer could run up a row of houses for his workers without water, drainage, access roads or any other amenity. In the second half the Building Regulations, and, to be fair, very often his own wish to improve their lot, insisted on a much greater outlay. Those companies which did continue to build for their workers did provide for them an improvement in their housing, giving both additional space and greater amenity, piped water and privy accommodation. But the improvement cost the worker a greater proportion of his wages. In Ebbw Vale, for instance, and it would seem to be a fairly general experience, the cost of a worker's house rose from £36 in the late eighteenth century to £164 in the late nineteenth century. A large part of this rise represented sanitary facilities and an increase in the number of rooms. The proportion of income spent on rent increased from 8.5 per cent in the eighteenth century to between 12 per cent and 14 per cent in the first half of the nineteenth century and between 14 per cent and 16 per cent in the second half.[1] In trades where real wages had advanced with the century, increased expenditure on rent was possible. But for the majority of the manufacturing population, especially in the textile areas where company towns had once provided a solution, subsistence wages allowed for little rent increase. Regulations against overcrowding, causing employers to frown on the taking of lodgers which they had once encouraged and even insisted upon, removed one means of finding the rent money.

Titus Salt had been able to command, as well as his 'steady, well disposed and well behaved work people', a return on capital of 4 per cent on his workers' housing.[2] Willingness to build for late-century workers was affected by three main financial considerations. The first was the recognition by employers that greater rents could not be extracted from workers' wages without a considerable increase in wages and their belief that competitive industry could not bear wage increases. In that situation the rise in the cost of even the cheapest housing made building impossible. The second was that progress, and increased foreign competition very often involved employers in increased outlay on machinery, industrial buildings and warehouses. This meant that, in periods of expansion, available funds went in directions other than housing. In periods of depression funds were available for neither technological improvement nor house-building. The third factor was the same temptation experienced by other former investors in housing—for industrialists to put the profits of manufacturing into speculative investment abroad rather than into company-town-building at home. Titus Salt had been thought admirably philanthropic for accepting as low a return as 4 per cent. In the later decades of the century he might have found it harder to be sure even of 4 per cent on new house-building and the opportunities for making much more elsewhere had widened.

The most important influences discouraging the building of workers' housing by employers were, therefore, certainly economic, but there were other factors. Increasing unemployment had made the need to attract labour by offering houses as an incentive quite unnecessary. People were sufficiently in need of employment to be willing either to live in slums near their work or to walk long miles to get to it. The return of a degree of prosperity for some at the end of the century brought also various forms of cheap public transport, workers' trains in the Metropolis, trams in provincial cities, which finally made it unnecessary for employers to provide housing close to the works.

One very clear advantage to employers in company towns had been the accessibility of workers. A sudden rush of orders, or the need to change from one process to another, could be speeded by knocking workers up from their sleep to come to work at any hour necessary. Especially in the days of water-powered industry—and it is often forgotten how long waterpower lingered on in pockets of Britain outside the main towns—it was necessary to call workers out to use the water as it became available. Legislation to regulate working hours made this all-round-the-clock accessibility of workers less easily taken advantage of and removed one incentive to build.

The possibility of enclosing employees in a community not open to outside influences was removed almost entirely by the growth of towns, the coming of cheap newspapers, and the more effective organisation of trade unions. Company towns like Saltaire, once isolated on an empty moor, were, first, met by the spread of neighbouring cities, then swallowed by them, so that the once closed community became only part of a swarming industrial population. It was no longer possible to preserve company employees from the corrupting influence of less paternally protected workers. Newspapers and travelling union men taught the workers allegiance to class instead of to employer. For the employer the possibility of keeping control over a dependent and docile labour force had been an important incentive to building. That incentive seemed, to most owners, now removed.

The experience of Baxter Brothers of Dundee, the biggest flax manufacturers in the world, must have been common. Because one of their partners kept a very full journal, the mixture of reluctance and relief with which this firm gave up providing housing for its workers can be understood. Reluctance to give up paternalistic control, relief at shedding the responsibility for the living standards of the poor, mingled uneasily with a sense of Christian duty to accept that responsibility, not shed it. But the impossibility of raising economic rents out of the wages they paid their workers dealt firmly enough with Christian duty:

'1 October 1865'

'We are very ill off for work-peoples' houses in Dundee. They are so crowded that disease has broken out and although it is against our principle as employers to build houses yet necessity and humanity compel us to do something. I am told they are building such houses of *brick* in Glasgow and suppose from the urgency of the case that we will be driven to use the same material.'

'6 November 1865'

'I find that the price of brick has advanced so much in this district owing to the great demand at a season when they cannot be made that they are out of the question.[3] I have gone and examined some new buildings and find that most of them consist of two small apartments. I measured one, 10 feet square each room, and I could on my tiptoes just touch the ceiling. The two rooms let for 6 guineas per annum . . . . Not to mention ordinary decency or morality I asked a man where they said their prayers . . . .

'As an experiment about eighty houses of two and three rooms each were built and fitted with all needful conveniences, including grates with boilers. But it was found that the tenants did not take sufficient care of these and the plates were soon burned through.[4] The double relationship of master and landlord, too, was at times awkward and it was not always possible to limit the letting of houses to the workers. The intention of doing so was therefore given up and the houses, though conveniently situated for the workers, were let to any who were likely to prove good tenants; and the workers, while encouraged to choose good houses, were left perfectly free in their choice.'

They were left, in fact, perfectly free to live in crumbling slums while the houses originally built for their use were let to more regular rent-payers with less destructive habits.[5]

These workers were in the industrial area of Dundee where the supply of unskilled labour was always abundant enough to give employers a sufficient hold over employees because of their need to keep their jobs.

The power over employees given by the provision of tied housing, however, could still be a great advantage.[6] In isolated areas, where the needs of a particular industry brought about its location in districts away from the main centres of population so that the need to attract labour by housing still existed and the other disincentives did not operate, employers continued for to build their workers. Collieries, iron-works, bleach-works still maintained close communities of one-employer towns, dependent upon the employer not only for their wages but for their homes. Employers did not hesitate on occasions to use the power this gave them. Linen bleachers, in particular, held off the reduction of working hours, the advancement of wages, the introduction of trades unionism until many decades after these advantages had come to other trades, preserving in the bleaching villages complete dependence upon a paternal employer whose benevolence lasted until trouble started. In 1834 the owner of the new village built for the workers at a bleaching and printing field in the parish of Campsie found the 'operatives a little turbulent'.[7] He put a stop to this by calling in the military and not long afterwards the village was said to be as respectful to their employer as could be wished. More than a century later the great bleachers' strike of 1906 was broken after thirteen weeks by the threat of eviction from the company-owned workers' houses. After the strike the trouble-makers were sacked and evicted.[8]

For the most part, however, those industries which were still small enough in scale to feel the advantages of owning company housing were, by definition, not expanding industries. Continuing ownership of existing property was usually enough. New building was seldom necessary. There were, of course, exceptions to the rule. Small rows of company houses were built here and there at all periods. But the experience of Ebbw Vale, where from the 1850s the company which had once provided houses for its workers now leased land for building clubs to use, seems to point a general tendency to give up house-building.[9] Certainly there was a gap between the creation of the company towns of the mid-nineteenth century and the establishment of the modern company-owned garden villages of Port Sunlight and Bourneville. How far were the motives which inspired the builders and the situation experienced by the workers similar in the two phases of company-town-building? Were those factors which had prevented building in the greater part of the second half of the nineteenth century later removed? Were the new ideal communities inspired by new ideals rather than new economic necessities?

Bourneville was, in fact, begun as early as 1879 and the Quaker faith of its founder, George Cadbury, made it at first a fairly straightforward philanthropic venture with a paternal organisation. The later establishment of the Bourneville Village Trust was a much more important step in the history of housing, accepting as it did the two very important principles of the need for a planned environment and the desirability of a community voice on development.

W. H. Lever's intentions in building Port Sunlight were, like all his motives, as mixed as only his very complicated character could make them. His often voiced dislike of philanthropy was contradicted by actions with no possible purpose but philanthropy, such as his abortive attempt to introduce industry to the Hebrides. His shrewd business methods were hardly weakened by his genuine wish to leave the world a better place than he found it. His determination to improve industrial relations was limited by the narrowness of his understanding of ordinary human beings. Perhaps the most satisfactory explanation of his creation of a model community lies in his recognition of the need to give workers a real motive for caring about his product. He had, for various reasons, not least the dislike of the trade unions for the idea, rejected profit-sharing, but he still wanted to improve worker motivation. His notion of 'prosperity sharing', by which extra profits in good years were not given straight to the workers as a money share but ploughed back into a housing and amenity fund, was the theory which built Port Sunlight.

The fact that other industrialists did not, though they praised them, copy Bourneville and Port Sunlight, seems satisfactorily to dismiss the idea that economic necessity dictated them. Cocoa and soap, although these two products were going into millions more working-class homes than before, were not the only fast expanding industries, but more manufacturers neglected to house their workers than attempted to do so. It needed the faith of a Quaker or the very individual drive of a Lever to plan Utopia. Perhaps the one thing these two men had in common was an early understanding of industrial relations. Both understood that to maintain quality as well as production they must somehow imbue the workers with a sense that what they were doing was worth-while for their own sakes as well as their employers: to give them comfortable houses in thoughtfully planned communities seemed one way to convey this sense of common purpose. It should be remembered that these ventures were planned in a social climate, deriving from the successive government reports on housing, in which it had become accepted that industry had made the slums. To some extent Cadbury and Lever were atoning for a guilty belief that industrialists like themselves had brought about the evil conditions in which so many workers lived. It is now known to be not wholly true that slums were caused by industrial growth, except in the indirect sense that by feeding people industry made rapid population growth possible. Town decay was caused, as we have seen, by a chain of economic causes lying deep in the society existing before the Industrial Revolution. But in the last decades of the nineteenth century most people felt, and the agricultural aristocracy certainly encouraged the belief, that manufacturers were to be blamed for the creation of the slums. The burden of guilt this laid on men of faith or on muddled-thinking progressives was considerable. Not that Lever, at least, let it interfere with business. Like most other industrialists, as we saw earlier, he found it impossible to finance works expansion and house-building at the same time, and it was house-building that had to wait. 'We shall not', he told his guests at the opening banquet, 'be able to build those houses at present simply because it will require all the capital we can spare to build our works.'[10] When he did, and it was only two years later, get round to building, he did it with gusto, providing large, gardened, semi-detached cottages in what can only be called a wealth of styles. It is unfortunate that none of those men who had the money to create villages or the sense to understand their planning needs, were gifted with the ability to lead the way in architectural design. That their tastes ran to 'quaint nooks and corners and fascinating gables'[11] was, of course, partly a reaction to the austerity of the building styles commonly thought suitable for the poor. Their fancy for the 'ye-oldey' in design accorded well, after all, with the romantic streak in their character which made Utopia seem possible.

Bourneville and Port Sunlight should not be given too much importance, however, within the history of working-class housing. They proved only that one man with enough determination, given enough land over which he had complete control and enough money freely available, could build a healthy environment. But they were much more important in educating public opinion, in influencing future town planning development than in housing the working class. The fact that the housing development which followed them was an almost entirely middle-class affair shows the irrelevance to the needs of the working class in general. They were not really original in conception. Price's Bromborough Pool estate, situated indeed very close to Port Sunlight, preceded them, as many earlier industrial villages with low density development preceded it. The intention of their builders was not different, in any important respect, from that of those earlier agricultural landlords who liked to build well-planned villages on their estates. Their isolation within a period in which most employers had turned their backs on the idea of providing housing, their large scale, and the fact that they were followed by the Garden City movement, has given them their significance. But their very virtues, their good planning and low density, prevented their having any decisive influence upon low-cost housing designed by builders with profit-making in mind. Their real importance lies in what Mumford called 'a useful dissociation . . . they dissociated the processes of industry from the idea of human degradation in a filthy environment.'[12] Any dream of re-housing the workers which needed enlightened industrialists for its fulfilment was doomed to failure. Not only are enlightened industrialists necessarily few in number but there remains also the huge number of workers who could never fit under any paternal wing. 'Slums represent the presence of a market for local casual labour.'[13] Benevolent paternalism shelters the permanent worker and ignores the casual.

In 1898 Ebenezer Howard's book *Tomorrow: A Peaceful Path to Real Reform* was published. Later re-issued as *Garden Cities of Tomorrow* this important work brought together the strands of economic thought popularised by Henry George, the threads of town planning theories developing from the best company-towns, into a new social philosophy. Howard succeeded, perhaps, as Mumford says, because he was 'unfettered by those forms of specialised competence that paralyse creative thought', in influencing the future development of towns everywhere by his brilliant exposition of the need for a balanced urban environment. He gave a new direction to housing reform whose results were hardly seen until after the Second World War which, by devastating whole cities, gave the chance to re-plan whole environments. He emphasised the importance of planning a whole community at the outset of its development, thus creating a healthy environment with controlled siting of industry, rational traffic, a balanced and therefore economical arrangement of social functions, organised so as to prevent speculative land development. His ideas were taken up in England by a private association which formed the First Garden City Limited in 1903 and built first, Letchworth, then Welwyn Garden City. Letchworth did succeed in attracting some industrial development and in building houses for workers, but the creative drive was entirely middle-class and successive Garden City developments became exclusively middle-class settlements. The Garden City movement gave housing reformers an ideal to aim for and had a real and constructive influence on the education both of those architects and town planners who were later to build pioneer council-house estates and of those progressive Members of Parliament and town councillors who were to work for their financing. These were long-term effects. The deadlock between the acute need for housing in the nineteenth century and the lack of any real initiative towards building it had to be broken by another force. It was, even in the 1890s not clear what that other force should be.

Speculative building and company building had failed to impinge on the size of the problem of housing need. Attempts by other agencies had varying success.

Chapter 17

Building Societies

'We are the greatest social reformers of the day'
A building society secretary, 1871

The recognised impossibility of building for the poor at a respectable profit led many reformers to believe that the only hope lay in encouraging the poor towards self-help. The best means of a worker helping himself towards decent housing seemed to lie in societies established for the purpose of house-building. It was obvious that no low wage-earner could save a sum of money from his earnings large enough to build or buy a house. But it seemed to many that he could afford to invest a small weekly sum in a society which would help him towards that end.[1] Friendly Societies were precluded by their rules from the purchase of land but it seems to have been in those districts, like Birmingham, where Friendly Societies were already deeply rooted, that the terminating building societies took root most successfully. This was partly because the benefits of saving and co-operation had been demonstrated in the area to some effect rather than preached to the doubting and apathetic. It was also, of course, largely possible because there were in these areas sufficient numbers of steadily earning artisans for whom saving was a possibility.

The earliest and most primitive in organisation of the housing societies were the building clubs, formed from the end of the eighteenth century by groups of tradesmen who then co-operated to build their own houses with their own hands. They clubbed together to buy materials and land and then each exercised his own trade, whether brick-laying, carpentry, plastering, labouring or painting, to the advantage of the group.[2] Groups similar to these indulged in speculative building of the least desirable kind in London in the 1830s but in the provinces the possibility of making huge profits was perhaps less tempting.

In Nottingham working men's 'money clubs' employed builders to provide houses for their members from their savings as early as the 1790s but this, a product of the prosperity of the independent knitters, could not survive the mechanisation of their trade.[3]

These early societies differ from the later pattern of building societies in that they were begun on initiative from working people. Because they were small-scale, short-term enterprises they involved no complicated administration. They were not due to the inspiration

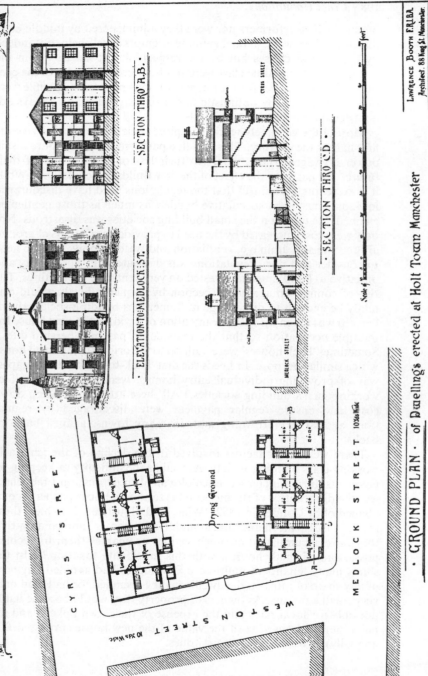

MANCHESTER & SALFORD WORKMENS DWELLINGS Cº Lᴰ

· SECTION THRO' A.B. ·

· ELEVATION·TO·MEDLOCK·ST. ·

CROSS STREET

Coal Bunkers

MEDLOCK STREET

Coal Bunkers

· SECTION THRO' C.D. ·

Scale of [ ] feet

Lawrence Booth F.R.I.B.A.
Architect. 88 Hug St. Manchester.

CYRUS STREET

Living Room   Bed Room   Bed Room   Living Room

Drying Ground

Bed Room   Living Room   Living Room   Bed Room

MEDLOCK STREET   10 yds Wide

WESTON STREET   10 yds Wide

· GROUND PLAN · of Dwellings erected at Holt Town Manchester of middle-class reformers nor were they administered by middle-class directors. They were, in fact, genuine attempts at self-help, not indeed by the poorest classes but by the respectable artisan to whom the attentions of the middle class were so often directed. Later in the century building societies for the purpose of housing working people were most often begun by optimistic middle-class groups and always administered by middle-class officials.

Most of the genuinely worker-inspired societies did not survive the first half of the century. This was due partly to the fall in purchasing power of wage-earners, partly to their less optimistic view of their future, and partly to the effect of the new Building Regulations. While it is exceedingly doubtful that the regulations need have discouraged low-cost housing by speculative builders as much as those gentlemen claimed, the effect on the small building societies was disastrous. Not only were costs increased by the need to provide larger areas of ground around houses, drainage, ventilation and water supply, but the need to consider and obey regulations was discouraging. The energy and initiative to build must have rested on very tentative promptings. The risk of coming up against inspection by council officials would certainly be enough to discourage it. Sometimes building-society membership was taken up with the intention of dividing the new house for multiple occupation so that the rents could pay membership dues.[4] Sometimes 'back houses' were built on to the originally planned house with a similar purpose. In Leeds the first 'back-to-backs', the cheapest way of providing individual entry homes, were built on behalf of working men's building societies.[5] All these attempts to keep down costs and ensure regular payment were discouraged by regulations against overcrowding and, in many towns, against back-to-backs.

There were other factors involved in the decline of the genuinely working-class building society. As well as the difficulty of keeping up payments during increased unemployment in depression times there was the disincentive of the increased taxation on house property complained of by Cobden in 1852: 'What kind of justice is it to meet these men . . . frugal mechanics and humble tradesmen . . . immediately that they have accumulated as much savings as enables them to become possessors of small houses, with this inordinate taxation?'[6] In the slums many tenants in multi-occupied houses had avoided payment of any share of rates on the dwellings they occupied, or had paid only very small amounts. As owners of property they would become liable not only for local rates and the expense of their own upkeep and repairs, but for house-tax (if the value of the new house surpassed £10 annually) as well as their society dues.

They not only added very considerably to their outgoings but risked eliminating a source of income in time of need. Some unemployment relief committees refused to allow relief during distress to owners of property of any kind, to co-operative society members and to trade unionists.[7] This added the extra peril of being entirely without income to the always present fear of being unable to keep up payments during periods of being out of work.

To the injustices of taxation and withheld relief was added the injustice suffered by small shareholders in building societies which collapsed through the unwise and sometimes fraudulent financial activities of their directors. In Sheffield, working-class investors were said to have lost £2 million in building societies in the ten years 1878–88, a period in which societies were already much less popular and more suspiciously regarded than they had been during the years up to 1860.[8] In Manchester, the inefficiency and greed of middle-men and jerry-builders employed by the societies and the lack of wisdom shown by directors who invested in worthless property caused the building-society idea to fail as an organisation for working people.[9]

It was in an attempt to combat this kind of disaster, although as Sheffield's experience shows, the attempt was not wholly successful, that Parliament passed the Building Societies Act, 1874. This gave building societies the legal status of limited companies.[10] It was made necessary chiefly by the change in form and intention of the societies which had taken place since the Act of 1836, which extended Friendly Society regulations to building societies. Early societies had been 'terminating' building societies; formed by a group of men in need of houses, dissolved when the last man was housed. As the possibility of making money out of the idea began to be noticed by people who were not themselves in need of houses, the permanent benefit society was involved. The terminating societies had often run into trouble, partly because of their lack of understanding of actuarial science—the difference between compound and simple interest was only shakily grasped—but chiefly because their form made joining at any time other than the society's first foundation almost impossible. Early members did not always find it possible to keep up their payments and were forced to withdraw. Withdrawals could prove disastrous to the very small societies.[11] But, because it was necessary to demand back payments, new members were very hard to attract. The interest of actuaries, particularly of Arthur Scratchley,[12] produced the idea of a 'permanent' building society, the point being that the composition of the membership could change while the society itself remained in existence. This not only allowed for the likelihood of new members joining at any time but also for the development of managerial skills and financial knowledge over a longer period. The member who wished a place to deposit his savings was encouraged by the new character of the societies. While terminating societies continued to be popular, especially in the north-west, partly because they continued to seem psychologically within reach of the working man in a way that the permanent societies did not, many of the large permanent building societies were formed in the period after 1846. The Leeds Permanent began in 1848, the Woolwich Equitable in 1847, the Abbey National in 1849, the Bradford Equitable in 1851, the Halifax in 1853.[13] Their aim, to provide a sound investment for savings, was different in emphasis from the aim of the terminating societies, whose chief aim was to provide houses. The fact that among the first were many members who were not strictly working class and that among the second were some members who were genuinely 'frugal mechanics . . . happily bent on improving their dwellings',[14] does not affect the very different intentions of the founders.

Incorporation, with its necessarily more complicated organisation, enlarged the scale of enterprise. For the middle-class investor the new kind of building society became an attractive way to make his savings work for him, with the additional virtue that while his money was appreciating, it might also be helping to house the poor. By the 1870s the housing of the poor was a problem sufficiently aired to make many people glad to find a reasonably painless way of doing something about it. It is not unduly cynical to understand that while the energy to tackle the problem in any realistic way was lacking in most of Victorian society there was willingness to allow money to be used towards that end, with of course the assurance that the money would not be diminished but increased in the process. The building society idea, too, did not challenge any of the tenets dear to that society. It did not hand out charity, it encouraged self-help. It provided no haven for the undeserving, it encouraged those who worked to be respectable. And it showed the outward and visible signs of grace because it made money safely for its supporters.

It did not, however, have much success in housing the poor. The terminating societies had fallen in popularity for a number of reasons, but chiefly because the rise in costs had made it difficult to build houses cheaply enough for letting to those who needed them. Speculators had found the same thing. Some of the new permanent building societies began with splendid aims but soon found the wise investment of their clients' money and the housing of the poor to be inconsistent ideals. The 'Land, Building and Investment Company Ltd' of Sowerby Bridge was not untypical in its intention of 'promoting the erection of improved dwellings, *chiefly, but not exclusively, for the working classes;*

at the same time putting it in the power of the working man to become the owner of his own dwelling.'[15]

For the working man the payment of membership dues, however small, over a period of years was dependent upon steady employment and good health. Neither could be taken for granted. The chances of avoiding unemployment became even slighter in the last quarter of the century, and while the worst epidemics had been subdued in most places, the prevailing poor diet and insanitary housing ensured a level of health in townsmen that made them prone to infectious ailments of every kind, especially the respiratory diseases. Their own knowledge of this state of affairs made those few working men who found saving possible wary of building societies where failure to keep up payments might result in loss of membership benefits.[16] For the successful, investment in a building society had obvious advantages. James Hole proved that the workman who paid a deposit of £33 13s 8d, and then 4s 6d a week for thirteen years, could be the owner of his own house, a house with its own kitchen, scullery, garden, back-yard, private convenience and two bedrooms; whereas his neighbour, with the same number of rooms but no garden or back-yard, shared with four other houses, and a privy between two, after paying 3s a week for thirteen years would have paid out £101 8s for a house he still did not own and for which he would have to go on paying rent. But even Hole, a very enthusiastic evangelist of self-help, admitted that such schemes could help only the better-paid artisan, not the poorest, for whom, if steady payment might, at a stretch, be possible, the finding of the initial deposit was certainly beyond his ability. Such an achievement needed not only greater monetary resources but greater reserves of mental energy and initiative, greater powers of foresight, than could commonly be expected among a class of underfed and uneducated labouring people.

Those societies which did have some success had to show, first, some genuine understanding of the kind of need existing in their areas, secondly a directorate with reasonably flexible aims, and thirdly a sound administration with acute financial sense. All these, however, were not enough unless they were dealing with a town in which a proportion of the working class were steadily employed, at good wages, with a reasonable prospect of future prosperity. The most successful, and the longest lived of the nineteenth-century building societies, was the Leeds Permanent Benefit Building Society. Some, at least, of its success was due to what the Royal Commission of 1885 called 'the opulence of the working classes here'.[17] This society was founded on 5 December 1848. It had at the outset 1,099 members which had grown to 6,782 by 1865. It did not itself build houses but provided facilities for those who wished to build. It was in this separation of functions that much of its success lay. Those who invested in it knew that their money was safely held. Those who borrowed from it trusted it to organise the financial side of their transactions while they concentrated on their aim of providing houses. Among those using it were the Model Cottage Society of Leeds, and the Society for the Erection of Improved Dwellings, Leeds. Here the original aim was to step aside from the much deprecated Leeds' habit of building back-to-backs. Leeds' streets were already laid out on the back-to-back principle but the society's intention was to escape this narrow planning by building one house on the ground laid out for two, using the extra space for gardens and yards. They were soon forced to lower their aims if they were to house the people they had set out to house and it is to their credit that they were flexible enough to do so. New model cottages in Leeds, then, were built in back-to-back rows, each row containing twelve two-storey houses. They had basements containing pantries with fixed stone tables, coal cellars and w.c.s, ground-floors with living-room and scullery which had 'good cooking apparatus, set-pot, sink-stone, closet for pots, water, and gas'. Upstairs were a large bedroom with two closets and a smaller single bedroom. They were built of brick in a 'plain domestic Gothic style' with ornamental string courses of black and white bricks and a quatrefoil panel in the gables. These houses, and similar ones in other parts of Leeds, could be built for between £160 and £200 per house.

The Leeds Society showed flexibility and a determination to put its houses within reach of working people by abolishing the need for a deposit, making houses available, without a deposit, for 2s 6d a week in addition to rent, the house remaining the property of the society and the purchaser legally a tenant until a quarter of the purchase price had been paid.[18]

Another society surviving until the present day, and in its time successful in housing fairly low wage-earners, was the Halifax Building Society. A share in the company could be bought for as little as £1. Purchase could be made over sixteen or twenty years. No initial deposit was required, and the society was administered in a manner suited to working-class members, membership dues being collected weekly by the rent-collectors. Realistic assessment of working-class needs was made at the planning stage where many building societies, with dreams of pretty cottages, went astray. The Halifax built four-storey blocks, the ground floor was divided into twelve single rooms for widows and aged persons letting at 1s 3d a week, plus a few front shops with living rooms and bedrooms attached, letting at 8s a week. Thus, right away, those who could not pay an economic rent were compensated for by the more profitable shop rents and it became possible to cater for the really low income groups. On the first floor were nine two-roomed houses letting at 2s a week, on the second floor nine more at 1s 9d a week, on the third floor another nine at 1s 3d for two rooms or 9d for one room. On land costing 5s a yard these houses were reckoned to give a return of 9 per cent. This appeared to prove that low payers could be both cheaply and profitably housed. The society was sufficiently certain of its own profitability to be able to open branches in other towns. It had considerable success, for instance, in Hull where the reluctance of the corporation to use the powers, the money and the land they held for the purpose of re-housing slum-dwellers caused middle-class reformers to look to the 'Halifax' for help. Working-class benefit societies in Hull were reported in 1884 as having £100,000 for investment at 5 per cent which they were willing to put into housing. The Halifax would lend at 4 per cent. With them a working man could purchase his own house in twenty years at 3s 6d per week.[19]

Dundee's experience was not untypical of the way in which middle-class interests combined to encourage working men in self-help towards better homes. On 2 November 1864, Dr James Begg, Free-church man and social reformer, was invited to address a meeting on 'Working Men's Houses and the Advantage of Building Societies'.[20] A large provisional committee was formed and a prospectus drawn up for 'The Dundee Working Men's Houses Association Ltd'. Its purpose was 'the providing of dwelling houses within the Town of Dundee suited for the occupation of the working classes; the acquisition of land . . . the purchase of houses already built . . . and the letting, sale or disposal of said houses.' 1,043 shares of £1 each were subscribed by 113 shareholders. Fifty-three of these were reported to be working men who between them took 113 shares. The other 930 shares were taken by 'merchants and others'. Lord Kinnaird along with some important manufacturers in Dundee gave donations amounting to £130 18s.[21] Ten two-storey tenement houses were erected in a street named Blyth Street after yet another manufacturer who gave much personal attention to the business of the association. Each block contained four houses and the plan was to offer them for sale. The first few went briskly (Dundee enjoyed a sensational boom during the American Civil War). The last went very slowly, remaining two years unoccupied in spite of an acute housing shortage, and the price had to be lowered. The smallest houses cost, at first, £105, later £85, the larger £146, later £125. Loans were arranged, for the small houses at an extra cost of £1 10s, for the large of £2.

Ten years later the promoters of a new campaign for working men's building societies were warned of the financial failure of the Blyth Street venture.[22] In 1874 James Cox, chief partner in the biggest jute firm in the world, purchased thirty copies of Begg's *Happy Homes* for distribution to the Working Men's Club 'to try to get the workmen interested in the scheme',[23] and was instrumental in persuading Lord Kinnaird to address the Club on 'Ventilation and Concrete Building'. In the same month the Dundee Independent Liberal Association held a meeting to discuss the question of providing houses for the working classes, at which Mr John Robertson, a local architect, presided.[24] Three housing societies resulted from this initiative. The Dundee Land and Building Association built a five-storey block with shops on the ground floor and eighteen houses on each storey, seven of them two-roomed, ten of them three-roomed, and one four-roomed. The Working Men's Building Company Ltd, Dundee, built in 1874 two three-storey blocks of two- and three-roomed houses each with a parlour, a w.c. and a scullery with bed-closet. The next year they built one three-storey block of two-roomed houses with a shop on the ground floor, with one shared w.c.[25] This lowering of standards points the difficulty experienced in making the proposition pay. During the same period the Concrete Building Company, which was reported as 'endeavouring to give cheap and substantial cottages to working men', pioneered the use of concrete for low-cost housing, building a number of two-storey cottages which 'look exceedingly well outside and are quite as comfortable inside as those built of stone'.[26] The company was not financially successful, nor did these three associations make any impression on the state of Dundee's housing problem. For one thing the areas in which they built were not those in which the pressure of overcrowding was most felt. There were many empty houses in the city at the same time as the central slums overflowed with stressed and derelict human beings. For another the cost, even of these houses intended especially for working-class use, was too high for a low-wage town. There was a big demand for one-roomed houses for single mill girls, the work force which was the basis of Dundee's industry, or for two-roomed family houses. Bigger houses demanded rents beyond jute-workers' pockets.

The much greater financial success of two similar schemes in Edinburgh was, of course, partly explicable by the different industrial pattern of the two towns. The Edinburgh Working Men's Building Association and the Edinburgh Co-operative Building Company Ltd, would seem not only to have been commercially viable and successful in housing working people, but genuinely worker-inspired and worker-run as well. On 28 February 1860, the delegates to Edinburgh's Trades Council agreed that it was desirable to take up the question of Building Associations amongst the Working Classes. The Working Men's Building Association used the Trades Council's approval as an advertising feature when they publicised their aims. The Edinburgh Co-operative Building Company Ltd, was formed by the operative stone masons during the important masons' lock-out of 1861. Its directors were working masons and its purpose was the support of working people in their struggle against employers during the nine hours campaign. This would make it appear that the first aim of the company was the increase by investment of workers' savings rather than the housing of members. It was successful in both its first and incidental aims. In 1869 the stone masons of Vienna wrote to Edinburgh asking for information about the structure of the society.[27] The society had a nominal capital of £10,000 in shares of £1 each, with 200 founder members.

A much earlier co-operative for the purpose of building their own homes had been started by workers in Colinburgh in 1826. Six separate blocks of eight flats each were built in Canning Place, Causeway side, each house containing a room and kitchen: 'a light bed-closet and two dark bed-closets, with water supply, soil-pipe, sink and water-closet.' The cost of each house was £80 and *The Builder* reported them as being 'a fair example of what workmen's houses ought to be' in 1862 when they were still standing and some, at least, of the original co-operators were still in occupation.[28]

These Edinburgh societies were not only the product of working-class effort but were organised by working men who were active campaigners for electoral and social reform. The Edinburgh and Leith Joiners Building Company Ltd, formed in May 1868, was managed by Peter McNeill who was also secretary of the local branch of the Reform League. He was paid as a full-time employee by the society and was proposed as a working man's candidate at the 1870 municipal election.[29]

There were a number of influences present in the comparative success of working men's building societies in Edinburgh. Among them was the strong tradition of co-operation in the city. St Cuthbert's Co-operative Society was formed in 1859 and five other societies began in the next few years, while the Manchester c.w.s. was not established until 1863. The Scottish c.w.s., Glasgow, followed in 1868 and Manchester and Glasgow combined to form the Co-operative Permanent Building Society. The advantages of co-operative building societies were much extolled in the evidence to the Royal Commission of 1884 but there were then said to be successful societies worthy of imitation only in Leeds and Manchester. A branch for London was then being discussed.[30]

It should be noticed that building societies other than these working people's co-operative ventures were no more successful in Edinburgh than elsewhere. The Property Investment Association found that those few workers who used its resources usually sold their property on completion of payments, and bought inferior houses to live in themselves.[31]

The difficulties in the way of working-class membership of building societies were, and remained, enormous. They were not only financial. Although the permanent societies undoubtedly did offer help and encouragement to working-class members, their whole administrative set-up made approach by poor people difficult. The small scale of the terminating societies made administration by workers possible. The permanent societies, governed by legal considerations and beset by clerical work, were necessarily involved in dealings with lawyers and bankers which meant that administration had to be in the hands of men with more education, more time, and, more social confidence than the average working man could boast. The system of sanitary improvement which depended upon complaints from those affected had proved unworkable because the people most affected were too slow to broach awe-inspiring council offices to complain. In the same way the permanent societies' meeting places and premises were less welcoming to working men than the pubs in which the terminating societies commonly met. Building-society meetings on licensed premises had been sociable affairs. 'The working classes generally take an interest in attending the meetings for conversation and to see what is going on.' Three pence per share for refreshments was paid at the beginning of the meeting, but, while the atmosphere was convivial, there was not much drunkenness. The kind of man who joined a building society was bound to be reasonably steady and temperate even if he did 'take a glass' with his friends.[32] The new permanent societies, however, partly in an attempt to discourage intemperance, partly to raise their social status and financial respectability in the eyes of middle-class investors, met in mechanics institutes, which attracted only the superior artisan, or in non-conformist church halls.[33] This change not only made working-class approach more difficult, it struck at the working-class culture in which the original idea of the building society had its roots. It put the cold, sober, empty hall above the warm and noisy pub. In Oldham, where genuine working-class membership was very high (mill hands from Platts making the majority), attempts to change the meeting place to a Temperance Hall failed completely: 'It would not take.'[34] In other towns the change was made and the working-class membership lost.

In 1871 a Royal Commission into the State of the Law relating to Friendly Societies and Benefit Societies considered the allegation often made by the witnesses it called that, while the permanent societies were much better managed than most of the terminating societies had been, they had 'altogether changed the character and altered the sphere of the building-society movement; and that it tends to throw this more and more under the direction and into the hands of the middle classes and to secure to them its benefits'.[35] The commissioners found the evidence on the subject very contradictory. There were claims that in Birmingham 95 per cent of the membership was working-class, that in the North of England generally, in Oldham, Sheffield, Leeds, and in some of the Liverpool societies, working people formed the bulk of the membership. There were counter claims that few working people joined the permanent societies, that in Newcastle the working classes played very little part in the movement, that in London they formed a minority of the membership.[36] The conclusion of the commissioners was that, taking Britain as a whole, in 1871 the middle classes played a bigger part in the building-society movement than the working class for whom it was designed. Some of the contradictions can be explained by individual differences in the definition of working class. In Liverpool, for instance, one building-society director who claimed that most of his members were 'labouring men', 'the humbler classes', then elucidated further that they were 'policemen, people in the Post Office and Customs',[37] In Birmingham, where 95 per cent were said to be working class, they were later described as the sort of people who normally paid 3s 9d or 4s a week in rent. 'Those who live in houses much below that do not belong to us, they belong to a public house.'[38] The weight of evidence seems to suggest what one would expect, that the artisan élite benefited from the re-shaping of the building society movement, using it both as a way to finding a good house and as a safe investment for savings, but for the bulk of the working class of Britain the middle-class takeover shut them out. It was suggested at the time of the Commission that the more and more frequent large advances by building societies to middle-class members did in fact benefit the working classes by making the investment of their money safer. While this is possibly true it is irrelevant to our present study. Building societies were becoming better places for working-class savings but providing for them a smaller chance of becoming house-owners.

Chapter 18

Freehold Land Societies

'What we need is a place where the dream can meet with reality'
DOXIADIS

Freehold land and building societies had perhaps more immediate success in attracting working-class support. The reason lay in their political commitment. Bound up with the whole idea of raising the working man from his slum-dwelling slough to a moral independence based on political strength, the freehold societies originally advocated house-owning chiefly as a step towards enfranchisement. If the only way a working man could earn a vote was by becoming owner of a £10 house, then the means to make him an owner had to be found. The fact that, in the process, he should attain to comfortable living in wholesome surroundings was good, but incidental. The proof that improvement in living standards was not the chief aim of these societies lay in the shoddiness of the building they indulged in.[1] The chief thing was the vote. If jerry-building brought it closer, then jerry-building was forgivable. It was a point of view quite understandable when reformers in Parliament and out felt working against them the weight of an illiberal, property-owning electorate from which both the labourer and his interest were excluded by his lack of property.

The Samuel Smiles attitude to property had a great attraction for the society which feared the 'have-nots' and suspected that they were made more dangerous by their lack of material possessions, They had too little to lose. Smiles preached the advantages of land and building societies to the National Association for Promoting Social Science in September 1864, but he was only giving a clear voice to a feeling that had been growing increasingly common: 'The accumulation of property has the effect which it always has upon thrifty men—it makes them steady, sober and diligent. It weans them from revolutionary notions and makes them conservative.' When every one has a house 'it will no longer be possible to make political capital out of imaginary woes.'

While the freehold land movement as a whole had always the same basic aim, the extension of the franchise, it had at least three separate manifestations, attracting different degrees of attention from the established electorate, and different kinds of support. The first wave of interest in the idea followed the Reform Act, 1832, which, by giving a country vote to the forty-shilling freeholder, encouraged the founding of building clubs. The agricultural depression, the move to the towns, and, especially, the lack of freehold land in the countryside, brought disillusion. A few groups of houses, huddled on marginal land, were the only visible results. However, the important political consequences of widespread working-class house-ownership were well recognised. The first wave of interest was part of the attempt to revivify Chartism after the despair of the great petition, the second wave formed part of the prelude to democracy working up to the 1867 Reform Act.

Fergus O'Connor's Chartist Land Company, dreamed up in 1843, aroused more hopes in the working classes of Britain and more antipathy in the middle classes than any other housing movement. 60,000 working men bought shares in the company between 1844 and 1847, buying with their 26s hope not only of a home but of complete removal from their present environment, a state of independence, and a vote. O'Connor offered not only houses but land which would support a family without wage-earning. His alienation from the main stream of Chartism taught him to seek a new way of gaining influence for himself and political power for the masses. Having chosen settlement on the land as the most opportune means to mass enfranchisement he then made it his faith and his creed. He lectured and wrote and persuaded with such dream-inducing conviction that thousands of slum-dwelling workers who attended his meetings and read his articles in the *Northern Star* caught his faith like an infection. He was giving them, after all, a dream in which they wanted to believe, the dream that they could be extracted from their present miserable situation without any real effort or planning on their own behalf except a small, temporary, sacrifice of earnings. They were to be wafted away from cruel masters, daily drudgery, dismal streets, by the purchase of a share which could be paid for in instalments of as little as 3d a week.

And, of course, for some of them, it worked, and the villages of O'Connorville, Lawbands, Charterville, Snigs End and Great Bodford are still there to prove it.

Very poor people were indeed rescued from the city, some even from the poor-house itself, and given a new start in the country with a three-roomed cottage, a work-shop and pigsty, a sum of money to begin the new life, and a piece of land sufficient to make them self-supporting. But only a few of the many thousands who bought shares were, or ever could have been, rehoused by O'Connor's scheme. Houses were allotted to the winners of regular ballots, but ticket holders forgot that their share bought them not a house, but only a chance of a house. For many the gamble involved was perhaps an attraction, not committing them too drastically to a changed way of life, not demanding too much involvement in an effort to improve. For others the chance itself must have been an incentive to keep on living in a world which offered little in the way of chance or hope. But for most the crashing reality that after the ballot their chance, and their money, had gone, brought terrible disillusion.

It was because they were sensitive to the disillusion and despair which seemed bound to overtake most of O'Connor's followers that Parliament, social reformers and radicals were united in antipathy to his scheme. The lack of any sound basis of organisation for his company, the wild irregularity of its financing and administration, and its complete dependence on the personality of its leader for its success earned it general disapproval. O'Connor's refusal to be subjected to inspection, or even to criticism or advice, made it impossible for his company to be registered as a Friendly Society or as a joint-stock company, and without such registration his members had no protection of their interests from mismanagement or dishonesty. In fact, considering the scale of the opportunity for embezzlement or a little quiet profit-making on the side, the personal honesty with which the scheme was conducted was admirable. O'Connor, while he gained fame and temporary influence, certainly did nothing for his pocket by the enterprise.[2] But the mismanagement and lack of understanding of business affairs was catastrophic. It allied the genuine reformers who mistrusted the demagoguery, the form and the method of this particular enterprise with all those who disliked any attempt to organise the power dormant in the masses of working people for any purpose whatever. Individual self-help was praiseworthy and to be encouraged. Attempts at mass self-help threatened the established order, smacked of 'democracy', gave a taste of power to those whom it could only corrupt. O'Connor's land scheme not only failed to rehouse more than a tiny minority of those to whom it held out promise, but also it increased, by its failure, the workers' apathetic acceptance of the inevitability of their plight, so that they were loath again to put their money or their trust in other societies' schemes for their betterment; and it earned the hatred of a large portion of the middle class for all philanthropic housing schemes which could not be shown to have the honest, trustworthy, easily understood motive of profit-making. James Taylor's quite differently organised freehold society, was at a disadvantage from the start because of its association in the public mind with the O'Connor scandal.

It was true that the initiative and energy which had gone to the organising of the terminating building societies in the first half of the century had been the same initiative and energy, springing from the same self-respect, the same belief in the rights of the working man, which had attempted to work for political change. Because some of the 'Friendlies' had been used as a cover for Jacobinism and forbidden trade-union activity there was a section of middle-class opinion which continued to see in all workers' organisations the germ of revolution.[3] Only when most of that initiative and energy had been either suppressed by the worsening economic situation or re-directed into more acceptable channels did middle-class support become widest for societies aiming at house-ownership by working people. In this context O'Connor's open association of land and housing reform with Chartism was unfortunate.

The early building societies, organised by working people for working people, had been evidence of a genuine working-class culture. James Taylor's whole campaign for his freehold land society depended on dissociation from that sub-culture. It was not by chance that the society had its beginnings in Birmingham, which, although it had its slums, did not have a housing problem to match that of other industrial cities, where the skilled artisan class was numerous and still influential, and where the Christian Chartists and the middle-class campaigners for political reform had settled their differences. Joseph Sturge's Complete Suffrage Union had already succeeded in making the extension of the franchise a well-supported issue in the town before Taylor took up the cause. Taylor had only to make his society respectable to have it accepted. His own background as a non-conformist preacher and an evangelist for temperance and self-help, was impeccable. By stressing the moral improvement in the working class which was bound to follow the improvement of their living conditions he gained the acceptance of the non-conformist, Liberal manufacturers of Birmingham.[4] It was clearly in their interest that the much discussed degeneration of the workers should be halted and their moral improvement by some means begun. It seemed certain that only the most superior of the working men would, in any case, aspire to become members of the society, and equally certain that, should any less desirable slip through, they would be raised to a superior status by their new condition. 'There can, we think, be *no* question as to the amount of intelligence and forethought possessed by the man who has accomplished this act of prudence.'[5] There was, it followed, not too much danger in the extension of the franchise to working men of this superior type who would then, inevitably in view of the good sense they had already displayed, become Liberal voters. This, of course, was open to some doubt as the later creation of the Conservative Land Society, with the same declared principles but a different political persuasion, demonstrated. There is no evidence that house-ownership in itself made a man a Conservative or a Liberal any more than membership of yet another society, the Temperance Building Society, could make him an abstainer if his inclinations ran the other way.

Taylor was instrumental in forming six separate freehold land societies in Birmingham having between them 14,973 members. At the same time the National Freehold Land Society was formed. Because it was registered under the Benefit Building Societies Act, it ran into the problem which, because he refused to face it, began disaster for O'Connor's society: the Act did not allow the purchase of land. But where O'Connor had simply dodged the issue, Taylor made a strength out of the need to meet it. A new associate company, the British Land Company, was formed to buy and sell land and prepare if for building, while the Freehold Land Society received deposits and organised loans. It was a profitable arrangement. The original society succeeded in paying a steady 5 per cent, the Land Company a warming 15 per cent. And it was reassuring to investors that 'both company and society conduct the business on strict commercial principles, not a particle of philanthropy is mixed up with the business of either.'[6]

Within Birmingham itself, while it seems likely that in the earliest stages there was a proportion of working-class members, the later insistence on a minimum value for properties erected with society help soon ensured that the movement housed only the artisan élite. Some of the first owners had built 'in an irregular and reckless manner', probably very cheaply, but from about 1855 the houses built in Birmingham by society members were substantial terraced villas, with considerable garden ground, in areas of the city whose very exclusiveness might have been expected to discourage working-class aspirations even if money had played no part.[7]

In the country as a whole, however, the freehold land movement, if it did not directly provide housing for those most in need, gave hope and direction again to those who campaigned for housing reform. It aroused great interest both in the working class itself and among those who tried to influence it. Taylor himself, and Thomas Beggs, a fellow crusader, lectured at meetings throughout the country and aroused a long-lasting interest in the subject. In Sheffield a 'Reform Freehold Land Society' was formed on the Birmingham model in 1849 and resulted in the building of two low-cost housing estates with 258 members. Another Sheffield venture, the Walkley Land and Building Society, formed in January 1849, succeeded in building a workman's garden suburb with 3,000 freeholders, of whom the great majority were working-class. Their district became known as the 'Working Man's West End'.[8]

In London, the London and Metropolitan Benefit Building and Investment Society was formed in 1848, its aims chiefly political.[9]

By 1871, however, the working class made up only a minority of its membership, and its aims had become purely commercial.[10]

The Conservative Land Society had so much success in creating freeholders that its purchases soon extended to twenty-six counties, and it may be indicative of its flagging enthusiasm for playing politics that its name was then changed to the United Land Company.[11]

Land societies in towns outside Birmingham seem not to have completely understood Taylor's system of using two separate but complementary companies, one to buy land, the other to make loans for building. In many cases land societies registered, quite illegally, as building societies, apparently not entirely aware of the risks they ran of prosecution and dissolution.[12] This made easier the final merger of the whole freehold land movement with the building society movement.

The separate steps were, first, the forgetting of political considerations in the rush of commercial success; next the passing of the Joint Stock Companies Act in 1856, which, by making it possible for building societies themselves to purchase land, ended the necessity for separate land societies; third, the passing of the 1867 Reform Act which, by giving the vote to most of the urban male working class, took away the chief purpose of the freehold-creating societies.

From 1871 the movements were entirely merged, the political character lost, and their membership weighted by middle-class interests. Although in Birmingham at least, the societies could say 'we have created a great love for freeholds' and 'we are the greatest social reformers of the day', it was not by this means that the bulk of the working class in need were to be housed.[13]

Chapter 19

The Philanthropic Housing Associations: I
Octavia Hill and the Lady Collectors

'Lectures and a little charity'
WALT WHITMAN

We have seen that, by the middle of the nineteenth century, a new awareness of poverty was disturbing the middle classes. Slums lay so close to the commercial districts of most big towns that few men could reach their own place of business without passing miserable people waiting in the entrance archways to filthy courts and yards. The true extent of the misery hidden behind the respectable façades of shops and offices was barely known to the average passer-by, but inklings of it reached them not only through what their eyes could see of dirt and raggedness, but through the clamour for charity that stretched towards them through their churches. Alms-giving had so long and firm a tradition in British society that it came easily and automatically to most families to subscribe, in one form or another, to the maintenance of the poor. The idea that the threat that lay in the existence of so large a body of destitute people might be removed by a change in society which diminished the numbers of poor nagged at the Victorians but did not convince them. For most it was an accepted tenet that the burden of the poor was one which would always have to be borne by the superior classes. The middle of the century began to see a willingness to do more than subscribe. The Victorians, not all of them of course, not even most of them, but a large and influential number of them, began to feel a need for active participation in a campaign to relieve poverty. Business men who would once have felt satisfied in their consciences to contribute a sum of money, now were prepared to serve on committees. Young ladies who once would have passed on their second-hand clothes, sewed for their church bazaars, or carried round bowls of broth to the families of indigent servants, now felt a need to train themselves for real social work. There began to be preparedness to probe the sore, to see the worst, to enter in a spirit of helpfulness the worst of those back alleys.

It was in this spirit that Octavia Hill cajoled a large sum of money out of her friend John Ruskin and set up as a housing manager of cheap property in a poor London district. Her certainty that the poor needed example, tuition, inspiration and guidance in their everyday lives more than they needed charity drove her to spend her time in houses 'in a dreadful state of dirt and neglect, where the place swarmed with vermin, the papers, black with dirt, hung in long strips from the walls; the drains were stopped, the water supply out of order.' It led her to watch, guide and manage people in despair until they began to pick up hope, to sweep their floors, wash their children and pay their rent. This enviable Victorian certainty about what was right gave Miss Hill and others like her the strength to go among the poor without catching their despair, to insist on their self-improvement without becoming discouraged, to display her own behaviour, with the whole background of culture which induced it, as undoubtedly right, undoubtedly superior. Because she knew what was best for them she raised a number of London slum dwellers to respectability and a degree of comfort. The number of houses improved by her management, and the number of families led to a better way of life by her guidance, was not large. She worked as an individual and could effect only what was within an individual's power.

Her influence on middle-class opinion, however, was very considerable. She brought proof to bear against the most dispiriting arguments for inaction. She proved that the practical considerations against slum improvement were not insurmountable. The property could be bought, the changes necessary for its improvement were neither technically difficult nor even very expensive, the tenants could be made to pay their rents so that each scheme could become not only self-supporting but mildly profitable. She proved that moral argument could equally well be met with the example of her experience: the slum dwellers were not irredeemable. Money spent on house-improvement on their behalf was not charity flung down the drain. They could, with watchfulness and determination, be raised not only to a better way of living but to a better opinion of themselves. They would not necessarily destroy their new amenities, foul their new surroundings, and sneer at their benefactors as many feared, nor would they learn to batten upon those who helped them, demanding more and more charity in return for less and less self-help. Given the constant shining example of a Christian lady they could, and did, become self-respecting citizens.

One of Octavia Hill's great virtues was patience. She did not expect to rehouse London, only to show on a small scale what could be done. She hoped that many like her, working in the same small patient way, would eventually transform cities into places fit even for the poor to live in. She did not aim at wholesale transformation scenes. Because her eyes were open to the effect of clearance schemes on overcrowding she did not believe in pulling down houses in order to rebuild others. She set out only to redeem structurally sound houses which were deteriorating through neglect. Her repairs were 'mainly of a superficial and slight character; slight in regard to expense—vital as to health and comfort'.[1] They amounted chiefly to cleaning and mending. She was liberal with soap and white-wash. She had existing drains cleared and trapped, but seldom built new ones. She had water-butts and cisterns mended and replaced, but did not attempt to bring in piped water. She advised the Royal Commission of 1885 that it was unnecessary and unwise for the larger housing associations to spend as much as they did: one tap per floor was quite sufficient.[2] In her own property she made sure that water was clean and available. A certain amount of effort in fetching it was not to be deplored. Wood-work, grates and windows were repaired where necessary and back-courts flagged with evenly laid paving stones. This last was most necessary to make cleanliness possible. The foulness of the unpaved, muddy, sewage-laden back-courts was a feature most frequently commented on as making house-cleaning impossible for slum-dwellers. Beyond these improvements she did not go until she saw signs of a genuine demand for better things in a willingness to pay higher rents.

Her rules for management included regular rent-paying, and the maintenance of the standard of cleanliness set at the beginning of the tenancy. In every case she found, when she took possession of old property, that huge arrears of rent had been tolerated, arrears which made it impossible for the tenant ever to escape from the trap of debt and equally impossible for the landlord to profit from his property. Her insistence that not one week's grace in rent paying must ever be allowed proved in itself sufficient to ensure a steady return of 5 per cent interest on capital invested. Arrears were not in anybody's interest, but only the constant vigilance of a lady collector could ensure that they were not allowed.

Miss Hill had, in some ways, a sophisticated understanding of the possibilities of community interest and corporate life, in others she accepted the Victorian view of the necessity for a paternal relationship between the people and their middle-class guides. She believed that 'the spiritual elevation of a large class depended to a considerable extent on sanitary reform . . . that sanitary improvement itself depended upon educational work among grown-up people . . . that any lady would soon find them eager to learn her view of what was best for them'.[3] She placed her own unshakable conviction of what was best for them up against the listless uncertainty of slum dwellers and it is hardly surprising that her tenants fell into her way of thinking.

Her influence produced a flow of lady visitors and rent-collectors whose kindness, understanding and firmness must have had some effect on the districts under their management. We can learn how the lady visitors themselves felt about their work, how those less certain than Miss Hill, because they came later in the century and saw how little had been achieved, grew anxious for government action instead of individual effort. Beatrice Webb wrote of her predecessors' 'calm assumption of social and mental superiority over the poor whom they visited' and of Octavia Hill's 'exaggerated cordiality'.[4] We cannot know, because they leave no written record how those tenants felt whose homes were managed and whose rents were collected by these earnest ladies. Did they indeed look up to them as shining examples, did they aspire to model themselves upon their precepts? Or did they resent their interference, clean the front door step, pay the rent and swear at their departing bustles? It must have depended very much on the individual lady, the individual tenant, the individual district in which the managed property lay. The small-scale housing improvement scheme modelled upon Miss Hill's ideas was inevitably dependent upon the character of individuals, and inevitably it failed to effect any noticeable change in the standard of housing of working people as a whole.

We are now much less certain that it is a good thing, or a wise one, to attempt to impose the values of one class upon another. Those neighbouring tenants of slum clearance schemes who found room in their own full houses for the people evicted by improvements were giving evidence of values other than middle-class ones. They were putting neighbourliness, the shelter of homeless friends and relations before space, cleanliness and ventilation. Those whole streets of citizens who created minor riots and mobbed the factor when he came to evict tenants in arrears through unemployment were putting sympathy for friends above respect for property. These incidents display values different from those of the middle classes but not necessarily inferior. What Miss Hill and her followers taught was that respect for other people's property and payment of debts due to people of property must come before other considerations. Those who could not accept this different scale of values were not accepted as tenants by Miss Hill or by most of the other philanthropists. But they had to have homes of sorts and so those who were resistant to the effect of middle-class influence were those who continued to cause overcrowding by their insistence on remaining in the centre of their own communities, in touch with their own culture, unpatronised and unhelped.

If Octavia Hill's influence on those she hoped to improve was perhaps less than she hoped, her influence on her own kind was important and widespread. Her faith, her example, her power as a teacher, above all her practical approach affected not only young women from all over the country who wanted to do something useful with their lives, but also men as hard-headed as the Ecclesiastical Commissioners. Her practice was to allow young women who came to her for training to work with her in London, going about her daily round with her, taking over small tasks, learning to administer small properties. Those who did not fall by the wayside, and it was a tough enough path for a gently-reared girl, went on to manage new housing companies, either in London or in the provinces. Among them were Lily Walker, who became a founder of Dundee Social Union and manager of its housing properties, Emma Cons who later managed Surrey Buildings for the South London Building Company, whom Beatrice Webb described as 'not a lady by birth, (but) with the face and manner of a distinguished woman',[5] Beatrice Webb herself and her sister Kate Potter, and Ella Pycroft, who managed for the East End Dwelling Company. The remarkable result was, that, when by her work, by her journalism and by her personal influence on important men,[6] Octavia Hill had succeeded in persuading others to follow her in providing improved housing for the poor, there was a fund of trained and dedicated women ready to manage the new properties. Perhaps many of these social workers could be blamed for their lack of sensitivity towards the customs of the poor. But in the absence of any large body of trained, professional, caring social workers it was, to say the least, convenient that Miss Hill's followers existed and were willing. It could be argued that they held up social advance by giving government an excuse for not providing and training state-paid social workers, but there is no evidence that, in the absence of Miss Hill, anything but a vacuum would have been left.

The long-lease system on which much of London was let by its great estate owners ensured, in the last quarter of the century, that much of the slum property which had for some fifty to eighty years been allowed to moulder profitably in the hands of middle-men, fell to be recovered by the proprietors. This drew attention to its condition. In the climate of social criticism then existing it was an embarrassment for men in the public eye to be responsible for such acres of decaying property and their wish to demolish it, clear it away or at least improve it began to have an effect on the appearance of London. Among the large land-owners to whom considerables acres of slum property now fell due were the Ecclesiastical Commissioners who began to be uncomfortably criticised for the dilapidated condition of their houses and the misery of their tenants.[7] Their remedy was to ask for Octavia Hill's help in the improvement and management of their poorer properties. In this way she found herself in charge of from 5,000 to 6,000 houses. These were formed into groups, to be managed, as she had managed her first three courts of houses, with individual care and attention by ladies trained in her methods. Beatrice Webb gives in *My Apprenticeship* a detailed description of the day-to-day work, duties and doubts, of a lady rent-collector.

Octavia Hill was neither the first nor the last to attempt the improvement of the housing of the poor as a charitable enterprise. But very many of those who came before her found it impossible to survive and all those who came after her were affected by her example.[8] One of the housing associations which preceded her and had some success was the Hastings Cottage Improvement Society. It resulted from the publication of a plan by the Rev. Canon Girdlestone, the well-known sanitary reformer, who suggested, at a time when most reformers were more enthusiastic about sweeping away every last vestige of the old slums, that it was more practicable to renovate old cottages than to build new.

The available money would be made to go further, the speed with which property could be made ready would be greater, and the poorer type of tenant, the one who could not afford to leave his own district, would be more easily reached.

In 1857 a committee of Hastings' gentlemen led by Dr Greenhill started a society with a capital of only £850. It was their policy to buy very bad property because, they reported, that way they could hardly fail to show an improvement and to make a profit. They met criticism because their initials, C.I.H.S., were flaunted on such dilapidated walls, but their policy was successful in housing a much poorer class of tenant than most and in steadily returning a rate of between 5 and 6 per cent to their investors: their plan was 'most directly charitable, not in the eleemosynary [sic] sense of the word, but most distinctly charitable and, I may say, religious; but we made it a matter of duty that it was to succeed and be commercial.' By 1884 their £850 initial capital had multiplied to £30,000, they owned 250 houses and housed about 1,000 people. Like Miss Hill, they did not aim to do much more than put old houses in a decent state of repair and cleanliness and then to institute good, fair and efficient management. They did not introduce new amenities but simply made the old basic arrangements function properly. In this way they soon found themselves in a position to re-build three or four houses at a loss each year without affecting their profitability.

The Hastings society certainly aimed at housing those most in need and had no illusions about where the need lay. 'We never built for a class that could take care of themselves. We wished to reach the lowest and that is what we have done.' However their lowest rent was 2s a room per week and there were only a dozen let at that rate. Large families, then, and large families necessarily make up the largest number of those in need, should have paid between 6s and 10s a week for adequate space.

We have seen already that for too many people this would amount to almost 50 per cent of their income, leaving nothing like enough for food, and boots, and fuel. But there was another factor working against the offering of houses to the 'lowest' class of tenant. The committee were beset by the usual Victorian notion that to be deserving it was necessary to be respectable. When slum property was bought, existing tenants were told: 'If you like to stop here and behave properly and quietly and cleanly and not be a scandal and a disgrace, you may; if not, you had better go. It generally ends in their going . . . .. As soon as they are out we renovate . . . then, when that is done, we would not take in any but respectable people.'[9] The trouble, again, was that the less respectable must also find houses. If they cannot find decent houses they will crowd into bad ones, their presence will continue to cause town deterioration until their need to be accepted without character reformation is eventually recognised.

Following Octavia Hill's example, in 1884 a very interesting group of young intellectuals, teachers in the new University College in Dundee, started Dundee Social Union. Dundee had then an infant mortality rate worse than that of London, Glasgow and Liverpool: one child in every two died before it was a year old, four out of every five died before reaching 3 years of age. One of the new young professors brought North in the 1880s to this jute town, where the average wage for men was 16s a week and very many households were supported by women earning much less, was Alfred Ewing, who had worked under Fleeming Jenkin, founder of Edinburgh's Sanitary Association. Another was D'Arcy Wentworth Thomson who had worked with Canon Barnett in Cambridge. Through their academic walk of life these two, and a group of others, had been in contact with a more liberal attitude to the poor than was common in Scottish mill towns. One of their first acts on behalf of the Dundee Social Union was to buy up four small slum properties, adding to the number as they gained experience. Their problem was not to be sure they reached the poorest—the population was so overwhelmingly poor that it would be difficult to avoid them. But, because these men were scientists they looked upon the venture as an experiment, one from which they, themselves, could learn. It was a humble enough attitude, and, of course, incidentally, a number of families were introduced by it to a better way of living. But the attack was never commercial, the Union waned in importance as its brighter stars moved to posts of academic distinction elsewhere, and the scale of Dundee's housing problem was too great to be much affected by such individual effort. The importance of such attempts was their effect on official opinion. Dundee Social Union's reports certainly played an important part in showing town councillors and corporation officials why it was necessary for their town to take notice of the new housing legislation going unsteadily through Parliament, and in educating planners about the provision it would be necessary to make for the rehousing of slum dwellers.[10]

Chapter 20

The Philanthropic Housing Associations: II
The Model Dwellings Associations

'A minimum of schooling, a minimum of rest, a minimum of
cleanliness, a minimum of shelter, a grey pall of negative virtue
hung over the urban improvements of the period'
LEWIS MUMFORD

Concurrently with Octavia Hill's quiet work the larger-scale model
dwellings associations were setting about the business of housing the
poor much more noticeably. With a mixture of philanthropy and commercial optimism they hoped to show that model housing for the poor
could be built and rented while showing a respectable return on capital
invested. They led people and Parliament to believe that private enterprise, efficiently directed, could deal with the problems of unsanitary
housing, homelessness, and overcrowding, and perhaps held up the
progress towards state-controlled housing for decades by encouraging
that ill-founded belief. Each one of the associations, with varying degrees of reluctance, had to give up its original aim of housing the very
poor. Those which survive, as some of them still do, into the present
day do so by radical changes in their character. All of them together
made no real difference to the housing needs of the nation. Yet they
attracted attention in their day and deserve attention now. Their importance lies in their pioneering work on cost-related problems of
design, function and need. They came in on the tide of the sanitary
idea. The were called *model* dwellings because it was the intention of
those who caused them to be built that they should serve as a model of
the way regular water supply, adequate sewage disposal and proper
ventilation could be provided at low cost for low wage-earners. And,
in fact, their standard of amenity was very high for their day. The
earliest had not only sinks with constant water, inside water-closets for
each house, but dust-shafts for the removal of rubbish and ashes as
well. Some had gas-lighting, some had built-in ovens, ventilated meat-
safes, excellent cupboard space. They were not only more comfortable
houses than working-class people were used to, but a good deal better
than most of the lower middle class could find in big towns, and this
proved to be the downfall of their aim to house the neediest, because
there was always a more enterprising number of superior workers
ready to fill them and better able to pay for them.
  They are very significant in the history of urban architecture not,

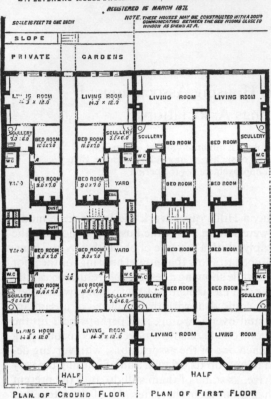

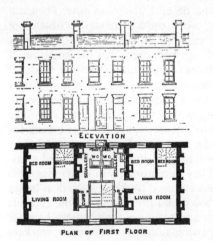

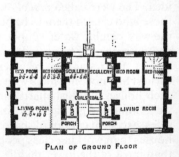

6. Plans for model dwellings for the industrial classes, 1871. The architect, Banister Fletcher, wrote that 'a proper economy has prevented the introduction of any expenditure and unnecessary embellishments'. The *Builder* thought the plan had some blemishes

regrettably, because they achieved any great distinction in exterior design, but because, from the start, they admitted the importance of design as a factor influencing the behaviour and attitudes of the occupants. The directors of the model dwellings associations were interested in the appearance of their buildings, recognising that it could affect the morale of their tenants, as well as in the functional quality of the design. They were right to suppose that the outward appearance of their buildings would be of interest even to those of the poor who were extricated from the most disgusting piles of slimy slum masonry. They were wrong to expect that it would meet with approval, for contemporaries universally condemned the street façades of the buildings. It was one of the few aspects of their housing on which the poor made their voices heard, and in every case it was to decry the barrack-like, Bastille-like, grim and unadorned façades of the model dwellings. They looked too much like the dreaded work-houses for comfort. 'There is not a working man in Glasgow but would turn up his nose at every such building in London',[1] wrote one Scottish minister considering the introduction of similar schemes to his own city. 'The working classes will never look upon a set of rooms in a great building in the light of a home'[2], was the summing-up by Her Majesty's Commissioners of a great deal of evidence about the dislike of the poor for model dwellings. The *Daily Telegraph* explained working-class dislike of the buildings: 'A small fault in the first buildings designed for the benefit of the labouring classes was a certain plainness, which, taken in connection with their designation of "model" was apt to associate them disagreeably with "model" work-houses and "model" prisons.'[3]

The middle classes were no happier about the design. George Godwin, editor of *The Builder*, professed his 'worst anticipations confirmed. The arrangement is a disgrace to the Society.'[4] Canon Barnett was sarcastically disapproving: 'Benevolence has had much to do with the erection of dwellings in the neighbourhood, and in the name of benevolence, so as to encourage benevolence, some argue that decoration must be given up, so that such dwellings may be made to pay.'[5] Twentieth-century architects have been equally inclined to run down the design of the model dwellings. John Nelson Tarn, for instance, writes that 'design, as a creative skill, played no part in the considerations of nearly all the societies and companies at work before 1880'; and that the work of the housing organisation between 1880 and 1890 'added little to the overall philosophy of working-class housing design'.[6]

Still, the design of model dwellings is worth consideration for a number of reasons. The first is that it was a conscious expression of

the Victorian attitude to poverty, spare and grim because to be anything else might seem to be encouraging the poor to 'take advantage'.
Because the attitude to poverty changed and developed from one of
fear and distaste to one of conscious-stricken anxiety and conde-
scension, the style of the model dwellings changed too. Those built up
to the 1850s were plain and repetitive in design but had some architectural merit, some little dignity. Those built after 1860, because they
then, fearing the poor less, could afford to pander a little to notions of
their likes and dislikes, allowed a little decoration, a modicum of
Gothic extravagance. The slapped-on, tasteless decorative detail of
this period, is more offensive to modern taste than the plainness of the
earlier façades. Waterlow's five-storey flats in Mark Street, Finsbury,
are typical of the hypocritical attempt to make tenement blocks more
acceptable to working people by the addition of ornamental features
which were supposed to give gentility to flats chiefly characterised by
their meanness and gloom. To suppose that the builders of these blocks
did not care about design is to misunderstand their overall intention.
They had, especially in the later period, little understanding of design,
very little sensitivity towards it. But they believed that it was necessary
for slum dwellers not only to be housed but to be morally uplifted and
they believed that the buildings they were designing could have an
uplifting effect. An architect could hardly ask for greater trust from
his client than the belief that he can by his design improve moral
character.

A much more important aspect of design is the work done on the
functional planning of large high-rise blocks for multi-occupancy.
There was, in England at least, no tradition of flat dwelling. The
problems of construction and design of multi-storey blocks had
hardly been considered until the architects of the first model dwellings
began to study the ways in which low-cost housing could best be
provided. Even within cities 'cottages' were the rule, huddled together
in rows rather than built singly as they might be in the country, but
not noticeably different in design from rural cottages nevertheless.
In the North of England problems of low-cost housing had been over-
come by the introduction of back-to-backs, which, in Leeds with the
approval of the council and in other towns in spite of the Building
Regulations, continued to be built till late in the century to meet the
needs of the poor.[7] In Scotland, although it was only in the old town
of Edinburgh that very high flats, of nine and ten storeys, were usual,
speculative builders customarily built four- or five-storey blocks for
working-class occupancy.[8] Perhaps because of these already existing
traditions of planning for flat dwelling the model dwellings associations were much less successful in the provinces than within London,

VI. Homes of the London poor:
Wild Court, as seen from Great
Wild Street

VII. Homes of the London poor: front view of House No. 2 in Wild Court

where their approach to the problems of low-cost design was a new
one. The handling of access to the separate flats, their lighting and
ventilation, the provision of water and drainage to above-ground
storeys, were all design problems faced by the first model-dwellings
architects. The extent to which costs could be cut without dangerously
weakening walls and foundations was hardly known. Strengths of
materials, many of them new and little understood, had to be studied.
The design which resulted from study of these problems was not distinguished, but even in its failures it broke ground for those who came
afterwards.

Had the design of model dwellings had no other significance it
would have been important for the reaction to it which followed. The
general Victorian dislike of the barrack-like exteriors certainly played
a part in bringing about the romantic movement in housing reform
which took up the Garden City idea with such enthusiasm. The fact
that Britain is covered with spreading acres of semi-detached and
begardened suburban council houses can be attributed in part to the
contempt for grim façades that followed the era of model dwellings.
Nikolaus Pevsner is on record as suggesting that those 'grim and grimy
barracks of the poor . . . succeeded in destroying any chance for the
block of flats to become popular in England with the class for which
they could be such a blessing.'[9] Housing reformers came to believe
that every working man had a right to something as nearly approaching a country cottage as the state could afford to give him. Politicians
came to believe that working men and women, now enfranchised and
therefore necessarily worth courting, would accept nothing less. The
result was that real consideration of the design problems of high-rise
housing was postponed for more than half a century, until the pheno-
menal rise in the cost of land after the Second World War forced it
upon the town authorities. The whole delay cannot be blamed on the
model dwellings, but their design did nothing to persuade Englishmen
to accept flat dwelling as desirable.

There were, of course, factors other than the taste of their directors
affecting the design of the model dwellings. The marked difference
between their design in the first half of the century and in the second
was brought about partly by a difference in concept, more by the
difference in the circumstances they had to face. At all periods the essential was that the buildings should be made to pay: 'elymosynary'
considerations were not to be pushed too far. But the impulse behind
the original designs was, as we have seen, sanitary reform. The chief
aim was that the buildings should be clean and ventilated, fortresses
against infection. The inexperience of their designers and the over-
optimism of their directors, who imagined that 7 or 8 per cent could

8

be wrung out of property that was also well-built, well-spaced and well-provided with amenities, meant that the planning was small-scale and the buildings low-rise. Henry Roberts, the most famous architect of nineteenth-century working-class housing, was not quick to grasp the problems involved. His model houses at Lower Road, Pentonville, were no real advance on the old cottage rows. But his Streatham Street houses, still in existence, are aesthetically satisfying while still fulfilling his own requirements of preserving domestic privacy and preventing the communication of contagious disease. Forty-eight families were housed in a five-storey block built around a spacious interior quadrangle. Prince Albert wrote to him: 'Mr Roberts, unless we can get 7 to 8 per cent, we shall not succeed in inducing builders to invest their capital in such houses.'[10] By 1853, only two years after the exhibition of his model cottages at the Great Exhibition had been greeted by such high expectations of their chances of solving the housing problem, Roberts had left to live abroad, disillusioned. In 1856 he officially resigned as architect to the Society for Improving the Condition of the Labouring Classes, and in 1861 Prince Albert, whose interest had helped to keep optimism alive, passed on.

The impulse behind the design of the model dwellings of the next decades was the new consciousness of poverty. The intention to comfort that poverty by providing good cheap housing was perhaps more genuinely philanthropic, because less optimistic, than it had been in the 1840s. Nobody now expected that it would be easy to earn 7 per cent on his investment in housing the poor.[11] At the same time there was more determination that the houses should be made to pay. Directors were not going to risk being called 'socialists' or open themselves to the accusation that 'development of the system will involve the provision of comfortable accommodation for the criminal and immoral classes'.[12] There was a new grim determination to do good profitably which was quite different from the happy zeal of those who first evolved the model-dwellings idea. The grimness showed in the design. Increasing land costs forced buildings to go higher so that they could accommodate more families on one site. Rising costs of labour and materials meant shrinkage of the accommodation offered. Rooms became both smaller and fewer than those in the flats offered by the early societies. Where each flat in the early tenements had been given a sink, tap and water-closet of its own, the later flats had only one per floor. This was the direct result of Octavia Hill's testimony before the 1885 Commission: 'I should not carry the water and the drains all over the place; I think that is ridiculous. If you have water on every floor, that is quite sufficient for working people.'[13] Miss Hill's economies, to give her her due, sprang from her determination to put first

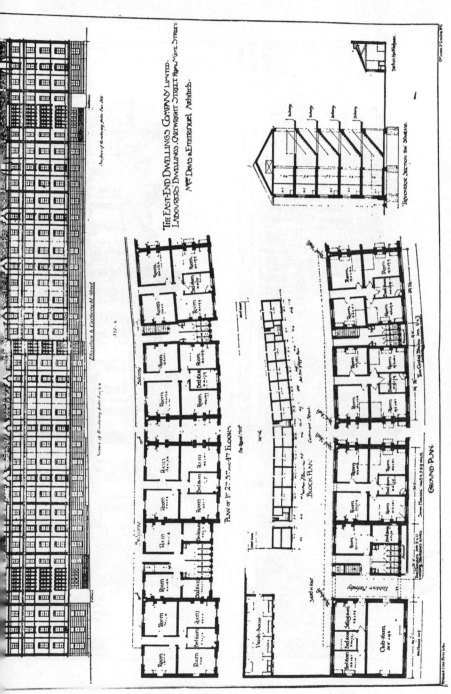

7. Labourers' dwellings, Cartwright Street: note the same staircase and closet facilities as St Katherine's buildings

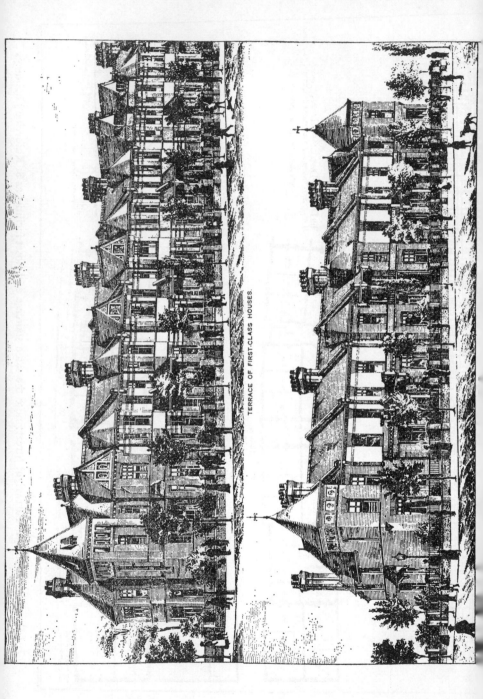

TERRACE OF FIRST-CLASS HOUSES.

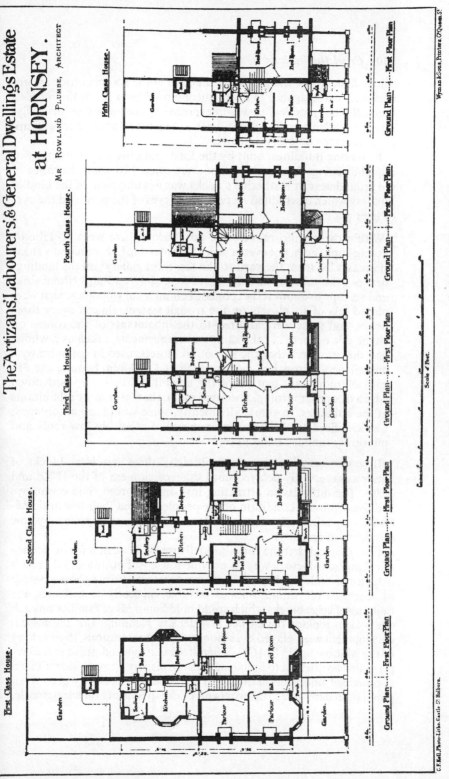

The Artizans, Labourers, & General Dwellings Estate at HORNSEY.

Mr Rowland Plumbe, Architect

First Class House.
Second Class House.
Third Class House.
Fourth Class House.
Fifth Class House.

Scale of Feet.

C.F. Kell, Photo-Litho Castle St Holborn.

Wyman & Sons, Printers O^s Queen S^t

9. The Artizans', Labourers' and General Dwellings Estate at Hornsey: plans

things first, to get the people housed, to allow no accusation of unnecessary extravagance to delay putting roofs over heads that needed them. But her practicality was interpreted by the more commercially-minded gentlemen who followed her as a recommendation for scrimping and saving on every amenity.

Katherine Buildings, built by the East End Dwellings Company as model dwellings for the dock labourers evicted by slum clearance of the ground near St Katherine's docks was not untypical of the kind of building which discredited its type in the eyes of the poor and the eyes of later planners:

'Within these uniform, cell-like apartments there were no labour-saving appliances, not even a sink and water-tap! Three narrow stone staircases led from the yard to the top-most gallery; on the landings between the galleries and the stairs were sinks and taps (three sinks and six taps to about sixty rooms); behind a tall wooden screen were placed sets of six closets on the trough system, sluiced every three hours, and these were allotted to the inhabitants of the rooms on either side of them . . . the sanitary arrangements, taken as a whole, had the drawback that the sets of six closets, used in common by a miscellaneous crowd of men, women and children, became the obtrusively dominant feature of the several staircases, up and down which trooped, morning, noon and night, the 600 or more inhabitants of the buildings. In short, all amenity, some would say all decency, was sacrificed to the two requirements of relatively low rents and physically sanitary buildings.'[14]

It was unfortunate that the building of these very large blocks of flats was necessarily delayed until the recession era of the 1870s and 1880s. The difficulty in attracting investment forced rigid economy; and the depressed condition of the people allowed their low anticipation to be taken advantage of: low demand was supplied by low standards of amenity.

It was logical that the early 'model' architects' search for an economical and satisfactory way to provide low-cost housing should result in high-rise building. Especially where it was necessary to house people as near their old slum homes as possible, on costly central sites, the building of large blocks which could hold hundreds of families on each site had to replace the earlier low density planning. But the logical development was delayed by, among other considerations, the working of the window tax.[15] In 1687, when it was introduced, this tax had represented an attempt to limit ostentatious display by mansion builders. It remained unobjectionable until the nineteenth-century growth of population demanded the provision of cheap housing on a large scale.

Then the limitation it imposed on the number of windows to each house prevented the cheap building of blocks of tenements. The iron galleries and wide open staircases of the early model dwellings, giving separate access to each flat, were designed to prove that the blocks contained numbers of completely independent houses. Without the galleries the block would be regarded, for the purposes of the window tax, as one dwelling, and its windows taxed accordingly. The additional space required for these extra features, as well as the materials involved, added considerably to the cost, although they did, in fact, add architectural interest to the façades when they were carefully handled. In the model houses for families in Streatham Street, Bloomsbury, by Henry Roberts, the iron-work galleries are interestingly detailed and give a character lacking in the later, unrelieved façades. In Scotland, of course, the traditional way to build, dictated by the cheapness of the local stone, was with outside stone staircases and access 'pletties' or platforms, and this did not change until the introduction of the modern multi-storey flats with lift access.[16]

In London the abolition of the window tax allowed for the first time the development of large-scale blocks of flats, economically planned. The era of the Peabody Buildings, called by Nikolaus Pevsner 'truly humanitarian in its pretentions, yet depressing in its results', was an era of monotony dictated by economy. The choice before the societies was to build high within the city where land was dear and getting dearer, or to build schemes of low-density cottages in the suburbs. Both were tried, the Peabody Trust and Waterlow's Industrial Dwellings building high central blocks until after 1900 and the Artisans pioneering suburban housing estates of semi-detached cottages.[17] Theoretically the extension of the suburban railway lines made possible the provision of cheap housing for workmen on the outskirts. In fact the jerry-built speculative cottages as well as the societies' solid rows attracted almost exclusively the rising class of skilled workmen.[18] For the poor the old pressures to stay in the centre remained, the need to pick up casual labour, the need for credit, the need to be near the cheap markets and the attraction of their own cultural centre.

From 1866 legislation on housing affected the work of the model dwellings associations. In 1865 Alderman Sidney Waterlow had written to *The Times* suggesting the desirability of making government loans to the model dwellings associations.[19] His idea was accepted and formed the basis for the 'Act to enable the Public Works Commissioners to make advances towards the erection of dwellings for the labouring classes.'[20] This allowed loans to local authorities, railway, dock or harbour companies, or housing societies for forty years at not

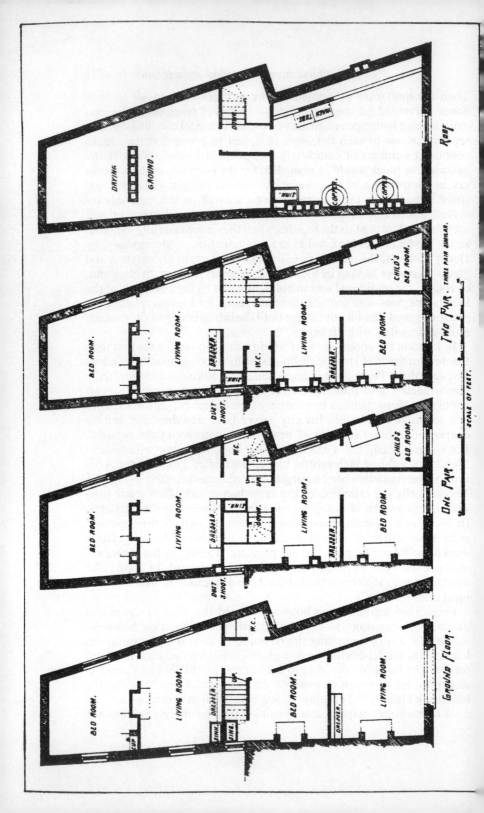

BED ROOM.   LIVING ROOM.   DRESSER.   SINK.   UP.   W.C.   BED ROOM.   DRESSER.   LIVING ROOM.

Ground Floor.

BED ROOM.   LIVING ROOM.   DUST SHOOT.   SINK.   DRESSER.   DOWN.   W.C.   LIVING ROOM.   KITCHEN.   DRESSER.   BED ROOM.   CHILD'S BED ROOM.

One Pair.

SCALE OF FEET.

BED ROOM.   LIVING ROOM.   DUST SHOOT.   SINK.   DRESSER.   W.C.   UP.   LIVING ROOM.   DRESSER.   BED ROOM.   CHILD'S BED ROOM.

Two Pair. THREE PAIR SIMILAR.

DRYING GROUND.   DOWN.   WASH TUBS.   SINK.   COPPR.   COPPR.

Roof.

less than 4 per cent. Money was thus made available to free the associations from the difficulty of attracting private investment, but the necessity of paying 4 per cent directed inflexible economy. The Slum Clearance Acts, 1867 and 1875,[21] freed central ground for rebuilding but resulted in some pressure to rehouse the tenants displaced by demolition. They gave recognition and new importance to the model dwellings movement because, from 1875, the Metropolitan Board of Works put the ground made available by their slum-clearance schemes into the societies' hands for redevelopment.

Overcrowding, at least in some areas, was increased with appalling effect by the clearances for slum demolition and for railway building. The model dwellings associations came in for some public criticism because, by their part in slum clearance, and by their failure to rehouse all the displaced, they added to the problem in contrast with their published aim of improving the housing conditions of the poor. The pressures on the societies all contributed towards the austerity of the later blocks of houses, the meanness of their internal arrangements and their character of comfortlessness. There had been over the years of the model dwellings associations' existence, a deterioration in the quality of housing offered to the poor by philanthropy, a narrowing of space, a limiting of amenity, an increasing cheerlessness. Not only an increasing insistence on economy was demonstrated by this decline but a disillusion about the amount of moral improvement which could be induced in the poor. In the first phase they were to be gently weaned from their apathy by light, airy, cheerful rooms, in the second no such inducement was offered to people who could only now be saved by their own grim determination.

The first were the Metropolitan Association for Improving the Dwellings of the Industrious Classes, formed in 1841, and the Society for Improving the Conditions of the Labouring Classes in 1844. Both built in cities, in the provinces, as well as in London,[22] but, like their later counter-parts, found provincial building commercially unattractive.[23] Their whole aim was to invite imitation by speculative builders: 'The committee, feeling that no description or reasoning, however accurate, is likely to make such an impression on the public as a real experiment, have resolved to build a certain number of houses, as models of the different kinds of dwellings which they would recommend for the labouring classes in popular towns.'[24] In spite of the interest of the Prince of Wales and Lord Shaftesbury, the approval of Edwin Chadwick and of George Godwin of *The Builder*, the publicity gained by display at the Great Exhibition, the invitation to imitate was not taken up commercially, although it was followed by other charitable groups. In fact the common response of public and

Parliament over the next forty years was to welcome the advent of the societies and gladly to leave the task of housing the poor in their hands. The approach of the later societies was more open-eyed. The Peabody Trust founded in 1862 had, as the intention of its founder, the amelioration of the condition of the poor, and the East End Dwellings Company was expressly intended to house the very poorest. Sydney Waterlow's Improved Industrial Dwellings Company, 1863, and William Austin's Artizans', Labourers' and General Dwellings Company Ltd, 1867, on the other hand, were commercial enterprises aiming to supply the apparent demand for low-rent housing without financial hazard, indeed with profit, to themselves. Waterlow justified his failure to attempt to house the poorest: 'The lowest of all, those comprising what may emphatically be called the lower orders, and who are least likely to appreciate the comforts of a decent home, will surely, receive their share of the benefits enjoyed proportionally by those above them.'[25] The better class of tenants housed by his society would vacate dwellings which would then become occupied by poorer people. It was a tempting and often-used argument, only belied by the increase rather than the decrease of overcrowding among the poor during the period of the societies' activities.

Each of the societies succeeded in housing some thousands of families in flats which, if grim, were substantially better than most city homes, and at rents often lower than those paid for filthy and cramped slum accommodation. Yet their contribution to the problem of housing the poor was very summarily dismissed by the Commissioners of 1885 and no evidence has yet appeared to lead us to suppose their importance was then misunderstood.[26]

There is no escaping the opinion of Sir Curtis Lampson, who ran the Peabody Trust, the society which probably made the greatest efforts to reach the poor, that no large scheme for housing those earning less than 12s a week could possibly succeed, and that those earning from 12s to 14s a week could only be housed in one room. It was unfortunate that a continuing demand existed from those earning under 14s a week and that until that demand was filled slums would continue to exist.[27] The associations attempted to fight off the accusation that they did less than they might to house the poorest. Peabody, for instance, had rooms to let for about 2s a week, but they would not allow large families to crowd into accommodation too small for them, and by this rule virtually excluded the neediest. Miss Hill's way, of allowing families to take one or two rooms at first and then gently tempting them to spare more money for more space, was more effective but not manageable without individual attention.

The poor were, in any case, not attracted by the prospect of living in model dwellings. The rules, which forbade noise and demanded temperance, regulated the hanging out of washing but insisted on cleanliness, refused house-room for work tools and storage for goods but required regular rent-paying, were too numerous and too repressive for the large majority of the noisy London poor. Certain trades, like coster-mongers, were excluded both by the rules, and by the lack of accommodation for their donkeys and carts. But the required standard of virtuousness, docility and respectability excluded many more.[28]

The importance of the model dwellings in the history of working-class housing is limited. In spite of their commercial pretensions they failed to persuade speculative builders to follow them. In spite of the large amounts of money put at their disposal[29] they never attracted enough money to allow experiment either in design or in management and so had to stick to narrow and unenterprising lines. In spite of their avowed philanthropy the idea of housing the undeserving still stuck in their throats and the blinkered Victorian definition of undeserving excluded many needy homeless people.

Their failures, however, were in themselves very important. The fact that these patently admirable, financially respectable, able and determined business men, working on the best commercial principles, should fail, had great influence on the future development of government housing policy. The development of social theory running parallel with the unfolding experience of the model dwellings associations led to a growing belief that state help must be essential for the shifting of the housing problem. The conviction grew that housing should not be left to charitable enterprise but should become a state responsibility. Even in the passionate voices raised against socialism and state interference there appeared a quavering of doubt.

The clause in the Act of 1866 which allowed loans to local authorities for the purposes of building houses for working people had gone almost unnoticed, but it opened the way for the development which would eventually supplant the work of the model dwellings associations and make them yield their role as chief providers of new low-cost housing.

PART 5

Legislation on Housing and the Assumption of Public Responsibility for the Housing of the Poor

Chapter 21

The Lodging Houses Acts

'little knowledge of beds'

JOHN SIMON

The first legislation concerned specifically with housing was passed in 1851. Some towns had earlier sought for and obtained private local Acts regulating buildings in their own districts; but the first attempt at general legislation was made in 1840 when, on 17 July, Slaney and Tufnell introduced into the House of Commons their 'Bill to improve the dwellings of the working classes', which became known as the Small Tenements Bill. It sought to prevent the building of houses below ground level, without drains, in close alleys or in back-to-back rows, and to insist upon the provision of privies, ash-pits and opening windows. It contained the interesting idea that 'house-wardens' should be appointed to enforce the regulations and would have inflicted heavy penalties for infringement. Not surprisingly, it got no second reading and when it appeared again next year, reframed as the Building Regulation Bill, 1841, it was soon dismissed. It had been brought in for reasons not wholly connected with housing and was thrown out for reasons not entirely connected with its own insufficiencies.[1]

Some Building Regulations were included in the Towns Improvement Clauses Act, 1847, and again in the Public Health Act, 1848.[2] But the Lodging Houses Act, 1851, later to be known as Shaftesbury's Act, was the first to be passed dealing with the housing of working people as its main object. It had been preceded by the Common Lodging Houses Act of the same year, which was entirely a public health measure. But the Lodging Houses Act attempted something much more radical. Indeed it is not generally realised just how radical were the proposals it contained.

Had it been energetically used it could have prevented the steady increase in overcrowding which characterised the century. It could have anticipated twentieth-century reforms, preventing the build-up of the housing problem to the unmanageable proportions which it reached before effective and inescapable legislation was finally passed sixty years later. Shaftesbury's Act illustrates as well as anything can how useless it is for Parliament to push through legislation too far ahead of the will of the people. Council-house building and the assumption of state responsibility for the housing of the poor became legislatively possible in 1851.

House-building for the poor by the State was, nevertheless, unthinkable. The Act remained on the statute book, a dead letter. The pursuance of its intentions was never at any time seriously contemplated. That such radical clauses could have been introduced to a mid-century Parliament, and accepted by it without much notice being taken of their potential, was due partly to the character and authority, the high-minded optimism, of the man that introduced them, partly to the fact that Parliament was at the time chiefly concerned with other things. The unsettled state of the parties after the Corn Law battle, the fact that Whig and Tory elements met on the common ground of conservatism against change, and that the radicals concerned themselves most with electoral improvement, education and religious liberty meant that there was no combined effort within Parliament to attempt housing reform. And yet there was hardly a session after 1851 when Parliament did not deal with some form of legislation on housing. Some of it was abortive, some positively harmful in its results. The fact remains that even in periods when interest in social reform was weakest, housing was a topic with which Parliament felt, if rather half-heartedly, that it ought to deal. The idea that the state might assume responsibility for housing, that government loans might be made available, that money would be raised as rates for local-authority spending on house-building, all found a hearing in mid-nineteenth-century parliaments. Bills fell like snow, following after one another as Parliament recognised the failings of one, fumbled towards better provision in another.

After the extreme simplicity, amounting to naivety, of Shaftesbury's attempt, the later Acts became more and more complicated in the effort to close all loop-holes and forestall self-interested wangling until it became almost impossible to understand them, and far too difficult to use them. Some little improvement in housing did take place during the nineteenth century, but what improvement there was came as the inevitable result of public health regulations and greater artisan prosperity. No real reform in housing was achieved by legislation during the nineteenth century. But it would be inaccurate to say that Parliament showed no concern with the housing of the nation. It was kept busy with the question throughout the century by Bill-promoters who, like Lord Shaftesbury in 1853, told the House of Lords: 'He would, with God's blessing, give their Lordships no rest until they had done something to remedy the evil he had brought under their notice.'[3]

The Housing of the Working Classes Act, 1885,[4] divided all previous Acts into three classes, the Lodging Houses Acts, 1851–85, the Artisans' Dwellings Acts, 1868–85, and the Artisans' and Labourers'

Dwellings Improvement Acts, 1871–82. This is an interesting classification because, in choosing to divide the Acts in a way other than their chronological order on the statute book, it gives some clues to the intention behind the Acts as it was understood in 1885. We shall deal later with the difference between Dwellings Acts and Dwellings Improvement Acts. For the moment it is necessary to break up the first group, the Lodging Houses Acts, into more detail. The most important of them, Shaftesbury's Act of 1851,[5] was not in fact concerned only with lodging houses as the term is now commonly understood and as the others were. It was Shaftesbury's first attempt to deal by legislation with an evil which he had fought by other means for a decade at least. The passing of the Ten Hours Act in 1847 had freed Shaftesbury, then Lord Ashley, for work in other fields of social reform. His appointment to the Board of Health, along with Chadwick, in 1848, at a time when public interest in sanitation and living conditions was keen, gave him authority and a position from which to attack. His succession to the earldom and to the House of Lords in 1851 gave him prestige and a new audience. His experience as a founder member of the Society for the Improvement of the Condition of the Labouring Classes[6] and his active participation in that society's attempts at providing model dwellings for the poor, had taught him the need for parliamentary interference.

Shaftesbury's Bill to encourage the establishment of lodging houses for the labouring classes was introduced on 8 April 1851. It allowed that income could be provided by boroughs either out of the borough funds, or by raising a rate for the purpose, or by borrowing on the strength of a mortgage of the rates, or by borrowing from the Public Works Loan Commissioners, for the purchase or renting of lands, the erection or purchase and repair of buildings suitable for lodging houses, their fitting and furnishing. If, after seven years in operation, the council found their lodging houses too expensive to keep up, the Act allowed for their sale. Powers were given for management and it was enacted that rents should not be 'too high for the means of the labouring classes nor so low as to be an indirect means of giving relief to the poor'.

It is clear that these new lodging houses, built by the boroughs, were intended to be something more than boarding houses for single persons. The need, as Shaftesbury plainly saw it, was for some respectable accommodation to replace the appalling 'ragged dormitories' so graphically described by John Simon: 'within your worst quarters, there is little knowledge of beds. The first hirer of the room may possibly have a pile of rags on which he lies, with his wife and children, in one corner of the tenement; but the majority of his sub-tenants (paying for their family lodging from 6d to 10d a week) lie on straw, or on the bare boards'.[7] In an 1853 report the model lodging houses were described: 'Each family is provided with rooms so arranged as to partake of the character of a private lodging'. But it is not certain whether those referred to were built under Shaftesbury's Act, more likely they were built by philanthropic action in the spirit of the Act.[8] That it was intended that families should be catered for is betrayed by Section XL of the Act forbidding entry to the lodging houses by persons in receipt of poor relief, and providing that 'such person and his family' shall be removed.

The fear shown here that the new lodgings should prove an easy escape from the poor-house unfortunately motivated the drawing up of the by-laws: It was laid down that the sexes must be segregated. So that, while the original conception of the Act was wide and general, springing straight from Shaftesbury's idealism, the drafters of the Bill and the watchful Members of Parliament between them made sure that the generosity of the first idea was gone before it reached the statute books. The part of the 1885 Act which dealt with the amendment of the Lodging Houses Acts finally provided the definition lacking from the 1851 Act: 'Lodging houses "shall be deemed to include separate houses or cottages for the labouring classes whether containing one or several tenements".'[9]

Shaftesbury had not clearly thought out the consequences of his Act. He was aware of the need, and he demonstrated it. He prepared an Act which, on the face of it, and without too much consideration, might have filled the need. But he was no nearer than the rest of his colleagues to accepting the inevitable corollary that the state would have to compel, rather than encourage, local authorities to adopt his Act. The building of model lodgings for the housing of the kind of people who in 1851 were living in the dens he wanted to abolish could never be profitable. Local councils were certainly not ready to face the unpopularity of building at a loss. The actual process of sanctioning additional expenditure from the rates for the purpose of building lodging houses was a cumbersome one involving the summoning of special meetings of rate-payers.[10]

An amendment added to Shaftesbury's Bill on 30 May 1851 made almost certain that the Act would never be adopted. The amendment provided that, where the council or the local Board of Health or the Improvement Commissioners, had decided to adopt the Act,[11] and to use public money for the building of house accommodation for the poor, rate-payers who were not in sympathy with the project could have the putting of the Act into force delayed until after the next local election. The possibilities of election-rigging inherent in that amendment were as great as the most reactionary rate-payer could require. The result was very little action, and none of the right kind.

Those towns which did adopt the Act provided no great encouragement for back sliders. It seemed to be possible to make a small profit from the lodging, in cheap but respectable dormitories, of single working men or women, but even then it was a profit so small as only to offer distant hopes of paying back borrowed capital. Districts like the City of London, where large numbers of homeless people demonstrated the crying need for some such place, discussed but delayed adoption of the Act.[12] Huddersfield included the provisions of the Act within its own Improvement Act and opened its Model Lodging House in 1854. In November of 1854 it housed 680 people, by November 1864, 2,870. The need was not declining. It was a stone-built, five-storeyed house providing eighty beds at 3d a night, forty-three at 4½d, and eleven for women at 3d, with twelve separate rooms for couples at 6d. The 3½d lodgers had a reading-room with improving daily papers provided, temperance lectures and religious services. The 4½d lodgers, mostly mill and warehouse workers, lived in a separate part which became known as 'The Mechanics Home', had their own reading-room, subscribed for their own choice of newspaper, and were given white coverlets on their beds. While the men were industrious, respectable fellows, it is interesting that 'the single females appear to give occasional trouble by conduct of an insurrectionary nature.'[13]

Huddersfield suffered from the excellence of its new lodging houses. Because other towns had not made the same provision, homeless people were attracted to Huddersfield by the prospect of a cheap roof over their heads. During the Lancashire distress, hundreds of out-of-work cotton workers drifted into the Model Lodging House. The likelihood of having to house people from less generous towns at the expense of the local rates was no incentive to make rate-payers press for lodging houses to be built. In fact, according to Lord Shaftesbury himself, writing in 1883, only one town had used the Act as he intended.[14]

The moral improvement of the poor was always as much the aim of the authorities who adopted the Act as the removal of the homeless from the streets. In Birmingham a new model lodging house, built fashionably with iron beams and supports, catered only for 'very respectable mechanics'.[15] In Dundee, where the Act was adopted (chiefly because of the interest taken in the subject by Lord Kinnaird) as soon as its application to Scotland became law in 1855, the three new houses were intended as a refuge for the unfortunate and a model of ideal house-keeping for the neighbouring inhabitants. 'Fallen women' were to be taught to wield a broom as an example to on-looking slum-dwellers as yet unrescued.[16] It is interesting that in this mill town, even so early as 1855, the need for accommodation for single women was more pressing than for men. Three model lodging houses were built, one for 90 men, and one for 220 women, and another in the Blackscroft for a smaller number of women.

In most towns, however, the Act was ignored and the building of model lodging houses was left either to philanthropists or to specu-lative builders. One of the best of the philanthropic efforts was Thanksgiving House, built in Gray's Inn Road, London, in 1849, as an offering in gratitude for the passing away of the 1848 cholera epidemic.[17] In Leeds, the council showing no sign of interest, a private philanthropist called William Denison of the well-known Leeds Tory family acting in the spirit of the Act, bought some old property and converted it into a lodging house for seventy men.[18] Leeds Council's inactivity was so whole-hearted that twenty-seven years later Denison renovated another property for the same purpose, the need still existing and himself still the only agent prepared to fill it.

But if council action was rare and philanthropic activity sporadic the purchasers of old property and the speculative builders were enthusiastically cashing in on the need for lodgings. From the worst slum dormitories, where a few pennies bought a corner to huddle in, the newly-built houses in which beds in packed rows were nightly let for a slightly larger sum, profits were made at little financial risk. The Whig Prime Minister, Palmerston, spoke on 17 August 1857 of 'monopolist builders ... who from a sordid love of gain ... built great dungeons for the poor' and 'kept the inmates in a state of misery, of dirt, and disease'.[19] There is very little other evidence of great activity by building speculators in the lodging house field. The houses described in Police Commissioners Reports would seem to have been old houses made over to the purpose.[20] It is possible that Palmerston had special knowledge that led him to talk of 'speculative builders who wished to overcrowd the houses they erected', and to declare that 'the builder's home is his dungeon'. Without more knowledge of the houses then existing we must guess that the late hour of the debate, it was almost two o'clock in the morning at the end of a wearisome parliamentary session, and the fact that his govern-ment was approaching defeat, led him to some slight exaggeration.

There was, of course, a long-term and pressing need for the building of new homes for the expanding town population and it was this need which Shaftesbury's first Act had aimed at filling. There was, however, an immediate and more easily filled need for regulation of the thous-ands of existing lodging houses in London and the provinces. The terrible conditions in those houses, the filth and disease, the over-crowding and degradation, the spread of crime were in themselves grave evils. More pathetic, however, because it was not an old and accustomed evil but a new one which might have been avoided, was the plight of provincial workers drawn to the cities in search of employment and led, because they could find no other home, to share lodgings with the rejects of society who traditionally filled such dens. Captain Hay of the Police Commissioners wrote, in his 1853 report on the lodging houses of Britain, of 'infamous brothels, harbours of criminals', who had among them 'industrious emigrant labourers with their wives and children, driven into them for want of other shelter'.[21] It was within the powers of government to see that lodgings which purported to accommodate such people should be relatively clean and not outrageously overcrowded.

The Common Lodging Houses Act, 1853, gave those powers.[22] In contrast to the earlier Acts it was enthusiastically adopted and applied by local authorities all over England.[23] While it could not, partly because the Act's definition of a common lodging house was not sufficiently precise and partly because the task of inspection was too vast for the number of police inspectors available, reach every such house in the country, it did make a sweeping improvement in the standards of accommodation available to those seeking temporary lodgings in cities. If the police reports can be believed, and they seem to be corroborated by middle-class evidence given to the 1884 Commission, lodging house-keepers were remarkably ready to clean, delouse and white-wash their premises and to limit the number of people sleeping there on any one night. Even more remarkable in view of the rise of rents which followed every succeeding attempt at housing improvement, the sprucing up of premises was done without an accompanying rise in the cost of accommodation.

Perhaps lodging house-keepers hoped to detract police attention from other more obviously criminal activities within their walls by showing willingness to co-operate over the new regulations about cleanliness and over-crowding. The right given to the police to enter lodging houses, inspect their sanitary provisions and ask questions about the numbers staying there is certainly likely to have driven the more practised criminals to further haunts. Their dispersal could clear the way for some of the more decent migrant labourers and so the general standards of respectability may have risen fairly quickly. The disreputable characters thus dispersed, and at this level almost certainly we are discussing those most inaccessible to improvement of any kind, moved as always into even worse lodgings.

One thing the reports following lodging house inspection make very clear is the extent of the need for this kind of accommodation. The artisan from the north 'tramping' the country in search of work, the vagrant, the immigrant Irish, all regularly sought accommodation paid for nightly rather than at longer intervals so that they could continually move in search of employment or a charitable hand out. In addition there was a multitude of city dwellers who, for a number of reasons, found it advisable to have no permanent address. In 1853, while 3,300 lodging house-keepers were under inspection in London alone, with something like 50,000 nightly lodgers, it was estimated that at least twice that number remained unregulated and uninspected.

In spite of the local authorities' quickness to adopt the Act, an alacrity no doubt connected with the fact that it involved them in little expense while disposing of a very considerable nuisance, two things limited its effectiveness. The first was the need for better definition of a 'common lodging house'. The worst abuses were reported in lodgings where large families of inter-related Irish immigrants were accommodated. The endless permutations of consanguinity among the Irish allowed a tenant to claim on occasions that as many as 37 individuals 'lying together on the floor like beasts' were members of his family and therefore not subject to inspection as lodgers. The second was the fact, not untypical of Victorian legislation, that the property owner had been spared at the expense of the keeper of the lodging house. The keeper could be forced to improve his lodgings as far as within his power, chiefly, it seems, by white-washing. The provision of water and sanitary facilities, however, which were even more necessary, involved structural changes which could only be accomplished with the co-operation of the owner of the property. The power to bring owners as well as keepers before the magistrates, and, the introduction of a penal clause to the Act were asked for by the police as necessary if the usefulness of the Act was to be extended.

These requests brought down a flood of oratory in support of the rights of Englishmen, property-owning Englishmen at least, against the encroaching tyranny of state authority. The police who, in fact, reports claimed to have acted moderately and temperately in their inspections of lodging house dwellers 'benevolently intruding upon their habits' were drawn as monsters on the dreaded French pattern, breaking into private homes at the behest of autocratic government. Any extension of the powers of the police would not be lightly given by mid-century parliaments, whatever the party in power. Too effective a police force could be, and was, represented as a threat to private property. As the police became increasingly involved in the enforcement of sanitary regulations, property owners felt themselves more and more threatened and a large body of public opinion would gladly have seen police activities not extended but rather confined to the pursuit of crime.

Shaftesbury's next attempt at housing reform was to call the attention of the House of Lords to the effect upon the housing conditions of the poor of the operations of railway companies and street planners. He rose in the House of Lords on 18 March 1853 to move

'that the following resolution be adopted as a standing order: that in every case of a Bill giving power . . . to take any houses the committee on the Bill shall require proof as to which of the houses are used wholly or in part as dwellings by persons of the labouring classes and whether those houses can be taken for the purposes of the Bill without occasioning pecuniary or other injury to such persons and without being likely to occasion any overcrowding of any other dwellings.'

If it were proved that hardship or overcrowding was likely to follow upon the passing of a Bill allowing demolition of houses in favour of railway-, dock- or street-building, the company involved must build within three years adequate housing at a convenient distance for 'at least as many' as had been displaced.[24] His Lordship explained that the order was necessary because, so far, Improvement Bills 'had invariably involved the displacement of large multitudes of the industrious classes'. He cited the instance of Church Lane, already overcrowded at an average density of twenty-four persons per house in 1841, whose population was doubled when New Oxford Street was driven through the old St Giles Rookery, dispersing its inhabitants to neighbouring slums. Those who praised the building of the new thoroughfare and the clearing of the Rookery did not look to either side of the new, clean, wide, shop-lined street to the houses even more densely packed than they had been before. For most Londoners the disappearance of a slum area from their daily paths allowed them to indulge the illusion that slum dwellers had miraculously vanished too. It was a popular notion that the suburbs of cheap houses beginning to spread outwards from the city were populated by ex-slum dwellers;[25] whereas, in fact, what evidence we have about the people in the suburbs suggests that they were those who had always kept their heads higher than the worst slum dwellers because it was economically possible for them to do so. Shaftesbury pointed out that within areas which had suffered large-scale demolition the same people continued to apply for charity, proving that they continued to find a corner to live in the same parish.

In spite of the evidence, their Lordships found the passing of a standing order impracticable. It was, again, a case of Shaftesbury's appreciation of the need and his fear of the consequences of inaction pushing him ahead before the practical details of his suggestion had been carefully worked out. Their Lordships noted immediately that there was no logical difference between requiring a railway company to rehouse people displaced by their activities and requiring an estate-owner to rehouse cottagers displaced by his estate improvements. It was a difference of scale, not of principle, and it was therefore unlikely that the principle would be allowed to become law. Leaders among the landed gentry were beginning to acknowledge the responsibility for rehousing people whose cottages had been destroyed in the course of modernising estates: they were, however, very far from accepting any compulsion to do so. It was natural, then, that they should be wary of forcing other bodies, even those large-scale demolishers like the railway companies, to do what they were unwilling to have forced upon themselves. They could see the danger in the precedent: so the Bishop of London's remark that 'in beautifying some parts of the Metropolis we are brutifying others' went unheeded.[26] A select committee was appointed and duly reported on 9 May with a recommendation which made it possible to pass a much weakened standing order. The demolition companies were to be required to draw up and deposit in the office of the clerk of Parliament a statement of the number of houses affected by any proposed work, their 'description and situation, the number (so far as can be estimated) of persons to be displaced and whether any and what provision is made in the Bill for remedying the inconvenience likely to arise from such displacement'. The new order applied only to schemes taking thirty or more houses in any one parish, which safely excluded all but the most sweeping estate improvements. Lord Shaftesbury gracefully accepted it as the best that could be achieved. 'Their Lordships had gone far towards instituting the very best relations between capital and labour that were capable of being made in relation to this subject.'[27]

The railway companies were not unduly dismayed by the new rules. The fact that they were now bound to report on their activities in some detail has made an interesting source of research material of which Professor Dyos had made good use. The effectiveness of the standing orders in limiting overcrowding caused by railway demolitions is summed up in two outstanding facts. Only once did a railway company make any scheme to rehouse the people displaced by its operations (that was at St Bartholomew's, built in 1859), and between 1853 and 1885, 56,000 people are reckoned to have been affected in this way in London. Provincial cities suffered similar upheavals.[28]

Not until 1874, when pressure by the Charity Organisation Society forced the drafting of new standing orders, was Shaftesbury's original plan requiring the provision of alternative accommodation adopted. But the 1874 orders presented no great difficulty to the railway promoters. The new requirements involved giving eight weeks' notice to tenants, the procuring of alternative housing and the drawing of the special attention of Parliament to each separate Bill involving demolition of housing. By one means or another it was usually possible to evict a large proportion of tenants before it became necessary to report on the numbers living in the acquired property. The means of evicting unwanted tenants open to unscrupulous landlords are still cruelly effective. They were unlimitedly so in 1874. The social consequences of widespread demolition were not limited to the destruction of homes. Small shopkeepers lost their trade, small jobbers their clients. Professor Dyos quotes the miserable charwoman whose circle of customers was driven away by the Marylebone Station demolitions, who hanged herself in desperation.[29] She ought, of course, to have had the initiative to move to a brighter district and build up a new clientele. But initiative was not overplentiful in the kind of slums through which the new railway lines thrust their imperative way.

Parliament was not unaware of the effect of city improvements on London's inhabitants, and after the 1885 Report members were no longer so able to push what they knew to the backs of their minds. The evidence heard before the select committee on the effect of railways on the city in 1892 showed an attitude to the unfettered operations of large companies quite different from that expressed in 1853. In 1892 it could be said that 'the people of London have a sort of right of control over the property on which the city stands'.[30] In 1853 even the discussion of such a right was unthinkable. The attitude of Parliament was best expressed by the Earl of Wicklow's distaste for the notion that companies should be forced to rehouse: 'they might', he said, almost incredulously, 'compel landlords to receive tenants whom they did not wish to have'.[31]

Social reform, even for the keenest radicals and the most dedicated evangelicals, was demoted in importance in Parliament by the threat of war. In January 1853 the Tsar's suggestion of the partition of Turkish territory awoke British suspicion of his long-term aims. In July a Russian army crossed the Prut. In October Turkey declared war on Russia. In March 1854 Britain made her declaration. W. H. Russell's dispatches to *The Times* diverted compassion from the poor at home to the suffering at Inkerman, and led, it can be argued, to a new conception of the relief of suffering, a new, more professional, direction for charitable enterprise. Temporarily, at least, the discussion of legislative action towards housing reform ceased, in spite of Shaftesbury's threat to give their Lordships no rest.

Chapter 22

Establishing Principles

'old, hackneyed political ground'

A. F. KINNAIRD

Lord Aberdeen's government fell at the beginning of 1855, brought down by the criticism of his conduct of the war. In the succeeding ten years under Palmerston, home affairs were always secondary in importance to Britain's foreign interests. The unsettled state of the parliamentary parties, however, allowed loosely formed groups of politicians to coalesce in temporary, almost fortuitous combinations. A group formed with common purpose during one parliamentary session would be disposed to opposing sides in the next. Palmerston's own interest in social reform, meanwhile, was kept fresh by the influence upon him of Shaftesbury, who was his wife's son in-law, and of William Cowper of the Board of Health, both frequent visitors to his table. During the 1850s, then, a considerable body of legislation touching on housing was put through Parliament.

1855 saw the passing of the Dwelling Houses for the Working Classes (Scotland) Act, 1855,[1] a new Nuisances Removal Act, 1855, the Metropolis Local Management Act, 1855, and the Labourers' Dwellings Act, 1855.[2] In 1856 the Nuisances Removal (Scotland) Act, 1856, and the Metropolis Management Amendment Act, 1856, were passed.

These were measures of great importance. The fact that they proved far from effectual in improving the housing of the poor should not be allowed to mask the significance of the principles contained within them. Parliament moves in waves. One session allows important principles to be introduced alongside clauses which make sure those principles cannot be acted upon; while in a succeeding session, referring confidently to the principles already established and accepted in earlier, inoperable Acts, the limiting clauses can be swept aside. Thus nineteenth-century legislative activity insinuated into the statute books the principle of state responsibility for housing while at the same time ensuring, with all the outrage of which Parliament was capable, that such unwarrantable intrusion upon private rights would not be tolerated.

The Dwelling Houses (Scotland) Act, 1855, for instance, gave power for associations of persons acting 'in the public interest'[3] to acquire dilapidated property at a price fixed by the sheriff. This was a forerunner of compulsory purchase and, if its opportunities were not widely taken, it was nevertheless important that Parliament accepted the idea.

The inclusion within these tentative Acts of such essential principles for housing reform made it possible for Parliament's advisers in later years to take for granted the rightness of underlying principles and to concentrate on solving practical difficulties. John Simon, for instance, in 1865, could write: 'the objects which such legislation would tend to compass are objects for which in principle, the Legislature has already declared itself . . ..'[4]

Alexander Dunlop, promoter of the Scottish Bill of 1855, could be said to be typical of those working for reform within Parliament in that he admitted no pledged allegiance to one party or another. From early Tory leanings he had veered towards Liberalism, but while in general he voted with the Liberals in the House he maintained an independent position and was never open to persuasion by offers of high office. A lawyer chiefly interested in the question of church patronage, he had stood for election in 1845 and 1847 but was not returned until 1852. From then until his resignation in 1868 he was Member for Greenock, his native town.[5] When he rose in the House on 21 February 1855 to bring in his Bill he was then relatively little known in Parliament. The general expectation was that his Bill would be merely a form of words extending to Scotland the provisions of the English Lodging Houses Acts.

In fact it was both wider in its scope and more practical in its provisions. Dunlop told the House that the steep increase in Scotland's population plus the decline in the number of available houses, a decline caused, especially in Edinburgh, by demolition of houses to make way for public buildings, had led to serious overcrowding. The object of his Bill was 'to induce capitalists to invest in the erection of suitable dwelling houses with a reasonable prospect of return'. His lawyer's experience had taught Dunlop some of the real difficulties deterring capitalists from investing in house-building. It was not a clear-cut issue of low profitability but one beset by legal complications. The three main obstacles were, he said, the unlimited liability of persons forming housing associations, the great expense of the conveyancing of land, and the difficulty of buying property when owners could not be traced. He proposed to remove all three by his Bill. Persons with plans approved by the sheriff as suitable for working-class housing were to be sheltered by limited liability.[6] The expense of conveyancing was to be reduced for the special purposes of the Bill from £7 or £8 to 5s or 10s, a very considerable inducement. And, as we have already seen, the power to acquire derelict property was given to local authorities. The Hon. John E. Elliott, Liberal Member for Roxburghshire, rose to say that 'he could not conceive anything more likely to raise the moral character of the people of Scotland'.[7]

It had been hoped that the provisions of the Act would encourage the forming of housing societies like London's model dwellings associations. In Dundee, as we have seen, there was quick action to build lodging houses but no follow up in single-family house-building. In Edinburgh and Glasgow small-scale philanthropic activity had built and improved lodging houses before 1855, and there seems little indication that the societies afterwards formed were inspired by the passing of the Act. Local authorities and private citizens alike were not ready to be dictated to by Parliament, which meant that general Acts whose clauses were adoptive rather than mandatory were unlikely to achieve much. Local improvement in the housing conditions of the poor took place in every case only after a private Local Improvement Act had been sought for and obtained from Parliament, only, that is, when local opinion and local initiative were ready for change. Dunlop's Act gave powers of improvement to those who chose to use them, it made no attempt to compel. Had it done so it would not have had such an easy passage through the House. It suffered only minor amendments by Lords and Commons and became law on 14 August 1855.[8] W. A. Wilkinson, Member for Lambeth, had expressed at the Bill's first reading the hope that such a measure would soon be extended to England,[9] as it immediately was, both Bills being given Royal assent on the same day. A similar Act for Ireland was deferred.

Sir Benjamin Hall's Metropolis Local Management Act, 1855, a Ministerial measure, made the first real attempt to co-ordinate the chaotic local administration of the overgrown huddle of decayed villages known as London. It established the Metropolitan Board of Works as the central administrative body. It was accompanied by a new Building Act for the city which, until the new model by-laws of 1875 out-stepped it, provided a standard of building practice superior to most of the country.[10] Among other provisions it made the appointment of medical officers throughout London compulsory, a step of great value because it was, in many cases, the reports of medical officers which first drew attention to the need for action on housing in their own areas.[11]

The Metropolitan Board was active and energetic in its first years, setting about the demolition of slum areas and the planning of new streets with sweeping, even heartless enthusiasm. Fifty improvement schemes were carried out by the Board during its thirty-three years of life, and only thirteen of them provided for rehousing the people made homeless by demolition. None of the slum-clearance schemes put in action before 1879 were followed by rehousing. The 10,340 working people rehoused between then and 1888, when the Metropolitan Board was replaced by the Local Government Board, represented a mere fraction of those whose homes had been destroyed.

This was exactly the kind of housing 'reform', so apparently praiseworthy, on the surface so satisfactory, which pleased middle-class voters. They saw the slums crumble to dust to be replaced by splendid thoroughfares, and they approved the local government reforms which made such a cleaning up process possible. But the housing situation was in no way improved by this kind of activity. The homeless and the overcrowded were merely eased out of sight to fester unnoticed till the next turn of 'improvement'. It was not so much the homelessness caused by its slum-clearance projects as the financial problems involved in the purchase of land with restrictions on its use which sapped the energy of the Board until it became, in Professor Tarn's words, 'moribund and discredited'.[12] By 1868 the Board 'did not possess the confidence of the rate-payers', Labouchère, the Radical Member for Middlesex, said in debate.[13] The Local Government Act, 1888, ended the official life of the Metropolitan Board. Its effectiveness had ended some twenty years earlier. But in 1855, when it was first set up, it was, or could have been, a useful instrument for reform. The 1855 Act gave wide powers to authorities who chose to use it, but John Simon found, ten years later, that it had not been 'universally adopted or properly applied'.[14]

1855 saw yet another piece of legislation significant in the history of housing reform.[15] The Nuisances Removal Act, 1855, is important because it contained, for the first time, the phrase 'unfit for human habitation'.[16] Sitting in the midst of a city where thousands of people were living in conditions much worse than farm animals, whose quarters at least were regularly 'mucked out', Britain's legislators at last took it upon themselves to say 'lower than this you shall not go'. The time had yet to come when Parliament could set a housing standard to be attained to, something to reach up to, but at least now the idea of fitness for humans was worked into the law. On 23 January a Bill 'to consolidate and amend the Nuisances Removal and Diseases Prevention Acts of 1848 and 1849' was introduced.[17] It suffered considerable opposition and amendment but gained Royal assent along with the two Dwellings Acts and the Metropolis Management Act on 14 August.

Existing Nuisances Removal Acts had already given considerable powers to authorities with a will to use them. The new Act, used in conjunction with the Metropolitan Board's appointment of medical officers, gave local authorities not only the power, but the duty to order the provision of adequate privies, the maintenance of premises in a safe and habitable condition, the cleansing and white-washing of insanitary houses and the closing of houses where the nuisance was 'such as to render the house unfit for human habitation'.

Vagueness of definition, lack of co-operation from local authorities and the unwillingness of medical officers to close houses when the occupants could turn only to worse conditions led to the Act's ineffectiveness. Arnold-Forster, explaining the existing laws on housing in 1883, thought the Nuisances Removal Act, 1855, a valuable measure[18] with provisions sufficient for the problem in hand. But he laid too much stress on the right and power of the ordinary 'man in the street' to order an inquiry into nuisances. The right was only a paper weapon in the hands of those who suffered most from nuisances: the inarticulate masses who were unlikely to seek any avoidable contact with authority. The man who lived in the damp and smelly cellar where the walls oozed sewage and the floor grew mould was not the man on whom to rely for the initiation of proceedings under the Act against his landlord.

Hole wrote in 1866 of the wide powers given under the consolidated Nuisances Acts, and of their comparative uselessness: 'If the cottage speculator chooses to ignore such regulations he may do so with impunity.'[19] Simon wrote of the 'evident unwillingness' of local authorities to apply the Acts: 'the Nuisances Removal Acts to which he [the labourer] might have wistfully looked for protection against some evil conditions of dwelling are probably a mere dead letter in the district.'[20]

'Unfit for human habitation' was a term not precisely defined and therefore open to any interpretation suiting those in power. For instance, construction which prevented the entry of light or air was not usually admitted to be a 'nuisance' under the Act. Dampness was not necessarily a nuisance. Even a generally ruinous condition need not lead to condemnation as a nuisance.[21] The use of cellars as dwellings was forbidden in those boroughs which had adopted the Public Health Act, 1848, or had made their own local regulations against it. It was by no means universally forbidden until 1909. Without a whole-hearted and zealous wish by a local authority to use it for the purpose of improving housing conditions the Nuisances Removal Act, 1855, was unlikely to have any marked effect. 1856 saw the extension to Scotland of the Nuisances Act, with certain adaptions made necessary by the different form of town government. But it was in 1857 that an abortive Bill on housing aroused debates in Parliament which most clearly illustrate the kind of thinking which made the pursuance of real reform in housing so difficult.

A report of the Police Commissioners on the working of the Lodging Houses Acts was received by Parliament in July 1857. It claimed very beneficial results from the system of inspection and regulation. Jack Shepherd's house, for instance, which, before the Acts, was 'frequented by such a desperate class of inmates that the police seldom dared to visit it', was now 'peaceful and orderly, sweet and clean'. Dens where half-naked women lay on filthy beds playing cards with drunken beggars and thieves now welcomed the visits of scripture missionaries. Such a reformation, such a victory for sweetness and light, however, was not claimed to be complete. There were too many overcrowded houses escaping regulation by the pretence that all lodgers were members of one family.[22]

Shaftesbury introduced into the House of Lords on 7 July 1857 a resolution that the 1851 and 1853 Lodging Houses Acts should be amended to deal with the problem. The Bill read: 'whereas it is expedient that further provision should be made for the prevention of overcrowding in dwellings of the poor . . . no house should be exempt from the provisions of the Lodging Houses Act' and overcrowding 'if it were dangerous and prejudicial to health . . . may be proceeded against as a nuisance under the Nuisances Act of 1855.'[23] The Lords can have spared the Bill little attention for they passed it without debate and sent it to the Commons on 24 July. There the implications of that first provision were more clearly seen. The idea that private houses should be liable to inspection of any kind aroused a holy, a fervent indignation in the spluttering breasts of the aggressively British Members of Parliament. The same period saw a similarly effective reaction to attempts to introduce a general system of police. Dislike of all interference with individual liberty, whether it was liberty to moulder in overcrowded dumps or to make money by drawing rents from the dumps, made furious opposition for the Bill. Fear of a strong bureaucracy like that endured by the suffering French added the fire of patriotism to the opposition. Lord Adolphus Vane Tempest, Tory Member for Durham, declared that he would have thought at first sight that the measure had emanated from the Tuileries![24] The Rt Hon. A. S. Ayrton, the Radical Member for Tower Hamlets, said the real aim of the measure was 'to place the dwellings of the poor under the surveillance of the police and to subject the country to an odious system of domiciliary visits.' The Tory F. W. Knight agreed with him: 'the same system of gradual encroachment which had enslaved the nations of the continent would be insidiously extended to this country.'[25] The speakers drew terrifying pictures of what might happen if the Bill were passed: working-men's houses burst into at dead of night by truncheon-wielding policemen.

After Ayrton had warned the House to take care not to 'place the people under the power and control of the executive officers of the government who were to regulate all their social affairs', the Bill was, not surprisingly, postponed to give Members an opportunity to collect the opinion of the country. Lord Palmerston, Home Secretary from 1852 to 1855, and now Prime Minister, reminded Members that it was not the property of the poor that was being regulated at all: the kind of people who lived in lodging houses had no property. It was indeed the *owners* of the lodging-house property, whose pockets were threatened by the legislation, who opposed it, but to use the argument of protecting the liberties of the poor was humbug. The Hon. A. F. Kinnaird, Liberal Member for Perth and brother of Lord Kinnaird, called the liberty of the subject 'old, hackneyed political ground' trodden over whenever no better argument offered.[26] While the government claimed 'the opponents of the Bill had power commensurate more with their pertinacity than with their numbers', there is no doubt the opposition drew support from genuine beliefs, dearly and closely held by lovers of the British political system. But in this case, at the end of the parliamentary session and in the small hours of the night, the great guns built by British parliamentarians to protect the people against tyranny were brought to bear on a tiny innocuous measure, a mere amendment to an Act of already acknowledged value, hammering it into oblivion with quite unnecessary vigour. Social reformers in British parliaments had commonly to face not only passive non-cooperation caused by meanness, ignorance and self-interest but active opposition of this kind with charges of despotism, un-Englishness and treachery.

The Bill was withdrawn. The savagery of its defeat explains the lapse of another ten years before any further determined attempt at general housing reform was made. But while the strength of the country's opposition to legislative interference with social conditions could delay general measures or large-scale improvement, the real, if

VIII. Housing near the mill, whose bell-tower and chimney dominate the sky-line, Dundee, *c.* 1890

IX. Model lodging house, Dundee, opened 1857 by Dundee Model Lodging House Association, President Lord Kinnaird

x. Demolition in London, 1866

XI. '. . . highly injurious to the moral and physical welfare of the inhabitants'

buried, pressure for social reform constantly nagged away at the opposition, gaining steadily, by means of small improvements and particular measures, a momentum for the housing reform movement. Each succeeding year saw parliamentary attention directed to measures touching on housing. Each year saw small victories, victories for principle and victories for more efficient practice of the existing powers. The impossibility of persuading Parliament to accept with any willingness the idea of inspection or enforcement meant that most legislation on housing was doomed to useless lingering on the statute books. But each step towards reform, however tentative, made the next one easier to take. And the existence in the law of the land of regulations about living conditions, however toothless the law, however easily ignored by the vast majority whose interest taught them to disparage it, made it possible for a few strong men to lead their local councils towards action. In 1858 with a minority Tory government in office, Parliament amended the Public Health Act, 1848, to make further provision for the local government of towns and populous districts,[27] and included within the provisions of this new Local Government Act a clause forbidding the building of new back-to-back houses. This was an important step in the history of housing and town planning. It set a limit, if a shifting one, to the land ravaging of the speculative builders whose efforts to make profits had packed so many thousands of tiny, drainless, airless houses on the edges of northern cities, eating into the moors and the valleys with schemes which did not need the deterioration of time to make them slums. Those councils who were already convinced of the evils of back-to-back building, could use the Act to plan their own town's further development. Those, like Leeds, who found arguments to defend back-to-backs could choose to ignore it. Sheffield, for instance, waited until 1864 to adopt the provision against back-to-back building as a by-law.[28] Manchester had banned back-to-backs by by-law as early as 1842.[29]

The years between 1858 and 1865,[30] with Palmerston as Prime Minister from mid-1859, saw no vigorous movement in Parliament towards the improvement of the people's living conditions. These were the last years of old Whig rule and it would have been difficult then to inflict on society the kind of state interference which alone could make any real difference. But even during these years small advances were made. The condition of the people was by now a topic no government could afford wholly to ignore. Whig governments allowed legislation on social reform when it was necessary to defend political advantage or when the measure was one tolerable to old fashioned landed gentlemen. For instance, the 1860 Act to facilitate

9

the building of labourers' cottages on entailed estates in Scotland, was designed to ease the path of improving landlords limited by the conditions of their inheritance.[31] An attempt to expand it into a more radical measure to facilitate the grant or sale of small portions of entailed lands near great towns as sites for dwellings for the working classes was defeated because legislative interference with entail was quite intolerable. A motion in the same year that a select committee should be appointed to consider the means of improving the dwellings of working classes in populous towns was withdrawn because the House made it clear that it had little wish to consider the subject again.[32]

Scotland was fortunate during this period in being represented in Parliament by a group of men committed to improving the lot of the working people. Robert Dalglish of Glasgow, a calico printer, Lord Kinnaird in the House of Peers and his brother, the Hon. A. F. Kinnaird, in the Commons, Alexander Dunlop of Greenock and N. D. Fordyce of Aberdeen County were all active in promoting housing reform. 1862 brought Scotland a Burgh Police and Improvement Act which gave Scotland burghs powers of improvement superior to those enjoyed anywhere in England until after 1868.[33] Dundee, Edinburgh and Glasgow all took advantage of it to plan improvement schemes and to set up special committees to which new building plans had to be submitted for approval.[34]

1863, 1864 and 1865 together saw no useful measures on housing but these years represent a lull of quietness before the bustle of a new kind of government, concerned, both through conviction and through knowledge of the insistence of the electorate, about the need to achieve social reforms.

Palmerston increased his majority at the General Election of July 1865 but died before he could take office. Russell, succeeding him as leader, was defeated on the Reform Bill in 1866 by the revolt of Adullamite Whigs. A Conservative leadership with Lord Derby as Prime Minister and Disraeli as its force, but with no majority in the House of Commons, was in office from 1866 to 1868. Disraeli's vision of Tory democracy, in which the good of the governed was the whole purpose of government, influenced Tory policy-making in the next years without being able to dominate it.

Outside Parliament the forces for reform were growing in strength and determination, shedding the image of genteel do-goodery for one of energetic activism. The founding of the Charity Organisation Society represented a resolute stepping away from the aristocratic paternalism of the evangelical approach to the poor. They shunned not only the sentimentalism of Shaftesbury's Christian endeavour, but its lack of precision. The new social reformers wanted, in Professor Best's words, 'to reduce the exuberant variety of his [Shaftesbury's] philanthropic empire to a simple, bonier, more business-like system.'[35] It was partly fear of what that 'bonier' system might mean if it were left in the hands of those resolute reformers, that drove Parliament to accept the government's own filleted legislation. Ministers guessed, and rightly as it turned out, that a Bill framed by these new and more formidable organisers could not be thrown out because it was 'imperfectly worded' and 'unintelligible' like that 'brought in by a noble Lord now in another place'.[36]

The Privy Council had ordered, in 1865, an inquiry into the Housing of the Poorer Population in Towns[37] to be carried out by John Simon's team as part of a systematic study of the distribution of disease. Simon's eighth report to the Privy Council[38] made it oppressively clear that the time for action had come. The return of King Cholera to Britain, ravaging the homes of East London especially,[39] as guest of the East End Water Company, but stepping throughout Britain with a tread heavy enough to alarm, increased Parliament's apprehensive feeling that the country expected action.

Once again cholera stalked alongside the fear of popular unrest as it had in 1832 and in 1848, political disturbance, radical pressure and disease serving together to edge Ministers into untenable positions. If neither the strength of the epidemic nor the threat of workers' uprisings was as much to be feared as in the earlier outbreaks they were enough to be useful weapons in the hands of the social reformers. Shaftesbury's way of thinking might have lost its appeal for advanced thinkers, but the words he later used on opening the Shaftesbury Park Estate made sense in 1866: 'People who are contented always give a government less trouble than those who are not.'[40] Disraeli himself put it this way: 'The palace is not safe when the cottage is not happy.'[41] It became necessary, in a Parliament inevitably, if reluctantly, moving towards some extension of the franchise, to find a new way of making the people contented.

The Labouring Classes Dwelling Houses Act, 1866, was framed with that intention. It had, in fact, a narrower scope than its title implied, its only effect being to empower the Public Works Loan Commissioners to make advances towards the erection of labourers' dwellings in populous towns.

The Act seems to have had its origin in a letter to the Rt Hon. Sir Frederick Peel at the Treasury[42] from Sir Sidney Waterlow, in which he suggested that the rehousing of people displaced by improvement in the Metropolis could best be encouraged by government loans at low interest to agencies prepared to build low-cost housing. In his reply the Financial Secretary held out hope that the government might be prepared to apply to Parliament for this purpose if the profit were not to exceed 5 per cent.[43] Alderman Waterlow sent a letter to *The Times* making the same proposal, and suggesting 4 per cent as a reasonable rate of interest on such loans. The Act finally allowed loans to be made 'for the purchase of land or buildings or the improvement of dwellings for the labouring classes' to 'any council, board or commissioners authorised under the Lodging Houses Act of 1851, any local authority . . . or to any railway, dock or harbour company, or any company established for the purposes of this Act.' The period of repayment was not to exceed forty years and the rate of interest to be not less than 4 per cent.[44]

Waterlow's own company, the Improved Industrial Dwellings Company, established in 1860, was said to have availed itself of the opportunity to the tune of £327,000.[45] A report to Parliament in 1874 on loans granted under the Act showed £84,000 to have been granted to the company between 1866 and 1874, in eight different sums. A further five applications by the company had been refused. Waterlow, in fact, had almost half of the total sum granted, £165,350. The other applicants were almost all model dwellings associations, sometimes large ones like the Metropolitan Association or the Highgate Dwellings Company, which were granted £18,000 and £2,500 respectively, sometimes smaller associations like the Cardiff Workmen's Cottage Company, which got £5,500, and the Briton Ferry Cottage Company which got £1,225. There were also a few private individuals, all from West Hartlepool, who applied for, and got, sums ranging from £750 to £1,750. Although the Act provided for borrowing by local authorities, the Corporation of Liverpool is the only one to appear in the list of successful applicants for loans, asking for and being granted £13,000 for the building of St Martin's Cottages in 1868.[46]

The Public Works Loan Commissioners cannot be blamed for the fact that local authorities did not use this Act for the improvement of their housing. Applicants were seldom refused. Apart from the extra sums asked for by Waterlow's company, which could hardly be said to have been harshly treated, the only applicants to be turned down were the Glasgow and Suburban Dwelling Company and a private individual called George Cuft, and these were refused on the grounds that their security for the loan was unsatisfactory. The amounts asked for were always granted in full, there was no haggling over the sum required, an open-mindedness which those concerned with building from public funds today might well envy.[47]

Potentially this Act could have set in train the building of working-class housing throughout Britain. No doubt Parliament was well aware of the unlikelihood of many local authorities being as courageous as Liverpool in saddling their rate-payers with the repayment of a large loan for such a purpose. No doubt, again, there might have been a more grudging attitude by the Public Works Loan Commissioners if the applications had been more frequent and more demanding. Local authorities were by no means ready to use this Act as it might have been used and Parliament felt safe in that knowledge when it passed the Act. The purpose was to help the model dwellings associations, which it was still thought were capable of building houses in sufficient quantity to solve the overcrowding problem in cities. The Act was intended to encourage private enterprise, not to subsidise the shiftless. Even among the model dwellings associations there were those, like the Artizans', Labourers' and General Dwellings Company, who prided themselves on not having borrowed any of their capital from the state.[48]

But while Parliament was backed by those in official positions throughout the country in delaying consideration of any Housing Act with general application and genuinely radical proposals there was in intellectual circles a noticeable move towards real understanding of the problems involved. The National Association for the Promotion of Social Science had set up a committee to consider how working-class living conditions, which the members recognised had been made worse by the extent of housing demolition, could be improved. Edwin Chadwick was put in the chair. McCullagh Torrens was one of the committee members. The Artisans' and Labourers' Dwellings Act, 1868, was the outcome of this committee's work.[49]

In the same year Chadwick was sent as official representative to the Paris Exhibition to report on any sanitary advances displayed there. His report, as well as containing a full account of the exhibits with his own typically ruthless comments upon them, contains most interesting comparisons between French and English living patterns, makes some very radical proposals, such as a complete re-thinking of building construction and a limiting of the profits made on building materials, and ends with a request 'to power' for research into building problems. His last words were: 'It is now generally admitted that moral and social advancement is dependent upon physical improvement and that on the sanitary improvement of dwellings.'[50] Chadwick's tone had not changed since his vigorous reporting of twenty years earlier, but his audience had changed. If his principles were still not generally admitted there was a growing body of opinion that not only agreed with him but went further, accepting the need for a degree of state interference and state subsidy very foreign to Chadwick's philosophy. Parliament under Palmerston had clearly been falling behind rather than leading the pace of social advancement.

In two great provincial cities the councils had faced the risk of alienating their rate-payers and begun to plan large-scale improvements. Liverpool had, as early as 1842, attempted to regulate the site-planning and construction of houses by its Liverpool Building Act. Under its Sanitary Act, 1846, it had appointed the first medical officer of health in the country, Dr Duncan. Its local Act of 1864, followed by a code of by-laws in 1865, put Liverpool, in theory if not in practice, ahead of the rest of the country in its housing policy, preventing the building of closed courts and laying down minimum space requirements around houses. In the same year the Health Committee of the Council recommended that the Finance Committee should give every facility for the erection of model cottages on land owned and cleared of slums by the corporation. In 1866 the borough engineer prepared plans for blocks of houses and the corporation decided to accept a tender for their erection at the council's expense. Liverpool was the first city to accept, however reluctantly, the principle that the rates could be used for the purpose of building houses for the poor.[51]

Glasgow was even more sweeping with its regulations against overcrowding in the local Police Act, 1862, and its comprehensive improvement scheme of 1866.[52] By 1865 £100,000 had been voted for improvement purposes in Liverpool, and Glasgow had asked Parliament to sanction the spending of £1,125,000. Glasgow's courage in planning for the future was not based on any expectation that well-to-do citizens would certainly accept the extra expenditure. The levying of the first 6d rate for improvement purposes cost the Lord Provost his seat on the council,[53] yet the rate of progress in slum purchase and demolition was not, or not immediately, slowed in deference to the angry electorate.

It was an example to Parliament not easily ignored, so that when McCullagh Torrens's Bill was first put forward in 1866 soon after the passing of the government's own Bill, Gladstone was not merely shelving the problem when he suggested a select committee[54] but accepting the need for further study of the issues involved. Neither Liverpool nor Glasgow achieved any real relief of the overcrowding in their cities, indeed the demolition of slum areas increased, as always, the pressure on neighbouring districts. The very first attempt at council housing, St Martin's Cottages in Liverpool in 1869, was not an ideal model for the rest of the country to follow nor was the enterprise large enough in scale to reduce Liverpool's own need. Both councils ran out of steam, and out of support, after the first impetus of slum purchase and demolition was passed. Rate-payers wanted to see the slums disappear. They would have liked the slum dwellers to disappear too. Glasgow Landlords' Association wrote to Sir Charles Dilke and their chief plea was the need for landlords to have more power to evict troublesome tenants. There was very little support, if any, for a programme of rehousing by the council at the rate-payers' expense.

But in 1866 the disappointing lack of achievement by these pioneer cities lay in the future. The plans put forward by their councils seemed courageous and inspiring. The sums of money voted to cover expenditure on improvement seemed, in the light of the whole country's inexperience of large-scale planning, generous and impressive. The acceptance of the responsibility for town improvement by these two local authorities was an important lead to Parliament and to the rest of the country.

Liverpool and Glasgow had to deal only with local issues. Parliament was burdened by the need not only to cope with the general business of government and with Britain's relationship with other countries, but by pressure to reform herself. Torrens and his friends were giving their attention to the particularities of the housing problem while Parliament was still reeling in the draught from Whiggery's petulant departure and bracing herself to meet Gladstone's 'restless, reforming Creed' of Liberalism.[55]

The Labouring Classes Dwellings Houses Act, 1866,[56] was presented by Mr Childers, Liberal Member for Pontefract, on 12 February and became law on 10 April.[57] The more radical Bill prepared by McCullagh Torrens, Locke and Kinnaird was presented on 20 February 1866, had its second reading on 12 March and was referred to a select committee of Messrs Torrens, Locke, Kinnaird, Goschen, Knatchbull-Hagessen, McLaren, Akroyd, Abel Smith, Henley, Adderley, Graves and Green, Lord Robert Montagu, Sir Colman O'Loghlend, Sir Minto Farquhar. The committee reported on 18 June. Derby's hold on his own party while he had no majority in Parliament was not safe enough for an attempt at the kind of reforming legislation the committee recommended, and the Bill was withdrawn on 31 July.

All legislation on housing up to 1867 was grouped by the authors of the 1885 Report on Housing under the heading 'Lodging Houses Acts 1851–85'.[58] Although the titles of the Dwellings Acts might lead one to expect definite proposals for the provision of housing, in fact the only real achievement lay in the provision and regulation of lodging houses and in some small encouragement to the model dwellings associations by the allowance of loans from the Public Works Loan Commissioners. Parliament was daring to calculate the effect of state interference in social conditions but had not yet gathered resolution enough for it. While the Acts allowed action by enlightened authorities or groups of people they made not even a gesture towards enforcement and gave no realistic encouragement to those who would have tried.

Certain limits on the jerry-builders' unscrupulous profiteering and the landlords' greed were set by nineteenth-century legislation. The Nuisance and Public Health Acts insisted upon the maintenance of reasonably sanitary conditions and made the building of new houses without adequate sanitary arrangements at least difficult. The new Sanitary Act, 1866,[59] took things an important step further by making overcrowding technically a nuisance, subject to the penalties incurred by creators of nuisances, and by empowering the Secretary of State to authorise local authorities to make regulations about the supply of water, overcrowding, cleanliness and inspection of premises, and to inflict penalties. The powers for improvement existed but they were, as was inevitable in the state of parliamentary feeling about the liberties of the subject, adoptive, not mandatory. Alone among the London boroughs Chelsea and Hackney were energetic in enforcing regulations. Outside London little or nothing was done. 'Even where the authorities have had their memories refreshed by energetic officers of health the result has often been the same.'[60]

Scotland's first comprehensive Public Health Act, the Public Health (Scotland) Act, 1867,[61] was passed in the following year, giving for the first time a sanitary code and a structure of administration covering drainage, water supply, overcrowding, appointment of sanitary officers, regulation of lodging houses and the enforcement of minimum requirements of lighting and ventilation for houses. It did not abolish but regulated cellar dwelling and it gave local authorities powers which they did not frequently make use of to insist on the supply of water to houses in cities. It was under this Act that towns like Dundee began to require approval by the Police Commissioners of plans for all new building within the boundaries. In fact they approved after this date the building of many thousands of tenement homes with only the most primitive of sanitary arrangements. Two things in general caused the Commissioners to disallow building, the construction of new houses below street level, and the provision of 'ash-pits'—a euphemism for open communal privies—without modesty screening. Otherwise the speculators were free. Glasgow used the Act to begin a system of 'ticketing' tenement houses in an attempt to control overcrowding by posting on doors the number of people each house was allowed to accommodate. It was effective enough in small areas but never comprehensively applied.[62]

If real improvement in the living conditions of the people was still distant, important advances in social theory had been made. The volume of protest at the possibility of state interference hints at the shouters' recognition that it inevitably approached. Enlightened thinkers, not all of them the wildest of radicals, were beginning to believe that action by the state and the expenditure of public money would become necessary. But in 1867 the belief that private enterprise would, with support and encouragement, be enough to rehouse the slum dwellers, seemed to have some foundation and the alternative was not to be frankly faced for a very long time.

Under the leadership of a Prime Minister who was convinced not only of the political expediency but of the real desirability and the moral need of improving housing conditions, a genuine attempt at a Housing Act was to be made in the next session. But Disraeli was as clearly opposed to compulsion as any Whig.

Chapter 23

The Torrens and Cross Acts

'The net result of the remedial legislation was to give the sanction of law to a low grade urban environment'
LEWIS MUMFORD, *Culture of Cities*

Lord Shaftesbury believed that the most necessary condition for the improvement of the homes of the people was a *rapprochement* between the aristocracy and the poor. If the aristocrat would step down from his carriage, enter the alleys and the back-courts, experience with his own senses the smell and the damp chill and the squalor, it would be enough to make him act. The finding of enough money from private pockets, the carrying out of the necessary work, the passing of the necessary legislation in Parliament would be bound to follow upon this acquiring of knowledge. Shaftesbury saw his peers as able and by duty bound to protect the poor and helpless. An alliance of the hereditary governing class and the needy labouring people was needed against the business classes, whose greed had built the slums and overcrowded them and now extracted extortionate rents from them.

Octavia Hill and the strong hearts of the Charity Organisation Society also believed in the need for first-hand experience of the misery of the poor. But they saw little hope of salvation from their Lordships alone. Their middle-class solution was work among the poor by dedicated professional men and women along with encouraging legislation from a Parliament enlightened by social idealism.

While peers and middle-class reformers talked of the need for a drawing together of the classes and a greater closeness with the poor, the separation had, in fact, never been greater. The housing conditions the well-to-do found necessary for themselves demonstrate the separation. Within the house the green baize door, the servants' staircase, separated one class from another. Shuttered and barred windows, ritually locked doors, spiked railings and padlocked gates protected those within from the unsafe streets outside. Policemen, chosen for their height and brawn, patrolled the pavements, 'moving along' any loiterer whose dress or manner betrayed his origin in a class other than that a genteel neighbourhood was built for. Large stores were peopled only by the middle classes; the poor bought at quite a different kind of shop. In theatres, concert halls, even in church, the well-to-do had their own comfortable areas firmly separated from the less respectable. Gardens and parks were railinged and locked at night. The whole structure of society maintained the separation of the middle classes from the submerged poor, the people Bright, who disliked the phrases commonly applied to the irredeemably poor, called 'the residuum'. The 'residuum' was what would always be left after charity, religion, education, factory legislation and improved public health had lifted those who could be saved out of the slough of slum dwelling into respectability. The residuum lived in the twilight areas which only the bravest dared to visit, where law hardly existed and could not be enforced.

The necessity for all this protective building of railings, this barricading of middle-class society, was the acknowledged existence of barely suppressed violence; violence contained by the vigilance of the police within the twilight areas, contained but not suppressed. Should it break through the surface calm of Victorian every-day living no one knew at whom it might be directed. They knew that a chink in the protective stockade would be immediately taken advantage of. *The Builder* reported, for instance, the frequency of looting by street mobs after fires in shops or houses.[1] The mob was still to be feared.

In this climate, where middle-class Victorian society constantly rejoiced in its prosperity, its freedom, its well-protected safety, and yet as constantly feared the threat which lay not entirely dormant in the slum areas of cities, it is not surprising that the legislation which Parliament was able to put through was concerned with the dispelling of the slums. The next era in the history of housing reform was the era of the Improvement Laws. The Lodging Houses Acts had been achieved. The Acts which would actually create housing were in the future. Between lay the period of the Improvement Acts.

The acknowledged purpose of the new Acts, the 'improvement' of our cities, the creation of better public health by the removal of the focus of disease, was almost unanimously approved. It was, in fact, for most people, if not for the immediate instigators of reform, not the real reason why they were prepared to suffer bureaucratic interference with private property. The first and most sweeping improvement schemes were deliberately driven through the most criminal areas, with the dispersal of criminals from their haunts, and the suppression of crime as the first motive. The fact that these haunts were in most cases also the most insanitary parts of the cities was a secondary consideration. The frequency with which the emotive phrase 'dens of vice' crops up is some indication of attitude.

In the first chapter the importance of *intention* in housing was looked at. Here is another example of its importance. The Improvement Acts of Torrens and Cross, although they were pioneering attempts at lifting the condition of the people, in fact increased the misery of the cities. By allowing and encouraging the demolition of homes without a rehousing policy they inevitably increased over-crowding and the ills attendant upon it. They did make the policing of the cities easier because anti-social elements were dispersed and took time to form again. They did not make the homes of the people more comfortable or more abundantly available. They achieved their first and unacknowledged aim and failed to achieve their second and proclaimed aim. Their real intention was to make the cities pleasanter in appearance by removing the worst eye-sores among the slums, and safer for the middle classes to walk in. It was not the intention needed for the real improvement of the housing of the working classes.

Those who later sat upon commissions to study the effects of these laws expressed surprise and disappointment at their failure; but the Torrens and Cross Acts were a direct answer to the demands of the society of their time and their failure was entirely consistent with the insufficiency of those demands. Until society could be led to demand reasonable living conditions for all its members, Parliament would answer with ineffective legislation; and in 1868 society was demanding only the appearance of improvement. In spite of this, the Acts of

Torrens and Cross are still significant, still represent a breakthrough. They represent a ground-work on which further legislation could be built. Their failure itself was important in demonstrating the lines which further reform would be bound to take.

On 20 November 1867 McCullagh Torrens, Kinnaird and Locke were ordered to prepare and bring in a Bill to provide better dwellings for artisans and labourers.[2] Although a Conservative government was in power, this important Bill was the work of Liberal Members of Parliament, many months of study and research having gone into its preparation without any noticeable encouragement from the leaders of their own party.

Under Disraeli the Bill found parliamentary time. It had a second reading on 11 March and then ran into a minor storm of amendments. This Bill had at first the assurance of the support of government Ministers, but it would seem that support was less enthusiastically given after the first few months of position and counter position. Torrens certainly thought so, and spoke of the government's 'astonishing change of tactics' with regard to the Bill.[3] Perhaps the opposition from the Metropolitan constituencies was stronger than expected; more likely Disraeli's own attention was taken up by other urgent matters and the support of his Ministers was less willingly given. On 6 May the third reading was allowed after a very short debate and the Commons passed the Artisans' and Labourers' Dwellings Act, 1868, on the 9th.

But it was not during the Commons debates that this Bill suffered its most serious disfigurement. The select committee of 1866 had already analysed and expanded every provision in it so that Torrens was more than justified in his indignation in 1868 when further adaptations were required, the Bill having already, as he said, occupied the attention of the House and of the select committee at great length. The 1866 Committee, however, had reported to the House on 18 June of that year, a day so taken up with the important debate on the representation of the people, the re-distribution of seats and the consequent need for Ministerial changes, that recommendations about housing were barely nodded at. Torrens's original Bill as presented to Parliament had eighteen clauses. By the time the select committee had finished with it there were forty-four. Many of the new clauses were concerned with safeguarding the owners of property or limiting the extent of spending by local authorities, although the recommendation of concerned witnesses to the select committee had assured the inclusion of other clauses to increase the Bill's chances of success. One major change introduced by the committee escaped notice in 1866 only to arouse great resentment and opposition in 1868. Torrens had intended that in London the local vestries should be the authorities carrying out demolition and reconstruction under his new Act. Doubts about the efficiency and good intentions of the vestries led the committee to substitute the Metropolitan Board of Works as the operating authority. In the years since 1855 the Board had rubbed too many parish officials the wrong way. This extra usurping of their authority with the threatened over-riding of parochial interests accounted for a great deal of opposition to the new presentation of the Bill in 1868. Members of Parliament for Metropolitan districts, particularly Tower Hamlets and Marylebone, had had time to become aware of their electorate's hostility to the Bill. They were now in a difficult position. Only a short time past 'they had gone to the hustings with professions of anxiety for the welfare of the working man on their lips'.[4] Now the strong interest vested in slum property in their parishes forced their opposition to the first Bill of a Parliament openly in favour of social reform. Their subsequent twistings in debate to delay without openly opposing the Bill caused some derision in the House.

What now seems extraordinary is that Torrens's original firm intention that demolition should be followed by rebuilding suffered neither change nor even any real opposition either by the select committee or through the debates in the House of Commons. Some clauses which in fact represented much less earth-shaking changes in the social organisation of the country had to be battled for. For instance, the clause allowing medical officers to enter, inspect and report upon insanitary or overcrowded premises was very much disliked, and the old cry of 'continental despotism' was brought against it.[5] But the very important Clause 28 which stated unequivocally that: 'The purposes of the Act shall be deemed to be, first, the providing by the construction of new buildings or the repairing and improving of existing buildings, the labouring classes with suitable dwellings', seems hardly to have attracted attention. A minor amendment by Mr Powell whose deeper purpose was guessed by Members to be an attempt to relieve local authorities of the responsibility of erecting new buildings for the working classes was quickly defeated.[6]

Parliament behaved as if council-house building by local authorities was a quite unsurprising idea easily accepted into the social order. Did Members know that this clause would, in fact, never be acted upon and that there was, therefore, no need to oppose it? It is certainly not the case that the general principle had been accepted that houses for the poor should be provided from public funds. That would be fought over for many decades to come. The explanation of the almost apathetic acceptance of this significant clause can only be that, because the Act contained no element of compulsion to rebuild, Parliament did not feel threatened by it.

Indeed they had no need to fear Clause 28 because, after the Act had been passed by the Commons, this and all subsequent clauses were expunged by the Lords before the Act gained Royal assent. The preamble to the Act as printed still read: 'whereas it is expedient to make provision for taking down or improving dwellings occupied by working men and their families which are unfit for human habitation,[7] *and for the building and maintenance of better dwellings for such* persons'. The levying of a 2d rate for the purposes of the Act was still allowed. But the important clause which defined the first purpose of the Act as providing housing was deleted. Two pence would, in any case, have proved even more insufficient for the purpose of building than it did for the purpose of demolition.

Another amendment by the Lords served to weaken the Bill even further. By changing the word 'street' to the word 'premises' they limited very much the powers of medical officers.[8] The power to deal with insanitary areas rather than insanitary houses was thereby withheld until Cross's Act of 1875; and to pick out one house more insanitary than another in a warren of slums was a task of some nicety.

As amended and passed by both Houses of Parliament Torrens's Act allowed officers of health to enter premises on their own initiative (this was an important step forward, allowing a progressive health officer to go ahead in spite of an unhelpful council), and gave them the duty of reporting insanitary premises to the local authority.[9] The authority was then bound to report to the owner of the property the work which their surveyors found necessary to make the place habitable. If the owner neglected to carry out the work the local authority was given power to shut up or demolish the property and to charge the cost to the owner. If the local authority failed to act, the Secretary of State was given the power to compel it to proceed. The levying of a 2d rate was allowed and the Public Works Commissioners could make loans to the local authorities for the purpose. This last way of raising money was, of course, already open through the Act of 1866. The new Act applied without further legislation to Scotland and England.

This Act, deriving from the work of the National Association of Social Science and of the Society of Medical Officers,[10] which made Torrens an honorary member, was planned as a real solution to the housing of the poor. In its passage through Parliament, through handling by people of less disinterested concern for its original intention, it became something far short of a solution. Its only effect was to empower, but not compel, local authorities to demolish individual insanitary houses. Most authorities chose to ignore it, as it was very easy for them to do. In the first place the whole mechanics of the new improvement legislation was to be put in motion by the report of the medical officer. Medical officers were of variable quality, not by any means, for instance, always qualified doctors. The Public Health Act, 1872, provided for the first time that medical officers who were legally qualified medical practitioners must be appointed in place of the old officers of health.[11] Sir J. Clerk Jervoise, Liberal Member for Hampshire South, was not being so very unjustifiably condescending when he said in the House during the debate on the third reading that 'it would be very difficult to find an officer of health whose discretion would warrant their entrusting him'.[12] But the 'medical police' were, for the most part, compassionate men, and their compassion, in fact, hindered the effective working of the Act. Medical officers knew that if they recommended the closure of an overcrowded house its evicted tenants would not have their situation improved by that action. Even if replacement housing were to be built it would never by built before demolition. The evicted could move only to similar, or worse, accommodation. It was, at least in part, as Professor Wohl has shown, 'due to the sensitivity of medical officers to the plight of the poor that [the Act] was not more vigorously pursued'.[13]

The doctors' reluctance to order closure or demolition was surpassed of course by the owners' reluctance to lose or to spend money.[14] Torrens's Act contained no compensation clause—the only return the owner of demolished slum property received under the Act was the amount raised by the sale of materials. He was not compensated for the loss of income from his house. The Artisans' and Labourers' Dwellings Amendment Act, 1879, contained a compensation clause but its existence was so little publicised that it was never used. Faced with the threat of compulsory purchase or forced demolition and the consequent drop of income from rents, owners most frequently chose to carry out the minimum of repairs necessary to keep the house open and productive of rents. The economics of slum proprietorship, then, made the Act unlikely to be very effective as an instrument of slum clearance, because owners chose to hang on to their property at the cost of some small, and usually temporary, spending on improved amenity.[15] This perhaps did a little to improve conditions in some properties but did not make progress, as the Act had intended, towards the replanning and improvement of the whole slum area.

The landlord class was not the only vested interest working against the intention of Torrens's Act. Speculators in property saw in the Act an opportunity for self-enrichment. Labouchère informed the House of the operations of 'a notorious bill-discounter' who was busily buying up slum properties which he hoped local authorities would be forced to buy from him again to his profit.[16] In the event the gentleman must have been disappointed because the reaction of most local authorities was to do nothing. They did not dare to offend their electorate by raising the necessary rate, they did not dare to offend the influential property owners, many of whom were local councillors, by interfering with private property, nor were they, in any case, convinced of the rightness of the principle that those who did not help themselves should be helped by public action and public expenditure. The report to Parliament by the Public Loans Commissioners in 1874 on the sums granted under the terms of the 1868 Act showed no grants to have been made, or *asked* for, for the purposes of that Act.[17] Liverpool and Glasgow raised rates for the purpose of slum clearance, but few local authorities followed their example.[18]

Unwillingness to offend rate-payers, and reactionary beliefs, were not the only characteristics braking local authority action. The Act allowed for compulsion by the Metropolitan Board in London and by the Secretary of State in other areas when individual local authorities failed to take action after a representation. This provision actually decreased the chances of local authorities' adoption of the Act. Their hatred of interference by the central government was such as to make them hostile to any Act containing such a provision. The Royal Commission of 1884–5 found that local authorities were always reluctant to apply regulations forced upon them by central authority.[19]

One of the major hold-ups to reform of any kind and to Torrens's Act, as to the 1866 Sanitary Act, was the pressing need for the reform of local government, especially in London. Petty parochialism, the insurmountable power of local vested interests, the overlapping of responsibilities, the unequal distribution of burdens, the sheer inefficiency of the system, all made reform under whatever enlightened legislation difficult to the point of being extremely unlikely.

Add to these reasons, that is to the doctor's compassionate reluctance, the landlord's greedy reluctance, the local authority's slothful reluctance, the difficulty of carrying out improvement schemes with insufficient funds, and it is little wonder that the Artisans' and Labourers' Dwellings Act, 1868, was not the success Torrens had hoped.

In succeeding years various amending Acts attempted to make it more effectual, for Parliament was not left unaware of its failure. Section 14 of the amending statute of 1879 put back the important clause defining the purpose of the Act as: 'The providing, by the construction of new buildings, or the repairing of existing buildings, the labouring classes with suitable dwellings.'[20] But in that lost decade since the original clause of 1868 had been deleted, the economic situation had worsened so much that house-building had passed its peak of activity, in 1876, and began a decline from which it did not quickly recover. The chance of council building while economic conditions were still reasonably favourable towards the building industry was lost. Section 6 of the Public Works Loans Act[21] of the same year, in any case, destroyed hopes of borrowing from government funds by raising the rate of interest demanded.

A further important amendment was later given by the Artizans Dwellings Act, 1882, which widened the powers of taking property to include not only buildings *unfit for habitation*[22] as the original Act did, but also *obstructive* buildings, those so situated as to prevent the entrance of light and air to other buildings, or to prevent their repair and improvement.[23]

The 1879 Amendment Act had to wait not only upon a greater understanding of the weaknesses inherent in the Torrens Act as passed but also upon the return of a Conservative government. Disraeli's short term of power ended in November 1868. Gladstone's period as Prime Minister lasted until February 1874 when the General Election returned the Conservatives to power and Disraeli to office. During the years 1869–73 there was no attempt at further legislation on housing.[24] This was partly, of course, because it took time to show that the Torrens Act was insufficient in itself to achieve major changes in the direction of urban redevelopment. It was partly because bodies like the Charity Organisation Society were determined that future reports prepared by them should be researched with such thoroughness that they could not easily be waved aside. They finally presented to Parliament in 1874 a memorial on the improvement of the dwellings of the poor in London which led to the Government Act on housing in 1875. More important than these two factors in causing delay, however, was Gladstone's absorption in other affairs, his indifference, not perhaps to the condition of the people, but to legislation about it, his aloofness even from the social reformers of his own party, his belief that moral resurgence would come by other means.

This spell of parliamentary inactivity gave time for some new assessment of the effect of legislation up to that date. Most noticeable is the wealth of provisions and the paucity of effect. Abortive legislation up to 1868 has been considered here with a detailed attention which may seem to bear little relation to its effectiveness and importance. But effectiveness and importance do not necessarily co-exist. The Acts up to and including Torrens were not effective. They were, however, important, because they contained within them, and established in the minds of politicians, every principle, except one, which was necessary for the solving of the housing problem; and even that one, the principle of compulsion, could be aired in Parliament with surprisingly little reaction.[25] Not only the principle but the mechanics of the necessary legislation were already there. The structure of housing law was established; the first assessment of need, the process of survey, purchase and construction, the method of financing had all been thought out. Local authorities had by now power to inspect and report, to close and demolish; to enforce drainage, the provision of water, cleansing and ventilation; to make regulations about building standards, to limit overcrowding, to provide lodgings and, under the 1851 and 1866 Acts, to build houses for working people. It seemed as though it was not further legislation that was needed, but a change of heart. Until compulsion could be introduced into housing law, and that was far distant, no parliamentary action could make any real difference. The change of heart was unlikely to come under a Gladstone government.

When Disraeli assumed power after the election of 1874 he did so with confidence in his majority in the House of Commons, a comfort he had lacked in 1866–8. He had a strong Cabinet, a sympathetic sovereign, and a firmly planned programme of social reform. The 1874 election had brought Parliament its first Labour Members, Alexander Macdonald and Thomas Burt, a slight indication of the country's wish for change. The Queen's Speech on opening Parliament referred with concern to the Health of the People, and the Honourable Edward Stanhope took up the subject when he moved the address; Alexander Whitelaw, iron-master of Gartsherry and Member of Parliament for Glasgow, seconded with reference to the new housing in Glasgow and the pollution of the Clyde, although Disraeli wrote afterwards that while the strength of his subject gave him 'a becoming position in the business of the evening' he 'unfortunately spoke in the language of his country and so soon lost the house'.[26]

The new Prime Minister divided the great subject of the condition of the people into three main lines of attack: housing, savings and the relation between master and servant. He was later to refer to the Cross Act as 'our chief measure', and it is certainly true that the improvement of the housing of the people was of real personal importance to him and that he believed it could be effected by legislation in Parliament. These were the most auspicious circumstances for the passing of an effectual Housing Act which had yet obtained.

Information on which to base new legislation was beginning to accumulate too. Latest among the relevant reports was the evidence of the Royal Commission on Building Societies of 1871. In 1873 a Building Societies Bill was presented to the then Liberal Parliament. Three attempts at reframing it were defeated and each time it was withdrawn. In April 1874 the Conservative, Sir Charles Russell, presented a new Building Societies Bill which went smoothly through Parliament.

1873 had seen other abortive attempts at useful housing legislation, W. D. Fordyce, the Liberal Member for East Aberdeenshire, had presented a 'Bill to facilitate the erection of labourers' cottages and other buildings by agricultural tenants in Scotland'. It was not successful in getting a second reading that year and Fordyce presented it again to Disraeli's Parliament on 3 March. It was withdrawn on 7 July, presented again on 8 February 1875 and withdrawn again on 7 July of that year. Other Liberal measures had better luck. John Whitwell, Liberal Member for Kendal, and Wren Hoskins had also tried to present a Housing Bill under Gladstone. Their 'Bill for facilitating the acquisition of land and its transfer for cottages for the manual labour class' was presented on 13 February 1873. Like the Labourers Cottages (Scotland) Bill, it got no second reading then. It was presented again in March 1874 by Whitwell and Morley in slightly different form and passed without much difficulty on 23 June[27] as the Working Men's Dwellings Act, 1874.

On 1 July 1874 the first Conservative measure on housing was presented by Sir Percy Burrell, member for Shoreditch, in the form of a 'Bill to give increased facilities for the erection of labourers' and artizans' dwellings'. It also got no second reading and had to be withdrawn.

The Liberal Morley brought in on 28 April 1875 a 'Bill to enable the Public Works Loan Commissioners to make advances for building labourers' cottages in rural districts'. It was withdrawn without a second reading on 5 July at 1.30 in the morning.

This confusion of frustrated legislation might seem to point to unwillingness by the reigning government to come to terms with the problem or to reluctance to allow opposition Members the credit for progressive measures under a Conservative government which they had been unable to have passed under their own leader. Disraeli's expressed opinion, on the contrary, was that the Liberal measures had been introduced only as delaying tactics. 'The plot was to waste the session and then hold the government up to scorn, for their imbecility, during the recess.'[28] In fact, however, these Bills were rejected because the Bill that Richard Cross, Disraeli's Home Secretary, was working on, was planned to draw all their separate threads together in one more comprehensive measure. Together with the great Public Health Act,

1875, which as we have seen laid down an enlightened code of Building Regulations,[29] the Cross Act was to represent the Conservative effort at real improvement of the condition of the people. As the 'Bill for facilitating the improvement of the dwellings of the working classes in large towns' it was presented on 8 February and passed on 30 April 1875, as the Artisans' and Labourers' Dwellings Improvement Act, 1875. 'Late at night, without any one being aware of it', wrote the Prime Minister to Lady Bradford, 'we passed the third reading of the Artizans Dwellings Bill, our chief measure, which now goes to the Lords.'[30]

The Cross Act[31] recognised that one of the impediments to the effectual working of the 1868 Torrens Act had been the uselessness of attacking slum areas in a piecemeal fashion. Its chief purpose, therefore, was to allow, and to encourage, slum clearance on a larger scale, the purchase and demolition by the local authority of large areas of 'unfit' property. It was in this respect, if in few others, an advance on the earlier Improvement Act.

It also recognised in its wording that wholesale demolition would increase homelessness and paid lip-service to the notion of rehousing as a public responsibility: 'Whereas various portions of many cities are so built . . . as to be highly injurious to the moral and physical welfare of the inhabitants . . . and whereas it is necessary for much demolishing and for provision to be made for those displaced . . .' But while it did allow for the possibility of rehousing by local authorities it was quite clear in its expression of government disapproval of the idea.

The local authority was to draw up schemes for the improvement of slum areas, carrying out the street planning, paving and sewering of the land itself and granting or leasing the land to persons who would build upon it under conditions imposed by the authority. If the authority did build houses it was to sell them to private owners within ten years. Parliament was simply not ready to accept the idea of government, whether central or local, accepting any long-term responsibility for housing, Nor was it prepared to accept the notion of subsidy. While the local authority was allowed to *use* public money by raising rates or borrowing for the purposes of the Act, it was taken for granted that this should not entail a loss to the rate-payers. So unrealistic was the approach that the need for raising money was only contemplated 'if there is an excess of expenditure over receipts'.[32] It was still imagined that the local authority could purchase slums, lay out land, and build houses for the poor without loss.

Cross's Artisans' and Labourers' Dwellings Improvement Act was, therefore, less of an advance than it might seem. Even had local authorities vigorously pressed on with rebuilding there would necessarily have been a time-lag between demolition and rehousing during which people rendered homeless by slum clearance increased overcrowding in neighbouring areas. Medical officers were, therefore, as reluctant as they had been under the Torrens Act to recommend closure and demolition. The financial arrangements for action by the local authority were not new. The important step in that field had been taken by the Public Health Act, 1875, which laid down principles for the purchase of land by local authorities. Both the Cross Act and the Housing of the Working Classes Act, 1890, use the phrase 'in like manner as if those purposes were the purposes of the Public Health Act of 1875'.

Local authorities were, in any case, far from vigorous in their chase after improvement. All the same disincentives remained, the apathy, the fear of offending the electorate, the vested interests within the corporation and the pressure groups among slum proprietors. Some slum landlords saw in the Act a great opportunity for money-making. By making sure that property was crammed beyond capacity when the surveyor came to assess its value before compulsory purchase by the council, landlords could put in exaggerated compensation claims based on takings for rent. These excessive demands for compensation were important in limiting the working of the Act.

But the most important disincentive was the extremely cumbersome nature of the machinery of the Act. Had it been easily workable it would have been at least difficult for all the excuses motivated by greed, laziness and power-seeking to be as effectively delaying as they turned out to be. Given the complications, the inevitable slowness and, above all, the intrusion of central bureaucracy into local affairs, all the other reasons for delay were reinforced by the argument of administrative difficulty. For each attempt at improvement a local authority had to submit a scheme to Parliament. In each case the House of Commons had to consider a 'Bill to confirm provisional orders of the Local Government Board (Artizans' and Labourers' Dwellings)'. In Scotland similar orders were usually made under the general Burgh Police and Improvement Act, 1862, or under local Acts until after 1883 when the Act for constituting a Local Government Board for Scotland was passed. This was cumbersome enough and meant the kind of submission of local interests to state scrutiny which caused parochial resentment. But should the scheme be found to need modification, and in almost every instance this proved to be the case, representation had again to be made to the Secretary of State requesting that he make an order permitting the modifications. The chance of a local body acting independently in answer to local initiative might be small enough. The certainty that such an initiative would immediately involve the local council in prying by the central government often removed what little chance there was.

The trouble was that once an official representation had been made, no matter how unwilling the local council might be to admit its justification, the affair became the business of the Local Government Board. An entertaining correspondence between the Secretary of that body and Dover's town clerk, who bore the imposing name of Wollaston Knocker, illustrates parochial attitudes very well. In 1876 fifteen rate-payers of Dover complained to the medical officer of the condition of a group of houses on Harbour Road property. These houses were not only dilapidated, insanitary, ill-ventilated and ruinous but actually below the level of high tides and liable to flooding. The medical officer not unnaturally recommended action by the town council. The town council asked the town clerk to inform them of their legal responsibilities and of the probable cost of accepting them, and meanwhile allowed Dover to be listed as one of the towns considering adoption of the Cross Act.

Mr Knocker's report in which he dwelt at some length on the complexities of the Act and emphasised the difficulties experienced elsewhere in obtaining borrowing powers was not encouraging. It is most likely that town clerks everywhere tended to hold back progress by discouraging adoption of reforming Acts. The town clerk, after all, was the man on whom much of the extra work would fall, as well as being the man most able to see the difficulties and expenses into which councils could be led.

Dover town council, rather than actually refuse to purchase the property, chose to doubt that it was in as bad a state as was reported. They claimed that 'they were not satisfied with the correctness of the representation' and then sat back, justified in inaction.

But, having received from the medical officer an official representation about uninhabitable property the Local Government Board was now bound to inquire what steps had been taken to improve the area: the reply they received shows both how unused to such central interference local authorities were and how unwilling they were to accept it. There was no apology or excuse for inaction. Wollaston Knocker wrote back: 'I am to ask you to be good enough to inform me by what authority your inquiry is made.'[33]

The Royal Commissioners of 1884–5 reported that between the passing of the Cross Act and 1884 only eleven towns had sought for and obtained provisional orders and only nine had begun improvement schemes. Actually there were twelve listed in the Return with respect to the 1875 Act of the number of official representations made between 1875 and 1882.[34] They were Birmingham, Derby, Devonport, Liverpool, Newcastle, Norwich, Nottingham, Swansea, Walsall, Wolverhampton, Greenock and Leith. Newcastle decided, after the provisional order had been confirmed, to act under its own local Act instead, and carried out a plan of street improvement paid for out of the rates. Derby had its order confirmed and then took no further action. Devonport pulled down five streets of houses, rebuilt houses on two-fifths of the area and, in 1883, had approved plans for more houses. This was without any loan. Liverpool pursued, as we have seen, a relatively vigorous campaign of clearing and rebuilding with the help of a Public Works Loan of £50,000. Norwich quickly completed a limited scheme of street improvement. Nottingham made two separate schemes. The first, in 1875, was a simple slum-clearance scheme paid for out of the rates, and the cost recouped by the sale of land and materials. Their 1881 scheme was more ambitious. Land was leased by the corporation for building houses and in 1883 dwellings were in the course of being erected. In Swansea all the houses included in their 1876 scheme had been demolished by 1883 and new houses were being built on a portion of the cleared property. Swansea borrowed £120,970 from the Public Works Loan Commissioners. Walsall purchased slum property with a loan of £15,000, cleared the land and relet it. Wolverhampton used a loan of £207,330 to purchase slum property and drive new streets through it.

It will be noticed that only four towns were replacing the houses they demolished.

Of all the schemes, only Birmingham's, with a loan of £1,500,000, was of any size, And Birmingham had important special advantages. To begin with, while it had areas of severe overcrowding they were of nothing like the extent of the worst affected cities. Birmingham was still an artisan town with a tradition of self-respecting independence which stemmed from well-paid skills and relatively steady employment. Most important of all it had as its mayor, Joseph Chamberlain, whose radical beliefs, energetic campaigning and brilliant strategy not only gave the town a compelling leadership and a co-ordinated attack but succeeded in obtaining what Chamberlain himself called 'exceptional terms which were not enjoyed by any other corporation in the kingdom.'[35]

Birmingham corporation purchased factories as well as houses in the areas it wished to improve and arranged for the rebuilding of those factories in the suburbs. So, by providing work in the suburbs for displaced people, it avoided the necessity for rehousing them in the central areas, and the Local Government Board was persuaded by Chamberlain to waive the rehousing clause. Speculative builders found it profitable enough to build houses where there was steady employment. The cleared central areas could therefore be let to commercial developers with high profits for the corporation.[36] So Birmingham could enjoy the clearing of slums from her town centre, the building of fine new shopping streets, without increasing the burden of homelessness. But few towns were in the lucky position of having factories in sufficient numbers within the worst crowded slum areas and it was the removal of those factories to the suburbs as an attraction for labour which made Chamberlain's scheme possible. Even then, the compensation demanded by the factory owners nearly crippled the plan.

One of the effects of improvement schemes which was much resented by those towns which had adopted the Cross Act and certainly discouraged other towns from so doing was that expensive council clearance schemes raised the value of neighbouring areas at no profit to the council. Chamberlain, by wangling much more extensive powers of purchasing land than other towns obtained, made sure that Birmingham council profited by its own schemes. Other town councils saw speculators buying up and profiting from land on the borders of their schemes without being able to prevent such profiteering. The subject of a 'betterment levy', which would subtract from neighbouring proprietors' slum-clearance profits a portion for public funds, was raised in most discussions about town improvement in the next decades. The real need, however, was for towns to be given much more extensive purchasing powers so that they could buy land for future needs and, incidentally, take for themselves the immediate benefits of bettering property near improvement schemes.

Both the Cross and the Torrens Acts were 'Improvement Acts',[37] chiefly concerned with slum clearance and town centre improvement. Cross, the Conservative, and Torrens, the Liberal, both believed not only that private enterprise *should* provide housing, but that it was likely to do so. They believed that it was not really the business of the state to build houses and that it was not, in any case, necessary for the state to attempt it. Birmingham's experience, where private housing speculators were quickly able to fill the demand created by demolition under the improvement scheme, appeared to prove them right. Few other towns put the theory to any searching test. Without fairly sophisticated analysis it was very easy in 1875 to suppose that charitable endeavour and speculative enterprise together, would soon have the need for housing well in hand. Ventures like the Artizan and General's Shaftesbury Park seemed hopeful forerunners of future schemes for housing the less well to do.[38] The peak of house-building activity was to be reached in 1876. In 1875 it could not have been possible to know that the decline was soon to begin, it was only possible to note the activity and to count on its being sustained.

Thousands were being housed in decent new villas either by the model dwellings associations or, increasingly as the suburban railway lines pushed out, in new suburbs built by speculators. It was not immediately apparent in the 1870s that those people moving into the new houses were too seldom those displaced from the old, and that a substantial section of the population was becoming unhousable by private enterprise.

Chapter 24

The Royal Commission

'not a safe sort of people'
Evidence given to Select Committee on Housing, 1881

When the end of the house-building boom began eventually to be recognised for what it was, the enthusiasm for slum clearance began to seem less enlightened. The era of the Town Improvement Acts, which were really demolition-directed, came to an end. Up to this time all legislation had aimed at demolition or regulation, it had been restrictive and destructive. Gradually the need for a constructive Housing Act began to be recognised.

In the meantime, however, the chief business of government was to make the Acts already passed more workable. On 6 December 1878 William Torrens presented to the House a Bill to extend the powers of the Torrens Act by provisions for compensation and rebuilding. The original Bill, it will be remembered, had made no provision for the compensation of proprietors whose condemned houses were to be demolished. This clause brought it into line with the Cross Act. Torrens's original provisions for rebuilding and re-housing were replaced. There was no smooth passage through the House for this independent measure and it suffered considerably through amendment and delay before being passed by the House of Commons on 9 August 1879 as the Artisans' and Labourers' Dwellings Act (1868) Amendment Act, 1879.[1] In contrast, the Bill presented by the Home Secretary, Richard Cross, to amend the 1875 Act was presented on 6 August 1879 and passed on the 9th.[2] Its chief purpose was to limit the amounts of compensation which, under Cross's Act, could be claimed by slum-property owners forced to sell. The new amendment clipped the claims by providing that, where overcrowding constituted a nuisance, the compensation should be based on the value of the house after the nuisance had been abated. So a proprietor could no longer take a house which had been judged technically overcrowded with thirty inhabitants, cram another twenty tenants into it and claim compensation for the value of the increased rental. He must, after 1879, reduce the original overcrowded thirty to a more reasonable number and base his claim on that reduced rental.

Another clause sought to relieve local authorities of the obligation laid down in the original Act to re-house displaced people on the sites where their demolished homes had stood. The expected difficulty of finding a lessee or buyer for cleared land with this condition hung on it had deterred slum clearance in many towns. Local authorities were now permitted to rehouse on alternative sites and to let cleared central land more profitably for commercial purposes. There was no shortage of takers for commercial building on central town sites, and it was argued that new modes of transport made central housing less essential for labourers. The new clause made slum clearance potentially profitable for town councils instead of cripplingly expensive.

These changes might have made Cross's Artisans' and Labourers' Dwellings Improvement Act, 1875, more workable by making it less expensive for local authorities to adopt it. But in the same year Disraeli's Chancellor, Sir Stafford Northcote, in his Public Works Loans Act, 1879,[3] dealt Cross another blow by raising the interest rate on all Public Works Commissioners' Loans. Northcote's difficulty in balancing his budget in a period of depression and unemployment left him little alternative. Nevertheless the increased cost of loans inevitably acted as a disincentive to local authority building.[4] The Artisans' and Labourers' Dwellings Improvement (Scotland) Act, 1875, was not amended until 1880 when it became law as the Artisans' and Labourers' Dwellings Improvement (Scotland) Act, 1880.[5]

Torrens did a little more tidying up of his 1868 Act which he presented on 9 February 1880, and then saw successfully through the Commons a 'Bill to explain and amend the 22nd Section of the 1868 Amendment Act, 1879'.

It was, however, becoming clear that more than pernickety amendment was needed. Disraeli, now Lord Beaconsfield, had chosen to go to the country in the spring of 1880. Parliament met again on 29 April with Gladstone as Prime Minister and the Liberal majority sorely divided into Gladstonians and Nationalists. One of the steps taken by this government was the appointment in May 1881 of a select committee whose purpose was 'to consider the working of the 1875 and 1879

Acts with a view of considering how the expense and delay and difficulty in carrying out these Acts may be reduced and also of inquiring into any causes which may have prevented the reconstruction of dwellings for the artizan class to the full extent contemplated and authorised by these Acts'. This committee seems to have been the government's answer to awkward questions asked in the House about the effectiveness of the 1879 Amendment Act to which Mr Dodson, for the government, had been forced to reply that action had been taken in only one or two cases. Neither Chamberlain at the Board of Trade nor Shaw-Lefevre at the Board of Works could cheerfully accept responsibility for this kind of failure. Among those appointed to the committee were Sir Sydney Waterlow, William Torrens and Richard Cross.[6]

On 2 August they made an interim report. The evidence so far collected had impressed the committee with the urgency of the need for action and, while they wished to hear more evidence, they were anxious not to hold up progress by causing doubt about the outcome of their work. They therefore recommended that

'with a view of lessening the expense of carrying out the intentions of the Act of 1875 . . . the confirming authority will be justified in giving a liberal interpretation to the relaxing power in the 4th Section of the Amending Act of 1879 and may take into account as in part fulfilment of the obligation to provide equally convenient accommodation and suitable existing facilities of transport to a reasonable distance and at reasonable prices by water, tramways, or workmen's trains.'[7]

The evidence certainly showed that the anticipated expense of adopting the 1875 Act had frightened off local authorities. However, it also showed that very, very few had ever given it any serious consideration. In addition to the small group of towns using the Act only another five could claim to be considering adoption.[8]

The reconstituted committee meeting during 1881/2 heard evidence not only from local authority officials and housing proprietors but from representatives of the working people and of their trades councils, showing deference to the strength of the new urban voters. Its report, issued on 19 June 1882, showed clearly that the Acts had not been used as fully as they might have been and that the need for housing for working people was still very severe in spite of the efforts of the charitable housing societies. The new report concluded that the chief reason for widespread failure to adopt the Acts was that the cost of operation was too high. The cost was too high because of the amount of compensation demanded and granted, the expense of the procedure, including low charges, and the obligation to sell or re-let for artisans' dwellings.[9] The committee decided that the evidence showed that there was no real need for insisting on rebuilding houses on land cleared under the Improvement Acts in the provincial cities. The experience of Edinburgh, Glasgow and Liverpool proved, they felt, that the displaced could easily be found adequate housing on alternative sites. It is possible that further inquiry into the condition of the people cleared from provincial slums might have shed doubts on this conclusion but it was not too closely examined and the report recommended that provincial cities should be relieved of the obligation to house on cleared sites.

In the Metropolis it was clear that there existed a continuing need for some classes of labourers, notably dockers and coster-mongers, to live in the central areas close to their work. Even the special workmen's trains did not come in from the new workmen's suburbs at an hour early enough to catch the earliest markets or the taking on of casual hands at the dock gates. But because the obligation to rehouse was obviously delaying action in the Metropolis it was recommended that the rule should be relaxed and that it should be necessary only to rehouse a portion of those displaced.

So that the day might be advanced when the displaced could safely not be housed in the centre, it was recommended that cheap transport should be encouraged, that central sanitary provisions should be extended to the suburbs, and that existing sanitary regulations in the new suburbs should be more vigorously enforced.[10] Thus with trains not too dear for labourers' pockets and speculative builders prevented from building new slums on the outskirts, the possibility of cheap and pleasant suburban living for the poor would become a reality.

What emerges most clearly from the evidence is that the body of existing legislation on housing had already become too confusing. A medical officer having decided on the need for improvement in his area had to choose between five different sets of machinery before he made his official representation recommending action. To deal with an insanitary group of houses he could use the 1855 Nuisances Act, the 1868 Torrens Act, the 1875 Cross Act or the two 1879 Amending Acts. It was not at all clear when an area became too large for the Torrens Act or too small for the Cross Act. Where owners might be expected to be at all co-operative the Nuisances Acts seemed simpler and cheaper to operate.

There was an obvious need for a consolidating Act which would bring all existing legislation into a more easily understood and more manageable form. Yet Cross's committee did not recommend new legislation of a general kind.

On 25 July 1882, Shaw Lefevre, Chief Commissioner at the Board of Works, and Sir William Harcourt, the Home Secretary, presented to Parliament a Bill to amend the Cross and Torrens Acts, which was passed on 7 August to become the 'Artisans' Dwellings Act, 1882'.[11] It was a weak and nibbling measure, altering the terms of compensation to allow the levying of an improvement rate on properties 'bettered' by neighbouring improvements and reducing the obligation to rehouse so that it affected only half of those displaced.

But if work towards housing reform within the Gladstonian Parliament was half-hearted and ineffective, the period was notable for the hardening of opinion outside. In 1883 three influential journals carried important articles on housing: Lord Salisbury's 'Labourers and Artizans Dwellings', in the *National Review* in November, Joseph Chamberlain's reply to it in the *Fortnightly Review* in December, and H. O. Arnold-Forster's 'The Dwellings of the Poor—the Existing Law' in the *Nineteenth Century*, also in December. These demonstrated editorial assessment of the current importance of the subject in the public mind and they were significant in declaring the presence within each political party of an important protagonist for reform.

The proposals in Salisbury's article were not wildly radical. His suggestion that the system of government loans for housing should be extended so that the cost of borrowing could be lowered and funds made more generally available hardly put him at the head of a socialist campaign, as Goschen, the stern Liberal apostle of *laissez-faire* implied. But the article represented an astonishing desertion of the *laissez-faire* position and an unexpected conversion to the need for state intervention in a Tory who had often suspected the social reforms of others as being sops to democracy. Was it a genuine conversion based on a new knowledge of the living conditions of the working people or a shrewd political move guided by a new assessment of the demands of the expanded electorate?

At any rate, the declaration of Salisbury's hand was decisive in affecting the conduct of the campaign for housing reform in Parliament. The setting up of the exhaustively conducted Royal Commission of 1884–5 was not only the logical but the inevitable consequence of the publication of this article.

Joseph Chamberlain relished his position at the head of those campaigning for the most extreme of reforms. He attacked 'property' with enthusiasm and enjoyed advocating swingeing taxes on land.[12] With an eye to the thousands of voters swayed by the popular economic theories of Henry George he declaimed against Salisbury's modest suggestions and mocked at 'the spectacle of Lords demolishing the economists and entering into conflict with the Liberty and Property

League'.[13] He may have frightened members of his own following by his very radical proposals. Until 1885, however, the presence within the Cabinet as President of the Board of Trade of this improving mayor of Birmingham had an encouraging effect on the morale of campaigners for housing reform.

1883 saw not only these three serious studies of the problem but also the sensational and very effective *Bitter Cry of Outcast London* whose widespread popularity and availability did perhaps more than anything else to arouse the middle-class conscience about housing.

There were other forces learning the principles of warfare for reform. The mid-1880s saw the beginnings of the Fabian Society and the working together of liberal intellectuals like George Bernard Shaw and the Webbs. They saw the founding of the Social Democratic Foundation by H. M. Hyndman. Sir Charles Dilke presided over an Industrial Remuneration Conference in 1884 at which the depressed condition of the working people was well publicised. The 1884 extension of the franchise to the rural labourer greatly increased the proportion of the working classes in the total electorate. The effects of the commercial recession were beginning to drive working people together in attempts to find expression for their resentment and despair. In 1885 John Burns, standing as an Independent Labour Party candidate, polled nearly 600 votes at Nottingham in the parliamentary election. Twenty years later, as Member for Battersea, he was to be President of the Local Government Board. The workers in the 1880s were beginning to find leaders. In February 1885 the Local Government Board received a deputation of unemployed which claimed that destitution was now so severe that the government within the next weeks would be responsible for murder if something was not done.

So on the one hand the intellectuals were developing a social theory dependent upon the assumption of state responsibility for the welfare of the people; the politicians were posturing for places in the procession towards social reform without any real intention of assuming uncomfortable responsibilities; while all the time among the officials who had to administer the existing law there was the same attitude towards the poor as had always existed. The poor were shiftless, undeserving, and to be feared. 'You can tell when you open the door what sort of people live in the house—you can tell they are not a safe sort of people,'[14] one medical officer said.

Everybody above the level of the poorest felt threatened by the existence of this unsafe sort of people. Opinions about how to meet the threat differed widely but as the strength of the working-class vote began to be assessed, the need to gentle this unsafe people into docility by improving their condition began to seem urgent.

Not, however, urgent enough in 1884 to change the dislike of Parliament for any kind of 'interference with the liberty of the subject'. A Bill for the sanitary inspection of dwellings presented by Francis Monckton, Tory Member for Staffordshire West, on 6 February failed to get a second reading. On 4 March the motion was made that 'in the opinion of this House the evils of overcrowding cannot in all cases be adequately met by the enforcement of purely sanitary regulations and that it is therefore expedient that, in the case of certain public trusts having for their object the improvement of the dwellings of the working classes, some relaxation should be made in the rules under which loans are at present granted by the Public Works Loan Commissioners.' Contained within these words was the long needed recognition of the fact that housing was something more than a public health issue, that even if epidemic disease were entirely swept away by sanitary regulations the housing problem would remain, that poverty and the need for the public financing of housing lay behind the appalling overcrowding of slum dwellings. But it was four o'clock in the morning. Fewer than forty members were present. The motion was withdrawn and the House adjourned.

It was in this climate that early in 1884 Lord Salisbury, from the House of Peers, moved the appointment of a Royal Commission on Housing. By this move he raised the status of the problem. Gladstone's government could only refuse to make the appointment at the risk of seeming to despise and neglect the condition of the people.

In the middle of the 1884 session, however, the Liberals were turned out by a combination of the Conservatives and the Irish members. Because the new electoral registers were not yet ready no General Election could be held. Salisbury became Prime Minister in a House in which he had no majority.

Three reports were eventually published by the Housing Commissioners, the first dealing with England and Wales, the second and third with Scotland and Ireland. What the evidence chiefly and shockingly showed was how dangerously overcrowded the big cities were. People who had imagined that the big charities had house-building well in hand, that cheap transport and slum clearance had removed the slum dwellers to the suburbs, and that the end of the killer epidemics meant the end of disease due to bad housing had their illusions snatched away. The reports showed plainly that the cities were still appallingly overcrowded with that unsafe sort of people.

Although, for instance, the population of old London had begun to decline from 1861 and in other cities the pace of growth had at least slackened, two major causes were combining to raise rents beyond the pockets of the poor and to force them to overcrowd cheap property.

First, extensive demolition of housing and the pressure of commercial demand for central sites forced rents of scarce houses up to compete with possible commercial incomes from the same sites. Even when model dwellings associations got sites for one-third less than the commercial price, the cost was still enough to make rents higher than they had been before demolition.

Secondly, the middle-class flight to the suburbs presented builders with a speculators' paradise which made them both disdain low-cost building and raised their expectation of profits if they did build for the artisan class. The result was that now an absolute and inescapable shortage of houses was shown to exist in certain areas. In spite of the much emphasised existence of empty houses in other areas, in spite of the workmen's trains and the workmen's suburbs, in spite of shorter hours and the rise in real wages of a larger section of the community there were not enough of the right kind of houses in the places where they were needed.

The commission stepped no nearer to the brink of a new housing policy. It found no way out of the jungle of difficulties and merely emphasised, as Arnold-Forster and John Simon had already done, the existence of legislation which might have been used and had not been used to drive a way through to a Britain where every man was decently housed. 'The provisions of these enactments cannot be said to be vexatious', said the report, commenting on the failure of local authorities even to enforce the rules against cellar dwelling. No town was spared criticism. Even in the exemplary Liverpool there were houses 'in the last stages of dilapidation . . . the walls were crumbling away, exuding a green slime and so rotten that a stick might be thrust through'.[15]

There was still among the commissioners no notion of a housing policy for the poor in general. It was accepted, as of course it had been since 1875, that those deliberately displaced by improvement schemes had the right to expect that their homes should be replaced at public expense. But that other homeless people, people whose homelessness was caused not by local authority clearance schemes, but by their own poverty, should have a similar right was not seriously contemplated. For all Lord Salisbury's conversion to the cause of the homeless poor, he still found 'very grave objections to the provision of cottages at the cost of public taxation'.[16]

In this, reality had stepped ahead of policy. The evidence clearly showed that housing built for the special purpose of rehousing those displaced by slum demolition was in fact rarely taken up by the displaced. The people cleared from the destroyed slums sifted away into the interstices of the remaining slum areas. The new houses became the homes of a different class of person altogether, the kind of families who wished to better themselves and had the means of doing so. So that unwittingly, but quite inevitably, local authorities were led into being landlord to working-class tenants not displaced by slum clearance at all. Local authorities were to find themselves in the same fix as the model dwellings associations, landlords who, in spite of good intentions, left those most in need still out in the cold while they housed those with steady wages.

The report of the commission in 1885 offered them no way out of this situation. It backed up the shocking effect of the *Bitter Cry* with hard evidence. It appealed to the profit motive by suggesting that poor housing was the prime cause of absenteeism and poor productivity: 'It was found that upon the lowest average every workman or workwoman lost about twenty days in the year from simple exhaustion.'[17]

What the Report did do was to put into easily understood form the great body of causes which combined to prevent reform, and to put unequivocally at the top of the list, as prime cause of the terrible housing, the poverty of the people: 'the relationship borne by the wages they receive to the rents they have to pay'. It had no useful suggestion to make about how this cause could be treated.

The next cause of inaction was the local authorities' dislike of central interference, and here the commissioners recommended that they should be given powers to make by-laws without previous action by the Local Government Board, and that *all* local authorities should now proceed to make by-laws 'although it is unlikely that action will be taken until the people show a more active interest in the management of their local affairs'. In other words the commissioners have demonstrated that through poverty, the failure of local authorities to protect their interests and the success of the landlord class in exploiting their need, the working people in Britain were as a class ill-housed to the point of destitution. Yet they could offer as remedy only that these same depressed people should begin to 'show an interest', to demand better treatment.

Apart from the suggestion that the existing law should be first consolidated, to make it more easily understood, and then very much more strictly enforced, this is the most constructive suggestion the commissioners were to make. It can hardly be called fortunate that the working people of Britain did not hear the incitement to make their demands felt. In an appended memorandum, George Goschen, E. Lyulph Stanley and S. Morley put on record their belief that the pressure of local opinion could not, in the prevailing conditions of poverty and chaotic local government, effect more than it already had done.

10

The Act which followed, the Housing of the Working Classes Act, 1885, introduced in the House of Lords by Salisbury and sent from there to the Commons on 24 July 1885 did attempt a consolidation of the existing law. It revived the neglected Shaftesbury Acts and where they had intended, but failed, to allow house-building, now gave them new force by clearly defining 'lodging houses for the labouring classes' to include separate houses or cottages. It lowered the interest and increased the period of years at which loans for improvement schemes could be made; it emphasised the duty of every local authority to put into force the powers with which they were entrusted. It severely limited compensation and deprived owners of the right to require local authorities to purchase property against which demolition orders had been made. It thus limited the speculators' chance of buying land and houses in the hope of making a quick and easy profit when the property was condemned.

There was no new principle contained in this Act. Yet it did meet opposition. In the Commons an attempt was made, against the extension of loans clause, to add the wrecking words: 'It is inexpedient at this stage of the Session to initiate legislation involving the principle of a National Subsidy towards aiding any locality in providing dwellings for the labouring classes.' The Bill went very swiftly through Parliament, however, in time to avoid being lost in the muddle of a new General Election in December 1885, followed by another Liberal government.[18]

In the country, however, those who feared the limitation of their activities grew incoherent with protest. The Act was 'pauperising and degrading'. It 'effectually blocked the path of the disinterested volunteer workers'.[19] Competition from local authorities would put private builders out of business.

A brief cooling period showed that nothing of the sort had happened, that, in fact, very little of any sort had happened. Local authorities did not rush to begin building houses.[20] Improvement schemes progressed in the same muddled and costly way. People remained inadequately housed and, apparently, unprotesting.

There is, obviously, recognition of the failure of the Royal Commission to promote action in the succession of Housing Bills presented to the House of Commons in the next three years. It is not, of course, unusual for a number of unsuccessful Bills to appear as heralds before an important new piece of legislation on any subject. By the presentation of a Bill to Parliament, even in the knowledge that it has no hope of acceptance, a reforming Member can both test and educate opinion in the House and, as a result, in the country. The first, simple, form of a Bill is thrown to the House as something to be tossed about, torn into shreds so that the form which may later prove acceptable can be discovered. In the process, clauses which will never be accepted can be removed or watered down, limits and safeguards can be added in amendments. If the matter is important it can be taken up by the newspapers, journals and pamphleteers so that the country has an opportunity for comment.

But while opinion is being tested it is also being led. Ideas which seemed sensational when first exposed can become so familiar after long and successive debates that they slip comfortably into the final framework of the Bill. So the persistence of Bill promoters in pushing forward measures unlikely to be passed in a Parliament not favourably disposed to more interference in social affairs is easily understood. They were demonstrating to those outside Parliament that the pressure was being kept up and they were gently leading Parliament itself to the point where a new and effective Housing Bill would gain a sympathetic hearing.

1887 brought a 'Bill to provide for the better housing of the working classes' presented on 28 January by Mr Pyne, Member for Waterford. This Bill had everything against it. Parliament was in turmoil over the Irish question and Mr Pyne was to die before a second reading could be arranged.[21]

Again, the information which would eventually give weight to the case for reform, was accumulating during these years in which Parliament remained unwilling to act. In 1887, for instance, a select committee on temporary dwellings,[22] produced evidence of the startlingly abject living conditions of travelling people in Britain. Legislation to protect them was attempted in 1884, 1887 and 1889, not surprisingly without success.

A report published in March 1887 was refreshingly original in that it actually solicited and passed on the opinions of working people about the houses in which they lived. By the time the statements reached Parliament they had been confined and restricted in tabulated form to take away their emotional impact, if not their truth; and they had been prefaced by a report which suggested that the statements should not be taken too seriously. 'It can hardly be expected that working men, all more or less in straitened circumstances . . . should be so far above all human weakness that they resist the temptation to exaggerate.'[23] Even so it showed that 13 per cent of dock labourers had only a share of a room for themselves and their families to sleep in and that 37 per cent had one room. Policemen were the best housed of the working people examined, dockers and coster-mongers the worst, a hardly surprising finding.

Early in 1888 the House received a Return relative to houses reported under the Acts of 1875–82. It was not encouraging, and Lord Henry Bruce, Conservative Member for North-West Wiltshire between 1886 and 1892 and later Marquis of Aylesbury, presented on 13 February a 'Bill to further amend the law relating to dwellings of the working classes and the Artizans and Labourers Dwellings Improvement Acts, 1875–85.'[24] This Bill got no second reading either.

Robert Reid, Member for Dumfries, a Gladstonian Liberal who was to become Solicitor General in 1892 and later, as Lord Loreburn, Lord Chancellor, presented on 15 February, that is only two days after Lord Henry's attempt, a 'Bill to facilitate the better housing of the working classes in London'. But this Bill, in spite of the narrowing of application, got no further than Bruce's.[25] The House was not to be allowed to forget housing, but it was not yet in the mood to deal with it either.

1889 brought a round of repeat performances. Bruce presented his Bill again on 22 February, only to withdraw it in June without a second reading.[26] Reid's came up again five days later and met the same fate.[27] James Stuart, Liberal Member for Shoreditch, presented a very similar Bill, slightly differently worded: 'A Bill to provide better housing for the working classes in the Metropolis'. He had no more success than the others.[28]

No one could be surprised that Bruce's Bill got an unenthusiastic reception. Its fifth Section threatened the whole basis of local power and prestige. Acknowledging that the Act of 1885 had laid on local authorities the duty of putting into force the existing housing law, it went on to emphasise that the Act contained no means of enforcing that duty. Bruce's Bill therefore provided that, where local authorities failed in their duty, a small group of rate-payers could demand a local inquiry and that, if the inquiry proved their complaint well-founded, the defaulting authority should be forced to dissolve. To ensure that a council newly elected after the dissolution should feel a more pressing sense of duty, the Bill provided that no previous council member should be eligible for re-election.[29]

The object of Reid's Bill had been to enable the newly-formed London County Council to acquire land, to build and to let houses and to provide open spaces for the benefit of the poorer classes. It proposed to make funds for the purpose available by allowing the rating of vacant land and by a cheap method of compulsory purchase.[30] James Stuart's Bill was no different in purpose, much the same in the wording of its preliminary sections, but with less simple provisions for compulsory purchase and more safeguards for the owner faced with a purchase order.

The years 1886–9 saw similar attempts to bring in new public health legislation relevant to housing. Monckton's Bill to allow the sanitary inspection of dwelling houses, rejected in 1884, came up only to be rejected again in 1888, and a similar Bill restricted to houses in the Metropolis was introduced in 1886 and again in 1887.

Beyond the shelter of the House of Commons a new horror lurked to make Londoners dread the slums and slum dwellers. In the autumn of 1888 Jack the Ripper disembowelled his first victim and wrote to the newspapers and to the police to announce his intention of slaughtering more. In Millers Court in Central London he killed an Irishwoman, cut her in little pieces and decorated the walls of her room with a pattern of entrails. The newspapers printed sensational stories which drew attention to the squalor of the streets in which the Ripper prowled. Bernard Shaw was heard to remark that if only the murderer had disembowelled a Duchess the slum-clearance programme might have moved with more speed.

The work of the 1880s came to fruition in 1890 which produced three useful Housing Acts and an important new Public Health Act.[31] The Public Health Amendment Act, 1890, extended the provisions of the 1875 Act to empower every urban authority to make by-laws about the keeping of w.c.s supplied with flushing water, the structure of floors, hearths and staircases and the height of rooms, the paving of yards, the provision of means of access for refuse removal; and to forbid the use as human habitation of rooms over privies, middens, cesspools and ash-pits. It will be seen that thought about the actual structure of houses, their form, size and layout, was still governed by 'the sanitary idea' and that legislation to regulate form was still contained in a Public Health rather than in a Housing Act.

The Housing of the Working Classes Act, 1890,[32] went further than the 1885 Act had done to meet the findings of the Royal Commission. It was a comprehensive Act consolidating all previous useful Housing Acts and making detailed provision for future action. It opened the way for progressive local authorities, already converted to a radical policy of housing, to begin development schemes in their areas. It did nothing to compel the laggard authorities to act. Outside London the next years proved most local authorities to be laggards. Its most useful provision was to allow authorities in the Metropolitan area to purchase as much land as might prove necessary for the long-term planning of an effective improvement scheme. It was not necessary for every house upon it to be proved 'unfit'.

As the Royal Commission had suggested, the 1890 Act kept the obligation to re-house one-half of those displaced by demolition in London but spared provincial cities where the housing need could easily be met. It allowed for, but did not encourage, the actual building of houses by the local authority (as opposed to the letting of ground to builders for the purpose of providing housing). It did not envisage continuing ownership of housing by local authorities, providing that where building was carried out it should be sold or disposed of to private owners within ten years.

While the Act made provision of a sort for the creation of finance for housing those who drew it up again betrayed their wilful ignorance of the problems of housing finance with the suggestion that expenditure should be 'defrayed out of the property dealt with' and with the optimistic notion that 'balances of profit' might be put to other uses. The rate of interest on loans was not diminished nor the term of repayment extended.

In many ways the Housing of the Working Classes Act, 1890, contained contradictory clauses. While Part 1 discouraged house-ownership by local authorities, Part 3, which referred to 'Working-Class Lodging Houses' and defined those to include separate houses and cottages, allowed authorities to erect houses, and alter, enlarge, repair and improve them, to fit up, furnish and supply them and to make by-laws for their regulation and management.

After 1890, therefore, it was legally possible for an enlightened local authority to pursue an enlightened housing policy, possible but not very much more possible than it had been since at least 1875 and, arguably, since 1851. The Act was very far from being imperative.

Yet uncompelling as this new legislation appeared, its effect was markedly different from the achievements of earlier Acts. In spite of the fact that it contained no relaxation of loans policy it stepped up the pace of borrowing for improvement purposes. Between 1875 and 1890 £2,500,000 had been borrowed. Between 1890 and 1904 this had risen to £4,500,000 borrowed by eighty different towns. The L.C.C. had embarked upon an energetic campaign of house-building which was not only to lead the way in design and humanity of conception but eventually to make council-house building seem the obvious way of housing the poor.

There was an important difference between the reception by the country of the Artisans' and Labourers' Dwellings Improvement Act, 1875, and the reception of the Housing of the Working Classes Act, 1890. The difference was caused not so much by the provisions contained within the Acts as by the different economic conditions prevailing, the changed attitude to social reform and the more confident demands of the electorate. But the difference in the effectiveness of the two Acts was caused by the improved machinery for implementing the Acts which had become available by 1890.

Chapter 25

Towards Compulsory Powers

'Rehousing may be looked upon as an insurance . . . paid by the
rich against revolution'
FRANK HARRIS

Clearly the most important factor for change in the last decade of the
nineteenth century was the effect of the Local Government Act, 1888,
which introduced the 'county council'. By putting the administration
of local affairs on a new and more efficient footing, by arranging units
of more economic size which allowed the appointment of permanent
trained officials and by introducing an electoral system which mini-
mised corruption and allowed the election of a new kind of representative, the 1888 Act made the efficient use of the 1890 Housing Act
possible. Most important of all, by bringing into existence the London
County Council, it allowed the creation of a progressive department
of architects who were to pioneer low-cost housing design.

In private house-building the architects William Richard Lethaby,
Norman Shaw and Philip Webb had broken a path away from the
pompous Victorian Gothic style, dependent for its effect on the hypocritical addition of illogical ornament, towards a new vernacular style
dependent upon respect for materials and straightforward.

The L.C.C. commendably chose from the start forward-thinking
members for its architects' department. Young men trained under
Norman Shaw and his contemporaries came to the planning of
council housing for the L.C.C. with enthusiasm for a style of architecture suited to the needs of the people, a humane regard for the quality
of life and a belief that that quality could be affected by their design
standards. This kind of zeal rescued low-cost housing design from the
bleakness to which it had been brought by commercial expediency as
judged by speculative builders. Immediately after the passing of the
Act in 1890 the L.C.C. set up a Housing of the Working Classes
Committee. Its first council-housing estate was built at Boundary
Street to rehouse those displaced by slum clearance in the East End.[1]
Millbank estate was to follow. In the next ten years the L.C.C. energetically set about the rehousing of people moved out of unfit houses
in the process of vigorously implemented improvement schemes.

But influential as the new system of local government became, the
new councillors could not have effected change through the machinery

of the 1890 Act without some shift in the attitude of the rate-payers who elected them. The twin levers engineering that shift were, first, signs of real demand by the working classes for improvement in their housing conditions and, secondly, a new toleration, even encouragement, of that demand by the middle classes.

After 1888 working people were given a greater say in the election of their county representatives, a better chance of electing men from among their own ranks to represent them. The new political groups organised to achieve the election of working men and, as in the case of John Burns in Battersea, were successful often enough to demand notice. In these circumstances a solution to the housing problem was to become an electoral campaign need.

In the next years the expression of a demand by working people for better housing was to become coherent. It is very noticeable that there seemed to be no depths of squalor to which the poor could not be reduced without protests, but when demolition brought about an absolute shortage of houses protest began. Dirty houses could be tolerated. The lack of houses could not be tolerated. Human beings apparently demand very little more than the most basic shelter from the elements and will endure conditions unfit for animals. But when shelter itself is not available they will begin to demand rather than endure. From the beginning of the twentieth century pressing demand by working people was more significant in effecting change than lobbying by social theorists. Conferences on housing in 1902, 1905, 1907 and 1909 were attended by trades council delegates from all over the country who returned to their own towns with determination to press for house-building. In 1909 a deputation from the mining counties of Scotland, formed after mass meetings had gathered and been heard at home, put the shortage of accommodation for miners before the Secretary of State for Scotland, Sir John Sinclair. They kept up the pressure until a new Royal Commission was appointed in 1912 to inquire into the Housing of the Industrial Population of Scotland. Similarly the Rent and Mortgage Restriction Act, 1915, was the direct result of protest and rioting in Glasgow about the shortage of low-rented housing.

Where this kind of demand would once have aroused a middle-class backlash with scares of rebellion, it now met encouragement. In the report of the 1885 commissioners there had been inherent a determination that, vile as their conditions were, the miserable classes must never be allowed to pressurise the respectable people into subsidising them. The 1917 commissioners, on the other hand, welcomed industrial unrest, which they saw as the expression of 'the desire of the workers to establish better conditions of life . . . we cannot but record

our satisfaction that, after generations of apathy, the workers all over
Scotland give abundant evidence of discontent with conditions that
no modern community should be expected to tolerate.'[2] The Great
War had had its effect by 1917 but the change in the attitude of the
middle-class public had been coming long before the war.

Partly the new tolerance for demand was based on new evidence.
The 1886 Commission on Depression had shown how helpless the poor
were in the face of changing economic conditions, how impossible it
was for Self-Help, Independence of Spirit or Trust in a Higher Authority, all hitherto much advocated, to lift an unemployed man into
respectability. In 1891, for the first time, the census gave figures on overcrowding, putting into alarmingly large figures the numbers of people
in the whole population living in overcrowded conditions, and dispelling for good the theory that the spread of suburban building was
really easing the pressure on areas where houses were most in demand.[3]
The 1911 Census showed that the situation was worsening rather than
improving. In 1907 a Report on the Housing of Navvies opened eyes
to the conditions in which workers on construction sites were living.[4]
The culmination of all the conscience-pricking built into twenty successive years of accumulated evidence on the hardships suffered by
working people in their homes was the 1914 Report of the Advisory
Committee on the Homeless Poor.[5]

The encouragement of strong demand by the poor was only one
aspect of a new tolerance of *democracy*. The word itself was losing its
overtones of horror. The middle classes were getting used to democracy,
forgetting very quickly the times when its introduction had been seen
as a prelude to violent mob rule. They were still comfortably on top.
For the present they had little need to fear democratic procedures.
They felt they could afford to encourage their proper use. Thirty years
of compulsory schooling had had some effect on the docility of the
mob.

Jingoism was another factor affecting the trend of the middle
classes towards acceptance of some responsibility for the housing of
the needy. The revelations of Boer War medical officers about the
physical condition of army recruits shocked a nation which liked to
believe in its 'fine fighting men'. Too many recruits were puny, rickety
and weak. Comparisons showed a shocking difference between recruits from Britain's manufacturing towns and those from her rural
areas, a difference of as much as four inches average height in boys of
the same age.[6] The ogre of the deteriorating race, so much feared in
the 1830s and 1840s, raised his head again, just when Britain, feeling
German competition, most needed to believe in the strength and fitness of her young men. Middle-class Britain could feel threatened by

the lack of health of the working classes as it had not done since the cholera scares.

When regular medical inspection of school children began in 1907 the army doctors' scare-mongering was reinforced by reports about the pale and chesty, undernourished children in the council schools. Gradually the middle classes approached some understanding of the difference between *poverty* and *pauperism*, and reached tentatively towards a new theory of public health and social security.

The Housing of the Working Classes Act, 1900,[7] extended to provincial boroughs the powers given to London in 1890, most important of which for our present interest was the power to establish lodging houses outside their own districts. Lodging houses, it will be remembered, had been defined in 1890 to include separate cottages and tenements for the working classes. In effect then, this clause gave boroughs the power to build houses not only on land cleared by town improvement but on other ground suitable for the purpose. The Act was interpreted as giving powers to *build* as opposed to *rebuild* for the poor.

Legislation up to this date had been interpreted as giving powers only for the rehousing of people displaced by slum clearance. In fact the laws could have been used to give much wider powers if authorities had chosen so to use them. But the interpretation was based on appreciation of what the country would tolerate. In spite of opposition it was fairly generally accepted that justice lay in the claim of evicted people to be rehoused. There was very little support for the notion of housing people unsatisfactorily housed for reasons other than slum clearance. The support was to grow in the next twenty years. In the meantime Parliament, by permitting house-building, threw the argument into the arena of local politics where it was to burn with varying effect in different towns.

There is, as yet, no general account of local authority building before 1918. It is necessary to look at local accounts and to attempt to draw a picture of the national situation from what is known of particular towns. Sheffield, still with a strong nucleus of respectable artisans in its population, was in the forefront of council housing. A meeting called in 1889 on the 'Housing of the Poor in Sheffield' was attended chiefly by working men and resulted in the formation of the 'Sheffield Association for the Better Housing of the Poor'. This society and the very active interest of Sheffield's trades council formed a pressure group pushing the town council towards action.

The first slum-clearance scheme was sanctioned in 1894 and 700 people were rehoused by the council on the same site. The high cost of the venture unfortunately caused the rejection of a second scheme in 1900. In the same year the council acquired a sixty-acre site for the purpose of building a workmen's garden suburb. The first 41 houses were completed in 1906 and by 1919 there were 617 houses on the site.

In 1909 the Town Planning Act gave a fresh impetus to Sheffield's social reformers. A sub-committee was formed in anticipation of the Act, to prepare plans for a comprehensive development scheme. Publication of the plans in 1911 meant that the 1911 municipal election was fought on the issue of housing reform. The parties divided on the issue of whether blocks of flats or self-contained cottages made the most suitable dwellings for the working classes. It was a pattern which was to become familiar throughout the country. Although there was, I think, no central party directive, Conservatives favoured central flat building, Liberals and Labour men wanted suburban cottages with gardens. It may have been a lower estimate of what the poor had a right to expect which made Tories prefer blocks of flats. It may equally well have been a better appreciation of the fact that working people, in spite of cheaper transport and shorter hours, still preferred to live near their work and the city centre. Almost certainly their laying of greater stress on the cost factor influenced Conservative policy.

The Liberal and Labour preference for cottages, on the other hand, was influenced by a vague and romantic attachment not only to the Garden City idea but to the whole ethic of Utopian Socialism and by an unacknowledged hankering after the days before the industrial revolution. The 'little master' in his own decent cottage was remembered, while the hind in his hovel was conveniently forgotten. This kind of disagreement did delay house-building by local authorities and explains, to some extent, why it was always easier to get town planning and improvement schemes passed than to pass house-building schemes.

Sheffield showed more enthusiasm for housing reform among its voters than almost any other town, and was praised both by the leaders of the Garden City movement and by the National Housing Reform Council. In 1905 the city council held a well-attended National Housing Conference to show other towns what could be achieved. Sheffield was a pioneer. And yet the total number of houses built by the corporation up to 1914 was only 409. 17,000 people were then still in back-to-backs, 8,000 in unfit houses.[8]

Liverpool was, as it had been since the middle of the nineteenth century because of its tradition of enlightened and vigorous medical officers, still leading the way. St Martin's Cottages, of 1869, had been followed in 1885 by Victoria Buildings at Nash Grove. The council could boast 'that the object was not to cover this site to its full capacity with dwellings, but to erect building of the best class for their purpose and of the highest sanitary standards'. Clement Dunscombe, the city engineer, had carefully avoided a barrack-like elevation by using a variety of coloured bricks, with contrasting terracotta detailing round doors and windows, and a mansard roof above the attic floor. Both St Martin's and Victoria estates were structurally sound and worth modernisation in 1953.[9]

Delegates to the International Housing Congress held in London in August 1907 were taken on the 'Special Housing Tour' of Sheffield, Liverpool, Port Sunlight and Bourneville. They came away especially impressed by Liverpool's achievement, not only in getting large estates of houses built, but in keeping the rents to the same level as those of the insanitary ones recently vacated by the new council tenants. One-roomed houses commanded 1s a week rent, two rooms 3s, three rooms 4s 3d, and four rooms 5s.[10]

In Bradford Fred Jowett first moved in the council for action on housing in 1894. His motion that the Sanitary Committee should take action under the 1890 Act got only five votes, one Liberal, one Tory-Labour, three I.L.P. In 1899 Jowett was appointed chairman of the Sanitary Committee and began a campaign with the support of an able, if alcoholic, medical officer, to enforce the sanitary regulations on housing proprietors. His first major improvement scheme, for the Longlands district, was put forward in 1898, but was delayed for three years by the opposition of property owners. Passed in 1899 by only one vote it was rescinded by the new council after the municipal election.

In 1901 Jowett managed to get a new scheme passed at last. It proposed the building of tenement flats for 432 people on a site cleared of slums by the council and the building of cottages in the near suburbs for 925 more. The scheme was to cost the city £980 a year for forty years.[11]

Manchester opinion was led towards housing reform by a very energetic Citizens Association. The first scheme of 200 houses to be built on a site at Blackley was planned in 1901 and influenced by the Citizens' suggestions on layout and type of house. It proved too expensive to meet majority approval in the council and was temporarily shelved. In 1904 the Citizens Association made a housing survey which exposed the degradation of housing condition in the city and urged the council to use the Acts of 1890 and 1900 'to erect in different parts of the town and country contiguous to the towns, groups of working-class cottages, with adequate yard space and small gardens'. They also succeeded in getting their secretary, Thomas Marr, elected to the council at the next municipal election. In 1905 the Blackley scheme was revised and the first houses built.

From then on, while agitation by the Labour party kept the housing issue lively in Manchester, and successive schemes for building were put before the council, the Rate-payers Association, equally vigorous, succeeded in opposing all schemes involving a charge on the rates. One scheme which was almost successful was cancelled because the opposition proved the existence of empty houses in the city and forced the council to conclude that there was therefore no need to build. The houses were, of course, as was the case in all cities where houses lay empty, in the wrong areas and at too high a rent, for the people in need of homes.[12]

Sheffield, Bradford, Liverpool and Manchester were all cities with some history of artisan strength. Dundee's situation was very different. It was a 'women's town', with low-paid work in the jute trade for female workers and hardly any opportunities for male employment. Weak to non-existent union organisation, and a middle class small in numbers and not very enthusiastic about social reform, meant that the town council was not subject to great pressure for housing improvement.

Yet Dundee had been among the first towns in Britain to adopt a town improvement scheme and, since the passing of its local Act in 1882, had been fairly vigorous in applying closure orders to unfit houses, enforcing the improvement of insanitary houses, and clearing slums. The first suggestion that the council should itself build houses was made in 1905. An enlightened city engineer and surveyor was appointed in 1906. A provisional order of £2,000 for the carrying out of the first housing plans was obtained in 1907. In 1908 the city engineer was instructed to prepare plans for the building of cottages on council-owned ground at Hospital Wynd and to proceed with the plan to the extent of £5,000.

The fairly progressive attitude of the town council in an apathetic town can be explained partly by the very great need for improvement,[13] a need enormous even by the measure of other slum towns, and partly by the existence within the uninterested majority of middle-class citizens of an alien and enlightened group of university people forming the Dundee Social Union.[14] A shocking report in 1901 by the sanitary inspector, Thomas Kinnear, gave a basis on which to work. His survey perhaps got more attention because of the nationally prevalent feeling that working people, even in this subdued town, were approaching the point of protest. In March 1901 the Sanitary Committee received a resolution from the 96 delegates of trades unions, Friendly Societies and Co-operative Societies of Forfarshire and Perthshire who had attended a conference on the Housing of the Working Classes held on Saturday 23 February: 'This conference urges the local authorities to use the powers they already possess under the Housing of the Working Classes Act, 1890, to borrow money for the purpose of acquiring land and erecting comfortable cottages and tenements thereon.'

From 1908 onwards, unhappily, the plans ran into trouble. Bitter in-fighting within the council chambers led to allegations of conspiracy in the Housing Committee almost as soon as it had been established as it was in November 1908 in anticipation of the 1909 Town Planning Act. The Act brought, as it did all over the country, a new enthusiasm for slum clearance and town improvement in preference to house-building. The beginnings of a Central Improvement Scheme, which would clear away the medieval houses in the closes of the Vault, were planned. Within the Housing Committee the parties settled down to a long wrangle on the merits of tenements or cottages for working people. As in Sheffield, the Right voted for tenements, the Left for cottages.

In 1909 the early scheme for cottage-building was rescinded and the city engineer told to prepare new plans for tenements. The tenement scheme itself was dismissed two months later and discussions about new sites began.

By 1912 no houses had been built, the enforced sanitary improvements had been used by landlords as an excuse for putting up rents and the overcrowded citizens looked apprehensively at the proposals for slum clearance in the city centre. The trades council sent a deputation to the Housing and Town Planning Committee begging 'that preferential consideration be given to a scheme of general housing for the workers and that such a scheme be proceeded with rather than any proposal of central improvement.'[15]

When the war came there were still no corporation houses. James Thomson, the city engineer, had prepared a comprehensive development plan involving clearance and house-building in 1912. This had to wait until 1918 for publication,[16] but its progressive clarity made it a model for other towns. Dundee's first housing scheme, the district-heated estate at Logie, earned the town praise as 'a paragon of civic excellence whose example other municipalities are asked to emulate'.[17]

Even the pioneering towns, then, had done very little in the way of house-building before the First World War. In 1914, of all the local authorities in the country only 179 had obtained sanctions for loans to build houses.[18] The Housing and Town Planning Act, 1909, has been consistently praised for its creative thinking on the planning of cities. In fact the public had always preferred slum clearance to construction. It remained preferable in the eyes of rate-payers to sweep away the visible horrors than to assume the expensive and uncomfortable responsibility of housing the poor. When the slums were pulled down it was easy to forget to worry about their inhabitants. It had been easy in 1851, just as easy in 1868 and 1875. In 1909 it became even easier because the scale of demolition could be larger, the improvement in town centres more noticeable, the poor could be swept more thoroughly away. The 1914 Report of the Local Government Board, praising the slum-clearance work of local authorities under the 1909 Act, added; 'we cannot profess to be satisfied with the progress which has been made in the direction of the provision of new housing by local authorities.'[19]

With the coming of National Health Insurance in 1911 it became easier still to suppose that no one was now so poor that he could not afford to house himself decently. Had it not always been the cry that periods of ill-health by interrupting wage-earning, made steady rent-paying impossible? Health Insurance was supposed to end all that although in fact its provisions reached only a small number of trades; for a large section of the population, not only the mass of voters but among the intellectual élite and the social reformers, it did end the pressure for subsidised housing for the poor. The Act of 1909 did no service to those who wished to see more houses built, the 1911 Act made it unlikely that there would be more people of influence who shared that wish.

Fortunately there was still within Parliament a small nucleus of Members who continued to press for housing reform. Their campaign between 1900 and 1911 had three fronts. The first, a moderate attack with fairly general support, aimed at easing the financial difficulties of local authorities considering house-building by extending the period of repayment of government loans. A 'Bill to extend the period of repayment of loans for housing for the working classes' was presented unsuccessfully in 1901, 1902 and again in 1903. But in 1903 a more general 'Bill to amend the law relating to the housing of the working classes' was presented for the government by Walter Long. It had to be fought through fierce opposition and a long series of amendments, but when, eventually, it was passed in August 1903 as the Housing of the Working Classes Act, 1903, it contained a clause extending the period of repayment of loans from sixty to eighty years.

The second front again contained moderate proposals but it was to gain no wide support. Dr F. C. Mackarness, Liberal Member for Berkshire South, and Sir Walter Foster, the Gladstonian Liberal representing Derbyshire Ilkeston, brought in a 'Bill to amend the Housing of the Working Classes Acts and to facilitate the building of houses for the working classes in rural districts' for the first time in 1904. It got no second reading. In 1906, when Foster presented his Bill again, it was referred to a standing committee, on whose report it was withdrawn. Foster tried again in 1908 but was still unable to persuade the House to give his Bill a second reading.

The third front was a radical one, with strong support from Labour and proposals of a more consequential kind. The 'Bill to amend the law relating to the housing of the working classes, to empower local authorities to levy rates on empty houses and to establish fair rent courts' was first brought in by Dr T. J. Macnamara, Liberal Member for Camberwell, and John Burns in 1901. It had no success. In 1902, rising in the House to complain that the King's speech contained no reference to housing, Burns said: 'At this moment within three hundred yards of the House of Commons the King is doing—what? why, inaugurating a county council housing scheme accompanied by his wife? . . .[20] I venture to say that if there is one man in England who would have been better pleased than another to have seen a paragraph on the improved housing of the poorer inhabitants of London, it is the King himself.'[21]

Burns may have felt sure of Royal support but he had not the support of the Commons. His Bill was presented again that year and yet again in 1903 without ever gaining second reading. John Burns was not one to stay with a loser, and he did not present that Bill again.

In 1902 Keir Hardie wrote an open letter to the Labour Leader accusing Burns of a 'halting spirit' and even of 'thinly veiled opposition' to the whole Labour movement. Burns had done good work on the L.C.C. but within Parliament he had been vacillating in support for the cause of the working man and strong only in his own ambition.[22]

But the Bill was not abandoned, even if Burns had deserted it. It was presented in the same form in 1904 by Nannetti with the support of, among others, Keir Hardie who by now found it pleasanter to work in alliances which did not include John Burns. The new promoters had no more success in 1904 and 1905 than their predecessors had had. In 1906 C. W. Bowerman, Independent Labour Party Member for Deptford, made the Bill his special interest and brought it in faithfully, but despite the large Liberal/Labour majority returned in 1906, with unrelenting failure, in 1906, 1907, 1908 and 1909.

In December 1905 Burns was made president of the Local Government Board. By May 1908 he had ready the Bill which, in his own eyes, was the peak of his achievement. He included some of the provisions planned by Bowerman but dropped the controversial clauses dealing with amendments to the law of rating and the establishment of fair rent courts. The Bill to amend the law relating to the housing of the working classes and to provide for town-planning schemes got as far as a second reading but was then referred to a standing committee on whose report it was withdrawn.[23]

Burns told the House that the object of the Bill was

'to provide a domestic condition for the people in which their physical health, their morals, their character, and their whole social condition would be improved; . . . to secure the home healthy, the house beautiful, the town pleasing, the city dignified, and the suburb salubrious . . . . On the housing side the Bill seeks to abolish, reconstruct and prevent the slum. It asks the Commons to do something to efface the ghettos of meanness and the Alsatias of squalor that can be found in many parts of the United Kingdom.'

But Walter Long, whose own Bill had resulted in the Housing of the Working Classes Act, 1903, told the House:

'It has been my business for many years now to have to read Bills and try to master them and I can safely say that never yet have I had to read a Bill that has given me such infinite labour, which left me with so appalling a headache, and even after the labour and with the headache, such a minimum of practical information as to what the Bill proposes to do . . . I protest against the government's hurling at our heads this enormous mass of undigested material.'[24]

The Bill was duly taken away and made a little more digestible. In 1909 it was presented again as a 'Bill to amend the law relating to the housing of the working classes, to provide for the making of town-planning schemes, and to make further provision for the appointment of medical officers and the establishment of public health and housing committees.' Even in its blander form the House found the Bill hard going. Its second reading was deferred nineteen times. Burns had to fight it through almost word by word until it gained consent at the end of November, as the Housing and Town Planning Act, 1909.

The new Act contained one clause important in housing history: Section 40 provided that 'Notwithstanding anything contained in the principal Act, [1890] it shall not be obligatory upon any local authority to sell or dispose of any lands or dwellings acquired or constructed by them.' Quietly the principle of local authority house-ownership crept in, even if it were not enthusiastically acted upon. The previous Acts had insisted that those authorities who did build should disencumber themselves of house-property within ten years so as to shed a responsibility generally considered the business of private enterprise. But as David Lloyd George was contemptuously to ask: 'Take for instance Mr Burn's Housing Act . . . . How many houses were built under that Act?'[25] Local authority expenditure on housing in England and Wales rose only from £580,000 in 1910 to £640,000 in 1913, a rise more easily accounted for by rising costs of materials and loan financing than by the effects of the 1909 Act.

More important, however, than any increase in spending, is the very marked increase in the number of local authorities responding after 1909, to pressure to undertake housing. Of the 179 urban authorities who received sanction for loans for house-building during the period 1890 to 1914, 112 of them acted between 1909 and 1914.[26] Lloyd George's question was not strictly a fair one because even after Burn's Act it was Part 3 of the 1890 Act which provided the machinery for house-building. What the 1909 Act did was to give the Local Government Board powers to prod local authorities into action. The Report of the Local Government Board for 1913–14 reckoned that some 18,000 houses had been built by local authorities under the 1890 Act.[27] The number of houses for which loans were sanctioned in any one year rose from 78 in 1910 to 2,465 in 1914.[28] Between 1910 and 1914 loans for the building of 6,780 houses were sanctioned, a figure which would have seemed more impressive without the corresponding figures for house-closure and demolition. For the four years ending 31 March 1912, 7,427 houses either had closure orders put upon them or were demolished as unfit for human habitation.[29] Sections 17 and 18 of the Act, which gave local authorities powers to deal with insanitary houses were most vigorously used after 1909. The result was that, in spite of an undeniable increase in house-building activity by local authorities, the country's stock of houses was diminished rather than increased by the 1909 Housing and Town Planning Act. When the general slump in speculative house-building and the almost complete stoppage of low-cost housing is remembered, the severity of the shortage can be appreciated.

From 1911 onwards it was necessary for housing reformers in Parliament to try a new tack. On the face of it so much had been achieved. In practice so little was being done. It was clear to those whose eyes were not blinkered that the best Acts possible were useless without powers of enforcement. So now a new Bill was to make an annual appearance in the House of Commons. Introduced by Sir Arthur Griffith-Boscawen, Kensington's Tory Member, the 'Bill to provide for the better application and enforcement of the Housing of the Working Classes Act', appeared in 1911, 1912, 1913 and 1914. In 1912 it was sent to a standing committee after a second reading. A report suggesting amendments was made in June but considerations of the amendments was deferred. In 1913, now shepherded by Captain D. F. Campbell, Unionist Member for North Ayrshire, and Major Harry Hope, it was again sent to a standing committee who reported in May that they 'could not with advantage proceed with this Bill'. Exactly the same thing happened in 1914.

A different kind of support, but not enough to earn it a second reading, was given to a 'Bill to encourage private ownership of dwelling houses and business premises by the working classes', presented in 1911 and 1913 by Montague Barlow, a future Conservative Minister.

In 1914, two Housing Acts were passed, but they were of little significance, their purpose being only to give the Board of Agriculture and Fisheries and the Local Government Board powers with respect to the housing of their own workers.

Actual achievements in housing, then, had been very slight up to 1914. Yet after the war the country found itself firmly set upon the way to council house dwelling as an ordinary rather than an exceptional way of life for working people. The war, of course, did a great deal to persuade the rate-paying public to accept the notion of subsidised housing. Awareness of the sacrifice of lives and health of young men in the trenches led to an enthusiastic if not very practical campaign for Homes for Heroes. As an undercurrent there ran the suspicion that soldiers returning from the Great War would refuse ever again to tolerate the living conditions of the pre-war years and would rise in rebellion if reforms were not made. In 1919 Lloyd George was using the danger of Bolshevism as a stick to prod the Cabinet into accepting his government housing programme.

But however galvanising the war to sluggard reformers it could not have brought about the Housing and Town Planning Act, 1919, without the planning and preparation of the pre-war period.

Most of the work of the Edwardian social reformers was concentrated upon the need for a central administrative system for public health. It will be remembered that the mid-nineteenth-century Central Board of Health had foundered on the national dislike for a central bureaucracy. Sixty years later greater knowledge of the diversity of causes for poverty and ill-health had led social theorists to see the need for comprehensive central planning.

But if the principle of a Ministry for Health was accepted, agreement on how far its powers should extend was slow in coming. Radicals wanted the new Ministry to take over not only preservation of health, the prevention of disease and the application of sanitary regulations, but the administration of the Poor Law, of National Insurance and of local government and housing as well. Strong instincts of self-preservation in the Poor Law Guardians, the Local Government Board and the Insurance and Friendly Societies delayed the creation of a Ministry of Health until 1919.

Concurrently with planning for a health ministry, the reformers supported Lloyd George's Land Campaign. National Health Insurance was supposed to have brought security to the life of the town labourer, the land scheme, by providing for the building of cottages from public funds, was expected to do the same for the rural worker. Lloyd George's attachment to the idea was based partly on a wish to tidy up legislation on the subject so that reforms could be said to cover the whole country, and partly on a wish to regain in 1915 the many rural constituency seats lost by the government in 1910. Like many other plans the Land Campaign was lost in the war.

By 1915 the lack of houses had become acute. Particularly in areas where war work concentrated labour, house rents rose steeply. The most dramatic demonstrations against high rents took place in Glasgow and came near enough to the appearance of revolution at home while the country faced war in Europe to frighten the government into passing the Rent and Mortgage Restriction Act, 1915.[30]

But if the new Act controlled rents it also put an end to what lingered of hopes for private-enterprise building of low-cost houses. With rents fixed at a level that was uneconomic in view of rising costs of building materials, no speculator would again attempt to build for the working classes.

The direct result of appreciation of this fact was the first Committee of Reconstruction, set up by Asquith on 18 March 1916 with instructions to prepare a survey of housing needs. In 1917 the Ministry of Reconstruction was established with Christopher Addison, later to be the first Minister of Health, at its head.

Addison drew on the recommendations of two important committees for his housing policy. The Salisbury Committee consisted of the Marquess of Salisbury, Beatrice Webb and B. Seebohm Rowntree. It was briefed to consider what might be expected to be the housing situation after the war, the probable availability of materials and the possibility of establishing priorities. Its report in August 1917 suggested that 300,000 houses would be needed immediately upon the end of the war and urged that preparations for their building should be begun immediately.[31] The 300,000 was a grave underestimate, but the urgency of the need for action was put into the report. Most important of all, the Salisbury Committee reported its belief that housing must, after the war, be made the *duty* of local authorities. The building of houses where a shortage existed was no longer to be a privilege or a power enjoyed by authorities if they wished, but to become a responsibility the law did not allow them to shirk.

The Carmichael Committee was concerned with easing the provision of building materials and the speedy demobilisation of building tradesmen after the war.

But the Ministry of Reconstruction was a planning, not an administrative department. It did not have the powers to fulfil what it had proved to be the need. When the war ended nothing was ready. Addison had been unable to get his plans accepted by a Cabinet whose attention was wholly occupied elsewhere. In 1920 he was to tell Lloyd George that he would rather sweep crossings than repeat his bitterly frustrating experience as Minister of Reconstruction.[32]

When the Ministry of Health was at last created and Addison, at its head, found himself with more power, he set about the preparation of a comprehensive Housing Act. The government's failure, in spite of Addison's anxious persuasion, to make any realistic assessment of the grave extent of the need for subsidised housing, or to accept the importance of making adequate financial provisions meant that the Housing and Town Planning Act, 1919, achieved much less than had been hoped for. Addison complained to Lloyd George of the emasculation of his proposals by the Cabinet: 'Apart entirely from the inherent difficulties of the task, in a time when there is great shortage of men, money and material, we have been compelled to work under restrictions imposed by the Cabinet itself, against my repeated advice on three of the most important branches of work.'[33]

The Act's failure must, even so, be at least in part blamed on Addison's own less than adequate understanding of the effect on the building industry of sudden and excessive demand. His determination to push ahead with house-building, what later Lloyd George called 'this very fatuous policy' of putting out contracts in advance of the trade's ability to cope with them, resulted in soaring and uncontrollable prices. Local authorities bombarded the Ministry of Health with complaints about the impossibility of carrying out the greatly expanded programmes pressed upon them with inadequate financial resources. In the next years the prospect of making any immediate improvement in the housing situation faded. The fall of the Geddes axe on government expenditure did not spare the housing programme. Lloyd George, when the moment came when he judged that his coalition government could be saved only by the sacrifice of Addison, was prepared even to join those most opposed to housing subsidies with the condescending criticism that he, Addison, 'was rather too anxious to build houses'.[34] Lloyd George, with those words, stepped aside from his friend, his principles and those millions of slum dwellers who had looked to him for help.

In spite of its own inadequacies, nevertheless, Addison's 1919 Act set in train a sequence of legislation which was eventually to transform not only the appearance of Britain's towns but the whole framework of her society. If council estates, brooding bleakly at the edge of our towns and swamping pretty villages, seem to have done nothing but harm to the shape and appearance of towns, they can only fairly be contrasted with what they replaced, a kind of squalor, a kind of misery even the most disparaged of council schemes has not yet achieved.

The tragedy is that, by the time the idea of compulsorily subsidised housing had been realised, it was almost too late for anything but wholesale destruction of a centuries-old environment, for the meanest replacement of it by the cheapest houses, the barest amenities, the bleakest layout. Only a few city architects found encouragement for a longer view, for more creative thinking, for more courageous planning and design. The idea that working people should in any way participate in the planning of the environment that is to be the setting for their lives is a new and to some people a startling one even in 1973. Poor Law thinking continued to affect the planning of council housing long after the Poor Law itself was dead.

Parliamentary Papers

ROYAL COMMISSIONS

First Report of the Royal Commission on the State of Large Towns and Populous Districts, 1844, Vol. 17, pp. 1–743.
Second Report, 1845, Vol. 18, pp. 1–287, 299–462.

First Report of the Royal Commission on Friendly and Benefit Societies, 1871, Vol. 25, pp. 1–269
Second Report, Vol. 26, pp. 1–906.

First Report of the Royal Commission on the Housing of the Working Classes, 1885, Vol. 30, pp. 1–1136.
Second Report, Scotland, Vol. 31, pp. 1–339.
Third Report, Ireland, Vol. 31, pp. 339ff.

Report of the Royal Commision on the Housing of the Industrial Population of Scotland, Rural and Urban, Edinburgh 1917, Vol. 14, p. 345ff.

SELECT COMMITTEES

Report of the Select Committee on the Health of Towns, 1840, Vol. 11, pp. 270ff.

Report of the Select Committee on Buildings Regulations, 1842, Vol. 10, pp. 133ff.

Report of the Select Committee on the Regulation of Buildings and the Improvement of Boroughs, 1842, Vol. 10, pp. 300ff.

Interim Report of the Select Committee on Artizans and Labourers Dwellings Improvement, 1881, Vol. 7, pp. 395ff.
Final Report, 1882, Vol. 7, pp. 249ff.

Report of the Select Committee on the Operation of the Common Lodging Houses Act, 1853, Vol. 78, pp. 525ff.

Report of the Select Committee on the Dwellings of the Poor by Edwin Chadwick, 1867–8, Vol. 117, c. 3968—11, Part 2, pp. 239–317.

Return of Monies Agreed to be Advanced by the Public Works Commissioners, 1866 7, Vol. 40, p. 60.

Accounts Showing Amounts Advanced under Labouring Classes Dwellings Acts, 1874, Vol. 35, p. 331.

Returns with Respect to 1875 Act of the Number of Official Representations Made, 1875–82, 1883, Vol. 58, pp. 1–28.

Tabulation of the Statements of Men Living in Certain Selected Districts of London in March 1887, Vol. 71, p. 303.

Reports of the Local Government Board, 1911–1914.

Bibliography of Books and Periodicals

ALISON, DR W. P., 'Observations on the Generation of Fever', *Report on the Sanitary Condition of the Labouring Population of Scotland* (London, 1842), p. 13.

ALLAN, CHARLES M., 'The Genesis of British Urban Redevelopment . . .', *Economic History Review*, 2nd ser. Vol. 18 (1965), pp. 598–613.

ARNOLD-FORSTER, H. O., 'The Dwellings of the Poor: The Existing Law', *Nineteenth Century* (December 1883), pp. 940–51.

ARNOTT, NEIL, M. D., 'On the Fevers which have Prevailed in Edinburgh and Glasgow', *Report on the Sanitary Condition of the Labouring Population of Scotland* (London, 1842), p. 24, and 'Remarks on Dr W. P. Alison's "Observations"', p. 34.

ARTIZANS AND GENERAL PROPERTIES COMPANY, LTD, *Artizans Centenary, 1867–1967* (London, 1967).

ASHWORTH, W., 'British Industrial Villages in the Nineteenth Century', *Economic History Review*, 2nd ser., Vol. 3, pp. 378–95.

ASHWORTH, W., *The Genesis of Modern British Town Planning*, (London, 1954).

BARNES, HARRY, *Housing; the Facts and the Future* (London, 1923).

BERESFORD, MAURICE, *The Lost Villages of England* (London, 1954).

BOARD OF AGRICULTURE, *General Views of the Agriculture of the Counties*, drawn up for the consideration of the Board of Agriculture (London, 1813; rep. Newton Abbot, 1969).

BOARD OF HEALTH, DUNDEE, *Reports*.

BOWLEY, MARIAN, *Housing and the State, 1919–1944* (London, 1945).

BOWLEY, MARIAN, *Innovations in Building Materials* (London, 1960).

BRADBURY, R., 'New Dwellings from Old: An Example from Liverpool', *R.I.B.A. Journal* (September 1953), pp. 452–4.

BROCKINGTON, C. FRASER, *Public Health in the Nineteenth Century* (Edinburgh, 1965).

BROCKWAY, FENNER, *Socialism over Sixty Years: The Life of Jowett of Bradford*, (London, 1946).

BUCKLE, G. T., *The Life of Benjamin Disraeli* (London, 1916–20), Vols. 4–6.

Builder, The.

BURTON, JOHN HILL, 'On the State of the Law as Regards the Abatement of Nuisances . . .', *Reports on the Sanitary Condition of the Labouring Population of Scotland* (London, 1842), pp. 40–65.

CAIRNCROSS, A. K., *Home and Foreign Investment, 1870–1913* (London, 1953).

CAIRNCROSS, A.K. AND WEBER, B., 'Fluctuations in Building in Great Britain, 1785–1849', *Economic History Review*, 2nd ser., Vol. 9, pp. 283–97.

CHALMERS, THOMAS, *On the Christian and Economic Polity of a Nation, More Especially with Reference to Its Large Towns* (Glasgow, n.d.).

CHAMBERLAIN, JOSEPH, 'Labourers' and Artizans' Dwellings', *Fortnightly Review*, new ser. (1 December, 1883), pp. 761–75.

CHAMBERLAIN, JOSEPH, *Mr Chamberlain's Speeches*, ed. C. W. Boyd (London, 1914), Vol. 1.

CHAMBERS, WILLIAM, *Improved Dwellings for the Humble and Other Classes* (London, 1855).

CHAPMAN, STANLEY D. (ed), *The History of Working-Class Housing* (Newton Abbott, 1971).

COCKBURN, JOHN *Letters to his Gardener, 1727–1744* (Scottish History Society publication, 1904).

COONEY, E. W., 'Capital Exports and Investment in Building in Britain and the U.S.A., 1856–1914', *Economica*, new ser., Vol. 16, pp. 347–54.

COONEY, E. W., 'Long Waves in Building in the British Economy of the Nineteenth Century', *Economic History Review*, 2nd ser., Vol. 13, pp. 257–69.

COONEY, E. W., 'The Origins of the Victorian Master Builders', *Economic History Review*, 2nd ser., Vol. 8, pp. 167–76.

COOPER, NICHOLAS, Housing the Victorian Poor. (1) 'The Myth of Cottage Life', *Country Life* (25 May 1967), (2) 'The Design of Estate Cottages', *Country Life* (8 June 1967).

CULLINGWORTH, J. B., *Housing and Local Government in England and Wales*, (London, 1966).

CULLINGWORTH, J. B., *Housing in Transition* (London, 1963).

CULLINGWORTH, J. B., *Scottish Housing in 1965* (Edinburgh, 1965).

D'ARCY THOMSON, SIR WENTWORTH, 'Fifty Years Ago and Now', presidential address to the 50th annual general meeting of the Grey Lodge Settlement (formerly Dundee Social Union) (27 April 1938).

DUNDEE POLICE COMMISSION, Plans approved by, 1867–1914.

DYOS, H. J., 'Railways and Housing in Victorian London', Parts 1 and 2, *Journal of Transport History*, Vol. 2, pp. 11–21, 90–100.

DYOS, H. J., 'The Slums of Victorian London', *Victorian Studies*, Vol. 11, pp. 5–40.

DYOS, H. J., 'Some Social Costs of Railway Building in London', *Journal of Transport History*, Vol. 3, pp. 23–30.

DYOS, H. J., 'The Speculative Builders and Developers of Victorian London', *Victorian Studies*, Vol. 11, supp. pp. 641–90.

DYOS, H. J. (ed.), *The Study of Urban History* (London, 1968).

DYOS, H. J., *Victorian Suburb: A Study of the Growth of Camberwell* (Leicester, 1964).

ERRAZUREZ, A., 'Some Types of Housing in Liverpool', *Town Planning Review*, Vol. 19, pp. 57–68.

FERGUSON, THOMAS, *The Dawn of Scottish Welfare* (Edinburgh, 1948).

FLETCHER, BANISTER, *Model Houses for the Industrial Classes* (London, 1871).

GEDDES, SIR PATRICK, *Cities in Evolution* (London, 1915).

GILBERT, BENTLEY B., *British Social Policy, 1914–1939* (London, 1970).

HABBAKUK, H. J., 'Fluctuations in House-Building in Britain and the United States in the Nineteenth Century', *Journal of Economic History*, Vol. 22, pp. 198–230.

HILL, OCTAVIA, *Homes of the London Poor* (London, 1875; rep. 1970).

HOBHOUSE, HERMIONE, *Thomas Cubitt, Master Builder* (London, 1970).

HOLE, JAMES, *The Homes of the Working Classes, with Suggestions for their Improvement*, published under the sanction of the Society of Arts (London, 1866).

HONEYMAN, JOHN, F.R.I.B.A., *The Dwellings of the Poor: Remarks on the Reports of the Royal Commission . . . 1885* (Glasgow, 1890).

JONES, G. T., *Increasing Return*, Part 2: *The London Building Industry* (Cambridge, 1933).

KEITH-LUCAS, B., 'Some Influences Affecting the Development of Sanitary Legislation in England', *Economic History Review*, Vol. 6, p. 290.

KELLETT, J. R., *The Impact of Railways on Victorian Cities* (London, 1969).

KELLETT, J. R., 'Property Speculators and the Building of Glasgow', *Scottish Journal of Political Economy*, Vol. 8, pp. 211–32.

KINNAIRD, HENRY, 9th Lord, Working Men's Houses, Dundee, 1874.

KINNEAR, THOMAS, 'Sanitation and Pure Air in Dundee, Fifty Years Ago and Now', *British Association Handbook* (1912).

LEAGUE OF NATIONS, *Urban and Rural Housing* (Geneva, 1939).

LEWIS, JOHN PARRY, *Building Cycles and Britain's Growth* (London, 1965).

LEWIS, R. A., *Edwin Chadwick and the Public Health Movement, 1832–1854* (London, 1952).

LEWIS, R. A., 'Edwin Chadwick and the Railway Labourers', *Economic History Review*, Vol. 3, pp. 109–10.

MACDOUGALL, IAN (ed.), 'The Minutes of Edinburgh Trades Council, 1859–1873', *Scottish History Society* (Edinburgh, 1968).

MACKINTOSH, J. M., *Housing and Family Life* (London, 1952).

MAIWALD, K., 'An Index of Building Costs in the United Kingdom', *Economic History Review*, 2nd ser., Vol. 7, pp. 187–203.

MEARNS, ANDREW, *The Bitter Cry of Outcast London: An Inquiry into the Condition of the Abject Poor*, (1883; rep. 1970).

MILLER, HUGH, *My Schools and Schoolmasters* (Edinburgh, 1881).

MORRIS, R. J., 'Leeds and the Crystal Palace', *Victorian Studies*, Vol. 13, p. 283.

PEVSNER, NIKOLAUS, 'Model Houses for the Labouring Classes', *Architectural Review*, Vol. 93, pp. 119–28.

POLLARD, SIDNEY, 'The Factory Village in the Industrial Revolution', *English Historical Review*, Vol. 79, pp. 513–31.

POLLARD, SIDNEY, *A History of Labour in Sheffield* (Liverpool, 1959).

POSTGATE, RAYMOND, *The Builders' History* (London, 1923).

PRIBRAM, KARL, 'Housing', *Encyclopedia of Social Science*.

PRICE, SEYMOUR J., *Building Societies, Their Origins and History* (London, 1958).

RASMUSSEN, STEEN EILER, *London, the Unique City* (London, 1948).

ROBERTS, HENRY, *The Improvement of the Dwellings of the Labouring Classes* (London, 1850).

SALISBURY, MARQUIS OF, 'Labourers' and Artizans' Dwellings', *National Review* (November 1883).

SAUL, S. B., 'House-Building in England, 1890–1914', *Economic History Review*, 2nd ser., Vol. 51, pp. 119–37.

SAVILLE, JOHN, *Rural Depopulation in England & Wales, 1851–1951* (London, 1957).

SCOTTISH DEVELOPMENT DEPARTMENT, Scottish Housing Advisory Committee, *Scotland's Older Houses* (H.M.S.O., 1967).

SIMON, SIR JOHN, *Public Health Reports* (London, 1887), 2 vols.

SIMON, SIR JOHN, *Sanitary Institutions*

SINGER, H. W., 'An Index of Urban Land Rents and House Rents in England and Wales, 1845–1913', *Econometrica*, Vol. 9, pp. 221–30.

SMITH, E. J., *Housing: The Present Opportunity* (Bradford, 1918).

SPRING, DAVID, *The English Landed Estate in the Nineteenth Century: Its Administration* (Baltimore, 1963).

SUTCLIFFE, ANTHONY, 'Nineteenth-Century Cities: The Study of Visual Evidence', *Local Historian*, Vol. 9 (1971), p. 400–6.

TARN, JOHN NELSON, 'Housing in Liverpool and Glasgow: The Growth of Civic Responsibility', *Town Planning Review*, Vol. 39, pp. 319–34.

TARN, JOHN NELSON, 'The Model Village at Bromborough Pool', *Town Planning Review*, Vol. 35, pp. 329–36.

TARN, JOHN NELSON, 'The Peabody Donation Fund', *Architectural Association Quarterly* (Winter 1968–9), pp. 32–47.

TARN, JOHN NELSON, 'Some Pioneer Suburban Housing Estates', *Architecture Review* (1968), p. 367.

TARN, JOHN NELSON, *Working-Class Housing in Nineteenth-Century Britain*, Architectural Association paper No. 7 (London, 1971).

VANCE, J. E., 'Housing the Worker: Determinative and Contingent Ties in Nineteenth-Century Birmingham', *Economic Geography*, Vol. 43, pp. 95–127.

VANCE, J. E., 'Housing the Worker: The Employment Linkage as a Force in Urban Structure', *Economic Geography*, Vol. 42, pp. 294–325.

VANCOUVER, CHARLES, *General View of the Agriculture of the County of Devon* (London 1813; rep. Newton Abbot, 1969).

WALTER, FELIX, 'Conversions', *Architects Journal* (11 and 18 March, 1954).

WEBB, BEATRICE, *My Apprenticeship* (London, n.d.).

WEBER, B., 'A New Index of House Rents', *Scottish Journal of Political Economy*, Vol. 7, pp. 232–37.

WEBER, B., 'A New Index of Residential Construction', *Scottish Journal of Political Economy*, Vol. 2, pp. 104–32.

WRIGHT, G. P. AND H. P., 'The Influence of Social Conditions . . .', *Journal of Hygiene*, Vol. 42, (October 1952), p. 451.

WOHL, ANTHONY, S. (ed.), *The Bitter Cry of Outcast London* by Andrew Mearns (Victorian Library, Leicester, 1970).

WOHL, ANTHONY, S., 'Unfit for Human Habitation', Dyos, H. J. and Wolft, M. W., *Victorian Cities: Images and Realities* (London, 1973).

APPENDIXES

Appendix 1
Rise in Population and Rise in Numbers of Inhabited Houses, England and Wales, 1801–1911

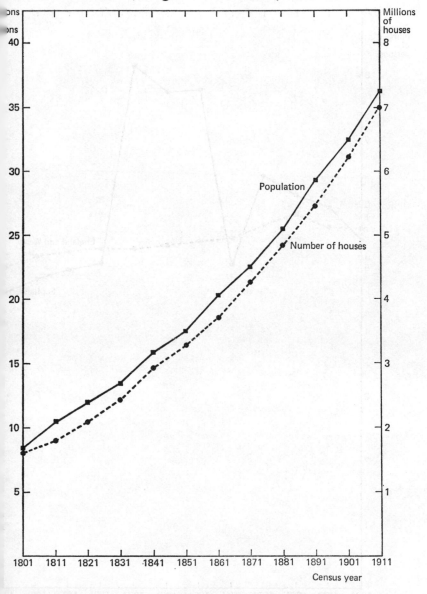

Appendix 2
Average Number of Persons per Inhabited House,
1801–1911

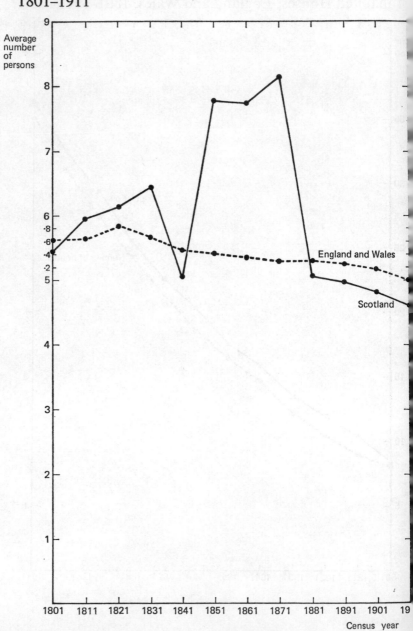

since the Passing of that Act

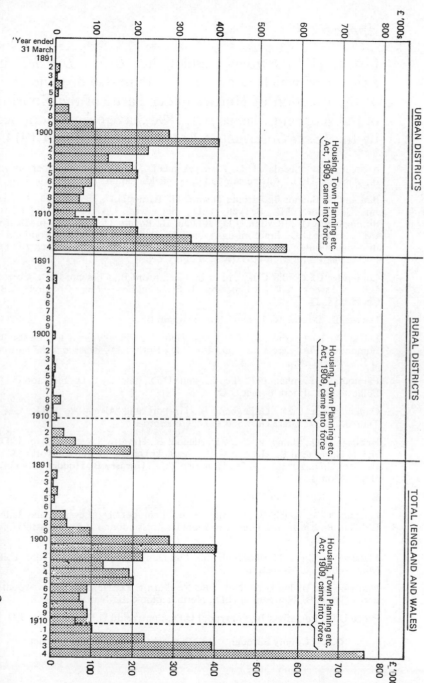

Appendix 4

List of (179) *Boroughs* and Other *Urban Districts* in Respect of which Loans for the Purchase of Land and/or the Erection of Houses under Part 3 of the Housing of the Working Classes Act, 1890, have been sanctioned by the *Local Government Board* up to 31 March 1914.

Abercarn U.D., Aberdare U.D., Abersychan U.D., Abertillery U.D., Aberystwyth B., Alnwick U.D., Altrincham U.D., Annfield Plain U.D., Aspatria U.D.

Banbury B., Bangor B., Barking Town U.D., Barnes U.D., Barnet U.D., Basingstoke B., Battle U.D., Bedwelty U.D., Biggleswade U.D., Birkenhead C. B., Birmingham C.B., Blaydon U.D., Bodmin B., Bognor U.D., Bolton-on-Dearne U.D., Bourne U.D., Bradford-on-Avon U.D., Brentford U.D., Brentwood U.D., Bridlington U.D., Bridport B., Brighton C.B., Bristol C.B., Briton Ferry U.D., Buckingham B., Burton-on-Trent C.B., Bury C.B.

Cambridge B., Cardiff C.B., Chard B., Chelmsford B., Chesham U.D., Chester C.B., Chiswick U.D., Cirencester U.D., Coventry C.B., Croydon C.B., Cuckfield U.D.

Darwen B., Devizes B., Droitwich B., Durham B.

Ealing B., East Grinstead U.D., East Ham B., Ebbw Vale U.D., Eccles B., Edmonton U.D., Egremont U.D., Ely U.D., Erith U.D., Esher and the Dittons U.D., Exeter C.B.

Falmouth B., Farnham U.D., Featherstone U.D., Finchley U.D., Flockton U.D., Folkestone B., Friern Barnet U.D.

Gainsborough U.D., Gillingham B., Gosport and Alverstoke U.D., Grays Thurrock U.D., Great Harwood U.D., Guildford B.

Hadleigh U.D., Hampton U.D., Hartlepool B., Haverfordwest B., Hayes U.D., Hemel Hempstead B., Hendon U.D., Hessle U.D., Heston and Isleworth U.D., Hexham U.D., Hinckley U.D., Holbeach U.D., Hornsey B., Huddersfield C.B., Huntingdon B.

Kendal B., Kirkburton U.D.

Leicester C.B., Leigh B., Leominster B., Lepton U.D., Levenshulme U.D., Lichfield B., Linthwaite U.D., Liverpool C.B., Llandudno U.D., Llanelli U.D., Lyme Regis B.

Manchester C.B., Marlborough B., Meltham U.D., Merthyr Tydfil C.B., Minehead U.D., Morpeth B.

Nantyglo and Blaina U.D., Neath B., Newburn U.D., Newbury B., Newcastle-upon-Tyne C.B., Normanton U.D., Northampton C.B., Northwich U.D.

Penge U.D., Pontefract B., Pontypool U.D., Pontypridd U.D., Prestatyn U.D.

C.B. = County Borough   B. = Borough   U.D. = Urban District

Radstock U.D., Rawtenstall B., Redditch U.D., Rhondda U.D., Rhyl U.D., Rhymney U.D., Richmond (Surrey) B., Risca U.D., Rishton U.D., Ruthin B.

Saddleworth U.D., St Austell U.D., Salford C.B., Seaham Harbour U.D., Selby U.D., Sheffield C.B., Sherborne U.D., Shipley U.D., Shrewsbury B., Sidmouth U.D., Southend-on-Sea B., Southgate U.D., South Molton B., Southwold B., Spalding U.D., Stafford B., Stanley (Durham) U.D., Stratford-upon-Avon B., Street U.D., Stretford U.D., Swansea C.B.

Tamworth B., Tauton B., Thetford B., Tiverton B., Tottenham U.D., Towyn U.D., Truro B., Tunbridge Wells B.

Wakefield B., Wallasey C.B., Wallingford B., Watford U.D., Wellington (Salop) U.D., West Ham C.B., Weymouth and Melcombe Regis B., Whitefield U.D., Whitehaven B., Whitley and Monkseaton U.D., Whitley Upper U.D., Wigan C.B., Wiveliscombe U.D., Wolverhampton C.B., Wood Green U.D., Workington B., Wrotham U.D.

Yeovil B.

Appendix 5

Loans Sanctioned to Local Authorities, 1891–1914

Year ended 31 March (1)	Urban Authorities			Rural Authorities			Totals—Urban and Rural Authorities		
	Number to which loans were sanctioned in the year (2)	Number to which loans were sanctioned in the year for the first time (3)	Amount sanctioned (4)	Number to which loans were sanctioned in the year (5)	Number to which loans were sanctioned in the year for the first time (6)	Amount sanctioned (7)	Number to which loans were sanctioned in the year (8)	Number to which loans were sanctioned in the year for the first time (9)	Amount sanctioned (10)
			£			£			£
1891	—	—	nil	—	—	nil	—	—	nil
1892	1	1	11,550	—	—	nil	1	1	11,550
1893	1	1	2,000	1	1	1,700	2	2	3,700
1894	1	1	17,350	—	—	nil	1	1	17,350
1895	2	1	8,200	—	—	nil	2	1	8,200
1896	—	—	nil	—	—	nil	—	—	nil
1897	5	3	34,487	—	—	nil	5	3	34,487
1898	4	3	36,800	—	—	nil	4	3	36,800
1899	7	2	94,833	—	—	nil	7	2	94,833
1900	18	14	279,967	1	—	1,800	19	14	281,767
1901	17	10	400,602	—	—	nil	17	10	400,602
1902	24	12	225,949	—	—	nil	24	12	225,949

(1)	(2)	(3)	(4)	(5)	(6)	(7)	(8)	(9)	(10)
1903	14	6	126,504	1	—	1,850	15	6	128,354
1904	18	6	187,760	2	2	2,250	20	8	189,920
1905	17	5	201,071	1	—	200	18	5	201,271
1906	13	6	8,910	1	1	2,500	14	7	91,410
1907	10	2	71,114	1	1	1,500	11	3	72,614
1908	11	2	58,727	1	1	21,500	12	3	80,227
1909	11	2	86,703	1	—	1,800	12	2	88,503
1910	11	3	47,824	2	1	12,230*	13	4	60,054
1911	12	7	101,342	1	—	250	13	7	101,592
1912	29	17	201,566	16	15	27,445	45	32	229,011
1913	46	26	335,875	22	14	59,557	68	40	395,432
1914	79	49	565,860	45	33	193,580	124	82	759,440
Totals	—	179	3,184,904	—	70	328,162	—	249	3,513,066
Averages for 1891–2 to 1913–14 (23 years)	15.3	7.8	138,474	4.2	3.0	14,268	19.5	10.8	152,742
Averages for 1899–1900 to 1902–3 (4 heaviest consecutive years prior to 1909–10)	18.3	10.5	258,256	0.5	0.3	912	18.8	10.8	259,168
Averages for 1891–2 to 1909–10 (19 years)	9.7	4.2	104,224	0.6	0.4	2,491	10.3	4.6	106,715
Averages for 1910–11 to 1914–14 (4 years)	41.5	24.8	301,161	21.0	15.5	70,208	62.5	40.3	371,369

* Including 11,960 sanctioned to County Council on default of Rural District Council.

Appendix 6

Loans by Public Works Loan Commissioners, 1891–1913

Year ended 31 March (1)	Amount Advanced (2)	Year ended 31 March (1)	Amount Advanced (2)
	£		£
1891	44,020	1904	16,185
1892	9,000	1905	36,490
1893	17,800	1906	27,050
1894	44,709	1907	18,536
1895	23,115	1908	51,010
1896	23,200	1909	67,292
1897	21,700	1910	95,411
1898	36,250	1911	283,969
1899	7,500	1912	198,336
1900	22,500	1913	175,085
1901	23,270		
1902	57,100	Total	£1,317,894
1903	18,375		

References

CHAPTER I

(1) Richard Cobden, *Speeches on Questions of Public Policy*, ed. John Bright and J. E. Thorold Rogers, 2 Vols (London, 1908), 3rd edn, Vol. 1, p. 81 (hereafter 'Cobden').

(2) Nicholas Cooper, 'The Myth of Cottage Life, Housing the Victorian Poor', 1, *Country Life* (25 May, 1967), p. 1,290; and Cobden, op. cit., p. 81.

(3) Cooper, op cit.

(4) S. Scott Alison, M.D., 'Report on the Sanitary Condition and General Economy of the Labouring Population in the Town of Tranent and Neighbouring District in Haddingtonshire', *Reports on the Sanitary Condition of the Labouring Population of Scotland, in Consequence of an Inquiry Directed to be made by the Poor Law Commissioners* (London, 1842), p. 89.

(5) Alison, op. cit., p. 90.

(6) James Caird, *English Agriculture in 1850–1851* (London, 1852), 2nd edn, p. 390.

(7) Edwin Chadwick, *Report on the Sanitary Condition of the Labouring Population of Great Britain, 1842* ed. M. W. Flinn (Edinburgh, 1965), p. 329.

(8) Cobden, op. cit., p. 84.

(9) See p. 44.

(10) Agriculture surveys of the counties of England drawn up for the consideration of the Board of Agriculture and Internal Improvement, 1807.

(11) Royal Commission on the Housing of the Working Classes, 1885, *Minutes of Evidence*, 14,495–14,496 and *Report*, p. 43.

(12) Royal Commission on Housing, 1885, *Minutes of Evidence*, 15,974 and *Report*, p. 43.

(13) R. H. Campbell (ed.), Board of Trustees for Manufactures in Scotland. States of the Annual Progress of the Linen Manufacture, 1727–1754 (Edinburgh, 1964), 1739–40, p. 62.

(14) John Cockburn of Ormiston, *Letters to his Gardener* (Scottish History Society, 1904), p. 79.

(15) *Old Statistical Account of Scotland* (henceforth *OSA*), Vol. 10, p. 168.

(16) Ibid., Vol. 19, p. 595.

(17) Ibid., Vol. 5, p. 421.

(18) Ibid., Vol. 5, p. 121.

(19) Barbara Cornford, 'Inventories of the Poor', *Norfolk Archaeology* (1970), No. 35, p. 118.

(20) A good first-hand description of the rise and fall in prosperity of hand-loom weavers can be found in Robert Chalmers, *Autobiography of Robert Chalmers, the Old Political and Social Reformer* (Dundee, 1872).

(21) Cockburn, op. cit., p. 83.

(22) Francis Home, *Experiments on Bleaching* (Edinburgh, 1781), p. 324.

(23) John Simon, *Public Health Reports*, ed. Edward Seaton (London, 1887), Vol. 2, p. 182. The seventh report to the Privy Council, 1864, *Distribution of Disease in England: I. House Accommodation*.

(24) Royal Commission on Housing in Scotland, 1917. *Parliamentary Papers*, Vol. XIV, p. 345.

(25) Simon, op. cit., p. 196n.

(26) This does not apply, of course, to the speculative building of the later period, see p. 93.

328   *Cruel Habitations*

(27) Cobden, op. cit., p. 81.
(28) W. P. Alison, M.D., 'Observations on the Generation of Fever', in *Reports of the Sanitary Condition of the Labouring Population in Scotland*, op. cit., p. 25
(29) Simon, op. cit., p. 183.

CHAPTER 2

(1) Arthur Young, Secretary to the first Board of Agriculture, *General View of the Agriculture of Oxfordshire* (London, 1813), p. 26.
(2) For Scotland the change took longer. There the population remained predominantly agricultural until after the 1851 census.
(3) H. J. Habbakuk, 'Population in the Eighteenth Century', *Economic History Review*, 2nd ser. (1953), pp. 117–33.
(4) C. Vancouver, *General View of the Agriculture of the County of Devon* (rep.) pp. 96–7.
(5) Arthur Young, *General View of the Agriculture of the County of Lincolnshire* p. 462.
(6) Colonel Dirom of Mount Annan, 'Remarks upon the Preceding Paper', *Prize Essays and Transactions of the Highland Society of Scotland*, Vol. 2 (1803).
(7) T. C. Smout, *A History of the Scottish People, 1560–1830* (London, 1969).
(8) William Cobbett, *Rural Rides*, ed. G.D.H. and Margaret Cole (London, 1930), Vol. 2, p. 370.
(9) Cobbett, vol. 2, p. 740.
(10) Bothies, see p. 66.
(11) See Royal Commission on Housing in Scotland, 1917, p. 173 for bad housing as cause of depopulation.
(12) *Old Statistical Account for Scotland* (henceforth *OSA*), Vol. 6, p. 237.
(13) J. Simon, *Public Health Reports*, ed. Edward Seaton (London, 1887), Vol. 2, p. 188; and see Nicholas Cooper, 'The Myth of Cottage Life', *Country Life* (25 May 1967).
(14) Simon, op. cit., Vol. 2, pp. 184, 187.
(15) J. L. and Barbara Hammond, *The Village Labourer* (London, 1932), p. 154
(16) Quoted E. P. Thompson, *The Making of the English Working Class* (Harmondsworth, 1968), pp. 244–5.
(17) Arthur Young, *General View of the Agriculture of Oxfordshire* (London, 1813), p. 26.
(18) This brought England into line with Scotland whose Poor Law system, depending as it did, not upon an assessment but entirely upon charitable giving, had never, at least in theory, allowed relief to the able-bodied unemployed.
(19) Thompson, op. cit., p. 296.
(20) An interesting discussion of the extent to which sanitary reform could be said to have followed Poor Law reform can be found in Professor Flinn's introduction to E. Chadwick, *Report on the Sanitary Condition of the Labouring Population of Great Britain, 1842*, ed. M. W. Flinn (Edinburgh, 1965), pp. 1–3.
(21) 'Report on the Sanitary Condition of the Labouring Population, 1842', in E. N. Williams (ed.), *A Documentary History of England* (London, 1965), Vol. 2, p. 237.
(22) Henry Hamilton, *Economic History of Scotland* (Oxford, 1963), p. 148, and Enid Gauldie, *Scottish Bleachfields* (unpublished thesis in Dundee University Library), pp. 191–5.
(23) Kenneth Hudson, *Industrial Archaeology* (London, 1965), p. 147

24) Simon, op. cit., Vol. 2, p. 190.
25) An interesting description of rural protest and its treatment can be found in Thompson, op. cit., pp. 248–58.
26) Harold Cattling, *The Spinning Mule* (Newton Abbot, 1970).
27) An interesting account of the difficulty of attracting labour to the new mills can be found in 'An Account of Some Flax Machinery', *Scots Magazine* (1766).
28) *Dundee Advertiser* (13 March 1823, 4 December 1823 and 25 August 1825).
29) Thompson, op. cit., p. 250.

CHAPTER 3

(1) E. Chadwick, *Report on the Sanitary Condition of the Labouring Population of Great Britain, 1842*, ed. M. W. Flinn (Edinburgh, 1965), p. 87.
(2) Nicholas Cooper, 'The Myth of Cottage Life', *Country Life* (25 May 1967).
(3) Costs and rents will be discussed in Chapters 13 and 14.
(4) The Duke of Bedford's brother, Lord John Russell, for instance, was largely responsible for the attempts to legislate for the health of towns which culminated in the Public Health Act, 1848.
(5) J. Simon, *Public Health Report*, ed. E. Seaton (London, 1887), Vol. 2, p. 188.
(6) *Household Words*, Vol. 16, pp. 84–6.
(7) Arthur Young, *General View of the Agriculture of the County of Norfolk* (rep. Newton Abbot, 1969), p. 24.
(8) Arthur Young, *General View of the Agriculture of Lincolnshire*, p. 39.
(9) 'stud and mud'; earth of any kind that will set tolerably hard, plastered on wattles or battens attached to a wooden framework, sometimes lashed to roof-beams with string. Joseph Wright (ed.), *English Dialect Dictionary*, Vol. 5.
(10) Arthur Young, *Lancaster*, p. 19.
(11) See *Builder*, Vol. 20 (1862), p. 925 for comparative cottage costs.
(12) James Caird, *English Agriculture* (London, 1852), pp. 437–9. By 1885 the cost of building had risen to about £500 a pair, the cost being partly due to the provision of more space and better accommodation. Royal Commission on Housing, 1885, *Minutes of Evidence*, 16415. The return on these, let at 1s 6d a week, had dropped to ½ per cent, 16414.
(13) J. Caird, *English Agriculture in 1850–1851* (London, 1852), 2nd edn., p. 442.
(14) Royal Commission on Housing, 1885, *Minutes of Evidence*, Appendix, p. 721.
(15) Act to facilitate estate improvement, 8 and 9 Vict. c. 56 (1845).
(16) For a very full and interesting account of the work of the Enclosures Commissioners see David Spring, *The English Landed Estate in the Nineteenth Century: Its Administration* (Baltimore, 1963).
(17) Simon, op. cit., Vol. 2, p. 186. There were, of course, many other landlords improving on a smaller scale, although most of these fall into the period after Simon's investigations.
(18) Simon, op. cit., Vol. 2, p. 186.
(19) Select Committee on Building Regulations, 1842, *Minutes of Evidence*, 1,392.
(20) Royal Commission on Housing, 1885, *Minutes of Evidence*, 13,945–13,956. Prince Albert was interested in the quality of bricks, advocating glazed surfaces.
(21) John Holt, *General View of the Agriculture of the County of Lancaster, 1795* (rep., Newton Abbot, 1969).
(22) Royal Commission on Housing, 1885, *Report*, p. 46. Weber's index shows a very slight upswing in rural house-building from 1841–71 with a downward movement for twenty years thereafter.

330   *Cruel Habitations*

(23) Even on the Bedford estates, which were exceptional for their generous provi
sion of housing, there were 714 old cottages as well as 1,116 modern ones in
1885. Royal Commission on Housing, *Minutes of Evidence*, 16,378.
(24) Two very interesting accounts of the efforts of Scottish landowners to im
prove the housing conditions on their estates are: John Cockburn, *Letters to
his Gardener, 1727-1744* (Scottish History Society, 1904), p. 79 and R. H
Matthew and P. J. Nuttgens, 'Two Scottish Villages', *Scottish Studies*, Vol. ?
(1969), Part 2, pp. 113–42; and Francis Garden, *Letter to the People o*
Laurencekirk (Edinburgh, 1780).
(25) *OSA*, Vol. 20, p. 176n.
(26) Rev. Robert Rennie, 'Plan of an Inland Village', *Prize Essays of the Highland
Society of Scotland*, Vol. 2, 1803.
(27) George Scott-Moncrieff, *The Stones of Scotland* (London, 1938), p. 90
Imperial Gazetteer of Scotland (n.d.), p. 663; and Thomas Sharp, *The Anatomy*
of the Village (Harmondsworth, 1946), *passim*.
(28) *OSA*, Vol. 13, p. 272.
(29) S. Scott Alison, M.D., 'Report on the Sanitary Condition . . . of the Labouring
Population . . . in Haddingtonshire'—*Reports on the Sanitary Condition o*
the Labouring Population of Scotland (London, 1842), p. 84. See also Henry
Graham, *Social Life of Scotland in the Eighteenth Century* (London, 1908)
p. 183.
(30) Royal Commission on the Housing of the Working Classes, 1885, *Minutes o*
Evidence (Scotland), Appendix E. Statement of the Highland and Land Law
Reform Association. Crofter Dwellings.
(31) Ibid.
(32) Chadwick, ed. Flinn, op. cit., p. 329. Royal Commission on Housing, 1885
op. cit., 15,974, shows evidence that this kind of cottage was still usual in
Buckinghamshire forty years later.
(33) Royal Commission on Housing, op. cit., 15,487, 15,508.
(34) Ibid., 16,380–16,382. By 1885 the estate was replacing thatch with slate as
repairs became necessary and gradually introducing earth closets and fire
ranges to the cottages. White-washing of the inside took place when a cottage
fell empty.
(35) Chadwick, ed. Flinn, op. cit., pp. 329–30.
(36) *Reports on the Sanitary Condition of the Labouring Population of Scotland*
(London, 1842), pp. 220–1.
(37) Chadwick, ed. Flinn, op. cit., p. 83.
(38) *OSA*, Vol. 19, p. 7.
(39) Ibid, p. 158.
(40) Select Committee on Building Regulations, 1842, *Minutes of Evidence*,
1,158.
(41) Royal Commission on Housing, 1885, op. cit., 17,085–17,087.
(42) Ibid., 17,088.
(43) Sidney Pollard, *Life and Labour in Sheffield* (Liverpool, 1969).
(44) Royal Commission on Housing, 1885, op. cit., 17,061.
(45) 'The dwellings of the poor are, in most counties, but mudcabins, with holes
that expose the inhabitants to the rigour of the climate', Arthur Young,
Sussex, p. 22.
(46) Royal Commission on Housing, 1885, op. cit., 17,328.
(47) Arthur Young, *Lincolnshire*, p. 46.
(48) Rennie, op. cit.
(49) Flinn, op. cit., p. 332.
(50) Royal Commission on Housing, 1885, 16,916.

CHAPTER 4

(1) J. Simon, *Public Health Reports*, ed. E. Seaton (London, 1887), pp. 194–6.
(2) Select Committee on Health of Towns, 1840, *Minutes of Evidence*, 110, 155; see also J. D. Marshall, 'Colonisation as a Factor in the Planning of Towns', in H. J. Dyos (ed.), *The Study of History*, p. 215 and Ashworth, 'British Industrial Villages', *Economic History Review*, Vol. 3, p. 378.
(3) *Old Statistical Account of Scotland* (henceforth *OSA*), Vol. 15, pp. 40–1. *New Statistical Account* (hereafter *NSA*), 1845, Vol. 6, pp. 12, 19, 22–3. See also John Butt, *Industrial Archaeology of Scotland* (Newton Abbot, 1967), pp. 70–1.
(4) *NSA*, Vol. 6, pp. 22–3; see also evidence given to the Factory Commissioners by Archibald Buchanan of Catrine, quoted E. Chadwick, *Report on the Sanitary Condition of the Labouring Population of Great Britain, 1842*, ed. Flinn (Edinburgh, 1965), pp. 301–2. *OSA*, Vol. 15, p. 42.
(5) C. S. Pollard, 'The Factory Village in the Industrial Revolution', *English Historical Review*, Vol. 79, pp. 513f.
(6) James Hole, *Homes of the Working Classes* (London, 1866), pp. 70–1 with plans and illustrations.
(7) J. N. Tarn, 'The Model Village at Bromborough Pool', *Town Planning Review*, Vol. 35 (1965), pp. 329–36.
(8) Hole, op. cit., pp. 67–8 and illustrations.
(9) Royal Commission on Housing (1885), *Minutes of Evidence*, 15,610.
(10) See E. P. Thompson, *The Making of the English Working Class* (Harmondsworth, 1968), pp. 246, 345, 473–6.
(11) A very interesting and full account of navvy shacks is in Terry Coleman, *The Railway Navvies* (London, 1965), pp. 72–82.
(12) See also A. A. Lewis, 'Edwin Chadwick and the Railway Labourers', *English Historical Review*, 2nd ser., Vol. 3, pp. 109–10. See also *Report of the Local Government Board on the Housing of Navvies, 1907*, 404.
(13) Ibid., p. 196n.
(14) Ibid., p. 194.
(15) S. Scott Alison, M.D., 'Tranent and Colliery Districts', *Reports on the Sanitary Condition of the Labouring Population of Scotland* (London, 1842), pp. 87–9.
(16) Royal Commission on Housing, 1885, op. cit., 7,521–7,522.
(17) Ibid., 8,173, 12,979–12,989.
(18) Simon, op. cit., Vol. 2, 193.
(19) Royal Commission on Housing, 1885, op. cit., 8,184–8,185.
(20) Ibid., 12,987–12,988.
(21) Alison, op. cit., p. 96.
(22) Quoted Simon, op. cit., pp. 192–3.
(23) Royal Commisson on Housing in Scotland, 1917, *Report*, p. 124.
(24) William Cobbett, *Rural Rides*, ed. G. D. H. and Margaret Cole (London, 1930), Vol. 3, p. 868.
(25) Ibid, p. 783.
(26) R. H. Campbell, *Scotland since 1707* (Oxford, 1965), p. 167.
(27) Enid Gauldie, *Scottish Bleachfields* (unpublished thesis in Dundee University Library), Chapter 6, Section 1. The housing of bleachers.
(28) Hugh Miller, *My Schools and School-Masters* (Edinburgh, 1881), p. 192.
(29) Royal Commission on Housing in Scotland, 1917, p. 187.
(30) E. Chadwick, *Report on the Sanitary Condition of the Labouring Population of Great Britain, 1842*, ed. Flinn (Edinburgh, 1965), p. 82.

(31) *Report of the Local Government Board, 1913–14,* Return as to Housing of the Working Classes, p. 545, and *Report,* p. xlvii.

CHAPTER 5

(1) John Simon, *English Sanitary Institutions, 1897,* p. 183 quoting Dr Southwood Smith's report to the Poor Law Commissioners of 1839.
(2) T. Southwood Smith, *A Treatise on Fever* (1830), p. 348.
(3) Select Committee on the Health of Towns, 1840, *British Sessional Papers,* Vol. 11. *Minutes of Evidence,* 2,511.
(4) Select Committee on the Health of Towns, 1840, *Minutes of Evidence,* 2,512.
(5) Ibid., 2,416.
(6) Report of a Conference held at Hull on 'Homes of the Poor', organised by the Charity Organisation Society (1 February 1884).
(7) Select Committee on the Health of Towns, 1840, *Report,* p. xiii.
(8) Neil Arnott, M.D., 'On the Fevers which have prevailed in Edinburgh and Glasgow', *Sanitary Report, 1842,* p. 8.
(9) Local Board of Health, Dundee, 1817. *Reports* (1847). In Lamb Collection of pamphlets (Dundee, Dundee Public Library), 308 (11).
(10) *Hansard,* House of Lords (30 April 1841). Debate on the Drainage Bill.
(11) First report of the Commissioners for Inquiring into the State of Large Towns and Populous Districts, 1844, *British Sessional Papers,* Vol. 17, p. xi.
(12) Select Committee on the Health of Towns, 1840, *Minutes of Evidence,* 1,678.
(13) State of Large Towns, 1844, *Minutes of Evidence,* 6,054.
(14) Evidence of Dr Angus Smith given at a public inquiry in Middleton in November 1853 in pursuance of the Public Health Act (11 and 12 Vict. c. 63), 1848. Middleton had shunned adoption of the general Act, like many other towns apprehensive of central government control, and had delayed application for a local Act. See John Simpson, 'A Public Health Petition', *Medical History,* Vol. 5 (October 1861), No. 4.
(15) Quoted E. Chadwick, *Report on the Sanitary Condition of the Labouring Population of Great Britain, 1842,* ed. M. W. Flinn (Edinburgh, 1965), p. 137.
(16) S. Scott Alison, M.D., 'Report on the Sanitary Condition and General Economy of the Labouring Population in the Town of Tranent and Neighbouring District of Haddingtonshire', *Reports on the Sanitary Condition of the Labouring Population of Scotland* (London, 1842), p. 7.
(17) Simon, *Public Health Reports,* ed. E. Seaton (London, 1887), Vol. 2, p. 287.
(18) Ibid.
(19) Royal Commission on Housing, 1885, *Minutes of Evidence,* 9,630–9,637.
(20) D. V. Donnison, *Victorian Studies,* Vol. 7, p. 106 in a review of Charles Loch Mawat, *The Charity Organisation Society, 1869–1913.*
(21) Royal Commission on Housing, 1885, *First Report,* pp. 13–15.
(22) Andrew Mearns, *The Bitter Cry of Outcast London* (London, 1883; rep. 1970), p. 17.
(23) Royal Commission on Housing, 1885, *First Report,* p. 18.
(24) Cf. F. M. Jones, 'The Aesthetic of the Nineteenth-Century Industrial Town', in H. J. Dyos (ed.), *Study of Urban History* (London, 1968), p. 176.
(25) 29 and 30 Vict. c. 90 (7 August 1866). *Law Reports, Statutes,* Vol. 1, p. 681.
(26) Sect. 11.
(27) Royal Commission on Housing, 1885, *First Report,* pp. 46–7.
(28) C. Fraser Brockington, *Public Health in the Nineteenth Century* (Edinburgh, 1965), p. 233.
(29) Where they did exist they were not reliably connected to the water supply. Royal Commission on Housing, 1885, *Minutes of Evidence,* 3,445.

(30) Ibid., 13,936.
(31) Select Committee on the Health of Towns, 1840, *Minutes of Evidence*, 2,816.
(32) 53 and 54 Vict. c. 70, and 53 and 54 Vict. c. 59. *Law Reports, statutes*, Vol. 2, pp. 470, 553.
(33) There were, of course, some very notable exceptions and local authority building was getting under way during this period. See Chapter 25.

CHAPTER 6

(1) Population census, 1841. *Parliamentary Papers, 1843*, pp. xviii, 10.
(2) B. R. Mitchell and Phyllis Deane, *Abstract of British Historical Statistics* (Cambridge, 1962).
(3) R. A. Lewis, *Edwin Chadwick and the Public Health Movement, 1832–1854* (London, 1932), p. 51 quoting Chadwick's *Sanitary Report*, ed. M. W. Flinn (Edinburgh, 1965), p. 7.
(4) B. Weber, 'A New Index of Residential Construction, 1838–1950', *Scottish Journal of Political Economy*, Vol. 2 (1955), pp. 104–32.
(5) H. A. Shannon, 'Bricks–A Trade Index, 1785–1849', *Economica*, Vol. 1, No. 103, pp. 300–18.
(6) See however S. D. Chapman (ed.), *The History of Working-Class Housing* (Newton Abbot, 1971), especially James H. Treble, 'Liverpool Working-Class Housing, 1801–1851', pp. 172–3, and John Parry Lewis, *Building Cycles and Britain's Growth* (London, 1965), pp. 37, 63–8, and Appendix 4.
(7) Chadwick, ed. Flinn, op. cit., p. 5.
(8) Quoted Lewis, op. cit., p. 51.
(9) Quoted R. W. Postgate, *The Builders' History* (London, 1923), p. 31.
(10) Overcrowding became for the first time technically a 'nuisance' under the Sanitary Act, 1866 (29 and 30 Vict. c. 90): 'Any house or part of a house so overcrowded as to be dangerous or prejudicial to the health of the inhabitants' made its owner liable to prosecution and after two convictions magistrates were given 'power to close the premises for such time as they think necessary'. The same provision was made for Scotland under the Public Health (Scotland) Act, 1867. In neither case was it effective.
(11) Typhus was said to be 'rarely found in English towns' in 1885 but was still prevalent in Dundee. Royal Commission on Housing, 1885, *Second Report*, p. 6 and *Minutes of Evidence*, 20,644.
(12) Interesting statistics on this subject can be found in an unpublished thesis in Dundee University Library by Dr William Lennox, 'Life in Dundee 1895–1903'.
(13) Charles M. Allen, 'The Genesis of British Urban Redevelopment', *Economic History Review*, 2nd ser., Vol. 18 (1965), No. 3, p. 612; but see also John Butt, 'Working-Class Housing in Glasgow, 1851–1914', in Chapman, op. cit., p. 80.
(14) Octavia Hill, *Homes of the London Poor. II Four Years' Management of a London Court* (London 1970, Cass Library of Victorian Times, new impression of 1883), 2nd ed., p. 25. This was first published as an article in *Macmillan's Magazine* (July 1869).
(15) James Hole, *The Homes of the Working Classes* (London, 1866), p. 42.
(16) Royal Commission on Housing, 1885, *Minutes of Evidence*, 54, 57, 5,977–5,980.
(17) Hole. op. cit., p. 6.
(18) State of Large Towns, *Minutes of Evidence. Parliamentary Papers*, Vol. 17, pp. 1–743. 6,050.
(19) H. J. Dyos, 'Railways and Housing in Victorian London', *Journal of Transport History*, Vol. 2 (1955–6), pp. 14–18.
(20) in Chapman, op. cit.

(21) Select Committee on the Health of Towns, 1840, *Minutes of Evidence*, 2,724–2,726.

(22) Ibid., 1,857–1,871.

(23) Mayhew, *Life and Labour of the London Poor* (1851), published as *Mayhew's London*, ed. Peter Quennell (London, n.d.), p. 539.

(24) This very steep rise was a response by Liverpool's builders to the threat of restrictions upon their activities by a new Building Act and represents the building of very shoddy houses at great speed, see J. N. Tarn, 'Housing in Liverpool and Glasgow', *Town Planning Review*, Vol. 39 (January 1961), No. 4, p. 321, and Weber, op. cit. See also Report of *Select Committee on Building Regulations* Appendix by James Woods, surveyor to north district of Liverpool, 1842, *Parliamentary Papers*, Vol. 10. See also Treble, op. cit., and Lewis, op. cit., p. 161.

(25) *Journal of Economic History*, Vol. 22, p. 198.

(26) See Appendix 1.

(27) Some towns had their own Building Regulations. Few, however, laid down standards for space around houses. For those who did see B. Keith-Lucas 'Some Influences Affecting the Development of Sanitary Legislation', *Economic History Review*, Vol. 6, p. 295.

(28) Select Committee on Building Regulations, 1009.

(29) Factory reports throughout the century include evidence on this subject. See, for instance, Royal Commission on Children's Employment, 1843, *Parliamentary Papers*, Vol. 75, p. 175, and Select Committee on Bleaching and Dyeing Establishments, 1856. 'One thing I found to prevail almost universally among them was a derangement of those functions peculiar to them as females'; for the spreading of information on contraceptives see E. R. Pike, *Human Documents of the Industrial Revolution* (London, 1967), p. 298–363.

(30) Roger Smith, 'Early Victorian Household Structure', *International Review of Social History*, Vol. 15 (1970), pp. 69–84.

(31) Hole, op. cit., p. 11. John Honeyman, *The Dwellings of the Poor* (Glasgow, 1890), p. 18. Royal Commission on Housing, 1885, *passim*.

CHAPTER 7

(1) Royal Commission on Housing, 1885, *Minutes of Evidence*, 6,080–6,081, 6,129–6,133, 6,154 and 'it very frequently happens that in the outskirts of London the houses are built upon the turf in a field'. *Building Regulations*, Vol. 10, 133.

(2) State of Large Towns, *Minutes of Evidence*, 6,045–6,047: 'Houses frequently fall down'.

(3) J. Hole, *The Homes of the Working Classes* (London, 1866), p. 125, quoting Richard Baker's report on Leeds. Hole reported that most of these houses built about 1840 still existed in the 1860s and that similar houses were still being built.

(4) Select Committee on Building Regulations, 217–18.

(5) Ibid., 1,790.

(6) Select Committee on the Health of Towns, 1840, *Minutes of Evidence*, 1,830.

(7) Select Committee on Building Regulations, 1842. *Parliamentary Papers*, Vol. 10. *Minutes of Evidence*, 1,127 and 1,132–1,133.

(8) There is, for instance, the surprising table in the Scottish Development Department's publication *Scottish Housing in 1965*, ed. J. B. Cullingworth, p. 11, which shows that 'Far more (42%) of dwellings built between 1881 and 1900 were regarded as having a life of less than 15 years than was the case with dwellings built between 1861 and 1880 (31%)'.

(9) Select Committee on the Health of Towns, 1840, op. cit., 2,797.
(10) Hull conference on 'Homes of the Poor', organised by the Charity Organisation Society (1 February 1884), p. 4.
(11) Mayhew, *Life and Labour of the London Poor* (1851), published as *Mayhew's London*, ed. P. Quennell (London, n.d.), p. 288.
(12) Ibid., p. 22.
(13) The collecting of evidence was undertaken by the Rev. Andrew Mearns (1837–1925), Secretary of the Congregational Union, in 1883 and the material written up by the Rev. William Carnall Preston (1837–1902), a Wigan Congregational minister who had been a newspaper editor. See Cass Library edition, 1970, 'Note on the authorship'.
(14) A. Mearns, *Bitter Cry of Outcast London* (London, 1833; rep. 1970), p. 7.
(15) R. A. Lewis, *Edwin Chadwick and the Public Health Movement, 1832–1854* (London, 1932), p. 222 quoting *The Times* (9 July 1849).
(16) Mayhew, op. cit., p. 272
(17) 'Sanitary Condition of Glasgow', in *Reports of the Sanitary Condition of the Labouring Population of Scotland*, 1842, op. cit., p. 72.
(18) E. Chadwick, *Report on the Sanitary Condition of the Labouring Population of Great Britain, 1842*, ed. M. W. Flinn (Edinburgh, 1965), p. 93.
(19) Select Committee on the Health of Towns, 1840, *Minutes of Evidence*, 1857–1871.
(20) S. Pollard, *Life and Labour in Sheffield* (Liverpool, 1969), p. 24.
(21) They were common at an earlier date in London than in the North. Mayhew mentions them among articles reluctantly pawned in 1851.
(22) R. Tressall, *The Ragged Philanthropist* (rep. 1962), p. 50.
(23) Fenner Brockway, *Socialism over Sixty Years* (London, 1946), p. 53.

CHAPTER 8

(1) Hull conference on the 'Homes of the Poor', organised by the Charity Organisation Society (1 February 1884), p. 5.
(2) William Farr 1807–83, trained in Paris and London, practised medicine in London from 1833, see E. Chadwick, *Report on the Sanitary Condition of the Labouring Population of Great Britain, 1842*, ed. M. W. Flinn (Edinburgh, 1965), p. 27.
(3) *Journal of the House of Commons*, 1841, p. 269 *et seq.*
(4) R. A. Lewis, *Edwin Chadwick and the Public Health Movement, 1832–1854* (London, 1932), p. 40.
(5) Among them Lord Calthorpe, Earl Howe and Sir Thomas Gooch. *Journal of the House of Commons*, 1841.
(6) Lewis, op. cit., p. 39.
(7) Chadwick, ed. Flinn, op. cit., p. 27.
(8) Cobden's evidence to Select Committee on Health of Towns, 1840, p. 106.
(9) The first influential use of the word 'statistics' in Britain had been by Sir John Sinclair in his 1791 *Statistical Account of Scotland*, an excellent source for the condition of the people. The *New Statistical Account of Scotland* began to appear in the early 1840s.
(10) *Hansard* (4 February 1840). The debate on 'Discontent among the Working Classes' was introduced by Richard Slaney and seconded by W. Smith O'Brien. The vote of the House, the earliest, as John Simon pointed out in English Sanitary Institutions, p. 189n to be made on the subject of health and housing, was not recorded in *Hansard*, although the debate was reported.
(11) Select Committee on the Health of Towns, 1840, *Parliamentary Papers*, Vol. 11 (1840)

(12) Slaney re-worded his motion 'to inquire into the circumstances affecting the health of the inhabitants of large towns, with a view to improved sanitary arrangements for their benefit'.
(13) *Hansard* (4 February 1840).
(14) See, for instance, Lewis, op. cit., pp. 113–14; S. Pollard, *Life and Labour in Sheffield* (Liverpool, 1969), p. 11.
(15) *Hansard* (4 February 1840).
(16) Ibid.
(17) Quoted Alice M. Hadfield, *The Chartist Land Company* (Newton Abbot, 1970), p. 16.
(18) Chadwick, ed. Flinn, op. cit., p. 266.
(19) *Report to Dundee Board of Health by Dr Carruthers, just returned from Sunderland* (29 December 1831).
(20) Select Committee on the Health of Towns, *Minutes of Evidence*, 1840, 1,678.
(21) Asa Briggs, 'Cholera and Society in the Nineteenth Century', *Past and Present*, No. 19 (1961).

CHAPTER 9

(1) Appendix to the First Report of the Commissioners of Inquiry into the State of Large Towns and Populous Districts. Abstract of the replies from fifty towns to questions about their condition. *British Sessional Papers*, Vol. 17 (1844). Only Bath and South Shields *ever* cleaned courts and alleys.
(2) Select Committee on the Health of Towns, 1840, *Minutes of Evidence*, 193.
(3) Rex *v*. Cross, 3 Camp., 227.
(4) The competence of the Scots law to deal with nuisance and its points of difference from English law are very clearly described by John Hill Burton, 'On the State of the Law as regards the Abatement of Nuisances . . .' (Edinburgh, 1840), *Reports on the Sanitary Condition of the Labouring Population of Scotland* (London, 1842), p. 40 (hereafter Burton).
(5) Select Committee on the Health of Towns, 1840, op. cit., 180, 3,034–3,042.
(6) See Edwin Chadwick, 'Recognised Principles of Legislation and State of the Existing Law . . .', in *Sanitary Condition of the Labouring Population of Great Britain, 1842*, ed. M. W. Flinn (Edinburgh, 1965), p. 360 in which he clearly says that the public health need not have been endangered 'had their powers been properly exercised, yet so complete was the desuetude of the machinery . . . that it appeared nowhere to be thought of as applicable'. See also John Simon, *English Sanitary Institutions* (1890), pp. 150ff.
(7) Select Committee on Building Regulations, 1842, *British Sessional Papers*, Vol. 10. *Minutes of Evidence*, 1,070–1,073.
(8) Charles Baird, 'The Law of Nuisance in Glasgow', *Sanitary Inquiry, Scotland*, p. 71n. See also Charles Allen, 'The Genesis of British Urban Redevelopment', *Economic History Review*, 2nd ser., Vol. 18 (1965), No. 3.
(9) Select Committee on Building Regulations, 1842, op. cit., 1,091–1,103.
(10) Burton, op. cit., p. 49.
(11) Ibid., p. 42.
(12) Select Committee on the Health of Towns, 1840, op. cit., 1,264.
(13) Ibid., 1,628–1,647.
(14) Abstract of petitions referred to the Select Committee on the Buildings Regulations and Boroughs Improvement Bills. *British Sessional Papers*, Vol. 101, p. 349.
(15) Select Committee on the Health of Towns, 1840, *Report*, p. xv.
(16) First Report of the Commission to Inquire into the State of Large Towns and Populous Districts, *British Sessional Papers*, Vol. 17, p. xiv.

(17) Select Committee on Buildings Regulations, 1842, *Minutes of Evidence*, 6,045–6,047.
(18) 3 and 4 William IV c. 46.
(19) Abstract of Petitions referred to the Select Committee on Buildings Regulations and Boroughs Improvement Bills, *British Sessional Papers*, Vol. 10, p. 349.
(20) Select Committee on the Health of Towns, *Minutes of Evidence*, 2,518.
(21) Ibid., 204.
(22) Chadwick, ed. Flinn, op. cit., p. 93.
(23) Constantine Henry Phipps, Normanby, 1st Marquess of Normanby, 2nd Earl of Mulgrave, 1797–1863, 1st President of the Health of Towns Association.
(24) Quotes Donald Southgate, *The Passing of the Whigs* (London, 1962), p. 154.
(25) John Simon, 'The Working of the Nuisances Removal Acts', from 7th Report to the Privy Council, *Public Health Reports*, Vol. 2, p. 198.

CHAPTER 10

(1) Octavia Hill, *Homes of the London Poor* (rep. London, 1970), p. 35.
(2) Select Committee on the Health of Towns, 1840, *Report*, p. iv.
(3) Ibid., p. ix.
(4) Ibid., p. x.
(5) Select Committee on the Health of Towns, 1840, *Minutes of Evidence*, 3,408.
(6) Sidney Pollard, *A History of Labour in Sheffield* (Liverpool, 1959), pp. 9, 11.
(7) *Dundee Advertiser* (10 May 1832 *et seq.*): £2 ratepayers could vote for Police Commissioners.
(8) Ibid. (31 January 1851).
(9) Ibid. (11 March 1851).
(10) Ibid. (11 March 1851).
(11) Select Committee on the Health of Towns, *Minutes of Evidence*, 3,409.
(12) E. Chadwick, *Report on the Sanitary Condition of the Labouring Population of Great Britain, 1842*, p. 380, Ed. M. W. Flinn (Edinburgh, 1965).
(13) James Hole, *The Homes of the Working Classes* (London, 1866), p. 110.
(14) John Simon, second annual City of London Report (26 November 1850), *Public Health Reports*, Vol. 1, p. 19.
(15) Select Committee on the Health of Towns, 1840, *Minutes of Evidence*, 3,408–3,409.
(16) Ibid., 3,427.
(17) Ibid., 242–243.
(18) Pollard, op. cit., p. 9.
(19) A. S. Wohl, 'The Housing of the Working Classes in London' in S. O. Chapman (ed.), *The History of Working-Class Housing* (Newton Abbot, 1971).
(20) Select Committe on Building Regulations, 1842, *Minutes of Evidence*, 1,091–1,092.
(21) A. S. Wohl, 'Unfit for Human Habitation', in H. J. Dyos and M. W. Wolff (eds), *The Victorian City: Images and Realities* (London, 1973).
(22) Simon, op. cit., Vol. 2, p. 199.
(23) Quoted by Wohl, op. cit.
(24) Select Committee on the State of Large Towns, *Minutes of Evidence*, 6,041–6,043.
(25) Of all papers published in the R.I.B.A. *Transactions* between 1835 and 1872 only three concerned themselves with the problems of contemporary house designers.

(26) Simon, op. cit., Vol. 2, p. 199.
(27) Chadwick, ed. Flinn, op. cit., p. 360.
(28) *Law Reports, Statutes*, Vol. 21, p. 377.
(29) Select Committee on Building Regulations 1842, op. cit., 1,073.
(30) Chadwick, ed. Flinn, op. cit., p. 384.
(31) Ibid., p. 385.

CHAPTER II

(1) M. Steig, 'Dickens's Excremental Vision', *Victorian Studies*, Vol. 13 (1969–70), p. 348.
(2) R. A. Lewis, *Edwin Chadwick and the Public Health Movement, 1832–1854* (London, 1932), p. 138; see also Keith Lucas, 'Some Influences Affecting the Development of Sanitary Legislation', *Economic History Review*, Vol. 6, p. 295.
(3) Lewis, op. cit., pp. 100–2.
(4) See A. S. Wohl, in H. J. Dyos and M. W. Wolff (eds), *Victorian City: Images and Realities* (London, 1973).
(5) See C. Fraser Brockington, *Public Health in the Nineteenth Century* (Edinburgh, 1965), pp. 137–8.
(6) This was not the figure suggested by Chadwick, but a small change in the percentage does not affect the principle.
(7) See Chapter 20 for an account of model dwellings societies.
(8) Machine-made bricks did not reach general use until after the introduction of patent kilns in the 1850s, see Singer, Charles, ed., *History of Technology*, Vol. 5, p. 442; see also Marion Bowley, *Innovations in Building Materials*, pp. 55–85.
(9) These were slabs constructed of Portland cement plastered on to a mat of straw, set in an iron frame, ready to be bolted together. They were exhibited in the English display of building materials at the Paris Exhibition of 1867.
(10) Reports on the Paris Universal Exhibition: Dwellings for the poor characterised by cheapness combined with the conditions necessary for health. *Parliamentary Papers, 1867–8*, c. 3968-III xxx Pt 11, p. 278.
(11) H. J. Dyos, 'Railways and Housing in Victorian London', *Journal of Transport History*, Vol. 11 (1955), No. 1, p. 94.
(12) Reports on the Paris Universal Exhibition, op. cit., p. 239.
(13) Ibid., p. 266.
(14) W. P. Alison, M.D., 'Observations on the Generation of Fever', *Report on the Sanitary Condition of the Labouring Population of Scotland* (London, 1842).
(15) 'Remarks on Dr W. P. Alison's 'Observations on the Generation of Fever'.
(16) Select Committee on the Health of Towns, 1840, pp. 38–9.
(17) *Hansard*, Debate on dwellings for the labouring poor (18 March 1853).
(18) J. Simon, *Public Health Reports*, Vol. 2, p. 206.
(19) Ibid., p. 207.
(20) Shaftesbury's Acts, 1851 and 1853, dealt only with houses intended for letting as lodgings and were, in any case, totally ineffective, see Chapter 5.
(21) His *English Sanitary Institutions* was published in 1890.
(22) 5 and 6 Vict. c. 104, Section 190.
(23) 29 and 30 Vict. c. 90, Section 35.
(24) 29 Vict. c. 28.

(25) 38 and 39 Vict. c. 55.
(26) 53 and 54 Vict. c. 59, Sections 23, 24, 25.

CHAPTER 12

(1) Census returns.
(2) Harry Barnes, *Housing: The Facts and the Future* (London, 1923), p. 370.
(3) Ibid., p. 413.
(4) Ibid., loc. cit.
(5) J. Simon, *Public Health Reports*, Vol. 2, p. 96.
(6) S. G. Checkland, *The Rise of Industrial Society in England, 1815–1885* (London, 1964), p. 232.
(7) John Honeyman, for instance, regarded it, along with the wellknown articles by Salisbury and Chamberlain, as having stimulated the establishment of the 1885 Commission. See also D. J. Oddy, 'Working-Class Diets in Late Nineteenth-Century Britain', *Economic History Review*, 2nd ser., Vol. 23 (August 1970), No. 2, p. 315.
(8) Nikolaus Pevsner, 'Model Dwellings', *Architectural Review*, Vol. 93, pp. 119–28.
(9) J. Hole, *Homes of the Working Classes* (London, 1866), p. 41.
(10) J. Honeyman, *Dwellings of the Poor* (Glasgow, 1890), p. 11.
(11) Ibid., p. 26.
(12) R. J. Morris, 'Leeds and the Crystal Palace', *Victorian Studies*, Vol. 13 (1970), p. 295.
(13) Beatrice Webb, *My Apprenticeship* (London, 1940), 2nd edn, pp. 155–6.
(14) Joseph Chamberlain, 'Labourers and Artizans Dwellings', *Fortnightly Review*, new ser., No. 204 (December 1883), p. 763.
(15) Royal Commission on Housing, 1885, *Minutes of Evidence*, 12,594–12,598.
(16) Hull conference on the 'Homes of the Poor', organised by the Charity Organisation Society (1 February 1884), p. 55.
(17) Ibid., p. 14.
(18) Chamberlain, op. cit., p. 501.
(19) Charles Booth, *Charles Booth's London*, ed. A. Fried and R. M. Elman (Harmondsworth, 1971), p. 416.
(20) Select Committee on the Health of Towns, 1840, *Minutes of Evidence*, 2,795–2,799.
(21) Hole, op. cit., p. 60.
(22) See pp. 197–9.
(23) See, for instance, J. H. Treble, 'Liverpool Working-Class Housing', in S. D. Chapman, *The History of Working-Class Housing* (Newton Abbot, 1971), pp. 167–70.
(24) Royal Commission on Housing, 1885, op. cit., 655–695; Select Committee on the Health of Towns, 1840, *Minutes of Evidence*, 809–818.
(25) See Gilbert Bentley, *British Social Policy 1914–1939* (London, 1970), p. 51.

CHAPTER 13

(1) 'An Index of Urban Land Rents and House Rents in England and Wales, 1845–1913', *Econometrica* (1941), p. 229, Table 4.
(2) Quoted Charles J. Singer, (ed.), *History of Technology* Vol. 5 (1954–8), p. 230.
(3) Shadwell, *Industrial Efficiency*, Vol. 2, p. 190.
(4) Singer, op. cit., p. 230, Table 5.
(5) A. S. Wohl, 'The Housing of the Working Classes in London, 1815–1914', in S. D. Chapman (ed.), *The History of Working-Class Housing* (Newton Abbot, 1971).

(6) Pollard, *Life and Labour in Sheffield* (Liverpool, 1969), p. 102.
(7) 53 and 54 Vict. c. 70 (18 August 1890), p. 588, Sect. 2, and 9 Edw. 7 c. 44 (3 December 1909), p. 173, Sect. 14.
(8) See *Economic History Review*, 2nd ser., Vol. 16, pp. 120ff.
(9) Industrial Remuneration Conference, *Report*, p. 86.
(10) Select Committee on the Health of Towns, 1840, *Report*, p.27.
(11) Royal Commission on Housing, 1885, *Minutes of Evidence*, 5,888–5,890.
(12) Wohl, op. cit., p. 26; John Butt, 'Working-Class Housing in Glasgow', in Chapman, op. cit., p. 78; *People's Journal* (13 April 1874).
(13) *Builder*, Vol. 47 (1884), p. 746.
(14) Royal Commission on Housing, 1885, *Minutes of Evidence*, 13,021–13,030, 13,110–13,115, 13,158, 13,166–13,168, 13,204–13,209, 13,196–13,199.
(15) Ibid., 5063.
(16) Royal Commission on Housing, 1885, *Report*, p. 54.
(17) J. Hole, *Homes of the Working Classes* (London, 1866), pp. 212–13.
(18) M. W. Beresford, 'The Back-to-Back House in Leeds, 1787–1937', in Chapman, op. cit., pp. 115–16.
(19) John Butt, 'Working-Class Housing in Glasgow, 1851–1914', in Chapman, op. cit., pp. 80–1.
(20) Royal Commission on Housing, 1885, *Minutes of Evidence*, 3,390, points out that rents of 'good' houses were no higher than bad.
(21) Butt, op. cit., p. 73; and Royal Commission on Housing, 1885, *Minutes of Evidence*, 1,321–1,324, 1,383–1,385, 3,146, 5,081, 5,254.
(22) J. H. Treble, 'Liverpool Working-Class Housing, 1801–1851', in Chapman, op. cit., pp. 198–9.
(23) Royal Commission on Housing, 1885, *Minutes of Evidence*, 12,877–12,882, 12,909–12,910.
(24) Ibid., 9,802–9,805, and Beresford, op. cit., pp. 115–16.
(25) B. P. Lenman *et al.*, *Dundee and Its Textile Industry* (Abertay Historical Society pamphlet).
(26) Royal Commission on Housing, 1885, *Minutes of Evidence*, 5,031–5,037, 12,311, 11,909, 11,960–11,967.
(27) Ibid., 7,392.
(28) Ibid., 6,805.
(29) Ibid., 7,896.
(30) Pollard, op. cit., p. 189.
(31) Wohl, op. cit., p. 18.
(32) B. Seebohm Rowntree, *Poverty: A Study in Town Life* (London, 1901), p. 133.
(33) D. J. Oddy, 'Working-Class Diets in Nineteenth-Century Britain', *Economic History Review*, 2nd ser., Vol. 23 (August 1970), No. 2, pp. 314–23.
(34) Sidney Pollard, 'Real Earnings in Sheffield', *Yorkshire Bulletin* (1957), p. 58, Table 2.
(35) Lenman B. P. Lythe and E. Gauldie, *Dundee and Its Textile Industry*, p. 83.
(36) K. Pribram, 'Housing', *Encyclopedia of Social Sciences*.
(37) Charles Booth, *Charles Booth's London*, ed. A. Fried and R. M. Elman (Harmondsworth, 1971), p. 415.
(38) Octavia Hill, 'Cottage Property in London', *Homes of the London Poor* (rep. London, 1970), p. 19.
(39) Royal Commission on Housing, 1885, *Report*, p. 55.
(40) R. Tressall, *The Ragged Philanthropist* (rep. 1962), pp. 54–6.
(41) Charles Booth, op. cit., pp. 415–16.
(42) H. Barnes, *Housing, The Facts and the Future* (London, 1923), quoting census figures, p. 412.

(43) Ibid., p. 371.
(44) Butt, op. cit., p. 71. The post-1891 figures are affected by boundary changes.
(45) Lenman *et al.*, op. cit., Appendix 1, p. 103.
(46) S. Pollard, *Life and Labour in Sheffield*, op. cit., pp. 188–9.
(47) S. B. Saul, 'House-Building in England, 1890–1914', *Economic History Review*, 2nd ser., Vol. 15, p. 136.
(48) John Parry Lewis, *Building Cycles and Britain's Growth* (London, 1965), Appendix 4.
(49) Barnes, op. cit., p. 359.
(50) Marian Bowley, *Housing and the State, 1919–1944* (London, 1945), p. 12.
(51) See 262, 279.
(52) Butt, op. cit., p. 80.

CHAPTER 14

(1) Beresford on Leeds, Butt on Glasgow in S. D. Chapman (ed.), *The History of Working-Class Housing* (Newton Abbot, 1971).
(2) See, for instance, J. B. Cullingworth, *Housing in Transition, A Case Study in the City of Lancaster, 1858–1962* (London, 1963), p. 16. The normal procedure in Lancaster was for the builder to provide a row of houses on 'spec.', selling to investors at a profit of about 12½ per cent.
(3) See H. J. Dyos, 'The Speculative Builders and Developers of Victorian London', *Victorian Studies*, Vol. 9 (1968), p. 652, and an answering 'comment' by E. W. Cooney, in Vol. 13 (1970), No. 3, p. 355.
(4) J. N. Tarn, 'Housing in Liverpool and Glasgow', *Town Planning Review*, Vol. 39 (January 1969), No. 4, and Treble, in Chapman, op. cit.
(5) H. W. Singer, 'An Index of Urban Land Rents and House Rents', *Econometrica* (1941), Table 4, pp. 228n, 229; and K. Maiwald, 'Index of Building Costs', *Economic History Review*, Vol. 7 (1954), No. 2, and B. Weber's, '*A New Index of House Rents*', *Scottish Journal of Political Economy*, Vol. 7, pp. 232–7.
(6) John Parry Lewis, *Building Cycles and Britain's Growth* (London, 1965), p. 161.
(7) R. Cobden, *Speeches on Questions of Public Policy*, ed. J. Bright and E. Thorold Rodgers (London, 1908), p. 272.
(8) Steen Eiler Rasmussen, *London, The Unique City* (1948), new edn., pp. 410–14.
(9) J. Hole, *Houses of the Working Classes* (London, 1866), p. 207.
(10) B. P. Lenman *et al.*, *Dundee and Its Textile Industry* (Abertay Historical Society pamphlet), p. 84. Scottish land is not bought outright but feued for a yearly sum.
(11) Select Committee on Building Regulations, 1842, *Minutes of Evidence*, 1,139, 1,168–1,177.
(12) Ibid., 217–228.
(13) Karl Pribram, 'Housing', *Encyclopedia of Social Sciences*.
(14) Maiwald, op. cit.
(15) Singer, *History of Technology*, Vol. 5, p. 442; see also Marian Bowley, *Innovations in Building Materials* (London, 1960), p. 63; see also *Builder*, Vol. 49, pp. 85–6.
(16) E. Gauldie and B. P. Lenman, 'Pitfour Brickworks', *Industrial Archaeology* (1969), p. 340.
(17) H. J. Dyos, 'The Speculative Builders and Developers of Victorian London', *Victorian Studies*, Vol. 9 (1968), p. 652 and comment by E. W. Cooney in *Victorian Studies*, Vol. 13 (March 1970), p. 355.

(18) Hermione Hobhouse, *Thomas Cubitt, Master-Builder* (London, 1971); and see also E. W. Cooney's review of this book in *Urban History Newsletter* (Spring 1972), p. 5.

(19) J. N. Tarn, 'Housing in Liverpool and Glasgow', *Town Planning Review*, Vol. 39, pp. 319–34, and J. H. Treble, 'Liverpool Working-Class Housing' in Chapman (ed.), op. cit., pp. 321, 194.

(20) Select Committee on Health of Towns, 1840, *Minutes of Evidence*, 340.

(21) Raymond Postgate, *The Builders' History* (London, 1923), p. 455.

(22) Ibid., p. 456.

(23) Which declared the signer not to belong to any trade society.

(24) Royal Commission on Housing, 1885, *Minutes of Evidence*, 13,616, 7,404.

(25) A. K. Cairncross, *Home and Foreign Investment 1870–1913* (1953), p. 16, Table 1.

(26) A. S. Wohl, 'The Housing of the Working Classes in London, 1815–1914', in Chapman (ed.), op. cit., pp. 26–7.

(27) M. W. Beresford, 'The Back-to-Back House in Leeds, 1787–1937', in Chapman (ed.), op.cit., p. 119.

(28) For instance Dundee Town Council.

CHAPTER 15

(1) J. B. Cullingworth, *Housing in Transition, A Case Study in the City of Lancaster, 1858–1962* (London, 1963), p. 15; B. P. Lenman *et al.*, *Dundee and Its Textile Industry* (Abertay Historical Society pamphlet), p. 104; S. Pollard, *Life and Labour in Sheffield* (Liverpool, 1969), p. 101; J. Hole, *Homes of the Working Classes* (London, 1866), p. 26; J. H. Treble, 'Working Class Housing in Liverpool' in S. D. Chapman (ed.), *The History of Working-Class Housing* (Newton Abbot, 1971).

(2) See p. 226.

(3) Henry Kinnaird, 9th Lord, 'Working Men's Houses' (Dundee, 1874), p. 3.

(4) J. N. Tarn, 'Some Pioneer Suburban Housing Estates', *Architectural Review* (1968), p. 36 and Nikolaus Pevsner, 'Model Houses', *Architectural Review* (1943), pp. 119–28.

(5) *Economic Journal*, Vol. 64, p. 256 reviewing Brinley Thomas, *Migration and Economic Growth* (Cambridge, 1954). See also Thomas, op. cit., pp. 183–9.

(6) 'Fluctuations in House-Building in Britain and the U.S. in the Nineteenth Century', *Journal of Economic History*, Vol. 22, p. 198.

(7) 'House-Building in England, 1890–1914', *Economic History Review*, 2nd ser., Vol. 15, p. 136.

(8) 'Fluctuations in the Glasgow Building Industry, 1856–1914', *Home and Foreign Investment, 1870–1913* (Cambridge, 1953), p. 36.

(9) Lenman *et al.*, op. cit., p. 88.

(10) J. Simon, *Public Health Reports*, p. 72.

(11) H. J. Habbakuk, 'Fluctuations in House-Building in Britain . . .', *Journal of Economic History*, Vol. 22.

CHAPTER 16

(1) S. D. Chapman (ed.), *The History of Working-Class Housing* (Newton Abbot, 1971), p. 298.

(2) J. Hole, *Homes of the Working Classes* (London, 1866), p. 66.

(3) The first patent brick kilns were introduced to the district in 1867. Before that bricks could not satisfactorily be made in frost.

(4) Grates with boilers were far from common (cf. Select Committee on the Health of Towns, 1840, *Minutes of Evidence*, 340, 598) and their proper use may well not have been understood. The boiler was at the side of the fire,

filled from the top, and emptied from a tap below. It would, of course, burn out if not kept filled when a fire was lit.

(5) Enid Gauldie (ed.), *The Dundee Textile Industry*, from the papers of Peter Carmichael of Arthurstone (Scottish History Society, 1969), pp. 189–90.

(6) J. D. Marshall, 'Colonisation as a Factor in the Planning of Towns', in H. J. Dyos (ed.), *The Study of Urban History* (London, 1968), p. 228.

(7) *OSA*, Vol. 15, p. 134, and John Cameron, *Parish of Campsie* (Kirkintilloch, 1891), p. 27.

(8) Enid Gauldie, *Scottish Bleachfields* (unpublished thesis), p. 553.

(9) F. J. Ball, 'Housing in an Industrial Colony: Ebbw Vale, 1778–1914', in Chapman (ed.), op. cit., p. 294.

(10) Charles Wilson, *The History of Unilever* (London, 1954), Vol. 1, p. 36.

(11) Ibid., p. 144.

(12) Lewis Mumford, *The Culture of Cities* (London, 1940), p. 392.

(13) H. J. Dyos, 'The Slums of Victorian London', *Victorian Studies*, Vol. 11, p. 34.

CHAPTER 17

(1) Alice Mary Hadfield, *The Chartist Land Company* (Newton Abbot, 1970), pp. 19, 50.

(2) S. Pollard, *Life and Labour in Sheffield* (Liverpool, 1969), p. 21; State of Large Towns, *Minutes of Evidence*, 6,041.

(3) S. D. Chapman (ed.), *The History of Working-Class Housing* (Newton Abbot, 1971), p. 143; 'Working-Class Housing in Nottingham'.

(4) Chapman, op. cit., p. 238–9: 'The Contribution of Building Clubs'.

(5) Ibid., pp. 101–2: 'Working-Class Housing in Leeds'.

(6) R. Cobden, *Speeches on Questions of Public Policy*, ed. J. Bright and J. E. Thorold Rodgers, (London, 1908), 3rd edn, p. 273 (13 December 1852).

(7) Ian MacDougall, *The Minutes of the Edinburgh Trades Council, 1859–1873* (Scottish History Society, 1968), p. 114.

(8) Pollard, op. cit., p. 105.

(9) Royal Commission on Housing, 1885, *Minutes of Evidence*, 13,852, 13,898–13,899.

(10) Seymour J. Price, *Building Societies, Their Origins and History* (London, 1958), p. 147.

(11) Twenty members were usual in the first societies, fifty to hundred after 1836. Two hundred and fifty was a common membership for the permanent societies. Ibid., p. 102.

(12) Arthur Scratchley, Secretary to Western Life Assurance and Annuity Society.

(13) Price, op. cit., p. 129.

(14) Cobden, op. cit., p. 273.

(15) J. Hole, *Homes of the Working Classes* (London, 1866), p. 180.

(16) One of the societies most successful in attracting working men, the Oldham Society, recognising the risk of mill hands, for instance, falling down on payment due to accident or depression, allowed for suspended payment in these circumstances. *Parliamentary Papers*, Vol. 25, pp. 1–260. Royal Commission on Friendly and Benefit Building Societies, *Minutes of Evidence*, 6,241–6,243.

(17) Royal Commission on Housing, 1885, *Report*, p. 50.

(18) Hole, op. cit., pp. 87–93, 172–85, 213.

(19) Hull conference on the 'Homes of the Poor', organised by the Charity Organisation Society (1 February 1884): *Report*, pp. 50–1 and Hole, op. cit., p. 87.

(20) Dr James Begg, D.D., 1808–83, had spoken on housing in Dundee six years

earlier when, appearing as 'Leader of the Freehold Land Movement in Scotland' he had, rather self-defeatingly, killed any such movement dead by announcing 'in Scotland the working man cannot reasonably hope to reach possession of a house worth £10 a year'.

(21) Owner of large estate in neighbouring county, friend of Lord Shaftesbury and constant campaigner for housing reform, author of '*Working Men's Houses*', (1874), he built some pretty cottages near his own grounds.
(22) *People's Journal* (16 May 1874).
(23) James Cox's *Letter-Book* (21 May 1874); ms very kindly lent by Miss Margot Cox, Seaton House, Nairn.
(24) *People's Journal* (16 May 1874).
(25) Dundee Police Commission Approved Building Plans.
(26) Lamb Collection, Dundee Public Library 227 (2). Joseph Tall patented the first system of shuttering for concrete in 1864. A handful of buildings were erected in concrete in England in the late 1860s and early 1870s. Beach Tower, Broughty Ferry, a mansion house of the early 1870s was the first house in Scotland to use concrete throughout.
(27) Ian MacDougall, *Minutes of Edinburgh Trades Council, 1859–1873* (Scottish History Society, Edinburgh, 1968), pp. 29–32, 54 and n, 277.
(28) *Builder* (28 December 1861), p. 899, and *Builder* (5 July 1862), p. 484.
(29) MacDougall, op. cit., pp. 303–5.
(30) Royal Commission on Housing, 1885, *Minutes of Evidence*, 13, 241–296, 10,954–10,956, 13,761, 13,766–13,824.
(31) *Builder* (28 December 1861), p. 899.
(32) Royal Commission on Benefit Building Societies, op. cit., 6,252–6,253.
(33) Price, op. cit., p. 117.
(34) Royal Commission on Housing, 1885, *Minutes of Evidence*, 6,244.
(35) Quoted Price, op. cit., p. 207.
(36) Royal Commission, 1871, *Minutes of Evidence*, 3,794, 4,864, 4,932, 5,125, 6,236–6,240, 6,424–6,425, 8,196–8,199.
(37) Ibid., 6,424.
(38) Ibid., 3,894.

CHAPTER 18

(1) J. Hole, *Homes of the Working Classes* (London, 1866), p. 85; Royal Commission on Housing, 1885, *Minutes of Evidence*, 13,852.
(2) The story of O'Connor's scheme is told in detail in Alice Mary Hadfield, *Chartist Land Company* (Newton Abbot, 1970). See also Royal Commission on Housing, 1885, op. cit., 15,011–15,141.
(3) E. P. Thompson, *The Making of the English Working Class* (Harmondsworth, 1968), p. 459.
(4) S. D. Chapman and J. N. Bartlett, 'The Contribution of Building Clubs and Freehold Land Society to Working-Class Housing in Birmingham', in S. D. Chapman (ed.), *The History of Working-Class Housing* (Newton Abbot 1971), p. 240.
(5) Hole, op. cit., p. 108.
(6) Ibid., pp. 84–5.
(7) Chapman and Bartlett, op. cit., pp. 241–4.
(8) S. Pollard, *Life and Labour in Sheffield* (Liverpool, 1969), pp. 22–3.
(9) S. J. Price, *Building Societies, Their Origins and History* (London, 1958), p. 208.
(10) Royal Commission, 1871, *Minutes of Evidence*, 2,888.
(11) Ibid., 7,348.

(12) Ibid., 2,888.
(13) Ibid., 3,692, 3,746.

CHAPTER 19

(1) Octavia Hill, *Homes of the London Poor, 1883* (rep. Cass, 1970), p. 18.
(2) Royal Commission on Housing, 1885, *Minutes of Evidence*, 15.
(3) Hill, op. cit., p. 1.
(4) Beatrice Webb, *My Apprenticeship* (London, n.d.), 2nd edn, p. 177n.
(5) Webb, op. cit., p. 229
(6) She was active, for instance, in the foundation of the London Charity Organi-
    sation Society, the Commons Preservation Society and the National Trust.
    Her articles on housing were published in the *Fortnightly Review* (November
    1866), *Macmillan's Magazine* (July 1869, October 1871, October 1872 and
    June 1874) and her influential book, a collection of the articles, was first
    published as *Homes of the London Poor* in 1875.
(7) Royal Commission on Housing, 1885, op. cit., 6,395–6,397, 6,439–6,443,
    6,637–6,639, 6,718–6,731.
(8) Ibid., 12,348.
(9) Ibid., 12,342–53.
(10) Sir D'Arcy Wentworth Thomson, *Fifty Years Ago and Now*, presidential
    address to Dundee Social Union, 50th Annual General Meeting (27 April
    1938).

CHAPTER 20

(1) Quoted Charles Allen, 'Genesis of British Urban Redevelopment', *Economic
    History Review*, 2nd ser., Vol. 18 (1965), p. 611 n 4.
(2) Royal Commission on Housing, 1885, *Report*, p. 55.
(3) Quoted J. Hole, *Homes of the Working Classes* (London, 1866), p. 57n.
(4) *Builder*, Vol. 3 (1845), p. 1.
(5) B. Webb, *My Apprenticeship* (London, n.d.), 2nd edn, p. 224.
(6) John Nelson Tarn, 'The Peabody Donation Fund', *Architectural Association
    Quarterly* (Winter 1968–9), p. 32.
(7) They were being built in Leeds until 1911, in Nottingham until 1874, in Bury
    until 1866.
(8) See also 'Building in Scotland', *Builder* (8 November 1851), Vol. 9, No. 457,
    p. 704.
(9) Nikolaus Pevsner, 'Model Dwellings for the Labouring Classes', *Architectural
    Review*, Vol. 93, pp. 119–28.
(10) Quoted Hole, op. cit., p. 56.
(11) Waterlow advertised his intention of earning 9 per cent from his Mark Street
    buildings but this was more to attract notice than belief; and, in any case, he
    had already stated his view that 'the wisest plan is to meet the wants of that
    portion of the working classes most worth working for, those earning from
    £1 5s to £2 per week'.
(12) Royal Commission on Housing, 1885, *Report*, p. 55.
(13) Royal Commission on Housing, 1885, *Minutes of Evidence*, 8,852.
(14) Webb, op. cit., p. 226.
(15) State of Large Towns, *Minutes of Evidence*, 1,501, 6,172; J. Simon, *Public
    Health Reports*, ed. E. Seaton (London, 1887), Vol. 2, pp. 51, 60; The tax was
    charged on a graduating scale rising by 8s 3d each window.
(16) 'Building in Scotland', *Builder* (8 November 1851), p. 704.
(17) See John Nelson Tarn, 'Some Pioneer Suburban Housing Estates', *Architec-
    tural Review* (1968), p. 367.

(18) The same thing happened in the provinces; the West Hill Park Model Dwellings near Halifax found that 'the inhabitants are of a higher class (than workmen) and as a natural result the ground floor arrangements have proved unsuitable.' It was necessary to add a parlour. Hole, op. cit., p. 76.
(19) Hole, op. cit., pp. 98–101 and Appendix. But see Chapter 22, p. 260.
(20) 29 Vict. c. 28 (18 May 1866). *Law Reports, Statutes,* Vol. 1, p. 249.
(21) 30 Vict. c. 28 (17 June 1867), 31 and 32 Vict. c. 130 (31 July 1868), and 38 and 39 Vict. c. 36 (29 June 1875). These Acts will be discussed in more detail in Chapter 23.
(22) See, for instance, John Nelson Tarn, 'Housing in Liverpool and Glasgow— the Growth of Civic Responsibility', *Town Planning Review,* Vol. 39 (1969), No. 4, p. 323.
(23) Royal Commission on Housing, 1885, *Minutes of Evidence,* 11,824.
(24) *Builder,* Vol. 2 (1844). See also Nikolaus Pevsner, 'Model Houses for the Labouring Classes', *Architectural Review,* Vol. 93, pp. 119–28.
(25) Hole, op. cit., p. 60 and Artizans and General Properties Co. Ltd, *Artizans Centenary,* 1867–1967.
(26) With the exception of Goschen, St Lyulph Stanley and Morley who appended to the Report their opinion that 'sufficient importance has scarcely been given in the Report to the work of the private companies for housing the working classes', p. 65. See also Select Committee on Housing, 1881, *Minutes of Evidence,* 167, and *Builder,* Vol. 20 (1862), p. 518: Peabody can house 'a mere drop in a bucket fraction'.
(27) Royal Commission on Housing, 1885, *Report,* p. 54 and *Minutes of Evidence,* Q 11, 643.
(28) Royal Commission on Housing, 1885, *Minutes of Evidence,* 763, 848, 849, 1,344–1,345, 4,740, 11,540, etc. See also *Builder,* Vol. 9 (1851), p. 632 where 'a new iron model lodging house for *very* respectable mechanics' is described.
(29) The Artizans started with £250,000 and increased it to £950,000 in thirty years. Peabody started with £15,000 and increased it to £500,000. Waterlow started with £327,000. *Artizans Centenary,* op. cit.; Hull conference on the 'Homes of the Poor', organised by the Charity Organisation Society (1 February 1884), pp. 47–8. J. N. Tarn, 'The Peabody Donation Fund', *Architectural Association Quarterly* (1968–9), p. 32. See also *Parliamentary Papers,* Vol. 40 (1868), p. 60 and Vol. 35 (1874), p. 331: Report on loans by Public Works Loan Commissions.

CHAPTER 21

(1) *Parliamentary Papers,* Vol. 3 (1840), p. 657. But see Chapter 8, pp. 103–7.
(2) The 1848 Act, and the Towns Improvement Clauses Act which preceded it, gathered together Building Regulations contained in earlier local Acts. See B. Keith-Lucas, 'Some Influences Affecting the Development of Sanitary Legislation', *Economic History Review,* Vol. 6, p. 295.
(3) *Hansard,* 3rd ser., Vol. 126 (18 March 1853), p. 400.
(4) 48 and 49 Vict. c. 72.
(5) 14 and 15 Vict. c. 34.
(6) This society was a revival, in 1841, by Shaftesbury, Southwood Smith and others of the earlier Labourers' Friendly Society founded in 1827.
(7) J. Simon, *Public Health Reports,* ed. E. Seaton (London, 1887), Vol. 1, p. 55.
(8) *Parliamentary Papers,* Vol. 78, p. 525.
(9) 48 and 49 Vict. c. 72, Part 3.
(10) H. O. Arnold Forster, 'The Existing Law', *Nineteenth Century* (December 1883), p. 940.

(11) *Parliamentary Papers*, Vol. 4 (1851), p. 119.
(12) Simon, op. cit., p. 54.
(13) J. Hole, *Homes of the Working Classes* (London, 1866), pp. 161–3, 52–4.
(14) *Pall Mall Gazette* (26 November 1883).
(15) *Builder*, Vol. 9 (4 October 1851), p. 632.
(16) *Dundee Advertiser* (2 February 1855).
(17) Nikolaus Pevsner, *Architectural Review*, Vol. 93, p. 123; J. N. Tarn, 'The Peabody Donation Fund', *Architectural Association Quarterly* (1968–9), p. 32.
(18) Tarn, *Working Class Housing in Nineteenth-Century Britain* (London, 1971), p. 7 and Hole, op. cit., p. 53.
(19) *Hansard*, during debate on Crowded Dwellings Bill, 17–18 August 1857, Vol. 147, 1471–1472.
(20) Report by Captain Hay on the operation of the Common Lodging Houses Act, March 1853, *Parliamentary Papers*, Vol. 78, p. 525.
(21) *Parliamentary Papers*, Vol. 78 (March 1853), p. 525.
(22) 16 and 17 Vict. c. 41.
(23) Hole, op. cit., pp. 51–3.
(24) *Hansard*, 3rd ser., Vol. 122 (18 March 1853), p. 400.
(25) See, for example, H. J. Dyos, 'Railways and Housing in Victorian London', *Journal of Transport History*, Vol. 2 (1955–6), p. 15.
(26) *Hansard*, 3rd ser., Vol. 122 (18 March 1853), p. 400.
(27) *Hansard*, 3rd ser., Vol. 126 (9 May 1853), p. 292.
(28) And once this converted court had served its purpose of confounding the Metropolitan Railway's critics it was converted into warehouses and its tenants evicted. Dyos, op. cit., p. 14. See also H. J. Dyos, 'Some Social Costs of Railway Building in London', *Journal of Transport History*, Vol. 3 (1957–8), p. 23. John R. Kellett, *The Impact of Railways on Victorian Cities* (London, 1969), p. 325).
(29) Dyos, 'Some Social Costs of Railway Building', op. cit., p. 25.
(30) Jack Simmons, 'The Pattern of Tube Railways in London', *Journal of Transport History*, Vol. 7 (1965–6), p. 235.
(31) *Hansard*, 3rd ser., Vol. 125 (1853), p. 417.

CHAPTER 22

(1) 18 and 19 Vict. c. 88.
(2) 18 and 19 Vict. c. 132.
(3) *Parliamentary Papers*, Vol. 11 (1855), p. 101.
(4) J. Simon, *Public Health Reports*, ed. E. Seaton (London, 1887), Vol. 2, p. 211.
(5) *Dictionary of National Biography*. But see a forthcoming thesis by Andrew Watterson dealing with parliamentary figures involved in early housing legislation.
(6) The Companies Act giving general limited liability was not passed until the following year.
(7) *Parliamentary Papers* Vol. 2 (1855), p. 101.
(8) *Parliamentary Papers*, Vol. 2 (1855), pp. 101, 117, 139, 161.
(9) *Hansard*, 3rd ser., Vol. 136 (17 February 1855), p. 1649.
(10) An Act to amend the law relating to the construction of buildings in the Metropolis. 18 and 19 Vict. c. 122.
(11) A. S. Wohl in *Victorian City: Images and Realities* (London, 1973), p. 6.
(12) J. N. Tarn, *Working-Class Housing in Nineteenth-Century Britain* (London, 1971), p. 46.
(13) *Hansard*, Vol. 191 (29 April, 1868), 2061.

(14) Simon, op. cit., Vol. 2, p. 200.
(15) 18 and 19 Vict. c. 121.
(16) Section 13.
(17) By Sir William Molesworth, the first Commissioner of Works and Public Buildings.
(18) Arnold-Forster, The existing law as it relates to the dwellings of the poor. *Nineteenth Century*, Vol. 14 (December 1883), pp. 942–3.
(19) J. Hole, *Homes of the Working Classes* (London, 1866), p. 129.
(20) Simon, op. cit., Vol. 2, p. 190.
(21) Ibid., Vol. 2, p. 211 and n.
(22) *Hansard*, 3rd ser., Vol. 146, 1542.
(23) *Parliamentary Papers*, Session 2, Vol. 1 (1857), p. 459.
(24) *Hansard*, 3rd ser., Vol. 147 (17 August 1857), 1761.
(25) *Hansard*, 3rd ser., Vol. 147 (18 August 1857), p. 1858.
(26) Ibid., Kinnaird succeeded his brother as Lord Kinnaird in 1878
(27) *Journals of the House of Commons* (14 July 1858).
(28) S. Pollard, *Life and Labour in Sheffield* (Liverpool, 1909), p. 100.
(29) *Urban History Newsletter* (Summer 1970), p. 3: a discussion of Professor Beresford's 'From Tenter Grounds to Building Ground', delivered at the Urban History Group Meeting, Birmingham (3 April 1970).
(30) Lord Derby, of course, headed a brief Conservative interregnum in 1858/9.
(31) Followed in 1861 by an Act to give the same powers in England.
(32) *Journal of the House of Commons* (1861).
(33) See Simon, op. cit., Vol. 2, p. 211. The Act provided for the lighting, cleansing, draining, supplying with water to and improving the same and also for promoting the public health thereof. The Bill was presented by Sir William Dunbar, Lord Advocate, on 21 March and passed by the Commons on 2 July. *Journal of House of Commons* (1862), p. 109.
(34) J. N. Tarn, 'Housing in Liverpool and Glasgow', in S. D. Chapman (ed.), *The History of Working-Class Housing* (Newton Abbot, 1971), pp. 329–30. Butt, Allan and Tarn op cit. on Glasgow; for Dundee, duplicate plans submitted to Police Commissioners.
(35) Geoffrey Best, *F.A. Shaftesbury* (London, 1964), p. 116.
(36) *Hansard*, 3rd ser., Vol. 147 (1857), 1767 and 1858.
(37) Preceded in 1864 by an inquiry into the housing of the rural poor.
(38) Simon, op. cit., Vol. 2, pp. 204–13.
(39) Norman Longmate, *King Cholera* (London, 1966), pp. 212–22.
(40) Best, op. cit., p. 112n, from *The Times* (5 August 1872).
(41) Quoted G. E. Buckle, *The Life of Benjamin Disraeli* (London, 1916–20), p. 369.
(42) 1823–1906, 2nd son of Sir Robert Peel, Liberal Member for Leominster 1849–52. Bury 1852–7, 1859–65, S.E. Lancs 1868, Financial Secretary at the Treasury 1800–65. Donald Southgate, *The Passing of the Whigs* (London, 1962), pp. 436–7.
(43) Hole, op. cit., Appendix, pp. 187–90.
(44) 29 Vict. c. 28 (18 May 1866), *Law Reports, Statutes*, Vol. 1, p. 249.
(45) Quoted at the Hull conference on the 'Homes of the Poor' organised by the Charity Organisation Society (1 February 1884), *Report*, p. 47.
(46) See also J. N. Tarn, 'Housing in Liverpool and Glasgow', *Town Planning Review*, Vol. 39 (1969), No. 4, p. 324.
(47) *Parliamentary Papers*, Vol. 35 (1874), p. 331. Report on cases in which loans have been granted by the Public Works Commissioners under the Labouring Classes Dwellings Act, 1866. See also *Parliamentary Papers*, Vol. 40 (1868), p. 60. Account showing amounts advanced.

(48) Royal Commission on Housing, 1885, *Minutes of Evidence*, 12,072–12,073, 12,243.
(49) 30 and 31 Vict. c. 28 (1867).
(50) *Parliamentary Papers*, Vol. 117 (1867–8), c. 3968–111, Part 2, pp. 239–317.
(51) Tarn (Liverpool and Glasgow), op. cit., pp. 323–4.
(52) The City of Glasgow Improvements Act, 1866. See Charles Allen, 'British Urban Redevelopment', op. cit., p. 604. Tarn, op.cit., pp. 328–9, and Chapman, op. cit., J. Butt, 'Working-Class Housing in Glasgow, 1851–1914', pp. 58–9.
(53) Allen, op. cit., p. 604.
(54) Royal Commission on Housing, 1885, *Report*, p. 7. Lord Derby's government's first session began on 1 February 1866.
(55) Southgate, op. cit., p. 327.
(56) 29 and 30 Vict. c. 28. This Act was amended in 1867 by the Act 30 and 31 Vict. c. 28, which made certain provisions about mortgages and extended the Act to Scotland.
(57) *Journal of House of Commons* (1866), pp. 57, 208.
(58) Royal Commission on Housing, 1885, *Report*, p. 377. None of these Acts was repeated until 1890.
(59) 29 and 30 Vict. c. 90.
(60) Royal Commission on Housing, 1885, *First Report*, p. 47 and *Minutes of Evidence*, 17,483. See also Wohl, op. cit., p. 21.
(61) 30 and 31 Vict. 101.
(62) Butt, op. cit., p. 68–9, 78.

CHAPTER 23

(1) *Builder* (3 August 1867).
(2) Torrens was Liberal Member for Finsbury. Born William McCullagh of Dublin, he was an independent Liberal, always interested in social questions and sitting originally as Member for Dundalk. He later assumed his mother's maiden name of Torrens. Robert Torrens of Australia was his uncle. The Hon. A. F. Kinnaird was Liberal Member for the city of Perth. He succeeded to the peerage as Lord Kinnaird in 1878, John Locke, Q.C., was Liberal Member for Southwark.
(3) *Hansard*, Vol. 191 (1 April 1868), 673.
(4) Ibid.
(5) Ibid.
(6) *Parliamentary Papers*, Vol. 1 (1866), pp. 43, 53; *Hansard*, Vol. 191 (1868), p. 677; *Parliamentary Papers*, Vol. 1 (1867–8), pp. 21, 43.
(7) *Law Reports, Statutes*, Vol. 3, p. 134. 31 and 32 Vict. c.130 (31 July 1868).
(8) *Parliamentary Papers*, Vol. 1 (1867–8), p. 65.
(9) The 'Duties of a medical officer outlined by the General Board of Health' of 12 February 1851 had already allowed the visitation of premises, the giving of instructions for the diminution of overcrowding and the making of annual reports (to the Board of Health) on the health of districts; C. Brockington, *Public Health in the Nineteenth Century* (Edinburgh, 1965), p. 179. See also *Parliamentary Papers*, Vol. 24 (1849), pp. 129–35, Instructions of the General Board of Health to the superintending officers.
(10) J. Wohl, *Victorian City: Images and Realities* (London, 1973), p. 32.
(11) Wohl, op. cit., p. 10. Public Health Act, 1872. 35 and 36 Vict. c. 79, Sections 10 and 11.
(12) *Hansard*, Vol. 191 (1868), 672.

(13) Wohl, op. cit., p. 8.
(14) Select committee on working of 1868 and 1875 Acts, Interim Report, *Minutes of Evidence*, 119–53. Final Report, *Minutes of Evidence*, 5,625–5,626.
(15) See also Charles Allen, 'The Genesis of British Urban Redevelopment', *Economic History Review*, 2nd ser., Vol. 18 (1965), p. 601.
(16) *Hansard*, Vol. 191 (1868), 1568.
(17) *Parliamentary Papers*, Vol. 35 (1874), p. 331. Return of applications for loans under provisions of 1868 Act Sessional Paper No. 235.
(18) See p. 279.
(19) Royal Commission on Housing, 1885, *First Report*, p. 51.
(20) 42 and 43 Vict. c. 64. Artizans and Labourers Dwellings Act (1868) Amendment Act, 1870.
(21) 42 and 43 Vict. c. 77.
(22) Artizans Dwellings Act, 1882. 45 and 46 Vict. c. 54, Section 5.
(23) 45 and 46 Vict. c. 54, Section 8.
(24) There was, however, a new Public Health Act in 1872. 35 and 36 Vict. c. 79, amended in 1874.
(25) *Hansard*, Vol. 191 (1868), 673.
(26) G. E. Buckle, *The Life of Benjamin Disraeli* (London, 1916–20), Vol. 5, p. 362.
(27) As a 'Bill to facilitate the erection of dwellings for working men on land belonging to municipal corporations. *Journal of House of Commons* (1874), p. 33, 253. 37 and 38 Vict. c. 59.
(28) Buckle, op. cit., Vol. 5, p. 377.
(29) For the country outside London, which had to wait until 1891 for an equally progressive measure. The Sanitary Law Amendment Act, 1874 (37 and 38 Vict. c. 59), had already authorised regulations about ventilation of rooms and paving and drainage of premises.
(30) Buckle, op. cit., p. 377.
(31) 38 and 39 Vict. c. 36. The Artizans and Labourers Dwellings Improvement Act, 1875.
(32) *Law Reports, Statutes*, Vol. 10, p. 255.
(33) *Parliamentary Papers*, Vol. 58 (1883), pp. 19–24.
(34) Ibid., p. 14. See also D. A. Hames, (ed.), *The Radical Programme* (Brighton, 1971), p. 85.
(35) Chamberlain, 'On the Sanitary Condition of Large Towns', speech given at Birmingham (13 January 1875) to conference of municipal authorities in Charles W. Boyd (ed.), *Mr Chamberlains's Speeches* (London, 1914), Vol. 1, p. 355.
(36) Royal Commission on Housing, 1885, *Minutes of Evidence*, Chamberlain, 12,398, 12,594, 12,597. See also Tarn, in S. D. Chapman (ed.), *The History of Working-Class Housing* (Newton Abbot, 1971), p. 43.
(37) The preamble to the Royal Commission of 1885 groups 'Torrens' with the 'Dwellings' Acts and 'Cross' with the 'Dwellings Improvement' Acts. Torrens' original intention was to include housing replacement within its function but, as we have seen, the essential clause was deleted by the Lords. This left both 'Torrens' and 'Cross' with demolition as their chief function.
(38) See *Artizans Centenary, 1867–1967*, p. 9.

CHAPTER 24

(1) 42 and 43 Vict. c. 64.
(2) 42 and 43 Vict. c. 63.

(3) 42 and 43 Vict. c. 77.
(4) See Chamberlain, 'Labourers and Artizans Dwellings', *Fortnightly Review*, new ser., No. 204, (1 December 1883), p. 774. In Swansea and Greenock new houses for working people were built on land cleared by the town councils with Public Works Loans. But the houses were not built by the council and the loans were made before 1879. 'Returns of the Number of Representations Made', *Parliamentary Papers*, Vol. 58 (1883), p. 14.
(5) 42 and 43 Vict. c. 8.
(6) *Journal of House of Commons* (1881), p. 225. *Hansard*, Vol. 261 (9 May 1881), pp. 858, 1135, 1535.
(7) Interim Report of Select Committee. *Parliamentary Papers*, Vol. 7 (1881), p. 395.
(8) They were Brighton, Dover, Exeter, Hastings and Sheffield, *Parliamentary Papers*, Vol. 58 (1883), p. 17.
(9) Select Committee, *Final Report* (1882), *Parliamentary Papers*, Vol. 7 pp. 249, vi.
(10) Ibid., p. x.
(11) 45 and 46 Vict. c. 54.
(12) Chamberlain, op. cit., pp. 762–3. See also D. A. Hames (ed.), *The Radical Programme* (Brighton, 1971), pp. 62–91 for Frank Harris's 'Housing of the Poor in Towns', which discusses Chamberlain's approach.
(13) In his speech to the Eighty Club (28 April 1885).
(14) Select Committee, 1881, *Minutes of Evidence*, 1601.
(15) *First Report* (1885), pp. 15–16.
(16) Memorandum by the Marquess of Salisbury appended to the 1885 *First Report*, p. 63.
(17) *First Report* (1885), p. 18.
(18) *Journal of the House of Commons* (1884–5), p. 362.
(19) J. Honeyman, *The Dwellings of the Poor* (Glasgow, 1890), pp. 28–31.
(20) Liverpool was the only town to take advantage of extended loans under the Act.
(21) *Journal of the House of Commons* (1887), p. 21. McCalmont, *Parliamentary Poll Book*, p. 248.
(22) *Parliamentary Papers*, Vol. 13 (1887), p. 1.
(23) Tabulation of the statements of men living in certain selected districts of London in March 1887. *Parliamentary Papers*, Vol. 71 (1887), p. 303.
(24) *Journal of the House of Commons* (1888), p. 33, 464.
(25) *Journal of the House of Commons* (1888), p. 44. McCalmont's, *Parliamentary Poll Book*, p. 73.
(26) *Journal of the House of Commons* (1889), pp. 16, 266.
(27) Ibid., p. 42.
(28) Ibid., p. 18.
(29) *Parliamentary Papers*, Vol. 3 (1889), p. 229.
(30) Ibid., p. 233. The cheap method was a very much simplified system of administering compulsory purchase.
(31) Public Health Amendment Act, 1890: 53 and 54 Vict. 59. The two less significant were (a) 53 and 54 Vict. c. 16, 17. An Act to facilitate gifts of land for dwellings for the working classes, which gave exemption from the clauses of the Mortmain Act, and (b) 53 and 54 Vict. c. 69. An Act to amend the Settled Land Acts, 1882–9, which allowed the application of capital money to improvements and which extended the definition of *working classes* to include all those who earn their living by wages or salaries.
(32) 53 and 54 Vict. c. 70.

CHAPTER 25

(1) A. S. Wohl, 'Housing of the Working Classes in London', in S. D. Chapman, *The History of Working-Class Housing* (Newton Abbot, 1971), pp. 28, 40 and J. N. Tarn, 'Some Pioneer Suburban Housing Estates', *Architectural Review* (1968), p. 367.

(2) Report of the Royal Commission on the Housing of the Industrial Population of Scotland, Rural and Urban (1917), pp. 345–6.

(3) See, for instance, A. S. Wohl, 'Housing of the Working Classes in London, 1815–1914', in S. D. Chapman (ed.), op. cit.

(4) *Parliamentary Papers*, Accounts and Papers (1907), No. 404.

(5) *Parliamentary Papers*, Accounts and Papers (1914), No. 456.

(6) See, for instance, John Lennox, 'Working-Class Life in Dundee, 1895–1903', unpublished thesis in University Library, Dundee.

(7) 63 and 64 Vict. c. 59. An Act to amend Part 3 of the Housing of the Working Classes Act, 1890.

(8) Pollard, *Life and Labour in Sheffield* (Liverpool, 1969), pp. 184–8.

(9) Tarn, op. cit., p. 326. See also Dr R. Bradbury 'New Dwellings from Old: An Example from Liverpool', *R.I.B.A. Journal* (September 1953), p. 452, and Bradbury, 'Liverpool: Improvements to Sub-standard Houses', *Architects' Journal* (18 March 1954), p. 336.

(10) Report of Baillie Mitchell, Dundee's representative to the Congress, to the City Council, *Council Minute Books* (3 October 1907).

(11) Fenner Brockway, *Socialism over Sixty Years: The Life of Jowett of Bradford* (London, 1946), pp. 48–53.

(12) Shena D. Simon, *A Century of City Government, Manchester 1838–1938* (London, 1930), pp. 295–7.

(13) The percentage of one-roomed houses occupied in all Scotland was 12.8, compared with 16.9 for Dundee. In Dundee 70 per cent of all occupied houses were of two rooms or less.

(14) See p. 220.

(15) Letter from the Secretary, Dundee and District United Trades and Labour Council, to Dundee town council (7 March 1912).

(16) *Report on the Development of the City*, 1917–18.

(17) *Spectator* (9 May 1925).

(18) Annual Report of the Local Government Board, 1914, *Housing and Town Planning*, pp. xl, 47.

(19) L.G.B., *Report* (1914), p. v.

(20) The scheme was Millbank and the Queen criticised the architect for not providing more cupboards.

(21) William Kent, *John Burns: Labour's Lost Leader* (London, 1950), pp. 123–4.

(22) Ibid., p. 125.

(23) *Journal of the House of Commons* (1908).

(24) Kent, op. cit., pp. 184–5.

(25) Ibid., p. 261.

(26) List of local authorities, Appendix 4.

(27) L.G.B., Report (1913–14), p. xxxvii.

(28) Ibid., p. xxxlx.

(29) Ibid., loc. cit. See also *Reports* (1911 and 1912).

(30) A slightly earlier strike in Glasgow in 1914 was started by Woolwich torpedo workers brought to the Clyde by war work and disgusted with tenement living conditions. Sir Patrick Geddes, *Cities in Evolution* (London, 1915), pp. 140–1.

(31) M. Bowley, *Housing and the State, 1919–44* (London, 1945), p. 12.
(32) Bentley B. Gilbert, *British Social Policy, 1914–1939* (London, 1970), pp. 137–58.
(33) R. J. Minney, *Viscount Addison, Leader of the Lords* (London, 1958), p. 172.
(34) Ibid., p. 189n.

Index